ELEMENTS OF MATHEMATICAL LOGIC

(MODEL THEORY)

STUDIES IN LOGIC

AND

THE FOUNDATIONS OF MATHEMATICS

NORTH-HOLLAND PUBLISHING COMPANY
AMSTERDAM

ELEMENTS OF MATHEMATICAL LOGIC

(MODEL THEORY)

G. KREISEL
Stanford University

J. L. KRIVINE
Université de Paris

1967

NORTH-HOLLAND PUBLISHING COMPANY
AMSTERDAM

Library of Congress Catalog Card Number: 67-20006.

PRINTED IN THE NETHERLANDS

PREFACE

This book presents the principles of the Axiomatic Method, here formulated in set theoretic, also called: semantic, terms.

The basic notions involved are: different kinds of *languages*; their *realizations* (types of mathematical structures); and *models* (of a formula in the language considered, i.e., the realizations of the language which satisfy the formula). From them are derived the notions of *consequence* (a conclusion A being a consequence of "axioms" $\mathscr{A}$, formulated in a language $\mathscr{L}$, if every realization of $\mathscr{L}$ which satisfies each formula of $\mathscr{A}$ also satisfies A) and of *definability* (in a realization of $\mathscr{L}$ by means of a formula of $\mathscr{L}$). Consequence and definability are the two main topics here studied.

The most general results on the Axiomatic Method known, apply to axiomatic systems formulated in the language of *predicate logic of first order* restricted to finite formulas. Much of this theory can be generalized to suitable infinite formulas of first order, less to languages of higher order, even when they are restricted to finite formulas. The last chapter contains some information on such generalizations.

The treatment is set theoretic in that the basic notions above are defined in the vocabulary of current set theory: sets, membership relation, logical operations.

This book contains the elementary, more or less classical, results of its subject. Each of its eight chapters is preceded by a summary which not only indicates the general content of the chapter, but also the relation of the exercises to the main theorems.

Appendix I gives an idea of the kind of applications to current mathematics that can be expected from a general theory of the Axiomatic Method. Knowledge of the main text is not assumed.

Appendix II is intended for readers with some interest (and background!) in the philosophy of mathematics. Parts A and B sketch the so-called semantic and syntactic (better: set theoretic and combinatorial) foundations with special reference to Gödel's completeness and incompleteness theorems, of which proofs are given in Part A. Part C discusses the relation between these foundational schemes: semantic analysis is developed, and not superseded, by syntactic analysis, which, incidentally, is a reason for adopting a semantic introduction to logic, as in the present text. The Introduction to Appendix II may be of use to those readers who, consciously or unconsciously, are influenced by positivistic, in particular formalistic philosophical doctrines which are widely quoted. If one accepts the doctrines, which reject the foundational notions of both Parts A and B, one is bound to be ill at ease with these notions and hence to find them difficult. (It is true that a *consistent* formalist would also be ill at ease with mathematical practice where the same notions occur constantly; however, with this psychologically important difference: they function as a tool, and not as a principal object of study.) The introduction, by pointing out, without technicalities, some of the most obvious weaknesses of the formalist position, is intended to overcome this, quite unnecessary difficulty. The knowledge acquired by study of these notions then permits a more searching criticism of the formalist position; cf. Parts A, B *in fine*. Appendix II can be read without specialized knowledge of mathematical logic, except for certain passages in square brackets ([ ]) which concern questions that are either raised or solved by results established in the main text.

This text developed from a graduate course ("Cours de troisième cycle") first given in 1960/61, and hectographed in 1962, at the University of Paris. The present version of Chapters 0–5, except for some exercises, is due to J. L. Krivine; it is, in most respects, a definite improvement on the original. More recently I added Chapters 6 and 7 which bring the course up to date and contain material needed in Appendix II. J. P. Ressayre, who translated into French an earlier version (or, rather, several versions) of Parts A–C of this appendix, has helped me much by his questions and constructive criticism.

Chapters 0–7 and Appendix I were translated from the French by A. Slomson except for some additions and changes made after he had completed the translation.

The collaboration of my friends Hubert Faure and Raymond Queneau deserves special notice. Faced with the translation (into French) of a hopelessly long preface, they led me, by acute questions, to separate the material into the present preface and the introduction to Appendix II; Hubert Faure helped me with the former, Raymond Queneau with the latter. Finally, my old friend Christopher Fernau translated the French text of this introduction, changing and suppressing freely whatever displeased him.

Uses of the book. Experience with students suggests the following comments. The (very natural) idea of keeping the treatment purely model theoretic really seems to work: for instance, rules of inference would not have helped the presentation. Also the separation of the main theorems from illustrations and refinements in the form of exercises seems successful. By way of criticism: some relatively small changes in Chapters 0–7 (which, however, would have required a good deal of work by somebody) could have much improved the whole presentation, in particular Appendix II, Part A. Specifically, Chapter 0 could establish the properties of formal languages needed for Gödel's incompleteness theorems, and a separate chapter containing a brief formal development of set theory would certainly be preferable to the relevant exercises in Chapter 5 and Appendix II, Part A. Concerning more technical points, the theory of p-adic fields should probably replace the theory of (certain) Boolean rings considered in Chapter 4; the elimination of quantifiers for the latter was given to stress two points not well illustrated by the other axiomatic systems studied in that chapter: (i) the need for introducing 'many' new relations; (ii) a theory that permits elimination of quantifiers but is 'far' from being saturated. Both points would equally well be illustrated by the elimination of quantifiers for p-adic fields, which is mathematically much more interesting and worth some extra labour. In the exercises of Chapter 5 the only (non principal) models of languages of higher order are provided by various systems of hereditarily finite sets: some specific models used in A. Robinson's Non-standard Analysis would be more interesting.

Originally a companion volume was planned, as purely proof theoretic as the present text is model theoretic: Part B of Appendix II would have properly belonged there. Though such a volume is both feasible and desirable, I doubt whether I shall write it. In the absence of such a book, Part B might be of use to somebody in preparing a course in proof theory, in conjunction with recent detailed literature on the subject.

G. KREISEL

CONTENTS

CHAPTER 0

PRELIMINARIES

This chapter contains elementary results about classes of functions defined by finite schemas. Such schemas are frequently used in mathematics (e.g. polynomials over a given ring, rational functions over a given field); here they are mainly used for the construction of languages. Theorem 2 establishes the existence of bracket-free notations.

The notions of this chapter can also be defined using only (hereditarily) *finite* sets; see Chapter 5, Exercise 6 or Appendix II, pp. 169–170.

We begin with a countable family $F_n (n=0, 1, \ldots)$ of disjoint sets. An element of F_n is called an *n-ary function symbol.*

We let $F = \bigcup_n F_n$ and $\sigma(F)$ be the set of all finite sequences of elements of F. (A finite sequence of elements of F is, for example, $(f_1, f_2, \ldots, f_k)$ written for short as $f_1 \ldots f_k$.) We consider those subsets M of $\sigma(F)$ which have the following property:

If $a_1, \ldots, a_n$ are elements of M and $f \in F_n$ then $fa_1 \ldots a_n \in M$. (We will call this property "property S".)

All intersections of sets which have the property S also have this property. Hence the intersection of all the subsets of $\sigma(F)$ having property S has this property. This intersection is called the *functional closure* of the family (F_n) and is denoted by $\bar{F}$. An element of $\bar{F}$ is called a *function schema* (constructed by means of symbols in F). *$\bar{F}$ is not empty if and only if F_0 is not empty.* (That is, if F contains 0-ary function symbols. 0-ary function symbols are also called *constants.*) For suppose that F_0 is not empty and that $a \in F_0$. Then a is in all the sets which have the property S and so $a \in \bar{F}$. Conversely if F_0 is empty, the empty set $\emptyset$ has the property S and so $\bar{F} = \emptyset$.

All the elements of $\bar{F}$ are of the form $fa_1 \ldots a_n$ with $f \in F_n$ and $a_1, \ldots, a_n \in \bar{F}$. For suppose E is the set of all elements of this form. Since $\bar{F}$ has the property S it is clear that all the elements of E are in $\bar{F}$. Conversely, since E also has the property S, $\bar{F} \subseteq E$. This concludes the proof.

If x and $y \in \bar{F}$, $a \in F_0$ and (the finite sequence) *z is obtained by replacing an occurrence of a in x by y then also $z \in \bar{F}$.*

The proof is by induction on the length of x, which we may take to be $= f_n a_1 \ldots a_n$. If $n=0$ either $x=a$ and $z=y$ or $x \neq a$ and $z=x$: in each case $z \in \bar{F}$. If $n>0$, each a_i has length less than that of x, and $\in \bar{F}$. So, if b_i is the result of replacing the occurrence of a considered by y, also $b_i \in \bar{F}$; $z = f_n b_1 \ldots b_n$.

LEMMA 1: *If $a \in \bar{F}$ and $u \in \sigma(F)$ with $u \neq \emptyset$ then $au \notin \bar{F}$.*
PROOF: The proof is by induction on the length of a. If a is of length 1 then we must have $a \in F_0$. So if $au \in \bar{F}$ it follows that $au = fa_1 \ldots a_k$ with $f \in F_k$, $a_1, \ldots, a_k \in \bar{F}$ and hence $a=f$. (Equating the first symbol of each expression.) Hence $k=0$, so $au=a$ and therefore $u=\emptyset$.

Now suppose that the lemma is true for all $x \in \bar{F}$ of length less than n and let a be an element of $\bar{F}$ of length n. Then $a = fa_1 \ldots a_k$ with $f \in F_k$ and $a_1 \ldots a_k \in \bar{F}$. If $au \in \bar{F}$ we have $au = gb_1 \ldots b_l$ with $g \in F_l$ and $b_1, \ldots, b_l \in \bar{F}$. Hence $fa_1 \ldots a_k u = gb_1 \ldots b_l$ and so $f=g$. Let i be the least integer such that $a_i \neq b_i$. Therefore $a_i a_{i+1} \ldots a_k u = b_i b_{i+1} \ldots b_l$. Hence for some $v \in \sigma(F)$ with $v \neq \emptyset$ we have either $a_i v = b_i$ or $a_i = b_i v$. But the length of a_i is less than that of a and so is less than n. Hence $a_i v = b_i \in \bar{F}$ contradicts our induction hypothesis. If $b_i v = a_i$ then the length of b_i is less than the length of a_i and since $b_i v \in \bar{F}$ we again have a contradiction.

THEOREM 2: *Each $x \in \bar{F}$ can be written uniquely in the form $fa_1 \ldots a_n$ with $f \in F_n$ and $a_1, \ldots, a_n \in \bar{F}$.*
PROOF: If there were two ways of writing x in this form we would have $fa_1 \ldots a_n = gb_1 \ldots b_p$ with $f \in F_n$, $g \in F_p$ and $a_1, \ldots, a_n, b_1, \ldots, b_p \in \bar{F}$. Thus $f=g$. Let i be the least integer such that $a_i \neq b_i$. Then $a_i \ldots a_n = b_i \ldots b_p$ and so $a_i = b_i v$ or $b_i = a_i v$ with $v \neq \emptyset$. But in either case this would contradict Lemma 1.

We will find that the next Theorem proves to be very useful.

THEOREM 3: *Let X be a set and for each integer n let $f \to \hat{f}$ be a mapping from F_n to the set of maps of X^n into X. Then there is a unique map $x \to \bar{x}$ from $\bar{F}$ into X such that for all $f \in F_n$ and all $a_1, \ldots, a_n \in \bar{F}$ we have*

$$\overline{fa_1 \ldots a_n} = \hat{f}(\bar{a}_1, \ldots, \bar{a}_n).$$

PROOF:

Uniqueness: suppose that there are two such maps from $\bar{F}$ to X. Let U be the set of all those elements of $\bar{F}$ for which these two maps agree. Then U has the property S and hence $\bar{F} \subseteq U$. Therefore $\bar{F} = U$ and so the two maps are the same.

Existence: let Φ_n be the set of elements of $\bar{F}$ which have length n. We define by induction on n, a map ϕ_n from Φ_n to X as follows: for $n=1$, since $\Phi_1 = F_0$, for all $x \in F_0$ we put $\phi_1(x) = \hat{x}$. Suppose now that ϕ_i has been defined for all $i<n$. If $x \in \Phi_n$, x can be written uniquely in the form $fa_i \ldots a_k$ with $f \in F_k$ and for $i \leqslant k$ each a_i is an element of $\bar{F}$ of length $l_i < n$. Therefore we put

$$\phi_n(x) = \hat{f}\,(\phi_{l_1}(a_1), \ldots, \phi_{l_k}(a_k)) .$$

The desired map $x \to \bar{x}$ is then given by $\bar{x} = \phi_n(x)$ if x is of length n. It follows at once that this map satisfies the conditions of the Theorem.

In particular we have the case when, for each $f \in F_n$, $\hat{f}$ is the n-ary function on $\bar{F}$ defined by $\hat{f}(a_1, \ldots, a_n) = fa_1 \ldots a_n$ for all $a_1, \ldots, a_n \in \bar{F}$. This function f is called the *natural value* of f on the functional closure of F.

CHAPTER 1

PROPOSITIONAL CALCULUS

This chapter treats grammatical connectives (or operators) such as negation, conjunction and disjunction. These connectives are used to form new propositions from given ones. The particular connectives considered here are called "Aristotelian", "classical" or "two-valued", because they were first brought into prominence by Aristotle and because they are applied to propositions with well defined values (true or false) and not to indeterminate propositions. Further, we restrict our attention to those connectives which produce propositions whose truth or falsity depends only on the truth or falsity of the propositions to which they are applied. This condition is not satisfied by, for example, the usual meaning of implication (A implies B) where the hypothesis A is supposed to have "something to do" with the conclusion B.

We call the operators considered "truth-functions". The structure which these operators make up is that of the class of all functions from $\{0,1\}^n$ into $\{0,1\}$. Exercise 1 shows the precise sense in which the collection of all these operators can be built up by superposition of the connectives mentioned in the text. Since the structure in question is very simple the only mathematically interesting questions are those about *infinite* sets of propositional formulas.

The basic notions we use are those of "propositional formula", which is defined in terms of the notions of the previous chapter, and of "model" of a given collection of formulas. This second notion is a particular case of the general concept of model in predicate logic. The main result is the Finiteness Theorem which can be proved by a simple application of compactness (there is also a proof by transfinite induction which generalises to languages considered in Chapter 7). Some algebraic applications are given in Exercises 4 and 5 (they are special cases of Theorem 13 in Chapter 3).

Let P be a given set. We denote by Prop(P) the set of function schemas constructed from the following symbols (supposed to be distinct from one another):

1) The 0-ary function symbols are $\top$, $\bot$ and the elements of P ($\top$ is read "true" and $\bot$ "false").

2) $\neg$ (read "not") is the only unary function symbol.

3) $\vee$ (read "or") is the only binary function symbol.

The elements of P are called *propositional variables*. The elements of

Prop(P) are called *formulas*. We call Prop (P) "the propositional calculus on P".

For A, $B \in$ Prop(P), we will usually denote $\vee AB$ by $(A) \vee (B)$; $\neg((\neg A) \vee (\neg B))$ by $(A) \wedge (B)$; $(\neg A) \vee (B)$ by $(A) \rightarrow (B)$ and $((A) \rightarrow (B)) \wedge ((B) \rightarrow (A))$ by $(A) \leftrightarrow (B)$. We read $\wedge$ as "and", $\rightarrow$ as "implies" and $\leftrightarrow$ as "is equivalent to". For readability we sometimes omit (round) brackets if no confusion is likely, and use square brackets; e.g. $[(A) \rightarrow (B)]$ for $((A) \rightarrow (B))$.

A *realization* of the propositional calculus on P is a map δ from P to $\{0,1\}$ (or, more generally, from P to an ordered set of two elements).

It follows from the fundamental theorem on function schemas (Theorem 0.3) *that each realization δ can be extended to a mapping (also denoted by δ) from* Prop(P) *into* $\{0,1\}$ if $\top$ is given the value 1, $\perp$ is given the value 0 and $\neg$, $\vee$ are given the following values (functions with values in $\{0,1\}$, defined on $\{0,1\}$ and $\{0,1\}^2$): $\neg 0 = 1$, $\neg 1 = 0$; $\vee 00 = 0$, $\vee 01 = \vee 10 = \vee 11 = 1$. We say that a realization δ of Prop (P) *satisfies* a formula A in Prop (P) or is a *model* of A if $\delta(A) = 1$.

We say that a realization δ satisfies a set $\mathscr{A}$ of formulas, or is a model of $\mathscr{A}$ if δ satisfies each formula in $\mathscr{A}$.

A formula A in Prop (P) is said to be a *theorem* of propositional calculus if it is satisfied by all realizations. Two formulas A and B are said to be *equivalent* if $A \leftrightarrow B$ is a theorem or if $\delta(A) = \delta(B)$ in all realizations, which is obviously the same thing.

LEMMA 1. THE INTERPOLATION LEMMA FOR PROPOSITIONAL CALCULUS: *If $A \vee B$ is a theorem of* Prop (P) *there is a formula C whose propositional variables occur in both A and B such that $A \vee C$ and $\neg C \vee B$ are theorems of* Prop (P).

PROOF: The proof is by induction on the number k of propositional variables which occur in A but not in B. If $k = 0$ it is sufficient to put $C = \neg A$. Now suppose that the lemma has been established for $k = n - 1$. Let A be a formula such that $A \vee B$ is a theorem and A contains exactly n propositional variables which do not occur in B. Let p be one of these variables and let A_1 and A_2 be the formulas obtained by substituting $\top$ and $\perp$ for p in A. $A_1 \vee B$ and $A_2 \vee B$ are theorems and so $(A_1 \wedge A_2) \vee B$ is a theorem to which we may apply the induction hypothesis. Thus there is some formula C, containing only propositional variables common to $A_1 \wedge A_2$ and B, such that $(A_1 \wedge A_2) \vee C$ and $\neg C \vee B$ are theorems. It follows from the definitions of A_1 and A_2 that $A \vee C$ is also a theorem. This completes the proof. (Cf. also Exercise 2.)

If we replace A by $\neg A$ in this lemma we get the following result:

If $A \rightarrow B$ *is a theorem of* Prop (P) *there is a formula* C*, containing only propositional variables common to* A *and* B *such that* $A \rightarrow C$ *and* $C \rightarrow B$ *are also theorems of* Prop (P).

We call C an *interpolation formula* for A and B. As a corollary of this result we have

THEOREM 2. THE DEFINABILITY THEOREM FOR PROPOSITIONAL CALCULUS: *Let* $A(p)$ *be a formula which contains the propositional variable* p*, and let* $A(p')$ *be the result of substituting* p' *for* p *in* $A(p)$*, where* p' *is a propositional variable which does not occur in* $A(p)$*. Then, if* $(A(p) \wedge A(p')) \rightarrow (p \rightarrow p')$ *is a theorem there is a formula* F *containing only propositional variables which occur in* $A(p)$*, but not* p *nor* p'*, such that* $A(p) \rightarrow (p \leftrightarrow F)$ *is a theorem.*

PROOF: Since $(A(p) \wedge A(p')) \rightarrow (p \rightarrow p')$ is a theorem we also have that $(A(p) \wedge p) \rightarrow (A(p') \rightarrow p')$ is a theorem. Hence by the Interpolation Lemma there is a formula F, not containing p nor p', such that $(A(p) \wedge p) \rightarrow F$ and $F \rightarrow (A(p') \rightarrow p')$ are both theorems. It follows that $A(p) \rightarrow (p \leftrightarrow F)$ is a theorem.

We can be precise about the form of the formula F. If we replace $(A(p) \wedge p) \rightarrow (A(p') \rightarrow p')$ by $(\neg A(p) \vee \neg p) \vee (\neg A(p') \vee p')$ the proof of the Interpolation Lemma yields $(A(\top) \wedge \top) \vee (A(\bot) \wedge \bot)$ for F, which reduces to the formula $A(\top)$. Thus F is $A(\top)$, the result of substituting $\top$ for p in $A(p)$. (More directly, we could argue as follows. For all A, $A(p') \rightarrow (p' \rightarrow A(\top))$, is a theorem; substituting $\top$ for p we have $A(p') \rightarrow (A(\top) \rightarrow p')$ is a theorem, and hence $A(p') \rightarrow (p' \leftrightarrow A(\top))$.)

We will make use of the next Theorem for the elimination of quantifiers.

THEOREM 3: *Each formula* A *of* Prop (P) *is equivalent to a formula of the form* $A_1 \vee A_2 \vee \cdots \vee A_k$ *where each* $A_i (1 \leqslant i \leqslant k)$ *is of the form* $\alpha_1 \wedge \cdots \wedge \alpha_{r_i}$ *where* $\alpha_j (1 \leqslant j \leqslant r_i)$ *is either* p *or* $\neg p$*, and* p *is either one of the propositional variables occurring in* A *or is* $\top$.

Thus we say that A can be written as a "disjunction of conjunctions". The Theorem is also true for a "conjunction of disjunctions" and can be proved in the same way.

PROOF: The proof is by induction on the number k of propositional variables occurring in A. If $k=0$, A is equivalent to $\top$ or $\bot$, i.e. $\neg\top$.

Suppose now that the Theorem has been proved for $k=n-1$ and let $A(p)$ be a formula containing n propositional variables of which p is one. Let B and C be the results of substituting $\top$ and $\bot$, respectively, for p in $A(p)$. B and C each contain $n-1$ propositional variables and clearly $A(p)$ is equivalent to $(p \wedge B) \vee (\neg p \wedge C)$.

By the induction hypothesis B is equivalent to $B_1 \vee \cdots \vee B_k$ and C is equivalent to $C_1 \vee \cdots \vee C_l$. Therefore $A(p)$ is equivalent to $(p \wedge B_1) \vee (p \wedge B_2) \vee \cdots \vee (p \wedge B_k) \vee (\neg p \wedge C_1) \vee \cdots \vee (\neg p \wedge C_l)$ which is of the desired form.

This completes the proof.

THEOREM 4. THE FINITENESS THEOREM FOR PROPOSITIONAL CALCULUS: *Let $\mathscr{A}$ be a set of formulas of* Prop (P) *such that every finite subset of $\mathscr{A}$ has a model. Then $\mathscr{A}$ has a model.*

PROOF: We will first prove the result for the most commonly occurring case, namely when P (and hence also $\mathscr{A}$) is countable.

Let $p_1, \ldots, p_k, \ldots$ be an enumeration of P. Suppose that we have found a map δ of $\{p_1, \ldots, p_n\}$ into $\{0,1\}$ such that each finite subset of $\mathscr{A}$ has a model in which $p_1, \ldots, p_n$ take the values $\delta(p_1), \ldots, \delta(p_n)$. Then we show that we can extend δ to $\{p_1, \ldots, p_n, p_{n+1}\}$ so that this same property holds. For suppose that this is not true if we put $\delta(p_{n+1})=0$. Then there is some finite subset U_0 of $\mathscr{A}$ such that there is no model of U_0 in which $p_1, \ldots, p_n, p_{n+1}$ take the values $\delta(p_1), \ldots, \delta(p_n)$, 0. Let U be any arbitrary finite subset of $\mathscr{A}$. Then $U_0 \cup U$ is a finite subset of $\mathscr{A}$ and so by hypothesis it has a model in which $p_1, \ldots, p_n$ take the values $\delta(p_1), \ldots, \delta(p_n)$. By the choice of U_0, in this model p_{n+1} must take the value 1. Hence if $\delta(p_{n+1})=1$ every finite subset U of $\mathscr{A}$ has a model in which $p_1, \ldots, p_{n+1}$ take the values $\delta(p_1), \ldots, \delta(p_{n+1})$.

Thus we can define, by recursion on n, a realization δ of Prop (P) such that, for each n, every finite subset of $\mathscr{A}$ has a model in which $p_1, \ldots, p_n$ take the values $\delta(p_1), \ldots, \delta(p_n)$. It follows that δ satisfies $\mathscr{A}$: for suppose A is a formula of $\mathscr{A}$; in order to see that δ satisfies A it is sufficient to take n so large that all the propositional variables occurring in A appear among $p_1, \ldots, p_n$.

Clearly this proof can be extended to the general case when P is not countable provided that we have a well-ordering of P. For the general case we also have the following proof.

For each formula A of Prop (P) the set of realizations which satisfy A is open in the space $\{0,1\}^P$, with the product topology, since A only contains a finite number of propositional variables. This set is also closed since the realizations which do not satisfy A are precisely those which satisfy $\neg A$. For each formula A of $\mathscr{A}$ let $\bar{A}$ be the set of realizations which satisfy A. It follows from the hypothesis of the theorem that all finite intersections of the sets $\bar{A}$ are non-empty. Since $\{0,1\}^P$ is compact the intersection of all the sets $\bar{A}$ for $A \in \mathscr{A}$ is non-empty.

This completes the proof.

The Finiteness Theorem can also be expressed in the following form:

THEOREM 5: *If each realization satisfies one of the formulas of a set $\mathscr{B}$ of formulas then there are formulas $B_1, \ldots, B_n$ in $\mathscr{B}$ such that $B_1 \vee \cdots \vee B_n$ is a theorem.*

PROOF: Suppose such a set $\{B_1, \ldots, B_n\}$ does not exist. Then for each finite subset $\{B_1, \ldots, B_n\}$ of $\mathscr{B}$ there is some realization which does not satisfy $B_1 \vee \cdots \vee B_n$ and which therefore satisfies $\neg B_1 \wedge \cdots \wedge \neg B_n$. Let $\mathscr{A}$ be the set of formulas $\neg B$ for B in $\mathscr{B}$. Then every finite subset of $\mathscr{A}$ has a model and so, by the Finiteness Theorem, $\mathscr{A}$ has a model. This contradicts the assumption that each realization satisfies some formula of $\mathscr{B}$.

A formula A is said to be a *consequence* of a set $\mathscr{A}$ of formulas if each realization which satisfies $\mathscr{A}$ also satisfies A. In particular, the consequences of the empty set are the theorems. The consequences of a finite set $\mathscr{A} = \{A_1, \ldots, A_n\}$ are those formulas A such that $(A_1 \wedge \cdots \wedge A_n) \rightarrow A$ is a theorem.

THEOREM 6: *A is a consequence of a set $\mathscr{A}$ of formulas if and only if A is a consequence of some finite subset of $\mathscr{A}$.*

PROOF: The condition is clearly sufficient. It is also necessary since to say that A is a consequence of $\mathscr{A}$ is equivalent to saying that the set $\mathscr{A} \cup \{\neg A\}$ does not have a model. This set does not have a model only if some finite subset $\mathscr{A}'$ of $\mathscr{A}$ exists such that $\mathscr{A}' \cup \{\neg A\}$ does not have a model. And this set does not have a model only if A is a consequence of $\mathscr{A}'$.

Exercises

1. Clearly each formula A having $p_1, \ldots, p_n$ as its propositional variables defines a map of $\{0,1\}^n$ into $\{0,1\}$. Show that each map of $\{0,1\}^n$ into $\{0,1\}$ is obtainable in this way.

Let U_k be the set of maps of $\{0,1\}^k$ into $\{0,1\}$ and let $U=\bigcup_{k\in N} U_k$. A subset S of U is said to be *complete* if all the elements of U can be obtained by composition from the elements of S.

Show that the sets $S=\{\phi\}$, where $\phi(p, q)=\neg p\wedge\neg q$, and $\{\to, \bot\}$ are complete and that the sets $S=\{\top,\to\}$ and $\{\top, \to, \wedge, \vee\}$ are not complete.

Answer. We prove that all maps from $\{0,1\}^n$ into $\{0,1\}$ can be obtained, by induction on n. Suppose that the result has been established for $n=k$ and let $f(p_1, \ldots, p_k, p_{k+1})$ be a mapping from $\{0,1\}^{k+1}$ into $\{0,1\}$. By hypothesis $f(p_1, \ldots, p_k, 1)=A(p_1, \ldots, p_k)$ and $f(p_1, \ldots, p_k, 0)=B(p_1, \ldots, p_k)$ where A and B are two formulas whose variables are $p_1, \ldots, p_k$. It can be seen at once that $f(p_1, \ldots, p_k, p_{k+1})$ is given by the formula

$$[p_{k+1}\to A(p_1, \ldots, p_k)]\wedge[\neg p_{k+1}\to B(p_1, \ldots, p_k)].$$

This shows that the set $\{\neg, \vee\}$ is complete. Now $\neg p=\phi(p, p)$ and $p\vee q=\neg\phi(p, q)=\neg p\to q$ and so the sets $\{\phi\}$ and $\{\to, \bot\}$ are also both complete.

Now consider the function schemas that can be constructed from $\{\top, \to\}$ and a set P of propositional variables. These represent all the functions that can be obtained from $\{\top, \to\}$ by composition. Let $A(p)$ be one such function schema which contains only the propositional variable p. It can be seen by induction on the length of $A(p)$ that either $A(p)\leftrightarrow\top$ or $A(p)\leftrightarrow p$ is a theorem as follows: if $A(p)$ is of length n then $A(p)=B(p)\to C(p)$, where $B(p)$ and $C(p)$ are both of length less than n. It follows that $A(p)$ is equivalent to one of the formulas $p\to p$, $\top\to p$, $p\to\top$, $\top\to\top$, i.e. to $\top$ or p.

Consequently the function $\neg$ cannot be obtained by composition from $\{\top, \to, \vee, \wedge\}$.

2. Let $A_1, \ldots, A_n\in\text{Prop}(V)$ where V is a set of propositional variables. The class of formulas built up from the propositional connectives (defined by) $A_1, \ldots, A_n$ is, by definition, the least class $\mathscr{C}$ such that

(i) each $A_i\in\mathscr{C}$ $(1\leqslant i\leqslant n)$, and $\top$ and $\bot\in\mathscr{C}$ if there is a formula $A\in\mathscr{C}$ such that A, resp. $\neg A$ is a theorem of Prop (V);

(ii) if $A\in\mathscr{C}$ and $B\in\mathscr{C}$ and C is obtained from A by substituting either a variable $\in V$ or the formula B for each occurrence of a variable in A, then $C\in\mathscr{C}$.

Show that, if P, Q, R are disjoint subsets of V, $A \in \mathscr{C}$, $B \in \mathscr{C}$, $A \in \text{Prop}\,(P \cup R)$, $B \in \text{Prop}\,(Q \cup R)$ and $A \to B$ is a theorem, then there is a formula $C \in \mathscr{C}$, $C \in \text{Prop}\,(R)$ such that $A \to C$, $C \to B$ are theorems. (Interpolation Lemma for arbitrary sets of propositional connectives.)

Answer. If $P = \emptyset$ or $Q = \emptyset$ there is nothing to prove.

Case 1: $R = \emptyset$. In this case either B is a theorem or $\neg A$ is a theorem (and $C = \top$ or $C = \bot$ satisfies the condition above). Suppose $\neg A$ is not a theorem; then there is a realization ρ_P of P for which $\bar{A} = 1$, and since $A \in \text{Prop}\,(P)$, $\bar{A} = 1$ for every extension ρ $(= \rho_P \cup \rho_Q)$ of ρ_P. Since $A \to B$ is a theorem, $\bar{B} = 1$ for ρ. Hence, since $B \in \text{Prop}\,(Q)$, for any ρ' whose restriction to Q is ρ_Q, $\bar{B} = 1$. Since ρ_Q was arbitrary, this means that B is a theorem.

Case 2: $R \neq \emptyset$. We consider first the case when $\top$ or $\bot \in \mathscr{C}$. Suppose $P = \{p_1, \ldots, p_n\}$, $Q = \{q_1, \ldots, q_m\}$. If $\top \in \mathscr{C}$ and $n = 1$, or $\bot \in \mathscr{C}$, and $m = 1$, we write $A = A(p_1)$, $B = B(q_1)$ and $C = A(A(\top))$ or $C = B(B(\bot))$ is a solution. By Lemma 1 it is enough to show that

$$(A(\top) \vee A(\bot)) \leftrightarrow A(A(\top)) \quad \text{and} \quad (B(\top) \wedge B(\bot)) \leftrightarrow B(B(\bot))$$

are theorems, since both $A(\top) \vee A(\bot)$ and $B(\top) \wedge B(\bot)$ are interpolation formulas. Let ρ be any realization of V, and so $\overline{\top} = 1$, $\overline{\bot} = 0$, and either $\overline{A(\top)} = 1$ or $\overline{A(\top)} = 0$; if $\overline{A(\top)} = 1$, $A\overline{(A(\top)} = \overline{A(\top)}$, i.e. $= 1$, and also $\overline{A(\top) \vee A(\bot)} = 1$; if $\overline{A(\top)} = 0$, $\overline{A(A(\top))} = \overline{A(\bot)}, = \overline{A(\top) \vee A(\bot)}$; in both cases, $\overline{A(\top) \vee A(\bot)} = \overline{A(A(\top))}$; since ρ is arbitrary this shows that $A(\top) \vee A(\bot) \leftrightarrow A(A(\top))$ is a theorem. The proof for $(B(\top) \wedge B(\bot)) \leftrightarrow B(B(\bot))$ is similar. (Note that Lemma 1 itself provides a solution only if both $\top$ and $\bot \in \mathscr{C}$ and either $\vee$ or $\wedge$ occurs in $\mathscr{C}$.)

To treat $n > 1$, we define a sequence $C_i (1 \leqslant i \leqslant n)$ where (i) each $C_i \in \text{Prop}$ $(\{p_{i+1}, \ldots, p_n, v\} \cup R)$ $(i < n)$, $C_n \in \text{Prop}\,(\{v\} \cup R)$ and $v \notin P \cup R$ (e.g. $v \in Q$ since $Q \neq \emptyset$), (ii) each C_i is obtained from A by substitution for the variables $p_1, \ldots, p_i$. We write $C_i = C_i(p_{i+1})$, $C_i = C_i\,[v]$ and denote by $C_i(F)$, $C_i[F]$ the result of substituting F for *each* occurrence in C_i of p_{i+1}, resp. of v,

$$C_1 = A(A(v)), \quad C_{i+1} = C_i(C_i(v)) \quad (1 \leqslant i < n).$$

Then, for $1 \leqslant i < n$, $A \to C_i[\top]$, $C_i[\top] \to C_{i+1}[\top]$; $C_i[\top] \to B (1 \leqslant i \leqslant n)$.

For $i=1$, we have the case above because $C_1[\top]$ is $A(A(\top))$. Suppose true for $i<j$, and write $C_j[\top]=C'_j(p_{j+1})$; since $C'_j\to B$, again $C'_j(C'_j(\top))$ is an interpolation formula, and this, by definition, is $C_{j+1}[\top]$.

If $\bot\in\mathscr{C}$, a similar construction of $D_i\in\text{Prop}(\{q_{i+1},\ldots,q_m,w\}\cup R)$ $(w\notin Q\cup R)$ yields a formula $D_m[\bot]$ where $D_1=B(B(v))$, $D_i=D_i(q_{i+1})=D_i[w]$, and $D_{i+1}=D_i(D_i(w))$.

For the general case, note first that, for any formula F, $C_n[F]\to B$ is a theorem because $C_n[v]$ is got from A by substitutions for $p_1,\ldots,p_n$ and the p do not occur in B. In particular, for $F=B_0$ where B_0 is obtained from B by substituting elements of R for $q_1,\ldots,q_m$. We shall show that $A\to C_n[B_0]$.

Let ρ_R be any realization of R. We distinguish two cases: (i) There is a realization ρ_P^* on P such that $\bar{A}=1$ for $\rho_P^*\cup\rho_R$, (ii) for each extension ρ_P, $\bar{A}=0$ for $\rho_P\cup\rho_R$. In case (i), since $A\to B$ in a theorem, for each realization ρ_Q of Q, $\bar{B}=1$ for $\rho_P^*\cup\rho_R\cup\rho_Q$; since the p do not occur in B, $\bar{B}=1$ for each extension of ρ_R, and, in particular, $\bar{B}_0=1$. So $\overline{C_n[B]}=\overline{C_n[\top]}$, and we know that $\overline{A\to C_n[\top]}=1$. In case (ii), since for all ρ_P, $\bar{A}=0$ for $\rho_R\cup\rho_P$, and hence for all $\rho_R\cup\rho_P\cup\rho_Q$, A being in Prop $(P\cup R)$, $\overline{A\to C_n[B_0]}=1$ for all extensions $\rho_R\cup\rho_P\cup\rho_Q$. Since ρ_R is arbitrary, $A\to C_n[B_0]$ is a theorem.

Similarly, $D_m[A_0]$ is an interpolation formula if A_0 is obtained from A by substituting elements of R for $p_1,\ldots,p_n$.

3. A set $\mathscr{A}$ of formulas is said to be *independent* if no formula A in $\mathscr{A}$ is a consequence of $\mathscr{A}-\{A\}$. Show that

a) a set $\mathscr{A}$ of formulas is independent if and only if each finite subset of $\mathscr{A}$ is independent;

b) each finite set $\mathscr{A}$ of formulas has an independent equivalent subset $\mathscr{B}$ (in the sense that each formula of $\mathscr{A}$ is a consequence of $\mathscr{B}$, and conversely);

c) each countable set of formulas $\mathscr{A}$ has an independent equivalent set of formulas.

We remark that there is a countable set $\mathscr{A}$ of formulas which does not have any equivalent independent *subset*. Let $p_1,\ldots,p_n,\ldots$ be a sequence of distinct propositional variables and let, for example, $\mathscr{A}=\{p_1,p_1\wedge p_2,\ldots,p_1\wedge\cdots\wedge p_n,\ldots\}$. Clearly each independent subset of $\mathscr{A}$ consists of a single formula and $\mathscr{A}$ is not equivalent to any single formula in $\mathscr{A}$.

Answer.

a) This is an immediate consequence of the Finiteness Theorem.

b) We prove the result by induction on the number of elements k in $\mathscr{A}$. If $k=0$ the result is trivial; suppose it is true for $k=n$ and let $\mathscr{A}=\{A_1, \ldots, A_n, A_{n+1}\}$ be a set of $n+1$ formulas. If this set is already independent we are home. If not, then A_{n+1}, say, is a consequence of $\{A_1, \ldots, A_n\}$ and it is sufficient to apply the induction hypothesis to this set.

c) Let $A_1, \ldots, A_n, \ldots$ be an enumeration of the formulas of $\mathscr{A}$. Let A_i be the first formula in this enumeration which is not a theorem. Put $B_1=A_i$ and in general let $B_{n+1}=B_n \wedge A_j$ where A_j is the first formula in the enumeration which is not a consequence of B_n. Clearly the formulas $B_1, B_2, \ldots, B_n, \ldots$ are all consequences of $\mathscr{A}$ and, conversely, each A_n is a consequence of the formulas $\{B_1, B_2, \ldots, B_n, \ldots\}$. In the sequence $B_1, \ldots, B_n, \ldots$ each formula is a consequence of the one following it but not of the one preceding it. If this sequence is finite let B_n be its last term. Then $\{B_n\}$ is the desired independent set of formulas. It is independent since if B_n were a theorem then, because $B_n \rightarrow B_1$ is clearly a theorem, B_1 would also be a theorem, which it is not. (If each A_n is a theorem, $\mathscr{A}$ is equivalent to the empty set.)

If this series is infinite, put $C_1=B_1$, $C_2=B_1 \rightarrow B_2, \ldots, C_n=B_{n-1} \rightarrow B_n, \ldots$. It follows at once that

i) no C_n is a theorem, and

ii) the set $\{C_1, \ldots, C_n, \ldots\}$ is equivalent to $\mathscr{A}$.

The set $\{C_1, \ldots, C_n, \ldots\}$ is, in fact, independent. For by i) there is a realization which satisfies $\neg C_n$, i.e. which satisfies B_{n-1} and $\neg B_n$. Since $\neg B_n \rightarrow \neg B_m$ for $n \leqslant m$ is a theorem, this realization also satisfies $\neg B_m$ for $n \leqslant m$ and hence satisfies C_m for $n \leqslant m$. But we also have that $B_n \rightarrow B_p$ is a theorem for $p \leqslant n$ and so this realization also satisfies C_p for $p<n$. That is, this realization satisfies all the formulas C_q for $q \neq n$ but it does not satisfy C_n. Therefore C_n is not a consequence of $\{C_1, \ldots, C_{n-1}, C_{n+1}, \ldots\}$.

This completes the proof.

4. a) A group G is said to be *ordered* if there is a total ordering $<$ of G such that $a \leqslant b$ implies $ac \leqslant bc$ and $ca \leqslant cb$ for all c in G. Show that a group G can be ordered if and only if every subgroup of G generated by a finite number of elements of G can be ordered.

b) Deduce that a commutative group can be ordered if and only if it is torsion free, i.e. no element other than the identity is of finite order.

Answer.

a) The condition is obviously necessary; we will show that it is also sufficient.

Consider the propositional calculus on $G \times G$, i.e. the propositional calculus having the elements of $G \times G$ as propositional variables. Let $\mathscr{A}$ be the set consisting of the following formulas:

i) (a, a) for all a in G,

ii) $(a, b) \vee (b, a)$ for all a, b in G,

iii) $(a, b) \to \neg(b, a)$ for all a, b in G with $a \neq b$,

iv) $(a, b) \wedge (b, c) \to (a, c)$ for all a, b, c in G,

v) $(a, b) \to (ac, bc) \wedge (ca, cb)$ for all a, b, c in G.

In any finite subset of $\mathscr{A}$, say U, there occur only a finite number of elements of G. If G_U is the subgroup which they generate, since G_U can be ordered, by hypothesis, there is a realization of the propositional calculus which satisfies U, namely the realization in which (a, b) gets the value 1 or 0 according as $a \leqslant b$ or $a > b$, for a, b in G_U, and which is arbitrary otherwise. By the Finiteness Theorem it follows that there is a model of the whole set $\mathscr{A}$. It is now sufficient to put $a \leqslant b$ when $(a, b) = 1$ in this model and $a > b$ otherwise to obtain an ordering of G.

b) If G is an ordered commutative group then G is clearly torsion free.

Conversely if G is torsion free the sub-groups generated by finite subsets of G are free groups which are isomorphic to $\mathbf{Z}^n$ for some integer n. But $\mathbf{Z}^n$ can be ordered by the lexicographical ordering where $(a_1, \ldots, a_n) < (b_1, \ldots, b_n)$ if i is the least integer such that $a_i \neq b_i$ and $a_i < b_i$.

5. A graph (a non-reflexive symmetric relation) defined on a set M is said to be *k-chromatic*, where k is a positive integer, if there is a partition of M into k disjoint sets $C_1, \ldots, C_k$, such that two elements of M connected by the graph do not belong to the same C_i. Show that for a graph to be k-chromatic it is necessary and sufficient that every finite sub-graph be k-chromatic.

Answer. The condition is clearly necessary since each partition of M induces a partition of each of its finite subsets. We will show that the condition is also sufficient.

Consider the propositional calculus on $\{1, 2, \ldots, k\} \times M$. Let $\mathscr{A}$ be the set of the following formulas

i) $(i, a) \to \neg(j, a)$ for all $i, j \leqslant k$ with $i \neq j$ and all $a \in M$,

ii) $(1, a) \vee (2, a) \vee \cdots \vee (k, a)$ for all $a \in M$,

iii) $(i, a) \rightarrow \neg (i, b)$ for all $i \leqslant k$ and all pairs (a, b) of elements of M connected by the graph.

If each finite sub-graph is k-chromatic it follows at once that each finite subset of $\mathscr{A}$ has a model. Hence $\mathscr{A}$ has a model. Then if we put $a \in C_i$ if and only if (i, a) has the value 1 in this model we obtain a partition of M with the required properties.

CHAPTER 2

PREDICATE CALCULUS

The discussion of the previous chapter is here extended by taking into account the quantifiers "for all" and "there exists". These quantifiers do not operate on propositions but on relations. They are applied to define n-ary relations from $(n+1)$-ary relations and, in particular, propositions (i.e. 0-ary relations) from unary relations. We also extend the use of the propositional connectives defined in the previous chapter so that they can be used as operations on relations.

The language obtained turns out to be adequate for the expression of most mathematical concepts and is therefore a useful framework for a general theory of axiomatic systems. For further analysis see also Appendix II, p. 169 and pp. 190–191.

Unlike the case of propositional calculus, when one defines the general notion of "quantifier" it is not true that all quantifiers can be defined in terms of the two quantifiers mentioned above. For more details about this see MOSTOWSKI, On a Generalization of Quantifiers, Fund. Math. **44** (1957) pp. 12–36.

The main notions used are those of "formula" and "language" of first order predicate logic, and that of a "realization" of a language, from which the notion of a "model" of a collection of formulas is defined. A particularly important case is that of "canonical" models in which each object (i.e. element of the model) has a *name* in the language under consideration.

The chief tool used in this chapter is that of the construction of canonical models by means of function schemas. This method leads to the following results:

i) Each model of a finite or countable set of formulas $\mathscr{A}$ has a countable subsystem which is also a model of $\mathscr{A}$.

ii) The Finiteness Theorem. This is proved by reduction to the case of propositional calculus.

iii) The Uniformity Theorem. Exercise 6 shows that this useful result is the best possible from several points of view.

Other results on the main topics of this chapter can be found in Chapters 3 and 5. This last chapter contains a second method for constructing canonical models (and alternative proofs of the main results of the present chapter).

The methods of this chapter permit an extension to predicate logic of the interpolation lemma, given in the preceding chapter for propositional logic; but its main interest derives from applications to definability such as those in Chapter 6.

For an interesting analysis of the special role played by the usual propositional operations applied to relations (and not only to truth values, discussed in Chapter 1, Exercise 1), see CRAIG, Boolean notions extended to higher dimensions, in: The Theory of Models (North-Holland Publ. Co., Amsterdam, 1965) pp. 55–69.

A *language* $\mathscr{L}$ consists of

1) A set $V_{\mathscr{L}}$ of elements called *variables*.

2) A sequence of sets $F^n_{\mathscr{L}}(n=0, 1, \ldots)$. The elements of $F^n_{\mathscr{L}}$ are called *n-ary function symbols*. $F_{\mathscr{L}}=\bigcup_n F^n_{\mathscr{L}}$ and is called the set of function symbols.

3) A sequence of sets $R^n_{\mathscr{L}}(n=0, 1, \ldots)$. The elements of $R^n_{\mathscr{L}}$ are called *n-ary relation symbols*.

We assume that the sets $V_{\mathscr{L}}$, $F^n_{\mathscr{L}}$, $R^n_{\mathscr{L}}$ are all pairwise disjoint.

The set of function schemas built up from $F^0_{\mathscr{L}} \cup V_{\mathscr{L}}$ as the set of 0-ary symbols and $F^n_{\mathscr{L}}$ as the set of n-ary symbols $(n=1, 2, \ldots)$ is called the set of *terms* of $\mathscr{L}$ and is denoted by $T_{\mathscr{L}}$. We denote by $T^n_{\mathscr{L}}$ the set of terms which contain n distinct variables.

The set $\bigcup_n [R^n_{\mathscr{L}} \times (T_{\mathscr{L}})^n]$ is called the set of atomic formulas of the language $\mathscr{L}$ and is denoted by $\mathrm{At}_{\mathscr{L}}$. Thus an atomic formula of $\mathscr{L}$ is a sequence $Rt_1 \ldots t_n$ where R is an n-ary relation symbol and $t_1, \ldots, t_n$ are terms of the language.

The set of formulas of the language $\mathscr{L}$, denoted by $\mathscr{F}_{\mathscr{L}}$, is the set of function schemas built up from the following list of symbols supposed to be distinct from one another:

i) The 0-ary symbols are the atomic formulas of $\mathscr{L}$, $\top$ (read "true") and $\bot$ (read "false"). Thus the set of 0-ary symbols is the set $\mathrm{At}_{\mathscr{L}} \cup \{\top, \bot\}$.

ii) The unary symbols are $\neg$ ("not") and the elements of a set Q, disjoint from the sets already mentioned, and in one-one correspondence with $V_{\mathscr{L}}$. The element of Q corresponding to the variable x is denoted by $\bigvee x$ (read "there is an x").

iii) A single binary symbol $\vee$ ("or").

We remark that $\mathscr{F}_{\mathscr{L}}=\mathrm{Prop}(P)$, in the sense of the previous chapter, where P is the subset of $\mathscr{F}_{\mathscr{L}}$ consisting of those elements (formulas) of $\mathscr{F}_{\mathscr{L}}$ whose first symbol is not a propositional constant ($\top$, $\bot$, $\neg$ or $\vee$).

A *realization* of the language $\mathscr{L}$ is defined to consist of

i) A non-empty set E called the *domain* of the realization.

ii) For each $n \geqslant 0$ a map of $F^n_{\mathscr{L}}$ into the set of functions defined on E^n and having values in E. From this we can derive (by Theorem 0.3) a map of $T^n_{\mathscr{L}}$ into the set of functions defined on E^n with values in E.

iii) For each $n \geqslant 0$ a map of $R^n_{\mathscr{L}}$ into $\mathscr{P}(E^n)$, the power set of E^n (or set of all subsets of E^n). From this we derive a map of $\mathrm{At}_{\mathscr{L}}$ into $\mathscr{P}(E^{V_{\mathscr{L}}})$ as follows: the image of the atomic formula $Rt_1 \ldots t_n$ in this mapping is the set $\{\delta \in E^{V_{\mathscr{L}}} : (\delta t_1, \dots, \delta t_n) \in \bar{R}\}$, where $\bar{R} \subseteq E^n$ is the image of R under the given map and δt_i is the value taken by the function derived from the term t_i when the variables take the values given by δ. ($\delta \in E^{V_{\mathscr{L}}}$ is a map of $V_{\mathscr{L}}$ into E.)

It follows from the fundamental theorem on function schemas (Theorem 0.3) that to each formula of the language $\mathscr{L}$ corresponds under the realization a subset of $E^{V_{\mathscr{L}}}$ if we define $\top$, $\bot$, $\neg$, $\vee$, $\bigvee x$ as functions on $\mathscr{P}(E^{V_{\mathscr{L}}})$ as follows:

$\top$ is the constant $E^{V_{\mathscr{L}}}$,

$\bot$ is the constant $\emptyset$,

$\neg$ is the map of $\mathscr{P}(E^{V_{\mathscr{L}}})$ into $\mathscr{P}(E^{V_{\mathscr{L}}})$ which sends each X into $\complement X$, the complement of X in $E^{V_{\mathscr{L}}}$,

$\vee$ is the map from $[\mathscr{P}(E^{V_{\mathscr{L}}})]^2$ into $\mathscr{P}(E^{V_{\mathscr{L}}})$ which sends (X, Y) into $X \cup Y$.

$\bigvee x$ is the map of $\mathscr{P}(E^{V_{\mathscr{L}}})$ into $\mathscr{P}(E^{V_{\mathscr{L}}})$ which sends X into the projection of X along x, i.e. to $\{\delta \in E^{V_{\mathscr{L}}}$: for some $\delta' \in X$, $\delta' = \delta$ except possibly at $x\}$.

(In Exercise 1 we give a simple example of a language and of a realization of this language which helps to explain the construction we have described here.)

Each time we are considering only a single realization of the language $\mathscr{L}$ we will denote by $\bar{A}$ the value taken by the formula A in this realization ($\bar{A} \subseteq E^{V_{\mathscr{L}}}$ if E is the domain of this realization.)

We say that a subset X of $E^{V_{\mathscr{L}}}$ *depends* only on the variables $x_1, \dots, x_n$ if there is a set $Y \subseteq E^{(x_1, \dots, x_n)}$ such that $X = Y \times E^{V_{\mathscr{L}} - (x_1, \dots, x_n)}$.

LEMMA 1: *Let A be a formula and let $x_1, \dots, x_n$ be the only variables occurring in the terms of A. Then in each realization, $\bar{A}$ depends only on the variables $x_1, \dots, x_n$.*

PROOF: This result is obvious if A is atomic. If it holds for formulas A and B then it holds also for $A \vee B$, since $\overline{\vee AB} = \bar{A} \cup \bar{B}$, for $\neg A$, since $\overline{\neg A} = \complement \bar{A}$, and also for $\bigvee xA$ since $\overline{\bigvee xA}$ is the projection of $\bar{A}$ along x. Therefore, by the definition of the set of formulas, the result is true of all formulas.

So that we can use this sort of argument easily we will call the *length* of a formula A the number of symbols occurring in A of types i), ii) and iii). That is, the length of A is the sum of the number of atomic formulas occurring in A and the number of symbols $\top$, $\bot$, $\neg$, $\vee$, $\bigvee x$ in A, separate *occurrences* being counted as distinct.

We associate with each formula A of the language $\mathscr{L}$ a finite set of occurrences of variables, called the *free* occurrences of variables in A. We do this by recursion on the length of A as follows: If A is of length 1, and so is an atomic formula or $\top$ or $\bot$, the free occurrences of variables in A are the occurrences of variables in the terms of A. Now suppose that we have defined the set of occurrences of free variables for each formula of length less than n and that A is a formula of length n. If A is of the form $\neg B$ the free occurrences of variables in A are those of B, and if A is of the form $\vee BC$ the free occurrences of variables in A are those in B together with those in C. Finally, if A is of the form $\bigvee xB$ the free occurrences of variables in A are those in B except x, if x has a free occurrence in B.

An occurrence of a variable which is not free in A is said to be *bound* in A.

A variable is called a *free variable* of A if it has a free occurrence in A, and bound if it has not. In particular, all those variables which do not occur in A are bound in A. Note that a free variable of A may have bound occurrences in A.

THEOREM 2: *Let A be a formula whose free variables are $x_1, \ldots, x_n$. Then in all realizations $\bar{A}$ depends only on the variables $x_1, \ldots, x_n$.*
PROOF: The proof is immediate by induction on the length of A.

A formula A is said to be *closed* if it has no free variables. It follows from Theorem 2 that in a realization with domain E, if A is closed, either $\bar{A}=\emptyset$ or $\bar{A}=E^{V\mathscr{L}}$.

We say that a realization, with domain E, *satisfies* a closed formula A if in the realization $\bar{A}=E^{V\mathscr{L}}$. In this case we say that the realization is a *model* of A. If $\mathscr{A}$ is a set of closed formulas of $\mathscr{L}$ we say that a realization of $\mathscr{L}$ satisfies $\mathscr{A}$, or is a model of $\mathscr{A}$, if it satisfies each formula of $\mathscr{A}$.

We will adopt the following notation. If A and B are two formulas of $\mathscr{L}$ we will write $(A)\vee(B)$ for $\vee AB$; $A\rightarrow B$ for $(\neg A)\vee(B)$ and $(A)\wedge(B)$ for $\neg((\neg A)\vee(\neg B))$. We write $\bigwedge xA$ for $\neg\bigvee x\neg A$, $\bigwedge x$ is read "for all x". If A is a formula whose free variables are $x_1, \ldots, x_n$, by the *closure* of A we mean the formula $\bigwedge x_1 \ldots \bigwedge x_n A$. Thus the closure of A is a closed formula.

We sometimes write $A(x_1, \ldots, x_n)$ for A and $A(t_1, \ldots, t_n)$ for the formula obtained by substituting the terms $t_1, \ldots, t_n$ for *each* occurrence of $x_1, \ldots, x_n$ respectively. By chapter 0, $A(t_1, \ldots, t_n)$ is a formula if A is one.

A (not necessarily closed) formula A is called a *theorem* of the language $\mathscr{L}$ if in each realization we have $\bar{A}=E^{V_{\mathscr{L}}}$, where E is the domain of the realization. This is equivalent to saying that each realization satisfies the closure of A.

If $A=A(x_1, \ldots, x_n)$ and no variable that occurs in $t_i (1 \leqslant i \leqslant n)$ has a bound occurrence in A then $A(t_1, \ldots, t_n)$ is a theorem provided A is one. The proof is immediate by induction on the length of A with use of Theorem 2.

QUANTIFIER FREE FORMULAS: A formula of the propositional calculus on $\mathrm{At}_{\mathscr{L}}$ is called a *quantifier free formula* of the language $\mathscr{L}$. Evidently such a formula is a formula of the language $\mathscr{L}$. It is called "quantifier free" because the symbols $\bigvee x$, $\bigwedge x$ are called "quantifiers".

PRENEX FORMULAS: A formula is said to be in *prenex normal form* or to be a *prenex formula* if it is of the form QA, where Q is a finite sequence of symbols $\neg$ and $\bigvee x_i$, $x_i \in V_{\mathscr{L}}$, and A is a quantifier free formula.

LEMMA 3: *If A and B are prenex formulas and $V_{\mathscr{L}}$ is infinite there is a prenex formula C which is equivalent to $A \vee B$.*

PROOF: The proof is by induction on the length of $A \vee B$. If A and B are quantifier free the lemma is obvious. Suppose, for example, that A contains quantifiers. Let $\bigvee x$ be the first quantifier occurring in A. It will be preceded by symbols $\neg$ which we may clearly assume to be not more than one in number.

Let x' be a variable not occurring in A nor in B. Since $V_{\mathscr{L}}$ is infinite such a variable exists.

If A is $\bigvee x A'$, let A'' be the formula obtained by replacing each occurrence of x in A' by x'. Then $A \vee B$ is equivalent to $(\bigvee x' A'') \vee B$ and so to $\bigvee x'(A'' \vee B)$ since x' does not occur in B. Since $A'' \vee B$ is shorter than $A \vee B$ and A'' and B are prenex formulas we can apply our induction hypothesis to obtain a prenex formula C' which is equivalent to $A'' \vee B$. Then $C = \bigvee x' C'$ is the required prenex formula equivalent to $A \vee B$.

If A is $\neg \bigvee x A'$, let A'' again be the formula which is obtained from A' by replacing each occurrence of x by x'. Clearly A is equivalent to $\neg \bigvee x' A''$, which is equivalent to $\bigwedge x' \neg A''$, and $\neg A''$ is shorter than A. Hence by the induction hypothesis there is a prenex formula C' which is equivalent to $\neg A'' \vee B$. Put $C = \neg \bigvee x' \neg C'$. Then C is equivalent to $\bigwedge x'(\neg A'' \vee B)$ which is equivalent to $\bigwedge x'(\neg A'' \vee B)$ since x' does not occur in B. Thus C is equivalent to $A \vee B$.

This completes the proof of the lemma.

We are now able to prove

THEOREM 4: *If $V_{\mathscr{L}}$ is infinite, then for each formula A there is a prenex formula A′ which is equivalent to A, i.e. $A \leftrightarrow A'$ is a theorem or $\bar{A} = \overline{A'}$ in each realization of $\mathscr{L}$.*

PROOF: We prove the theorem by induction on the length of A.

If A is an atomic formula we put $A' = A$. If A is $\neg B$ or $\bigvee xB$ then, by the induction hypothesis, there is a prenex formula B' which is equivalent to B. We put $A' = \neg B'$ or $A' = \bigvee xB'$. If A is $B \vee C$ then, by the induction hypothesis, there are two prenex formulas B' and C' equivalent to B and C respectively. We can apply Lemma 3 to obtain a prenex formula A' which is equivalent to $B' \vee C'$ and hence to A.

A prenex formula can always be written in the form $Q_1 x_1 \ldots Q_n x_n H$, where each $Q_i$is a quantifier, $\bigvee$ or $\bigwedge$, and H is quantifier free. The formula is said to be *existential* if each Q_i is $\bigvee$ and *universal* if each Q_i is $\bigwedge$.

Let $\mathscr{E}$ be a set of formulas of $\mathscr{L}$. The language of $\mathscr{E}$, denoted by $\mathscr{L}(\mathscr{E})$, is the language whose variables are those of $\mathscr{L}$ and whose relation and function symbols are those which occur in the formulas of $\mathscr{E}$.

A *canonical* realization of $\mathscr{E}$ is a realization of $\mathscr{L}(\mathscr{E})$ with domain $T_{\mathscr{L}(\mathscr{E})}$, the set of terms of $\mathscr{E}$, in which the function symbols are given their natural or canonical values as functions on $T_{\mathscr{L}(\mathscr{E})}$. The choice of values for the relational symbols is left free.

The aim of the theorems that follow, up to the Uniformity Theorem, is to answer the question of how we can tell whether a given formula is a theorem or not. We concern ourselves only with prenex formulas (see also Appendix II A, Lemma 3).

THEOREM 5: *Let $\mathscr{E}$ be a set of closed universal prenex formulas. If $\mathscr{E}$ has a model then it has a canonical model.*

PROOF: Put $\mathscr{L}' = \mathscr{L}(\mathscr{E})$. Each formula of $\mathscr{E}$ is, by hypothesis, of the form $\bigwedge x_1 \ldots \bigwedge x_n A$, where A is a formula of the propositional calculus on the set of atomic formulas of $\mathscr{L}'$. Let E be the domain of the given model of $\mathscr{E}$, and let $\bar{R} \subseteq E^n$ be the value in this model of the relational symbol R in $R^n_{\mathscr{L}}$. Let δ be an arbitrary fixed element of $E^{V_{\mathscr{L}'}}$. We derive from it a map $t \to \bar{t}$ of $T_{\mathscr{L}'}$ into E. We now define an canonical realization of $\mathscr{E}$ by giving to $R \in R^n_{\mathscr{L}}$, the value $\bar{\bar{R}} = \{(t_1, \ldots, t_n) \in T^n_{\mathscr{L}} : (\bar{t}_1, \ldots, \bar{t}_n) \in \bar{R}\}$. The map $t \to \bar{t}$ of $T_{\mathscr{L}}$ into E defines a map $\phi : T^{V_{\mathscr{L}'}} \to E^{V_{\mathscr{L}'}}$ and from this, the inverse map $\phi^{-1} : \mathscr{P}(E^{V_{\mathscr{L}'}}) \to (T^{V_{\mathscr{L}'}})$.

If A is a quantifier free formula of $\mathscr{L}$, $\bar{A}$ the value it has in the given model and $\bar{\bar{A}}$ its value in the canonical realization, then $\bar{\bar{A}}=\phi^{-1}(\bar{A})$. This is obvious if A is atomic and we know that ϕ^{-1} commutes with the operations of unions and taking complements.

Now let $\bigwedge x_1 \ldots \bigwedge x_n A$ be a formula of $\mathscr{E}$. By hypothesis $\bar{A}=E^{V_{\mathscr{L}'}}$. Hence $\bar{\bar{A}}=\phi^{-1}(\bar{A})=(T_{\mathscr{L}'})^{V_{\mathscr{L}'}}$. Therefore $\bigwedge x_1 \ldots \bigwedge x_n A$ is satisfied by the canonical realization we have constructed.

This completes the proof.

We have the following dual result.

THEOREM 6: *If A is a closed existential prenex formula then A is a theorem if and only if all canonical realizations satisfy it.*
PROOF: The condition is obviously necessary. It is also sufficient since if all canonical realizations satisfy A none satisfies $\neg A$. Hence by Theorem 5 $\neg A$ does not have a model.

THEOREM 7: *To each prenex formula F there corresponds a universal prenex formula $\hat{F}$, whose language does not differ from that of F except for the addition of a finite number of function symbols, such that*

a) *In each realization of $\mathscr{L}(\hat{F})$, $\bar{\hat{F}}\subseteq\bar{F}$, that is, $\hat{F}\rightarrow F$ is a theorem and*

b) *Each realization of $\mathscr{L}(F)$ can be extended to a realization of $\mathscr{L}(\hat{F})$ in such a way that $\bar{F}=\bar{\hat{F}}$.*

PROOF: The proof is by induction on the number of quantifiers in F. If F has no quantifiers in it we put $\hat{F}=F$.

If $F=\bigwedge xG$, then by our induction hypothesis, there is a formula $\hat{G}$ which satisfies the theorem for G. It is sufficient to put $\hat{F}=\bigwedge x\hat{G}$.

If $F=\bigvee xG$, we again let $\hat{G}$ be the formula which satisfies the theorem for G. Let $x_0, x_1, \ldots, x_n$ be the free variables of $\hat{G}$. If x is not free in G then in each realization $\overline{\bigvee x\hat{G}}=\bar{\hat{G}}$ and so it is sufficient to take $\hat{F}=\hat{G}$. If x is free in G, say x is x_0. Let ϕ be an n-ary function symbol which does not occur in $\mathscr{L}(\hat{G})$. Let $\hat{F}$ be the formula obtained from G by replacing each occurrence of x by $\phi x_1 \ldots x_n$. Clearly, because $\hat{G}$ is universal so is $\hat{F}$.

We first show that $\bar{\hat{F}}$ satisfies condition a). Let E be the domain of a realization of $\mathscr{L}(\bar{\hat{F}})$. $\hat{F}$ is the set of all $(a_1, \ldots, a_n)\in E^{(x_1, \ldots, x_n)}$, such that $(\bar{\phi}(a_1, \ldots, a_n), a_1, \ldots, a_n)\in\bar{\hat{G}}\subseteq\bar{G}\subseteq E^{(x_1, \ldots, x_n)}$. Thus for each element $(a_1, \ldots, a_n)$ of $\bar{\hat{F}}$, $(a_1, \ldots, a_n)\in\overline{\bigvee xG}=\bar{F}$. Hence $\bar{\hat{F}}\subseteq\bar{F}$.

Finally we show that $\hat{F}$ satisfies condition b). Let E be the domain of a realization of $\mathscr{L}(F)$. By hypothesis this realization can be extended to $\mathscr{L}(\hat{G})$ in such a way that $\bar{G}=\bar{\hat{G}}$. Thus we then have $\bar{F}=\overline{\bigvee xG}=\overline{\bigvee x\hat{G}}$. So $(a_1, \ldots, a_n)$ is in $E^{(x_1, \ldots, x_n)}$ if and only if there is some $a \in E$ such that $(a, a_1, \ldots, a_n) \in \bar{\hat{G}}$. We now define $\bar{\phi}$ as follows (since, by hypothesis, $\phi \notin \mathscr{L}(\hat{G})$, we still have this definition to make):

$$\bar{\phi}(a_1, \ldots, a_n) = a \quad \text{if} \quad (a_1, \ldots, a_n) \in \bar{F}$$

and $\bar{\phi}(a_1, \ldots, a_n) = a_0$ is an arbitrary element of E, otherwise.

In this way we obtain a realization of $\mathscr{L}(\hat{F})$. In this realization $\bar{\hat{F}}$ is the set of those $(a_1, \ldots, a_n)$ such that $(\bar{\phi}(a_1, \ldots, a_n), a_1, \ldots, a_n) \in \bar{\hat{G}}$. Hence $\bar{\hat{F}}= \overline{\bigvee x\hat{G}}=\bar{F}$.

This completes the proof.

We again have a dual result.

THEOREM 8: *To each prenex formula F there corresponds an existential prenex formula $\check{F}$ whose language does not differ from that of F except for the addition of a finite number of function symbols, such that*

a) *In each realization of $\mathscr{L}(F)$, $\bar{F} \subseteq \bar{\check{F}}$, that is, $F \to \check{F}$ is a theorem, and*

b) *Each realization of $\mathscr{L}(F)$ can be extended to a realization of $\mathscr{L}(\check{F})$ in such a way that $\bar{F}=\bar{\check{F}}$.*

PROOF: It is sufficient to put $\check{F}=\neg(\widehat{\neg F})$.

COROLLARY 1: *For a closed prenex formula F to be a theorem it is necessary and sufficient that $\check{F}$ be satisfied by all canonical realizations.*

PROOF: If F is a theorem then because $F \to \check{F}$ is a theorem, $\check{F}$ is also a theorem. Hence, in particular, $\check{F}$ is satisfied by all canonical realizations.

Conversely, suppose $\check{F}$ is satisfied by all canonical realizations. Then by Theorem 6, since $\check{F}$ is existential, $\check{F}$ is a theorem. Given any realization of $\mathscr{L}(F)$ it can be extended so that $\bar{F}=\bar{\check{F}}$. But $\check{F}$ is satisfied by this extension and so F is satisfied by the original realization and hence is a theorem.

COROLLARY 2: *Let $\mathscr{E}$ be a countable set of closed formulas. If $\mathscr{E}$ has a model then $\mathscr{E}$ has a countable model.*

PROOF: We may assume that $\mathscr{E}$ consists of prenex formulas. Let $\hat{\mathscr{E}}$ be the set of formulas $\hat{F}$ for F in $\mathscr{E}$. (We assume that the function letters added to $\mathscr{L}(\mathscr{E})$ for different formulas F are different.) If $\mathscr{E}$ has a model this model can be extended to a model of $\hat{\mathscr{E}}$. Now $\hat{\mathscr{E}}$ consists of universal prenex formulas and so if it has a model it has a canonical model. Clearly such a model is countable.

This concludes the proof.

Later (in Exercises 4 and 5) we shall give more precise formulations of this result.

Consider a language $\mathscr{L}$. If we have a canonical realization of $\mathscr{L}$ we have at the same time, for each $n \geqslant 0$, a map of $R^n_{\mathscr{L}}$ into $\mathscr{P}((T_{\mathscr{L}})^n) = \{0,1\}^{(T_{\mathscr{L}})^n}$. From this we can obtain a map of $R^n_{\mathscr{L}} \times (T_{\mathscr{L}})^n$ into $\{0,1\}$ and thus, for each $n \geqslant 0$, a map of $\mathrm{At}_{\mathscr{L}}$, the set of atomic formulas of $\mathscr{L}$, into $\{0,1\}$. Thus we have seen that

THEOREM 9: *Having a canonical realization of a language $\mathscr{L}$ is equivalent to having a realization of the propositional calculus on the set of atomic formulas of $\mathscr{L}$.*

LEMMA 10: *Let $F(x_1, \ldots, x_m)$ be a quantifier free formula of $\mathscr{L}$ with free variables $x_1, \ldots, x_m$ and let $t_1, \ldots, t_m$ be terms of $\mathscr{L}$. Then in a given canonical realization of $\mathscr{L}$, $(t_1, \ldots, t_m) \in \bar{F}$ if and only if the corresponding realization of the propositional calculus on $\mathrm{At}_{\mathscr{L}}$ satisfies $F(t_1, \ldots, t_m)$.*

PROOF: The lemma is obvious if F is atomic. Also if F satisfies the lemma then clearly so does $\neg F$.

Now suppose that G and H satisfy the lemma. $(t_1, \ldots, t_m) \in \overline{G \vee H}$ if and only if $(t_1, \ldots, t_m) \in \bar{G}$ or $(t_1, \ldots, t_m) \in \bar{H}$, that is, if and only if either $G(t_1, \ldots, t_m)$ or $H(t_1, \ldots, t_m)$ is satisfied by the corresponding realization of the propositional calculus on $\mathrm{At}_{\mathscr{L}}$, and hence if and only if $F(t_1, \ldots, t_m)$ is satisfied by this realization.

THEOREM 11. THE UNIFORMITY THEOREM: *Let $F(x_1, \ldots, x_m)$ be a quantifier free formula with free variables $x_1, \ldots, x_m$. Then $\forall x_1 \ldots \forall x_m F(x_1, \ldots, x_m)$ is a theorem if and only if there are terms $t^i_1, \ldots, t^i_m$, $1 \leqslant i \leqslant k$, of the language of F such that the formula*

$$F(t^1_1, \ldots, t^1_m) \vee F(t^2_1, \ldots, t^2_m) \vee \cdots \vee F(t^k_1, \ldots, t^k_m)$$

is a theorem of the propositional calculus on $\mathrm{At}_{\mathscr{L}(F)}$.

PROOF: The condition is sufficient. For suppose that the formula

$$F(t_1^1, \ldots, t_m^1) \vee F(t_1^2, \ldots, t_m^2) \vee \cdots \vee F(t_1^k, \ldots, t_m^k)$$

is a theorem of the propositional calculus on $\mathrm{At}_{\mathscr{L}(F)}$. Now consider an arbitrary canonical realization of $\mathscr{L}(F)$. In the corresponding realization of the propositional calculus on $\mathrm{At}_{\mathscr{L}(F)}$ the formula above is satisfied. Hence for some i, $1 \leqslant i \leqslant m$, the formula $F(t_1^i, \ldots, t_m^i)$ is satisfied in this realization. Therefore, by Lemma 10, in the given canonical realization $(t_1^i, \ldots, t_m^i) \in \bar{F}$, and so $\bigvee x_1 \ldots \bigvee x_m F(x_1, \ldots, x_m)$ is satisfied. Since this existential formula is satisfied by all canonical realizations it is a theorem.

Conversely, we will show that the condition is necessary. Suppose that $\bigvee x_1 \ldots \bigvee x_m F(x_1, \ldots, x_m)$ is a theorem, then it is satisfied by all canonical realizations. Thus for each canonical realization of $\mathscr{L}(F)$ there are terms $t_1, \ldots, t_m$ such that $(t_1, \ldots, t_m) \in \bar{F}$. By Lemma 10, it follows that for each realization of the propositional calculus on $\mathrm{At}_{\mathscr{L}(F)}$ there is a sequence of terms $t_1, \ldots, t_m$ such that $F(t_1, \ldots, t_m)$ is satisfied in the realization. Hence, by the second version of the Finiteness Theorem for propositional calculus (Theorem 1.5), there are terms $t_1^i, \ldots, t_m^i$, $1 \leqslant i \leqslant k$, such that $F(t_1^1, \ldots, t_m^1) \vee \cdots \vee F(t_1^k, \ldots, t_m^k)$ is a theorem of the propositional calculus on $\mathrm{At}_{\mathscr{L}(F)}$. This completes the proof.

These results give us the following method for verifying that a prenex formula A is a theorem. We construct the formula $\check{A}$ which, being existential, can be written in the form $\bigvee x_1 \ldots \bigvee x_m F(x_1, \ldots, x_m)$, where F is a quantifier free. Then it is sufficient to look at all the formulas of the form

$$F(t_1^1, \ldots\ t_m^1) \vee \cdots \vee F(t_1^k, \ldots, t_m^k)$$

where the t_j^i are terms of $\mathscr{L}(F)$ until you come across one which is a theorem of the propositional calculus on $\mathrm{At}_{\mathscr{L}(F)}$. (For each formula of this form we can test in a finite number of steps whether or not it is a theorem, by the definition of a theorem of the propositional calculus.)

Then A will be a theorem if and only if you finally discover a theorem of the propositional calculus in this way.

THEOREM 12. THE FINITENESS THEOREM FOR PREDICATE CALCULUS: *A set $\mathscr{E}$ of closed formulas has a model if and only if each finite subset of $\mathscr{E}$ has a model.*

PROOF: Trivially, if $\mathscr{E}$ has a model so does every finite subset of $\mathscr{E}$.

Now suppose that every finite subset of $\mathscr{E}$ has a model. We will prove that $\mathscr{E}$ has a model.

Let $\mathscr{L}$ be the language of $\mathscr{E}$. Clearly we can assume that all the formulas of $\mathscr{E}$ are in prenex normal form. Let $\hat{\mathscr{E}}=\{\hat{A}:A\in\mathscr{E}\}$. We will assume that the function symbols that we use to construct different $\hat{A}$ are distinct. Since $\hat{A}\rightarrow A$ is a theorem for each A, it will be sufficient to prove that $\hat{\mathscr{E}}$ has a model.

Each finite subset of $\hat{\mathscr{E}}$ has a model. For suppose $\{\hat{A}_1, \ldots, \hat{A}_n\}$ is a finite subset of $\hat{\mathscr{E}}$. Then, by hypothesis, $\{A_1, \ldots, A_n\}$ has a model and, by Theorem 7, this can be extended to a model of $\{\hat{A}_1, \ldots, \hat{A}_n\}$. Therefore we need only consider the case when $\mathscr{E}$ consists of universal prenex formulas.

Let each formula A of $\mathscr{E}$ be of the form $\bigwedge x_1 \ldots \bigwedge x_n A_0(x_1, \ldots, x_n)$, where A_0 is quantifier free. Let $\mathscr{A}=\{A_0(t_1, \ldots, t_n)\colon A\in\mathscr{E}$ and $(t_1, \ldots, t_n)\in (T_{\mathscr{L}})^n\}$. So $\mathscr{A}$ is a set of formulas of the propositional calculus on $\mathrm{At}_{\mathscr{L}}$.

Every finite subset of $\mathscr{E}$ has a model and so has a canonical model. Hence, by Lemma 10, every finite subset of $\mathscr{A}$ has a model, in the sense of propositional calculus. Therefore, by the Finiteness Theorem for propositional calculus, $\mathscr{A}$ has a model. It follows, again from Lemma 10, that the canonical realization corresponding to this model satisfies $\mathscr{E}$.

This completes the proof.

We will use the following notation in what follows:

1. Let $\mathscr{L}$ and $\mathscr{L}'$ be two languages. Then $\mathscr{L}\cup\mathscr{L}'$ will be used to denote the language whose function and relation symbols are those of $\mathscr{L}$ together with those of $\mathscr{L}'$ and $\mathscr{L}\cap\mathscr{L}'$ is the language whose function and relation symbols are those common to $\mathscr{L}$ and $\mathscr{L}'$. We write $\mathscr{L}\subseteq\mathscr{L}'$ to indicate that the function and relation symbols of $\mathscr{L}$ belong also to $\mathscr{L}'$. For example, $\mathscr{L}(A\vee B)=\mathscr{L}(A)\cup\mathscr{L}(B)$.

2. If $A_1, \ldots, A_k$ are formulas we write $\bigvee_{1\leqslant i\leqslant k} A_i$ for the formula $A_1\vee\cdots\vee A_k$ (and $\bigwedge_{1\leqslant i\leqslant k} A_i$ for the formula $A_1\wedge\cdots\wedge A_k$).

THEOREM 13. THE INTERPOLATION LEMMA FOR PREDICATE CALCULUS:

If $A\vee B$ is a theorem, there is a formula C such that $\mathscr{L}(C)\subseteq\mathscr{L}(A)\cap\mathscr{L}(B)$ and such that $A\vee C$ and $B\vee\neg C$ are theorems.

PROOF: We show first that it is sufficient to consider the case when A and B are both closed formulas. For suppose that we have proved the Theorem for this case and that $A(z_1, \ldots, z_k)$ and $B(z_1, \ldots, z_k)$ are two formulas whose free variables occur among $z_1, \ldots, z_k$ such that $A(z_1, \ldots, z_k) \vee B(z_1, \ldots, z_k)$ is a theorem. Let $a_1, \ldots, a_k$ be k constant symbols (0-ary function symbols) which are not in $\mathscr{L}(A) \cup \mathscr{L}(B)$. Then $A(a_1, \ldots, a_k) \vee B(a_1, \ldots, a_k)$ is a theorem and so, by hypothesis, there is a formula D such that $\mathscr{L}(D) \subseteq (\mathscr{L}(A) \cap \mathscr{L}(B)) \cup \{a_1, \ldots, a_k\}$ and such that $A(a_1, \ldots, a_k) \vee D$ and $B(a_1, \ldots, a_k) \vee \neg D$ are theorems. Let C be the formula obtained from D by substituting $z_1, \ldots, z_k$ for $a_1, \ldots, a_k$. Then clearly $A(z_1, \ldots, z_k) \vee C$ and $B(z_1, \ldots, z_k) \vee \neg C$ are theorems.

So from now on we shall assume that A and B are closed. We shall now show that it is sufficient to consider the case when they are existential formulas. For suppose that we have proved the theorem for this case and let A and B be two closed prenex formulas such that $A \vee B$ is a theorem. We construct the formulas $\breve{A}$ and $\breve{B}$ using distinct function symbols which do not occur in $\mathscr{L}(A) \cup \mathscr{L}(B)$, so that $\mathscr{L}(\breve{A}) \cap \mathscr{L}(\breve{B}) = \mathscr{L}(A) \cap \mathscr{L}(B)$. Since $A \to \breve{A}$ and $B \to \breve{B}$ are theorems, $\breve{A} \vee \breve{B}$ is a theorem. Therefore, by hypothesis, there is a formula C such that $\breve{A} \vee C$ and $\breve{B} \vee \neg C$ are theorems and $\mathscr{L}(C) \subseteq \mathscr{L}(A) \cap \mathscr{L}(B)$. All realizations of $\mathscr{L}(A)$ can be extended to realizations of $\mathscr{L}(\breve{A})$ in such a way that $\bar{A} = \bar{\breve{A}}$. Hence each realization of $\mathscr{L}(A \vee C)$ can be extended to a realization of $\mathscr{L}(\breve{A} \vee C)$ in such a way that $\overline{A \vee C} = \overline{\breve{A} \vee C}$. It follows that $A \vee C$ is satisfied by each realization and hence is a theorem. Similarly $B \vee \neg C$ is a theorem.

So we can assume that $A = \bigvee x_1 \ldots \bigvee x_m H(x_1, \ldots, x_m)$ and $B = \bigvee y_1 \ldots \bigvee y_n K(y_1, \ldots, y_n)$ where H and K are quantifier free. $A \vee B$ is a theorem, and so, by the Uniformity Theorem, there are terms t_i^h and u_j^k of $\mathscr{L}(A \vee B)$ such that if

$$A_1 = \bigvee\!\!\!\!\bigvee_h H(t_1^h, \ldots, t_m^h)$$

and

$$B_1 = \bigvee\!\!\!\!\bigvee_k K(u_1^k, \ldots, u_n^k)$$

then $A_1 \vee B_1$ is a theorem of the propositional calculus on $\mathrm{At}_{\mathscr{L}(A \vee B)}$. Then, by the Interpolation Lemma for propositional calculus, there is a formula C whose propositional variables occur both in A_1 and B_1 such that $A_1 \vee C$ and $B_1 \vee \neg C$ are both theorems of the propositional calculus.

Let $\xi_1, \ldots, \xi_l$ be the terms which occur in the atomic formulas of C. So $C = C_1(\xi_1, \ldots, \xi_l)$ where $C_1(z_1, \ldots, z_l)$ is a formula with free variables $z_1, \ldots, z_l$ which does not contain any function symbols and whose relation symbols are all in $\mathscr{L}(A) \cap \mathscr{L}(B)$.

We construct, by recursion on p, a sequence of quantifier free formulas $C_p(z_1, \ldots, z_{l_p})$ whose language is contained in $\mathscr{L}(A) \cap \mathscr{L}(B)$, and for each p a sequence $\xi_1^p, \ldots, \xi_{l_p}^p$ of terms of $\mathscr{L}(A) \cap \mathscr{L}(B)$ so that $C = C_p(\xi_1^p, \ldots, \xi_{l_p}^p)$, as follows:

For $p=1$ the formula is $C_1(z_1, \ldots, z_l)$ and the terms are $\xi_1, \ldots, \xi_l$. Suppose we have carried out this construction as far as p so that $C = C_p(\xi_1^p, \ldots, \xi_{l_p}^p)$. We choose a ξ_i^p of maximum length that begins with a function symbol $\phi \in \mathscr{L}(A) \cap \mathscr{L}(B)$, if one such ξ_p^i exists. If, say $\xi_{l_p}^p$ is this term, we have $\xi_{l_p}^p = \phi\eta_0 \ldots \eta_r$ where $\eta_0, \ldots, \eta_r$ are terms of $\mathscr{L}(A) \cap \mathscr{L}(B)$. We then put $C_{p+1}(z_1, \ldots, z_{l_p+r}) = C_p(z_1, \ldots, z_{l_p-1}, \phi z_{l_p} \ldots z_{l_p+r})$ and we let the corresponding sequence of terms be $\xi_1^p, \ldots, \xi_{l_p-1}^p, \eta_0, \ldots, \eta_r$.

Clearly when p is increased by one the sum of the lengths of the terms ξ_i^p decreases by one. Consequently this construction must stop after a finite number of steps. Thus we eventually obtain a quantifier free formula $M(z_1, \ldots, z_q)$ and a sequence of terms $\eta_1, \ldots, \eta_q$ such that $C = M(\eta_1, \ldots, \eta_q)$, the language of $M(z_1, \ldots, z_q)$ is contained in $\mathscr{L}(A) \cap \mathscr{L}(B)$ and none of the terms $\eta_1, \ldots, \eta_q$ begins with a function symbol of $\mathscr{L}(A) \cap \mathscr{L}(B)$.

Since $A_1 \vee C$ and $B_1 \vee \neg C$ are theorems of the propositional calculus on $\mathrm{At}_{\mathscr{L}(A \vee B)}$ it follows from Lemma 10 that $\bigvee x_1 \ldots \bigvee x_m H(x_1, \ldots, x_m) \vee M(\eta_1, \ldots, \eta_q)$ and $\bigvee y_1 \ldots \bigvee y_n K(y_1, \ldots, y_n) \vee \neg M(\eta_1, \ldots, \eta_q)$ are both theorems. Suppose that $\eta_1, \ldots, \eta_q$ are arranged in order of decreasing length (in such a way that no term can be a sub-term of any that follows it).

Put $D = Q_q z_q \ldots Q_1 z_1 M(z_1, \ldots, z_q)$, where $Q_i = \bigwedge$ if η_i begins with a symbol ϕ which is in $\mathscr{L}(B)$, and hence not in $\mathscr{L}(A)$, and $Q_i = \bigvee$ if η_i begins with a symbol ϕ which is in $\mathscr{L}(A)$, and hence not in $\mathscr{L}(B)$. We will see that D is the desired formula.

Clearly $\mathscr{L}(D) \subseteq \mathscr{L}(A) \cap \mathscr{L}(B)$ since $\mathscr{L}(M) \subseteq \mathscr{L}(A) \cap \mathscr{L}(B)$. Suppose that for $l \leqslant q$ we have shown that

$$A \vee Q_{l-1} z_{l-1} \ldots Q_1 z_1 M(z_1, \ldots, z_{l-1}, \eta_l, \ldots, \eta_q)$$

and

$$B \vee \neg Q_{l-1} z_{l-1} \ldots Q_1 z_1 M(z_1, \ldots, z_{l-1}, \eta_l, \ldots, \eta_q)$$

are both theorems. (Note that this is certainly true when $l=1$.)

Put $U(z_l) = Q_{l-1} z_{l-1} \ldots Q_1 z_1 M(z_1, \ldots, z_{l-1}, z_{l-1}, z_l, \eta_{l+1}, \ldots, \eta_q)$. So by our hypothesis $A \vee U(\eta_l)$ and $B \vee \neg U(\eta_l)$ are both theorems. Suppose, say, that η_l begins with a symbol ϕ of $\mathscr{L}(B)$, so $\phi \notin \mathscr{L}(A)$. Let $\eta_l = \phi\tau_1 \ldots \tau_r$, where $\tau_1, \ldots, \tau_r$ are terms of $\mathscr{L}(A) \cup \mathscr{L}(B)$. We have to show that both $A \vee \bigwedge z_l U(z_l)$ and $B \vee \bigvee z_l \neg U(z_l)$ are both theorems. Clearly the latter is because $B \vee \neg U(\eta_l)$ is a theorem.

Put $A \vee U(z_l) = V(z_l, \eta_{l+1}, \ldots, \eta_q)$ where

$$V(z_l, z_{l+1}, \ldots, z_q) = A \vee Q_{l-1}z_{l-1} \ldots Q_1 z_1 M(z_1, \ldots, z_{l-1}, z_l, \ldots, z_q).$$

Then we have to show that $\bigwedge z_l\ V(z_l, \eta_{l+1}, \ldots, \eta_q)$ is a theorem. This is a consequence of the following lemma.

Lemma 14: *Let $V(z, z_1, \ldots, z_q)$ be a formula with free variable z and let ϕ be a function symbol which does not occur in $V(z, z_1, \ldots, z_q)$. Let $\eta = \phi\tau_1 \ldots \tau_r$ be a term beginning with ϕ distinct from and at least as long as each of the terms $\eta_1, \ldots, \eta_q$. Then, if $V(\eta, \eta_1, \ldots, \eta_q)$ is a theorem so is $\bigwedge z\ V(z, \eta_1, \ldots, \eta_q)$.*

The lemma reduces to its special case of purely existential V. For, if $V(\eta, \eta_1, \ldots, \eta_q)$ is a theorem, so is $\check{V}(\eta, \eta_1, \ldots, \eta_q)$ and hence, by applying the lemma to this existential formula, so is $\bigwedge z \check{V}(z, \eta_1, \ldots, \eta_q)$. Let a be an individual constant or variable not occurring in $V(\eta, \eta_1, \ldots, \eta_q)$ (by assumption that there are infinitely many variables there always is such an a). So $\check{V}(a, \eta_1, \ldots, \eta_q)$, i.e. $[\bigwedge z\, V(z, \eta_1, \ldots, \eta_q)]^{\vee}$ is a theorem, and so is $\bigwedge z\ V(z, \eta_1, \ldots, \eta_q)$. Suppose then that $V(z, \eta_1, \ldots, \eta_q) = \bigvee x_1 \ldots \bigvee x_m\ W(z, \eta_1, \ldots, \eta_q, x_1, \ldots, x_m)$, and that a is a new constant or variable. We wish to show that $V(a, \eta_1, \ldots, \eta_q)$ is a theorem or, equivalently, that it is satisfied in each canonical realization $\mathfrak{M}$. Let $\mathfrak{M}'$ be the realization obtained from $\mathfrak{M}$ by changing the value of $\bar{\phi}$ at the place $(\tau_1, \ldots, \tau_r)$ by putting $\bar{\phi}(\tau_1, \ldots, \tau_r) = a$ instead of $\phi = \tau_1 \ldots \tau_r$ (its value in the canonical realization $\mathfrak{M}$). Now $\mathfrak{M}'$ satisfies $V(\eta, \eta_1, \ldots, \eta_q)$ since this is a theorem; also the values of $\eta_1, \ldots, \eta_q$ in $\mathfrak{M}$ and $\mathfrak{M}'$ are the same, namely $\eta_1, \ldots, \eta_q$ because none of these terms contains η as a part. Since $W(z, z_1, \ldots, z_q, x_1, \ldots, x_m)$ does not contain ϕ, its values in $\mathfrak{M}$ and $\mathfrak{M}'$ are the same: let $\bar{W}$ be the common value. Since $\mathfrak{M}'$ satisfies $\bigvee x_1 \ldots \bigvee x_m\ W(\eta, \eta_1, \ldots, \eta_q, x_1, \ldots, x_m)$ and the domain of $\mathfrak{M}'$ is the set of terms, there are terms $t_1, \ldots, t_m$ such that $(\bar{\eta}, \bar{\eta}_1, \ldots, \bar{\eta}_q, t_1, \ldots, t_m) \in \bar{W}$. But $\bar{\eta}_1 = \eta_1, \ldots, \bar{\eta}_q = \eta_q$ and $\bar{\eta} = a$. So $(a, \eta_1, \ldots, \eta_q, t_1, \ldots, t_m) \in \bar{W}$ which means, since $t_1, \ldots, t_m$ are also elements of the domain of $\mathfrak{M}$, that $\bigvee x_1 \ldots \bigvee x_m\, W(a, \eta_1, \ldots, \eta_q, x_1, \ldots, x_m)$ is satisfied in $\mathfrak{M}$ and hence also $V(a, \eta_1, \ldots, \eta_q)$.

This concludes the proof of the lemma and hence of Theorem 13.

In the Exercises we give an example where the formula C is obtained by following the above proof.

We can restate the result as

THEOREM 15: *If $A \to B$ is a theorem there is a formula C such that $A \to C$ and $C \to B$ are theorems and $\mathscr{L}(C) \subseteq \mathscr{L}(A) \cap \mathscr{L}(B)$.*

We have as a corollary

THEOREM 16. THE DEFINABILITY THEOREM FOR PREDICATE CALCULUS: *Let $\mathscr{A}$ be a set of formulas, R an n-ary relation symbol of $\mathscr{L}(\mathscr{A})$ and $\mathscr{A}'$ the set of formulas obtained by substituting for R in each formula of $\mathscr{A}$ an n-ary relation symbol R' which does not occur in $\mathscr{L}(\mathscr{A})$. Then if $(Rx_1 \ldots x_n \to R'x_1 \ldots x_n)$ is a consequence of $\mathscr{A} \cup \mathscr{A}'$, there is a formula F such that $\mathscr{L}(F) \subseteq \mathscr{L}(\mathscr{A})$, $R \notin \mathscr{L}(F)$ and $(F \leftrightarrow Rx_1 \ldots x_n)$ is a consequence of $\mathscr{A}$.*

PROOF: Since $(Rx_1 \ldots x_n \to R'x_1 \ldots x_n)$ is a consequence of $\mathscr{A} \cup \mathscr{A}'$, by the Finiteness Theorem, there is a finite subset $\mathscr{A}_1$ of $\mathscr{A}$ such that $(Rx_1 \ldots x_n \to R'x_1 \ldots x_n)$ is a consequence of $\mathscr{A}_1 \cup \mathscr{A}'_1$. If A is the conjunction of the formulas in $\mathscr{A}_1$ and A' is the conjunction of the formulas in $\mathscr{A}'_1$ then

$$(A \wedge A') \to (Rx_1 \ldots x_n \to R'x_1 \ldots x_n)$$

is a theorem and hence so too is

$$(A \wedge Rx_1 \ldots x_n) \to (A' \to R'x_1 \ldots x_n).$$

Therefore, by the Interpolation Lemma there is a formula F such that $\mathscr{L}(F) \subseteq \mathscr{L}(A) \cap \mathscr{L}(A')$, and both

$$(A \wedge Rx_1 \ldots x_n) \to F \qquad \text{and} \qquad F \to (A' \to R'x_1 \ldots x_n)$$

are theorems. Therefore $A \to (Rx_1 \ldots x_n \to F)$ and $A' \to (F \to R'x_1 \ldots x_n)$ are theorems, which gives the desired result.

Exercises

1. The language $\mathscr{L}$ is given as follows:

$V_{\mathscr{L}}$ is the two element set $\{x, y\}$,

$R_{\mathscr{L}}$ contains two elements, a unary symbol U and a binary symbol R,

$F_{\mathscr{L}}$ contains one unary symbol f.

Consider the following realization of $\mathscr{L}$. The domain is $\mathbf{R}$, the set of real numbers, the value of U is the closed interval $[0,1]$, R has the value $\bar{R} = \{(x, y) \in \mathbf{R}^2 : x < y\}$, the value of f is given by $\bar{f}(t) = t^2 + 1$.

What is the set of terms of $\mathscr{L}$?

The values of the formulas of $\mathscr{L}$ can be represented as subsets of the plane $\mathbf{R}^{\{x, y\}}$. Which subsets of the plane correspond to the following formulas:

$$Ux,\ Ufx,\ \bigvee xUfx,\ R(x, fy),\ \bigwedge xR(y, fx),\ \bigwedge xR(x, fy),$$
$$\bigwedge xR(x, fx),\ \bigwedge y(Uy \to R(fy, x)).$$

2. Give a formula in prenex normal form which is equivalent to $\bigwedge x \bigvee y \bigwedge z Axyz \to \bigwedge y \bigvee z Byz \quad (A \in R^3_{\mathscr{L}},\ B \in R^2_{\mathscr{L}})$.

3. Consider the formula $F = \bigwedge x \bigvee y \bigvee z \bigwedge u \bigvee v\, A(x, y, z, u, v)$, where A is a 5-ary relation symbol.

Give two formulas $\hat{F}$ and $\check{F}$ which satisfy Theorems 7 and 8.

Answer. The proofs of these Theorems give the following formulas

$$\hat{F} = \bigwedge x \bigwedge u\, A(x, fx, gx, u, h(x, fx, gx, u))$$

where f and g are unary function symbols and h is a 4-ary function symbol.

$$\check{F} = \bigvee y \bigvee z \bigvee v\, A(a, y, z, \phi(a, y, z), v)$$

where a is a 0-ary function symbol and ϕ is a ternary function symbol.

4. Let $\mathscr{E}$ be a set of formulas of cardinal $\aleph \geqslant \aleph_0$. Show that if $\mathscr{E}$ has a model then, for each cardinal $\aleph' \geqslant \aleph$, $\mathscr{E}$ has a model of cardinal $\aleph'$.

Answer. Let $\hat{\mathscr{E}} = \{\hat{F} : F \in \mathscr{E}\}$, where we use distinct function symbols not occurring in $\mathscr{L}(\mathscr{E})$ to form $\hat{F}$ for different F. $\mathscr{E}$ has a model and this can be extended to a model of $\hat{\mathscr{E}}$. We add to $\mathscr{L}(\mathscr{E})$ a set C of constant symbols of cardinal $\aleph'$. Since $\hat{\mathscr{E}}$ has a model it has a canonical model for this new language. Clearly this canonical model is of cardinal $\aleph'$.

5. If $\mathfrak{R}$ is a realization of a language $\mathscr{L}$ with domain E, a realization $\mathfrak{R}'$ of $\mathscr{L}$ with domain $E' \subseteq E$ and such that for each $\phi \in F^n_{\mathscr{L}}$, $\bar{\phi}(E'^n) \subseteq E'$ and the values of the function and relational symbols are the restrictions to E' of their values in $\mathfrak{R}$ is called a *sub-realization* of $\mathfrak{R}$.

a) Show that if $\mathscr{E}$ is a set of universal prenex formulas then every sub-realization of a model of $\mathscr{E}$ is a model of $\mathscr{E}$.

b) Let $\mathscr{E}$ be a set of prenex formulas of cardinal $\aleph \geqslant \aleph_0$. Show that if $\mathscr{E}$ has a model then this model has a sub-realization, whose domain is of cardinal $\leqslant \aleph$, which is a model of $\mathscr{E}$.

Answer.

a) Let F be a quantifier free formula, $\bar{F}$ the value which it has in the realization $\mathfrak{R}$, $(\bar{F} \subseteq E^{V_{\mathscr{L}}})$, and $\bar{\bar{F}}$ the value which it has in the sub-realization $\mathfrak{R}'$ of $\mathfrak{R}$, $(\bar{\bar{F}} \subseteq E'^{V_{\mathscr{L}}} \subseteq E^{V_{\mathscr{L}}})$.

Then we show that $\bar{\bar{F}} = \bar{F} \cap E'^{V_{\mathscr{L}}}$. This is clear if F is atomic; also if it is true for F and G then it is true also for $\neg F$ and $F \vee G$ and hence for all quantifier free formulas. Now suppose that $A = \bigwedge x_1 \ldots \bigwedge x_n F$, where F is quantifier free, is a formula of $\mathscr{E}$. It is satisfied by the realization $\mathfrak{R}$ and so $\bar{F} = E^{V_{\mathscr{L}}}$. Therefore $\bar{\bar{F}} = E'^{V_{\mathscr{L}}}$ and so A is satisfied also in the sub-realization $\mathfrak{R}'$.

b) We construct the set $\hat{\mathscr{E}} = \{\hat{F} : F \in \mathscr{E}\}$ using distinct function symbols not in $\mathscr{L}(\mathscr{E})$ for different formulas F. The given model $\mathfrak{R}$ of $\mathscr{E}$ can be extended to a model of $\hat{\mathscr{E}}$. Let E be the domain of this model and let T be the set of terms of $\mathscr{L}(\mathscr{E})$. Clearly the cardinal of T is less than or equal to $\aleph$.

Let δ be an arbitrary fixed element of $E^{V_{\mathscr{L}}}$. From δ we can derive a map $t \to \bar{t}$ of T into E such that $\bar{x} = \delta(x)$ for each variable x, and $\overline{\phi t_1 \ldots t_n} = \bar{\phi}(\bar{t}_1, \ldots, \bar{t}_n)$ for each ϕ in $F^n_{\mathscr{L}}$, where $\bar{\phi}$ is the value of ϕ in the model $\mathfrak{R}$ of $\hat{\mathscr{E}}$. Let E' be the image of T under this map. Clearly E' is of cardinal $\leqslant \aleph$. Also if ϕ is an n-ary function symbol of $\mathscr{L}(\hat{\mathscr{E}})$ and $a_1, \ldots, a_n \in E'$ then $\bar{\phi}(a_1, \ldots, a_n) \in E'$. Consequently there is a sub-realization $\mathfrak{R}'$ of $\mathfrak{R}$ with domain E.

By a) $\mathfrak{R}'$ satisfies $\hat{\mathscr{E}}$ and so $\mathfrak{R}'$ is a model of $\mathscr{E}$.

6.a) If R is a binary relation symbol, show, by using the method on page 24, that the formula $\bigwedge x \bigvee y \bigwedge z (R(x, y) \vee \neg R(x, z))$ is a theorem.

b) Give an example of a quantifier free formula $A(y)$ such that $\bigvee y A(y)$ is a theorem but for no term t of $\mathscr{L}(A)$ is $A(t)$ a theorem.

c) Give an example of a quantifier free formula $A(x, y, z)$ such that $\bigwedge x \bigvee y \bigwedge z A(x, y, z)$ is a theorem but for each sequence $t_1(x), \ldots, t_n(x)$ of terms of $\mathscr{L}(A)$ having only x as free variable the formula $A(x, t_1(x), z) \vee \cdots \vee A(x, t_n(x), z)$ is not a theorem.

Answer.

a) It is obvious that this formula is a theorem; in fact it is the closure of $\bigvee y R(x, y) \vee \bigwedge z \neg R(x, z)$ which is of the form $A \vee \neg A$.

If $F = \bigwedge x \bigvee y \bigwedge z (R(x, y) \vee \neg R(x, z))$ then $\check{F} = \bigvee y (R(a, y) \vee$

$\neg R(a, \phi y))$, where a is a constant symbol and ϕ is a unary function symbol. It follows from the Uniformity Theorem that there are terms $t_1, \ldots, t_k$ formed from a, ϕ and variables such that

$$(R(a, t_1) \vee \neg R(a, \phi t_1)) \vee \cdots \vee (R(a, t_k) \vee \neg R(a, \phi t_k))$$

is a theorem of the propositional calculus. In this case it is clear that we need only take $t_1 = a$ and $t_2 = \phi a$ to obtain the formula

$$R(a, a) \vee \neg R(a, \phi a) \vee R(a, \phi a) \vee \neg R(a, \phi\phi a)$$

which is obviously a theorem of the propositional calculus.

b) Put $A(y) = R(a, y) \vee \neg R(a, \phi y)$. Clearly $\bigvee y A(y)$ is a theorem. But for any term t, $A(t) = R(a, t) \vee \neg R(a, \phi t)$ is a theorem only if it is a theorem of the propositional calculus on $\{R(a, t), \neg R(a, \phi t)\}$ which it plainly is not.

c) Put $A(x, y, z) = R(x, y) \vee \neg R(x, z)$. We have seen that $\bigwedge x \bigvee y \bigwedge z\, A(x, y, z)$ is a theorem. However $A(x, t_1(x), z) \vee \cdots \vee A(x, t_n(x), z)$ is equivalent to $\neg R(x, z) \vee R(x, t_1(x)) \vee \cdots \vee R(x, t_n(x))$ which cannot be a theorem if none of the terms $t_k(x)$ is equal to z.

7. Consider a formula F. Let $\hat{F}$ and $\check{F}$ be constructed using distinct function symbols. Show that $\hat{F} \to \check{F}$ is a theorem. Which is the corresponding interpolation formula?

Let $F = \bigwedge x \bigvee y \bigwedge z\, A(x, f(y), z)$, where A is a ternary relation symbol and f is a unary function symbol. Find the corresponding interpolation formula given by the proof of the Interpolation Lemma.

Answer. We have already shown that $\hat{F} \to F$ and $F \to \check{F}$ are both theorems. It follows that $\hat{F} \to \check{F}$ is a theorem. On the other hand since $\hat{F}$ and $\check{F}$ are constructed with distinct function symbols we have $\mathscr{L}(F) \subseteq \mathscr{L}(\hat{F}) \cap \mathscr{L}(\check{F})$ and so F is an interpolation formula.

If $F = \bigwedge x \bigvee y \bigwedge z A(x, f(y), z)$ then $\hat{F} = \bigwedge x \bigwedge z A(x, f(\phi x), z)$ and $\check{F} = \bigvee y A(\alpha, f(y), \psi(\alpha, y))$, where α, ϕ, ψ are, respectively, 0-ary, unary and binary function symbols. Thus the theorem $\neg \hat{F} \vee \check{F}$ is

$$\bigvee x \bigvee z \neg A(x, f(\phi x), z) \vee \bigvee y A(\alpha, f(y), \psi(\alpha, y))$$

which, in order to follow the proof of the Interpolation Lemma, we can write as $\bigvee x \bigvee z H(x, z) \vee \bigvee y K(y)$.

It can be seen at once that $H(\alpha, \psi(\alpha, \phi\alpha)) \vee K(\phi\alpha)$ is a theorem of the propositional calculus. (It can be written in the form $N \vee \neg N$ where N is $A(\alpha, f(\phi\alpha), \psi(\alpha, \phi\alpha))$.) The corresponding interpolation formula is N.

We write $N=C(\xi_1, \ldots, \xi_p)$, the formula $C(z_1, \ldots, z_p)$ in this case is $A(z_1, z_2, z_3)$ with $\xi_1=\alpha$, $\xi_2=f(\phi\alpha)$ and $\xi_3=\psi(\alpha, \phi\alpha)$. We choose the longest ξ_i beginning with a function symbol common to $\hat{F}$ and $\check{F}$ (here ξ_2) and put $C_2(z_1, z_2, z_3)=C_1(z_1, fz_2, z_3)=A(z_1, fz_2, z_3)$. Thus we have $\xi_1^2=\alpha$, $\xi_2^2=\phi\alpha$ and $\xi_3^2=\psi(\alpha, \phi\alpha)$, and the sequence of formulas C_p stops here. The formula $M(z_1, \ldots, z_q)$ in this case is therefore $A(z_3, fz_2, z_1)$ and $\eta_1=\psi(\alpha, \phi\alpha)$, $\eta_2=\phi\alpha$ and $\eta_3=\alpha$, the η being arranged in descending order of length. Therefore the interpolation formula we seek is $Q_3z_3Q_2z_2Q_1z_1\ A(z_3, fz_2, z_1)$ with $Q_1=\bigwedge$, because η_1 begins with $\psi\in\mathscr{L}(\check{F})$, $Q_2=\bigvee$ because η_2 begins with $\phi\in\mathscr{L}(\hat{F})$, and $Q_3=\bigwedge$, because η_3 begins with $\alpha\in\mathscr{L}(\check{F})$. Thus the interpolation formula is $\bigwedge z_3 \bigvee z_2 \bigwedge z_1\, A(z_3, fz_2, z_1)$ which is equivalent to $\bigwedge x \bigvee y \bigwedge z A(x, fy, z)$. Thus we have again arrived at the same interpolation formula.

8. A formula A is said to be a *consequence* of a set $\mathscr{E}$ of formulas if all realizations of $\mathscr{E}$ which satisfy $\mathscr{E}$ also satisfy A.

a) Show that A is a consequence of a finite set $\{A_1, \ldots, A_n\}$ of formulas if and only if $(A_1 \wedge \cdots \wedge A_n) \rightarrow A$ is a theorem.

b) Show that A is a consequence of a set $\mathscr{E}$ of formulas if and only if it is a consequence of a finite subset of $\mathscr{E}$.

c) A set $\mathscr{E}$ of formulas is said to be *independent* if no formula of $\mathscr{E}$ is a consequence of the other formulas of $\mathscr{E}$. Show that $\mathscr{E}$ is independent if and only if every finite subset of $\mathscr{E}$ is independent.

d) Show that each finite set of formulas has an equivalent independent subset and that for each countable set of formulas there is an equivalent independent set.

Answer. The proofs of these results are similar to those already given for the case of propositional calculus.

CHAPTER 3

PREDICATE CALCULUS WITH EQUALITY

We now consider those languages studied in the preceding chapter which contain the symbol $=$, and we only consider those realizations in which $=$ represents the identity relation. It turns out that the study of these *normal* realizations can be reduced to the general theory of the previous chapter. It should be noted that when a given relation symbol is required to have some definite realization then the class of models so obtained will in general have a somewhat different theory, cf. the ω-models of Chapter 7, Exercise 4.

The chief result given in the text provides a convenient set of necessary and sufficient conditions for a given realization to be embeddable in a model of a given set of formulas. These conditions are, incidentally, also significant in the case of a language without equality. As an interesting consequence we have a general result about the existence of "symmetric laws" in the sense of Bourbaki, and purely algebraic conditions for the existence of an ordering compatible with a given structure.

The result on embeddability is a particular case of a general result on the equivalence of certain *second order* (or higher order) axioms and certain sets of first order axioms. (See Chapter 7 where the notion of "second order axiom" is studied.) Exercise 5 provides an example of a second order axiom which is equivalent to an infinite set of first order axioms (of the same language) but which is not equivalent to any finite set of such axioms. This proves the existence of an infinite set of first order axioms constructed from a *finite* number of relation symbols which is not equivalent to any of its finite subsets.

Exercises 1 and 2 establish some important non-categoricity properties of first order axiom systems (even for normal realizations). In fact, neither the notion of a finite set, nor that of a countable set, nor that of the set of natural numbers (with the successor relation) can be characterized by means of first order formulas. We shall show in Chapter 7 that the usual characterizations of these notions (those due to Dedekind and Peano) are in fact second order formulas. Thus these second order conditions are not equivalent (in the sense of having the same class of models) to any set of first order formulas.

A language $\mathscr{L}$ is said to be *with equality* if $R^2_{\mathscr{L}} \neq \emptyset$ and there is a singled out element E of $R^2_{\mathscr{L}}$ (called the *identity* or *equality* symbol).

A realization of a language with equality with domain U is said to be *normal* if in this realization $\bar{E}$ is the diagonal of U, i.e. the set of all pairs (x, x) with x in U.

A formula A of $\mathscr{L}$ is called a *theorem of the predicate calculus with equality* if in each normal realization of $\mathscr{L}$, $\bar{A}=U^{V\mathscr{L}}$, where U is the domain of the realization, i.e. if each normal realization of $\mathscr{L}$ satisfies A.

Given a language $\mathscr{L}$ with equality we denote by $\mathscr{E}_{\mathscr{L}}$ the set consisting of the following formulas

1. $$\bigwedge xExx.$$

2. For each $P \in R^n_{\mathscr{L}}$ (including $P=E$) the formula

$$\bigwedge x_1 \ldots \bigwedge x_n \bigwedge y_1 \ldots \bigwedge y_n((Ex_1y_1 \wedge \cdots \wedge Ex_ny_n \wedge Px_1 \ldots x_n) \to Py_1 \ldots y_n).$$

3. For each $\phi \in F^n_{\mathscr{L}}$ the formula

$$\bigwedge x_1 \ldots \bigwedge x_n \bigwedge y_1 \ldots \bigwedge y_n(Ex_1y_1 \wedge \cdots \wedge Ex_ny_n \to E(\phi x_1 \ldots x_n, \phi y_1 \ldots y_n)).$$

Clearly, each formula of $\mathscr{E}_{\mathscr{L}}$ is a theorem of the predicate calculus with equality.

Let $\mathfrak{M}$ be a realization of $\mathscr{L}$ which satisfies $\mathscr{E}_{\mathscr{L}}$. $\mathfrak{M}$ therefore satisfies the formulas $\bigwedge xExx$ and $\bigwedge x_1 \bigwedge x_2 \bigwedge y_1 \bigwedge y_2(Ex_1y_1 \wedge Ex_2y_2 \wedge Ex_1x_2 \to Ey_1y_2)$ which shows that $\bar{E}$, the value of E in $\mathfrak{M}$, is the graph of an equivalence relation on U, the domain of $\mathfrak{M}$. Since $\mathfrak{M}$ satisfies all the formulas of 2), for each $P \in R^n_{\mathscr{L}}$, $\bar{P}$ is closed with respect to the equivalence relation $\bar{E}$. That is, if $(a_1, \ldots, a_n) \in \bar{P}$ and $a_1 \sim b_1, \ldots, a_n \sim b_n$ under the relation $\bar{E}$, then $(b_1, \ldots, b_n) \in \bar{P}$. We let $\mathfrak{M}'$ be the following realization of $\mathscr{L}$. The domain of $\mathfrak{M}'$ is $U'=U/\bar{E}$, the quotient of U with respect to $\bar{E}$, that is, the set of equivalence classes of elements of U under the equivalence relation $\bar{E}$. For each $P \in R^n_{\mathscr{L}}$, $\bar{\bar{P}}$, the value taken by P in $\mathfrak{M}'$, is $\bar{P}/\bar{E}$. For each $\phi \in F^n_{\mathscr{L}}$, $\bar{\bar{\phi}}$ the value of ϕ in $\mathfrak{M}'$ is given by

$$\bar{\bar{\phi}}(a_1/\bar{E}, \ldots, a_n/\bar{E}) = \bar{\phi}(a_1, \ldots, a_n)/\bar{E}.$$

This is a good definition since $\mathfrak{M}$ satisfies all the formulas of 3).

LEMMA 1: *For each formula A of $\mathscr{L}$, $\bar{A}$, the value of A in the realization $\mathfrak{M}$, is closed with respect to the equivalence relation $\bar{E}$, and $\bar{\bar{A}}=\bar{A}/\bar{E}$.*

PROOF: We prove the lemma by induction on the length of A. The result is obvious if A is atomic. Also if the result holds for formulas B and C it holds also for $\neg B$ and for $B \vee C$. For example, if A is $\neg B$ then $\bar{A}=\complement\bar{B}$ and $\bar{\bar{A}}=\complement\bar{\bar{B}}$, therefore since $\bar{B}$ is closed so is $\complement\bar{B}$ and $\complement\bar{\bar{B}}=\complement\bar{B}/\bar{E}$.

Now suppose that A is $\bigvee xB$, where B satisfies the lemma and let $x, x_1, \ldots, x_n$ be the free variables of B. $\bar{A}$ is (up to a factor of $U^{V_{\mathscr{L}}-\{x_1, \ldots, x_n\}}$) the set of $(a_1, \ldots, a_n) \in U^{\{x_1, \ldots, x_n\}}$ such that, for some $a \in U$, $(a, a_1, \ldots, a_n) \in \bar{B}$. Now if $a_1 \sim a_1', \ldots, a_n \sim a_n'$ under the relation $\bar{E}$, since by hypothesis $\bar{B}$ is closed, if $(a, a_1, \ldots, a_n) \in \bar{B}$ then $(a, a_1', \ldots, a_n') \in \bar{B}$ and so $(a_1', \ldots, a_n') \in \bar{A}$. Hence $\bar{A}$ is also closed;

$$\bar{\bar{A}} = \{(\alpha_1, \ldots, \alpha_n) \in U'^{\{x_1, \ldots, x_n\}} : \text{ for some } \alpha \in U', (\alpha, \alpha_1, \ldots, \alpha_n) \in \bar{\bar{B}}\}.$$

Let $a, a_1, \ldots, a_n$ be elements of U whose equivalence classes under $\bar{E}$ are $\alpha, \alpha_1, \ldots, \alpha_n$. Since $\bar{B}$ satisfies the lemma, $(a, a_1, \ldots, a_n) \in \bar{B}$ and therefore $(a_1, \ldots, a_n) \in \bar{A}$ and so $\bar{\bar{A}} = \bar{A}/\bar{E}$.

THEOREM 2: *A set $\mathscr{A}$ of formulas has a normal model if and only if the set $\mathscr{E}_{\mathscr{L}} \cup \mathscr{A}$ has a model.*

PROOF: The condition is obviously necessary since each formula of $\mathscr{E}_{\mathscr{L}}$ is a theorem of the predicate calculus with equality.

Conversely if $\mathscr{E}_{\mathscr{L}} \cup \mathscr{A}$ has a model $\mathfrak{M}$, then in the normal realization $\mathfrak{M}'$ obtained from $\mathfrak{M}$ as above $\bar{\bar{A}} = \bar{A}/\bar{E}$ for all formulas A. Therefore since $\mathfrak{M}$ is a model of $\mathscr{A}$, $\mathfrak{M}'$ is also a model of $\mathscr{A}$.

COROLLARY 1: *A countable set $\mathscr{A}$ of formulas of $\mathscr{L}$ which has a normal model has a countable or finite normal model.*

PROOF: Since $\mathscr{E}_{\mathscr{L}(\mathscr{A})}$ is countable if $\mathscr{A}$ is, $\mathscr{E}_{\mathscr{L}(\mathscr{A})} \cup \mathscr{A}$ has a countable model. The domain of the normal model of $\mathscr{A}$ obtained from this model is the quotient of the domain of the original model with respect to an equivalence relation (see above). It follows that the domain of the normal model is finite or countable.

COROLLARY 2: *A formula A is a theorem of the predicate calculus with equality if and only if it is a consequence* of $\mathscr{E}_{\mathscr{L}(A)}$.

PROOF: The condition is obviously sufficient. It is also necessary. For suppose A is a theorem of the predicate calculus with equality, then $\neg A$ does not have a normal model. Hence, by Theorem 2, $\mathscr{E}_{\mathscr{L}(A)} \cup \{\neg A\}$ does not have any model. This shows that A is a consequence of $\mathscr{E}_{\mathscr{L}(A)}$.

THEOREM 3. THE FINITENESS THEOREM FOR PREDICATE CALCULUS WITH EQUALITY: *A set $\mathscr{A}$ of formulas of $\mathscr{L}$ has a normal model if and only if every finite subset of $\mathscr{A}$ has a normal model.*

PROOF: The condition is obviously necessary. It is also sufficient, since, if it holds then every finite subset of $\mathscr{E}_{\mathscr{L}(\mathscr{A})} \cup \mathscr{A}$ has a model. Therefore $\mathscr{E}_{\mathscr{L}(\mathscr{A})} \cup \mathscr{A}$ has a model and so $\mathscr{A}$ has a normal model.

THEOREM 4. THE INTERPOLATION LEMMA FOR PREDICATE CALCULUS WITH EQUALITY: *If $A \to B$ is a theorem of the predicate calculus with equality then there is a formula C such that both $A \to C$ and $C \to B$ are theorems of the predicate calculus with equality and $\mathscr{L}(C) \subseteq \mathscr{L}(A) \cap \mathscr{L}(B)$.*

PROOF: By an abuse of language we shall use $\mathscr{E}_{\mathscr{L}(A)}$ to denote the conjunction of all the formulas in $\mathscr{E}_{\mathscr{L}(A)}$, which is finite. Since $A \to B$ is a theorem of the predicate calculus with equality it is a consequence of $\mathscr{E}_{\mathscr{L}(A)} \wedge \mathscr{E}_{\mathscr{L}(B)}$. So $(\mathscr{E}_{\mathscr{L}(A)} \wedge \mathscr{E}_{\mathscr{L}(B)}) \to (A \to B)$ is a theorem and hence $(\mathscr{E}_{\mathscr{L}(A)} \wedge A) \to (\mathscr{E}_{\mathscr{L}(B)} \to B)$ is a theorem. Therefore, by the Interpolation Lemma for predicate calculus, there is a formula C, such that $(\mathscr{E}_{\mathscr{L}(A)} \wedge A) \to C$ and $C \to (\mathscr{E}_{\mathscr{L}(B)} \to B)$ are theorems and $\mathscr{L}(C) \subseteq \mathscr{L}(A) \cap \mathscr{L}(B)$. It follows that $\mathscr{E}_{\mathscr{L}(A)} \to (A \to C)$ and $\mathscr{E}_{\mathscr{L}(B)} \to (C \to B)$ are both theorems and hence $A \to C$ and $C \to B$ are theorems of the predicate calculus with equality. (See also Exercise 4 of Chapter 5.)

THEOREM 5. FIRST DEFINABILITY THEOREM FOR THE PREDICATE CALCULUS WITH EQUALITY: *Let A be a formula, R an n-ary relation symbol of $\mathscr{L}(A)$ and A' the formula obtained from A by substituting for R an n-ary relation symbol R' which does not occur in $\mathscr{L}(A)$. Then if*

$$(A \wedge A') \to (Rx_1 \ldots x_n \to R'x_1 \ldots x_n)$$

is a theorem of the predicate calculus with equality, there is a formula F such that $\mathscr{L}(F) \subseteq \mathscr{L}(A)$, $R \notin \mathscr{L}(F)$ and $A \to (F \leftrightarrow Rx_1 \ldots x_n)$ is a theorem of the predicate calculus with equality.

PROOF: The proof is the same as before, from the Interpolation Lemma.

THEOREM 6. SECOND DEFINABILITY THEOREM FOR THE PREDICATE CALCULUS WITH EQUALITY: *Let A be a formula, ϕ an n-ary function symbol of $\mathscr{L}(A)$ and A' the formula obtained from A by substituting for ϕ an n-ary function symbol ϕ' which does not occur in $\mathscr{L}(A)$. Then if*

$$(A \wedge A') \to (\phi x_1 \ldots x_n = \phi' x_1 \ldots x_n)$$

is a theorem of the predicate calculus with equality, there is a formula F of $\mathscr{L}(A)$ such that $\phi \notin \mathscr{L}(F)$ and such that $A \to (F \leftrightarrow y = \phi x_1 \ldots x_n)$ is a theorem of the predicate calculus with equality.

(Note that in the statement of this Theorem we have written $u=v$ instead of Euv: we shall continue to do so below.)

PROOF: $(A \wedge A' \wedge (y=\phi x_1 \ldots x_n)) \to (y=\phi' x_1 \ldots x_n)$ is a theorem and hence so is $(A \wedge y=\phi x_1 \ldots x_n) \to (A' \to y=\phi' x_1 \ldots x_n)$.

The result now comes by applying the Interpolation Lemma to this formula.

We have the following theorems which are immediate consequences of the analogous results of the previous chapter.

THEOREM 7: *For each prenex formula F there is a universal prenex formula $\hat{F}$ and an existential prenex formula $\check{F}$ such that* a) $\hat{F} \to F$ *and* $F \to \check{F}$ *are theorems of the predicate calculus with equality, and* b) *each realization of $\mathscr{L}(F)$ can be extended to $\mathscr{L}(\hat{F})$ and to $\mathscr{L}(\check{F})$ so that $\bar{F}=\overline{\hat{F}}$ and $\bar{F}=\overline{\check{F}}$.*

THEOREM 8. THE UNIFORMITY THEOREM FOR PREDICATE CALCULUS WITH EQUALITY: *The formula $\bigvee x_1 \ldots \bigvee x_n A(x_1 \ldots x_n)$, where A is quantifier free, is a theorem of the predicate calculus with equality if and only if there are terms $t_1^i, \ldots, t_n^i (1 \leqslant i \leqslant k)$, such that the formula*

$$\mathop{\mathrm{W}}_{1 \leqslant i \leqslant k} A(t_1^i, \ldots, t_n^i)$$

is a consequence, in the sense of the propositional calculus on $\mathrm{At}_{\mathscr{L}(A)}$, *of the following set of formulas:*

1) *For each term $t \in \mathscr{L}(A)$, $t=t$.*

2) *For each n-ary relation symbol R of $\mathscr{L}(A)$ and each pair of n-tuples $(t_1, \ldots, t_n)$ and $(t_1', \ldots, t_n')$ in $(T_{\mathscr{L}(A)})^n$*

$$(t_1 = t_1' \wedge \cdots \wedge t_n = t_n' \wedge Rt_1 \ldots t_n) \to Rt_1' \ldots t_n' .$$

3) *For each n-ary function symbol ϕ of $\mathscr{L}(A)$ and each pair of n-tuples $(t_1, \ldots, t_n)$ and $(t_1', \ldots, t_n')$ in $(T_{\mathscr{L}(A)})^n$*

$$(t_1 = t_1' \wedge \cdots \wedge t_n = t_n') \to \phi t_1 \ldots t_n = \phi t_1' \ldots t_n' .$$

PROOF: It is sufficient to apply the Uniformity Theorem to the formula $\neg \mathscr{E}_{\mathscr{L}(A)} \vee A$.

EXTENSIONS OF REALIZATIONS

Given a realization $\mathfrak{M}$ of the language $\mathscr{L}$ with domain U, by an *extension* of $\mathfrak{M}$ we mean a realization $\mathfrak{M}'$ of a language $\mathscr{L}'$ containing $\mathscr{L}$ such that

a) the domain U' of $\mathfrak{M}'$ contains U,

b) for each n-ary relation symbol R of $\mathscr{L}$, if $\bar{R}, \bar{\bar{R}}$ are its values in the realizations $\mathfrak{M}, \mathfrak{M}'$, respectively, then $\bar{R} = \bar{\bar{R}} \cap U^n$,

c) for each n-ary function symbol ϕ of $\mathscr{L}$, if $\bar{\phi}, \bar{\bar{\phi}}$ are its values in the realizations $\mathfrak{M}, \mathfrak{M}'$, respectively, then $\bar{\phi}$ is the restriction of $\bar{\bar{\phi}}$ to U^n.

LEMMA 9: *Let $\mathfrak{M}'$ be an extension of $\mathfrak{M}$. Let F be a quantifier free formula with values $\bar{F}$ and $\bar{\bar{F}}$ in $\mathfrak{M}, \mathfrak{M}'$ respectively. Then $\bar{F} = \bar{\bar{F}} \cap U^{V_{\mathscr{L}}}$.*

PROOF: The proof is by induction on the length of F. If F is atomic then $F = Rt_1 \ldots t_n$, say. Let $x_1, \ldots, x_k$ be the variables of F. $\bar{F} = \{(a_1, \ldots, a_k) \in U^{\{x_1, \ldots, x_k\}} : (\bar{t}_1, \ldots, \bar{t}_n) \in \bar{R}\} = \bar{\bar{R}} \cap U^n$. Since on $U^{\{x_1, \ldots, x_k\}}$, $\bar{t}_i = \bar{\bar{t}}_i$ $(1 \leqslant i \leqslant k)$ we certainly have that $\bar{F} = \bar{\bar{F}} \cap U^{\{x_1, \ldots, x_k\}}$.

Clearly if F and G satisfy the lemma then so too do $\neg F$, because $\overline{\neg F} = \complement \bar{F}$, and $F \vee G$, because $\overline{F \vee G} = \bar{F} \cup \bar{G}$. This completes the proof.

THEOREM 10: *If $\mathfrak{M}'$ is an extension of $\mathfrak{M}$ all closed universal formulas of $\mathscr{L}$ satisfied in $\mathfrak{M}'$ are satisfied also in $\mathfrak{M}$.*

PROOF: If $\bigwedge x_1 \ldots \bigwedge x_n A(x_1, \ldots, x_n)$, where A is quantifier free, is satisfied in $\mathfrak{M}'$ the value of A in $\mathfrak{M}'$ is $U'^{V_{\mathscr{L}}}$. Hence A is also satisfied in $\mathfrak{M}$.

For the remainder of this chapter we shall assume that all the languages we consider are languages with equality and that all realizations are normal.

Let $\mathfrak{M}$ be a realization of a language $\mathscr{L}$ whose domain is U. By the diagram of $\mathfrak{M}$, which we denote by $D(\mathfrak{M})$, we mean the set of the following formulas of the language $\mathscr{L}'$ which is obtained from $\mathscr{L}$ by adjoining the elements of U as constant symbols. (We assume that $U \cap \mathscr{L} = \emptyset$.)

a) for each $R \in R^n_{\mathscr{L}}$ and each $(a_1, \ldots, a_n) \in U^n$ the formula $Ra_1 \ldots a_n$ or $\neg Ra_1 \ldots a_n$ according as $(a_1, \ldots, a_n) \in \bar{R}$ or $(a_1, \ldots, a_n) \notin \bar{R}$,

b) for each $\phi \in F^n_{\mathscr{L}}$ and each $(a, a_1, \ldots, a_n) \in U^{n+1}$ the formula $a = \phi a_1 \ldots a_n$ or $a \neq \phi a_1 \ldots a_n$ according as $a = \bar{\phi}(a_1, \ldots, a_n)$ or $a \neq \bar{\phi}(a_1, \ldots, a_n)$. In particular $D(\mathfrak{M})$ contains for each pair $(a, b) \in U^2$ the formula $a = b$ or $a \neq b$ according as $a = b$ or $a \neq b$.

THEOREM 11: *A realization $\mathfrak{M}'$ of $\mathscr{L}$ is (up to isomorphism) an extension of $\mathfrak{M}$ if and only if $\mathfrak{M}'$ can be extended to $\mathscr{L}'$ so as to satisfy $D(\mathfrak{M})$.*

PROOF: $\mathfrak{M}'$ has a sub-realization isomorphic to $\mathfrak{M}$ if and only if there is a one-one map of U into U' which preserves the values of the function and relation symbols of $\mathscr{L}$ in the two realizations. The existence of such a map is equivalent to being able to extend $\mathfrak{M}'$ to $\mathscr{L}'$ so as to satisfy $D(\mathfrak{M})$.

THEOREM 12. THE EMBEDDING THEOREM: *Let $\mathfrak{M}$ be a realization of the language $\mathscr{L}_0$ and $\mathscr{A}$ be a set of formulas of a language $\mathscr{L}_1$. Then $\mathfrak{M}$ has an extension which is a model of $\mathscr{A}$ if and only if $\mathfrak{M}$ satisfies all the universal formulas of $\mathscr{L}_0$ which are consequences of $\mathscr{A}$.*

PROOF: The condition is necessary, since if $\mathfrak{M}'$ is an extension of $\mathfrak{M}$, $\mathfrak{M}$ satisfies all the universal formulas of $\mathscr{L}_0$ satisfied by $\mathfrak{M}'$.

Conversely suppose that there is no extension of $\mathfrak{M}$ which satisfies $\mathscr{A}$. Then, by Theorem 11, the set $D(\mathfrak{M}) \cup \mathscr{A}$ is inconsistent. Hence there is some finite subset Δ of $D(\mathfrak{M})$ such that $\Delta \cup \mathscr{A}$ is inconsistent. Let U be the domain of $\mathfrak{M}$ and $a_1, \ldots, a_n$ the elements of U which occur in Δ. Let $F(a_1, \ldots, a_n)$ be the conjunction of all the formulas of Δ. $F(x_1, \ldots, x_n)$ is a quantifier free formula of $\mathscr{L}_0$. Clearly $F(a_1, \ldots, a_n)$ is satisfied by $\mathfrak{M}$ if we put $\bar{a}_1 = a_1, \ldots, \bar{a}_n = a_n$. Hence $\bigvee x_1 \ldots \bigvee x_n\, F(x_1, \ldots, x_n)$ is satisfied by $\mathfrak{M}$. Now $\mathscr{A} \cup \{F(a_1, \ldots, a_n)\}$ is inconsistent and hence $\neg F(a_1, \ldots, a_n)$ is a consequence of $\mathscr{A}$. Since the constant symbols $a_1, \ldots, a_n$ do not occur in $\mathscr{A}$, $\bigwedge x_1 \ldots \bigwedge x_n \neg F(x_1, \ldots, x_n)$ is a consequence of $\mathscr{A}$. Thus we have found a universal formula, which is a consequence of $\mathscr{A}$, but which is not satisfied by $\mathfrak{M}$.

This completes the proof.

We have the following application of this result. We take as $\mathscr{L}_0$ the language which has a single binary function symbol $\times$. (We will write xy for $\times xy$). Then there is a (clearly countable) set $\mathscr{G}$ of closed universal formulas of $\mathscr{L}_0$ such that a monoid is embeddable in a group if and only if it satisfies $\mathscr{G}$.

Any monoid is a realization of $\mathscr{L}_0$. If $\mathscr{A}$ is the following set of formulas of $\mathscr{L}_1$, the language which has the binary function symbol $\times$, the unary function symbol $^{-1}$ and the constant e;

$$\bigwedge x \bigwedge y \bigwedge z\,(x(yz) = (xy)\,z), \qquad \bigwedge x\,(xe = x), \qquad \bigwedge x\,(xx^{-1} = e)$$

then Theorem 12 gives us the existence of the set $\mathscr{G}$.

We note that one of the formulas of $\mathscr{G}$ is the cancellation rule

$$\bigwedge x \bigwedge y \bigwedge u \bigwedge v\,(uxv = uyv \rightarrow x = y).$$

This formula is sufficient, by itself, if the monoid is commutative.

Let $\mathfrak{M}$ be a realization of a language $\mathscr{L}$ with domain U and let U' be a subset of U. U' is the domain of a sub-realization $\mathfrak{M}'$ of $\mathfrak{M}$ if and only if for each n-ary function symbol ϕ of $\mathscr{L}$ and each n-tuple $(a_1, \dots, a_n)$ of elements of U', $\bar{\phi}(a_1, \dots, a_n) \in U'$, where $\bar{\phi}$ is the value of ϕ in the realization $\mathfrak{M}$. Clearly the intersection of any collection of subsets of U having this property also has this property. We therefore give the following definition.

For each subset U' of U, *the sub-realization* $\mathfrak{M}'$ *of* $\mathfrak{M}$ *generated by* U' is the sub-realization whose domain is the smallest subset of U which contains U' and has the above property. The following Theorem generalizes Exercises 4 and 5 of Chapter 1.

THEOREM 13: *Let* $\mathfrak{M}$ *be a realization of a language* $\mathscr{L}_0$ *and let* $\mathscr{A}$ *be a set of formulas of a language* $\mathscr{L}_1$. *Then* $\mathfrak{M}$ *has an extension which is a model of* $\mathscr{A}$ *if and only if every sub-realization of* $\mathfrak{M}$ *generated by a finite set has such an extension.*

PROOF: The condition is necessary since, obviously, an extension of $\mathfrak{M}$ is an extension of every sub-realization of $\mathfrak{M}$.

Conversely, let $\mathscr{B}$ be the set of universal formulas of $\mathscr{L}_0$ which are consequences of $\mathscr{A}$. By the Embedding Theorem, if $\mathfrak{M}$ does not have an extension which is a model of $\mathscr{A}$, then there is some formula of $\mathscr{B}$ which is not satisfied by $\mathfrak{M}$. Let $F = \bigwedge x_1 \dots \bigwedge x_k\ G(x_1, \dots, x_k)$ be this formula, where $G(x_1, \dots, x_k)$ is quantifier free. Let $\bar{G}$ be the value of G in $\mathfrak{M}$. Then there are elements $a_1, \dots, a_k$ in E, the domain of $\mathfrak{M}$, such that $(a_1, \dots, a_k) \notin \bar{G}$. Let $\mathfrak{M}'$ be the sub-realization of $\mathfrak{M}$ generated by $\{a_1, \dots, a_k\}$. Let E' be the domain of $\mathfrak{M}'$ and $\bar{\bar{G}}$ be the value of G in $\mathfrak{M}'$. Since G is quantifier free $\bar{\bar{G}} = \bar{G} \cap E'^{\{x_1, \dots, x_k\}}$. Hence $(a_1, \dots, a_k) \notin \bar{\bar{G}}$ and $\mathfrak{M}'$ does not satisfy F. Hence $\mathfrak{M}'$ does not have an extension which satisfies $\mathscr{A}$.

This completes the proof.

We give some more applications of these results in the Exercises.

Exercises

(In these Exercises we shall write $=$, instead of E, for the identity symbol and $x = y$ for $= xy$.)

1. Two realizations $\mathfrak{M}$ and $\mathfrak{M}'$ of a language $\mathscr{L}$ with domains U and U' are said to be *isomorphic* if there is a one-one map ϕ of U onto U' such that for all $R \in R^n_{\mathscr{L}}$, $\bar{\bar{R}} = \phi(\bar{R})$ and for all $f \in F^n_{\mathscr{L}}$, $\bar{\bar{f}} = \phi(\bar{F})$, where $\bar{R}, \bar{f}$ are the values of R and f in $\mathfrak{M}$ and $\bar{\bar{R}}, \bar{\bar{f}}$ are their values in $\mathfrak{M}'$.

A set $\mathscr{A}$ of formulas of $\mathscr{L}$ is said to be *categorical* with respect to a set of realizations of the language $\mathscr{L}$ if all the models of $\mathscr{A}$ in this set are isomorphic.

a) Show that if a set $\mathscr{A}$ of formulas is categorical with respect to the class of all realizations then it does not have a model, i.e. $\mathscr{A}$ is inconsistent.

b) Show that if $\mathscr{A}$ is categorical with respect to the class of all normal realizations then all models of $\mathscr{A}$ have the same finite number of elements in their domains.

Answer.

a) Let $\mathscr{A}$ be a set of formulas which has a model. If $\aleph$ is the cardinal of this model we show that $\mathscr{A}$ has also a model of cardinal $\aleph' > \aleph$. This will prove that $\mathscr{A}$ is not categorical.

Let $\hat{\mathscr{A}} = \{\hat{A}: A \in \mathscr{A}\}$, where we use distinct function symbols not occurring in $\mathscr{L}(\mathscr{A})$ to construct different formulas $\hat{A}$. Let $\mathscr{L}'$ be the language which is obtained by adding to $\mathscr{L}(\mathscr{A})$ a set of constant symbols of cardinal $\aleph'' > \aleph$. Since $\mathscr{A}$ has a model so too does $\hat{\mathscr{A}}$. Hence $\hat{\mathscr{A}}$ has a canonical model with respect to the language $\mathscr{L}'$, i.e. a model with domain $T_{\mathscr{L}'}$. This model is of cardinal $\aleph' \geqslant \aleph'' > \aleph$.

b) Let $\mathscr{A}$ be a set of formulas of the language $\mathscr{L}$, with equality, which has an infinite normal model of cardinal $\aleph$. We shall show that $\mathscr{A}$ has a normal model of cardinal greater than $\aleph$.

We add to $\mathscr{L}(\mathscr{A})$ a set C of constant symbols of cardinal greater than $\aleph$. Let $\mathscr{B}$ be the set of formulas obtained by adding to $\mathscr{A}$ all the formulas $a \neq b$ for $a, b \in C$ with $a \neq b$. Clearly each finite subset of $\mathscr{B}$ has a normal model (e.g. the given normal model of $\mathscr{A}$, since this is infinite). Hence $\mathscr{B}$ itself has a normal model. Clearly the normal model is of cardinal greater than or equal to that of C and hence greater than $\aleph$.

2. Consider the following language $\mathscr{L}$ with equality. The only relation symbol of $\mathscr{L}$ is $=$, there is one constant symbol 0, a unary function symbol s (read "successor") and two binary function symbols $+$, $\times$. Given two terms t, t', we will write $t + t'$ for $+tt'$ and $t \times t'$ (or just tt') for $\times tt'$. The *standard realization* of $\mathscr{L}$ is the realization whose domain is **N**, the set of natural numbers, and in which the symbols 0, s, $+$, $\times$, take their natural values in **N**, namely zero, successor, addition and multiplication.

Now consider the following formulas, $\mathscr{A}$, of $\mathscr{L}$:

$$\bigwedge x(sx \neq 0), \quad \bigwedge x \bigwedge y(sx = sy \to x = y), \quad \bigwedge x \bigvee y(x = 0 \vee x = sy),$$
$$\bigwedge x(x + 0 = 0), \quad \bigwedge x \bigwedge y(s(x + y) = x + sy),$$
$$\bigwedge x(x \times 0 = 0), \quad \bigwedge x \bigwedge y(x \times sy = (x \times y) + y).$$

a) Show that the standard realization of $\mathscr{L}$ is a normal model of $\mathscr{A}$ (the *standard model* of $\mathscr{A}$) and that all normal models of $\mathscr{A}$ have a submodel isomorphic to the standard model. The elements of this submodel, i.e. the values of the terms 0, $s0$, $ss0$,... are called the *natural numbers of the model.*

b) Show that given any set $\mathscr{B}$ of formulas of $\mathscr{L}$ which contains $\mathscr{A}$ and has a model, there is no formula $A(x)$ of $\mathscr{L}$ with a single free variable whose value in *all* models of $\mathscr{B}$ is the set of natural numbers of that model.

c) Show that given any countable set $\mathscr{B}$ of formulas of $\mathscr{L}$ which contains $\mathscr{A}$ and has a model, there is a countable normal model of $\mathscr{B}$ which is not the standard model of $\mathscr{A}$(in particular, $\mathscr{A}$ is not categorical with respect to the class of all countable models).

d) (An improvement of b).) We obtain the system called *first order arithmetic* by adding to $\mathscr{A}$ the countable set of the following formulas: for each formula $A(x)$ having as free variables x, x_1, ..., x_k we include the formula

$$\bigwedge x_1 \ldots \bigwedge x_k[(A(0) \wedge \bigwedge x(A(x) \to A(sx))) \to \bigwedge x A(x)].$$

The set of these formulas represents the principle of induction for properties definable in the language $\mathscr{L}$.

Show that for each formula A of $\mathscr{L}$ with a single free variable and for all non-standard models $\mathfrak{M}$ of first order arithmetic, the value $\bar{A}$ of A in $\mathfrak{M}$ is not the set of natural numbers of $\mathfrak{M}$.

Answer.

a) Clearly the standard realization satisfies $\mathscr{A}$. Conversely if $\mathfrak{M}$ is a normal model of $\mathscr{A}$ the first three formulas of $\mathscr{A}$ entail that the values in $\mathfrak{M}$ of the terms of the form s^n0 form a set isomorphic to **N**, under the map $\overline{s^n0} \to n$, in which 0 and s have their natural values. The other formulas of $\mathscr{A}$ entail that $+$ and $\times$ have as values addition and multiplication on this set. This subset of $\mathfrak{M}$ closed under $\bar{s}$, $\bar{+}$ and $\bar{\times}$ is a sub-model of $\mathfrak{M}$.

b) Add the constant symbol a to $\mathscr{L}$ and consider the set of formulas $\{A(a), a \neq 0, a \neq s0, \ldots, a \neq s^n 0, \ldots\}$ where $A(x)$ is a formula of $\mathscr{L}$ with one free variable. If the value of $A(x)$ in each model of $\mathscr{B}$ is the set of natural numbers then each finite subset of this set has a model which satisfies $\mathscr{B}$ (it is sufficient to take for the value of a a sufficiently large natural number). Therefore the whole set has a model which satisfies $\mathscr{B}$. In this model $A(x)$ is satisfied by an element, the value of a, which is not a natural number.

c) Take as $A(x)$ in b) the formula $x = x$. The normal model which we have contains the standard model as a proper sub-model, since the value taken by a is different from all the natural numbers, which is not isomorphic to it.

d) If $\overline{\neg A(x)}$ is the empty set, $\overline{A(x)}$ contains non-standard elements since, by hypothesis, $\mathfrak{M}$ is non-standard. If $\overline{\neg A(x)}$ is not empty, since

$$(A(0) \wedge \bigwedge y(A(y) \to A(sy))) \to \bigwedge y A(y)$$

is equivalent to

$$\bigwedge x(\neg A(x) \to (\neg A(0) \vee \bigvee y(\neg A(sy) \wedge A(y))))$$

either $\bar{0} \notin \overline{A(x)}$ or there is a non-standard $\bar{y} \in \overline{A(x)}$ or there is a natural number $\bar{y}$ of $\mathfrak{M}$ such that $\bar{y} \in \overline{A(x)}$ and $\bar{s}\bar{y} \notin \overline{A(x)}$. In each case $\overline{A(x)}$ is not the set of natural numbers of $\mathfrak{M}$.

We can see now why Peano's postulates are categorical while those of first order arithmetic are not. Peano's axioms state that the induction principle can be applied to any property of the elements of the domain of the realization (of $\mathscr{A}$) we are considering. In particular it can be applied to the property of being a natural number of that realization. However this property cannot be defined in the language $\mathscr{L}$ for any realization of $\mathscr{L}$ other than the standard realization.

3. Consider the following language $\mathscr{L}$. The only relation symbol is $=$; there are two constant symbols 0 and 1 and two binary function symbols $+$ and $\times$. Show that given any formula A of $\mathscr{L}$ which is satisfied in all commutative fields of characteristic zero, there is an integer P such that A is satisfied in all commutative fields of characteristic $p \geqslant P$.

Answer. Let $\mathscr{C}$ be the following set of formulas of $\mathscr{L}$.

$$\begin{array}{ll} \bigwedge x \bigwedge y \bigwedge z(x+(y+z)=(x+y)+z) & \bigwedge x \bigwedge y \bigwedge z(x(yz)=(xy)z) \\ \bigwedge x \bigwedge y(x+y=y+x) & \bigwedge x \bigwedge y(xy=yx) \\ \bigwedge x(x+0=0) & \bigwedge x(x\cdot 1=x) \\ \bigwedge x \bigvee y(x+y=0) & \bigwedge x \bigvee y(x=0 \vee xy=1) \\ \bigwedge x \bigwedge y \bigwedge z(x(y+z)=xy+xz) & 1 \neq 0 \end{array}$$

(here we have written xy instead of $\times xy$).

Clearly the normal models of $\mathscr{C}$ are precisely the commutative fields. Let F_p be the formula $1+1+\cdots+1=0$, where 1 is repeated p times. Clearly the normal models of $\mathscr{C}\cup\{\neg F_p: p \text{ prime}\}$ are precisely the commutative fields of characteristic zero. Thus any formula A which is true in all commutative fields of characteristic zero is a consequence of $\mathscr{C}\cup\{\neg F_p: p \text{ prime}\}$. Hence it is a consequence of some finite subset $\mathscr{C}\cup\{\neg F_2, \ldots, \neg F_P\}$ of this set and hence is satisfied by all commutative fields of characteristic $p>P$.

4 (Steinitz's theorem). Consider a commutative field K. Show that there is an extension field L of K in which all polynomials with coefficients in K decompose into linear factors. Deduce from this the existence of the algebraic closure of K.

Answer. Consider the language $\mathscr{L}$ of Exercise 3. The field K is a realization of $\mathscr{L}$. Let the diagram of this realization be D_K. Clearly every normal model of $\mathscr{C}\cup D_K$, where $\mathscr{C}$ is the set of formulas defined in Exercise 3, is an extension field of K.

For each polynomial $P(x)=a_0+a_1x+\cdots+a_{n-1}x^{n-1}+x^n$, with coefficients in K, we consider the formula

$$\bigvee x_1 \ldots \bigvee x_n(a_0+\cdots+a_{n-1}x^{n-1}+x^n=(x+x_1)\cdots(x+x_n))$$

of the language $\mathscr{L}'$, in which the diagram of K is expressed. Let $\mathscr{A}$ be the set of all these formulas. For each finite subset $\mathscr{A}_0$ of $\mathscr{A}$ we know that there is a normal model of $\mathscr{C}\cup D_K\cup\mathscr{A}_0$, since we can construct an extension of K, of finite dimension over K, in which a given polynomial splits into linear factors. Thus every finite subset of $\mathscr{C}\cup D_K\cup\mathscr{A}$ has a normal model. It follows that $\mathscr{C}\cup D_K\cup\mathscr{A}$ has a normal model. This model, L say, is a commutative field which is an extension of K in which all polynomials with coefficients in K can be split into linear factors. Let

Ω be the subfield of L consisting of all those elements of L which are algebraic over K. Then clearly Ω is the algebraic closure of K.

5. Consider the language $\mathscr{L}_0$ which has a single binary relation symbol P. Show that there is a set $\mathscr{U}$ of universal formulas of $\mathscr{L}_0$ such that given a realization $\mathfrak{M}$ of $\mathscr{L}_0$, $\bar{P}$, the value of P in $\mathfrak{M}$, can be extended to an order relation if and only if $\mathfrak{M}$ satisfies $\mathscr{U}$. Give an example of such a set $\mathscr{U}$ and show that it is not equivalent to any finite subset of the consequences of $\mathscr{U}$. Show that $\bar{P}$ can be extended to a *total* ordering if and only if $\mathfrak{M}$ satisfies $\mathscr{U}$.

Answer. Consider the language $\mathscr{L}_1$ with two binary relation symbols P and $\leqslant$. Let $\mathscr{A}$ be the set of the following formulas of $\mathscr{L}_1$:

$$\bigwedge x \bigwedge y (Pxy \to x \leqslant y)$$
$$\bigwedge x (x \leqslant x)$$
$$\bigwedge x \bigwedge y (x \leqslant y \wedge y \leqslant x \to x = y)$$
$$\bigwedge x \bigwedge y \bigwedge z (x \leqslant y \wedge y \leqslant z \to x \leqslant z).$$

By the Embedding Theorem a realization $\mathfrak{M}$ of $\mathscr{L}_0$ can be extended to a model of $\mathscr{A}$ if and only if it satisfies the set $\mathscr{U}$ of universal formulas of $\mathscr{L}_0$ which are consequences of $\mathscr{A}$. But clearly $\mathfrak{M}$ can be extended to a model of $\mathscr{A}$ if and only if $\bar{P}$ can be extended to an order relation. Hence $\mathscr{U}$ is the desired set of universal sentences.

It is at once evident that $\mathscr{U}$ contains the formula

$$F_n = \bigwedge x_1 \dots \bigwedge x_n ((Px_1x_2 \wedge \dots \wedge Px_{n-1}x_n \wedge Px_nx_1) \to$$
$$\to (x_1 = x_2 = \dots = x_n))$$

for each $n \geqslant 1$. We now show that given a realization $\mathfrak{M}$ which satisfies all these formulas, F_n, $\bar{P}$ can be extended to a total ordering or, equivalently, that $\mathfrak{M}$ has an extension which satisfies

$$\mathscr{B} = \mathscr{A} \cup \{\bigwedge x \bigwedge y (x \leqslant y \vee y \leqslant x)\}.$$

To show that $\mathfrak{M}$ has such an extension it is sufficient to show that every sub-realization $\mathfrak{M}'$ of $\mathfrak{M}$, generated by a finite set, has such an extension. Any such sub-realization $\mathfrak{M}'$ has a finite domain E'. We prove that $\mathfrak{M}'$ can be extended to a model of $\mathscr{B}$ by induction on the number of elements, k, in E'.

If $k=1$ the result is trivial. Suppose it is true for $k=r-1$ and let E' contain the r elements $a_1, \dots, a_r$. There is some i, $1 \leqslant i \leqslant r$, such that for all

$j \neq i (a_i, a_j) \notin \bar{P}$, for otherwise there is a sequence $n_1, \ldots, n_p, \ldots$ of integers between 1 and r such that $(a_1, a_{n_1}), (a_{n_1}, a_{n_2}), \ldots, (a_{n_{p-1}}, a_{n_p}), \ldots$ are all in $\bar{P}$, which would contradict one of the formulas F_n.

We will therefore assume that a_r, say, is such that, for $1 \leqslant i < r$, $(a_r, a_i) \notin \bar{P}$. Since $E'' = \{a_1, \ldots, a_{r-1}\}$ contains only $r-1$ elements, by our induction hypothesis, $\bar{P}$ can be extended to a total ordering of E''. It is sufficient to put $a_i \leqslant a_r$ for $1 \leqslant i \leqslant r$ in order to extend $\bar{P}$ to a total ordering of E'.

Consider the relation $\bar{P}$ on the set $\{1, \ldots, n\}$, whose elements are the pairs $(1, 2), (2, 3), \ldots, (n-1, n), (n, 1)$. Clearly this is a model of $\{F_1, \ldots, F_{n-1}, \neg F_n\}$ which, by the Finiteness Theorem, shows that the set of all F_n's is not equivalent to any finite subset of its consequences.

6. a) Consider the language $\mathscr{L}_0$ which has the single binary function symbol $\times$. Show that there is a set $\mathscr{U}$ of closed universal formulas of $\mathscr{L}_0$ such that an arbitrary group G can be totally ordered if and only if it is a model of $\mathscr{U}$. Give such a set of formulas $\mathscr{U}$ for the case of commutative groups.

b) Consider the same problem for a field. In this case the language has two binary function symbols $+$, $\times$ and a single constant 0.

Answer. This is an easy consequence of the Embedding Theorem.

For the case of a commutative group the set of universal formulas sought for is $\{\bigwedge x \bigwedge y (x^n = y^n \rightarrow x = y) : n \geqslant 1\}$. The commutative groups which are models of this set are the torsion free groups.

In the case of a commutative field the desired set of formulas is $\{\bigwedge x_1 \ldots \bigwedge x_n (x_1^2 + \cdots + x_n^2 = 0 \rightarrow x_1 = \cdots = x_n = 0) : n \geqslant 1\}$. The commutative fields which are models of this set are the real fields.

7. Let $\mathscr{L}$ be a language with equality which contains a binary relation symbol R different from $=$. Show that there is no set $\mathscr{A}$ of formulas of $\mathscr{L}$ which has an infinite normal model and is such that in all normal models of $\mathscr{A}$, R represents a well-ordering of the domain.

Answer. Let $\mathscr{A}$ be a set of formulas of $\mathscr{L}$ and let $\mathfrak{M}$ be an infinite normal model of $\mathscr{A}$ with domain E, such that the value $\bar{R}$ of R in this model is a well-ordering of E. E therefore contains an infinite strictly increasing sequence of elements $\xi_1, \ldots, \xi_n, \ldots$. Therefore, for each integer i, $(\xi_i, \xi_{i+1}) \in \bar{R}$ and $\xi_i \neq \xi_{i+1}$. We add to $\mathscr{L}$ an infinite sequence of constant $a_1, \ldots, a_n, \ldots$. For each integer n the set

$$\mathscr{A} \cup \{Ra_2a_1 \wedge a_2 \neq a_1, \ldots, Ra_na_{n-1} \wedge a_n \neq a_{n-1}\}$$

has a model, namely the model $\mathfrak{M}$ with $\bar{a}_1=\xi_n, \ldots, \bar{a}_n=\xi_1$. Hence, by the Finiteness Theorem, the set

$$\mathscr{A} \cup \{Ra_{n+1}a_n \wedge a_{n+1} \neq a_n : n \geqslant 1\}$$

has a model. In this model the sequence $\bar{a}_1, \ldots \bar{a}_n, \ldots$ is an infinite strictly decreasing sequence and hence R does not represent a well-ordering.

8 (Existence of *free* models). Let $\mathscr{L}$ be a language with equality and $\mathscr{A}$ a set of closed formulas of $\mathscr{L}$ of the form $\bigwedge x_1 \ldots \bigwedge x_n [(A_1 \wedge \cdots \wedge A_m) \rightarrow B]$ where m is possibly zero, and all $A_i (1 \leqslant i \leqslant n)$ and B are atomic formulas.

a) Show that $\mathscr{A}$ is satisfied by the normal realization whose universe consists of (equivalence) classes of terms t' of $\mathscr{L}$ i.e. $[t]=\{t' : t'=t$ is a consequence of $\mathscr{A}\}$ for each term t of $\mathscr{L}$; for each function symbol f of $\mathscr{L}$, $\bar{f}([t_1], \ldots, [t_n])=[f(t_1, \ldots, t_n)]$; and for each relation symbol R of $\mathscr{L}$, $([t_1], \ldots, [t_n]) \in \bar{R}$ if and only if the formula $R(t_1, \ldots, t_n)$ is a consequence of $\mathscr{A}$.

b) Deduce that if each C_i is an atomic formula, possibly containing free variables, and if $C_1 \vee \cdots \vee C_p$ is a consequence of $\mathscr{A}$, some $C_i (1 \leqslant i \leqslant p)$ is a consequence of $\mathscr{A}$.

Answer.

a) The equality axioms for $\mathscr{L}$ have the form $\bigwedge x_1 \ldots \bigwedge x_n [(A_1 \wedge \cdots \wedge A_m) \rightarrow B]$ with $m=1$ and $m=2$. Consider $t_1, \ldots, t_n$: if $([t_1], \ldots, [t_n])$ satisfy each $\bar{A}_i (1 \leqslant i \leqslant m)$, each formula $A_i(t_1, \ldots, t_n)$ is consequence of $\mathscr{A}$ and so is $B(t_1, \ldots, t_n)$, i.e. $([t_1], \ldots, [t_n])$ satisfies $\bar{B}$.

b) Each C_i has the form $R_i(t_1, \ldots, t_{p_i})$ where R_i is a relation symbol of $\mathscr{L}$ and $t_1, \ldots, t_{p_i}$ are terms of $\mathscr{L}$ or C_i is $t_1=t_2$. Since $C_1 \vee \cdots \vee C_p$ is a consequence of $\mathscr{A}$, it is satisfied in the realization given in a), and so $C_1 \vee \cdots \vee C_p$ is true, i.e. either the formula C_1 is a consequence of $\mathscr{A}$ or the formula C_2 is a consequence of $\mathscr{A}$ ... or the formula C_p is a consequence of $\mathscr{A}$.

CHAPTER 4

THE ELIMINATION OF QUANTIFIERS

The general theory given in the previous chapters is here applied to axiomatic systems having the following property: each formula (in the language of the axiomatic systems considered) is equivalent to a quantifier free formula. The [illegible] systems given in the text are: certain discretely (and totally) ordered commutative groups; algebraically closed fields; real closed fields; certain Boolean rings. This property has the following important consequences:

1) A complete characterization of all those relations explicitly definable in the axiomatic systems considered;

2) (Usually) Completeness.

Among the useful applications of this second result we have: in the case of algebraically closed fields the "Nullstellensatz" of Hilbert (Exercise 4) and in the case of real closed fields Artin's Theorem on the representation of positive forms (Exercise 5).

A simple model theoretic condition is formulated (p. 50) which can often be used to show the impossibility of eliminating quantifiers. (Exercises 1 and 2 provide examples, even in the case of complete axiomatic systems.) A partial converse of this condition is given in Exercise 1 of Chapter 6. Exercise 5 contains an algebraic application obtained by combining the result 1) above with the theorem on definability given in the previous chapter.

In Exercise 3 we describe a method for proving that certain axiomatic systems are complete without eliminating quantifiers (using, instead, more strictly algebraic methods). For the use of the more general method of ultraproducts in dealing with this type of question, see KOCHEN, Ultraproducts in the Theory of Models, Annals of Maths. **74** (1962) pp. 229–261 and KEISLER, Ultraproducts and Elementary Classes, Proc. Kon. Ned. Akad. Wet. **64** (1961) pp. 477–495 and its application to p-adic fields in AX-KOCHEN, Diophantine Problems over Local Fields, Amer. J. of Maths. **87** (1965) pp. 605–648. (For an alternative treatment without the use of ultrapowers, see their paper, Annals of Maths. **83** (1966) pp. 437–456, where the method of Chapter 6, Exercise 1, is employed.) References to the older literature are to be found in ERSHOV, LAVROV, TAIMANOV and TAITSLIN, Elementary Theories, Russian Math. Surveys **20** (1965) pp. 35–106.

The results of this chapter are used below only for some counter-examples.

In this chapter all the languages that we shall consider will be languages with equality and all the realizations will be normal realizations.

Suppose that we have a language $\mathscr{L}$ and a set $\mathscr{A}$ of formulas of $\mathscr{L}$. We say that $\mathscr{A}$ *allows the elimination of quantifiers in a formula F* of $\mathscr{L}$ if there is a quantifier free formula F' of $\mathscr{L}$ such that $F \leftrightarrow F'$ is a consequence of $\mathscr{A}$ or, equivalently, such that $\bar{F} = \bar{F}'$ in every normal model of $\mathscr{A}$. $\mathscr{A}$ is said to *allow the elimination of quantifiers in* $\mathscr{L}$ if it allows the elimination of quantifiers in every formula of $\mathscr{L}$.

Clearly we can show, by induction on the number of quantifiers in F which we assume is in prenex normal form, that $\mathscr{A}$ allows the elimination of quantifiers in $\mathscr{L}$ if $\mathscr{A}$ allows the elimination of quantifiers in all formulas of the form $\bigvee xHx$, where Hx is quantifier free. By Theorem 1.3 of the propositional calculus, each quantifier free formula H is equivalent to a formula of the form $H_1 \vee \cdots \vee H_k$ where each H_i is of the form $\alpha_1 \wedge \cdots \wedge \alpha_r$, and each α_j is an atomic formula of the language $\mathscr{L}$ or the negation of such a formula. Therefore, because $\bigvee x(H_1 \vee \cdots \vee H_k)$ is equivalent to $\bigvee xH_1 \vee \cdots \vee \bigvee xH_k$, we have the following theorem.

THEOREM 1: *A set $\mathscr{A}$ of formulas of $\mathscr{L}$ allows the elimination of quantifiers in $\mathscr{L}$ if and only if it allows the elimination of quantifiers in all formulas of the form $\bigvee x(\alpha_1 \wedge \cdots \wedge \alpha_k)$ where each α_i is an atomic formula or the negation of an atomic formula of $\mathscr{L}$.*

A set $\mathscr{A}$ of formulas is said to be *complete for* $\mathscr{L}$ if for each closed formula F of $\mathscr{L}$ either F or $\neg F$ is a consequence of $\mathscr{A}$.

THEOREM 2: *If $\mathscr{A}$ allows the elimination of quantifiers in $\mathscr{L}$ and $D(\mathfrak{M})$ is the diagram of a model $\mathfrak{M}$ of $\mathscr{A}$ then $\mathscr{A} \cup D(\mathfrak{M})$ is complete (for the language $\mathscr{L}'$ of $\mathscr{A} \cup D(\mathfrak{M})$).*

PROOF: We first note that if $\mathscr{A}$ allows the elimination of quantifiers in $\mathscr{L}$ then it allows the elimination of quantifiers in all languages $\mathscr{L}'$ obtained from $\mathscr{L}$ by the addition of a set C of individual constants. For suppose F is a formula of such a language $\mathscr{L}'$. Let F_1 be the formula of $\mathscr{L}$ which is obtained by substituting for each a in C which occurs in F a variable x which does not occur in F, substituting distinct variables for distinct elements of C. There is a quantifier free formula F_1' which is equivalent to F_1. If we substitute back the constants in F_1' we obtain a quantifier free formula which is equivalent to F.

Now suppose that $\mathscr{L}'$ is the language of $\mathscr{A} \cup D(\mathfrak{M})$ and that F is a closed formula of $\mathscr{L}'$. If F is satisfied in the model $\mathfrak{M}$ then $\bar{F} = E^{V\mathscr{L}}$, where E is the domain of $\mathfrak{M}$. Now every model of $D(\mathfrak{M})$ is an extension of $\mathfrak{M}$.

Consider a model $\mathfrak{M}'$ of $\mathscr{A} \cup D(\mathfrak{M})$. In $\mathfrak{M}$ and $\mathfrak{M}'$, which are both models of $\mathscr{A}$, F is equivalent to a quantifier free formula. Hence by Lemma 3.9, if $\bar{\bar{F}}$ is the value of F in $\mathfrak{M}'$, we have $\bar{F} = \bar{\bar{F}} \cap E^{V\mathscr{L}} = E^{V\mathscr{L}}$. Hence $\bar{\bar{F}}$ is not empty, but F is a closed formula and so $\mathfrak{M}'$ satisfies F. Thus if F is satisfied by $\mathfrak{M}$ it is satisfied by all models of $\mathscr{A} \cup D(\mathfrak{M})$ and hence is a consequence of $\mathscr{A} \cup D(\mathfrak{M})$. But for each closed formula F either F or $\neg F$ is satisfied by $\mathfrak{M}$. Thus for each closed formula F either F or $\neg F$ is a consequence of $\mathscr{A} \cup D(\mathfrak{M})$.

This completes the proof.

We devote the rest of the chapter to the consideration of some particular cases.

I. Dense orders with first and last element

We consider the language $\mathscr{L}$ which has two constant symbols 0,1 and two binary relation symbols $<, =$. (We will write $x<y$ for $<xy$.)

Let $\mathscr{A}$ be the set of the following formulas of $\mathscr{L}$:

$\bigwedge x \neg(x<x)$ $\bigwedge x \bigwedge y \bigwedge z(x<y \wedge y<z \rightarrow x<z)$ $\bigwedge x \bigwedge y(x=y \vee x<y \vee y<x)$	Axioms for a total ordering.
$\bigwedge x \bigwedge y \bigvee z(x<y \rightarrow x<z \wedge z<y)$	Axiom for a dense ordering.
$\bigwedge x(x=0 \vee 0<x)$ $\bigwedge x(x=1 \vee x<1)$	Axioms for first and last elements.

We will show that $\mathscr{A}$ allows the elimination of quantifiers in $\mathscr{L}$.

Suppose that we have a formula of the form $\bigvee x(\alpha_1 \wedge \cdots \wedge \alpha_r)$ where each α_i is either an atomic formula of $\mathscr{L}$ or the negation of an atomic formula of $\mathscr{L}$. Thus for each α_i there are four possibilities: $t_1<t_2$, $t_1=t_2$, $\neg(t_1<t_2)$, $t_1 \neq t_2$, where t_1, t_2 are terms of $\mathscr{L}$ and so either 0,1 or a variable.

From $\mathscr{A}$ it follows that $\neg(t_1<t_2)$ is equivalent to $(t_2<t_1) \vee (t_1=t_2)$ and that $t_1 \neq t_2$ is equivalent to $(t_1<t_2) \vee (t_2<t_1)$. Using the facts that $A \wedge (B \vee C)$ is equivalent to $(A \wedge B) \vee (A \wedge C)$ and $\bigvee x(A \vee B)$ is equivalent to $\bigvee xA \vee \bigvee xB$ we can therefore reduce the problem to that of eliminating quantifiers in a formula of the form $\bigvee x(\alpha_1 \wedge \cdots \wedge \alpha_r)$ where each α_i is of the form $t_1=t_2$ or $t_1<t_2$.

We proceed by recursion on r. If $r=1$ the formula is $\bigvee x(t_1<t_2)$ or $\bigvee x(t_1=t_2)$ where t_1, t_2 are 0,1 or a variable. The elimination of the quantifier for this case is obvious.

Now suppose that we have eliminated quantifiers for all formulas where $r<h$, and consider the formula $\bigvee x(\alpha_1 \wedge \cdots \wedge \alpha_h)$. If one of the α_i, say α_1, does not contain x, the formula is equivalent to $\alpha_1 \wedge \bigvee x(\alpha_2 \wedge \cdots \wedge \alpha_h)$ and we are reduced at once to the case $r=h-1$. So we will assume that all the α_i contain x so that we can write the formula as $\bigvee x(x<t_1 \wedge \cdots \wedge x<t_k \wedge u_1<x \wedge \cdots \wedge u_l<x \wedge x=v_1 \wedge \cdots \wedge x=v_m)$ where the t, u, v are terms which we can assume are different from x (if, for example, $t_1=x$ the formula is equivalent to $\perp$, and if, for example, $v_1=x$ we are reduced to the case $r=h-1$).

If $k>1$ the formula is equivalent to

$$(t_1 < t_2 \wedge \bigvee x(x < t_1 \wedge x < t_3 \ldots)) \vee \\ \vee (\neg t_1 < t_2 \wedge \bigvee x(x < t_2 \wedge x < t_3 \ldots))$$

and we are again reduced to the case $r=h-1$.

We obtain a similar reduction if $l>1$.

If $k=l=1$ the formula can be written

$$\bigvee x(x < t_1 \wedge u_1 < x \wedge x = v_1 \wedge \cdots \wedge x = v_m)$$

which for $m\neq 0$ is equivalent to

$$(v_1 = v_2 = \cdots = v_m) \wedge (u_1 < v_1 < t_1)$$

and for $m=0$ is equivalent to $u_1<t_1$.

For $k=0$ the formula can be written

$$\bigvee x(u_1 < x \wedge x = v_1 \wedge \cdots \wedge x = v_m)$$

which for $m\neq 0$ is equivalent to

$$(u_1 < v_1) \wedge (v_1 = v_2 = \cdots = v_m)$$

and for $m=0$ is equivalent to $u_1 \neq 1$.

We obtain similar results when $l=0$.

This completes the proof.

The reader can investigate in a similar way dense orders with first but without last element (drop the constant 1 and add the axiom $\bigwedge x \bigvee y(x<y)$) with last but without first element, and without first or last element.

It should be noted that the quantifier free formula which is equivalent to $\bigvee x(\alpha_1 \wedge \cdots \wedge \alpha_r)$ contains the same variables as this formula, other than x. Thus for each closed formula F the quantifier free formula associated with it contains no variables. The propositional variables in it are therefore all equivalent to either $0<1, 0=1$ or $1<0$ which are in turn equivalent to $\top$ or $\bot$. Therefore F is equivalent to either $\top$ or $\bot$ and hence *the set $\mathscr{A}$ is complete for its language $\mathscr{L}$.*

II. Discrete orders without first or last element

We consider the language $\mathscr{L}$ which has one unary function symbol s (read "successor") and the two binary relation symbols $<$ and $=$. The terms of $\mathscr{L}$ are therefore of the form $s^p x$ (s repeated p times followed by a variable x).

Let $\mathscr{A}$ be the set of the following formulas: a) the axioms for a total ordering (see I above), and b) the formulas

$$\bigwedge x \bigwedge y (x < y \leftrightarrow (y = sx \vee sx < y))$$
$$\bigwedge x \bigvee y (x = sy).$$

We will show that $\mathscr{A}$ allows the elimination of quantifiers in $\mathscr{L}$.

As in I above, we need only consider a formula of the form $\bigvee x(\alpha_1 \wedge \cdots \wedge \alpha_r)$ where each α_i is of the form $t_1 < t_2$ or $t_1 = t_2$ i.e. $s^{p_1}x_1 < s^{p_2}x_2$ or $s^{p_1}x_1 = s^{p_2}x_2$.

We proceed by recursion on r. The case $r=1$ is trivial. Suppose we have dealt with the case $r<h$ and that we have a formula of the form $\bigvee x(\alpha_1 \wedge \cdots \wedge \alpha_h)$. As before it is immediate that in each atomic formula $s^{p_1}x_1 < s^{p_2}x_2$ or $s^{p_1}x_1 = s^{p_2}x_2$ at least one of x_1 and x_2 is x or else we can immediately reduce the problem to the case $r=h-1$. If both x_1 and x_2 are x in some α_i then this α_i is of the form $s^{p_1}x < s^{p_2}x$ or $s^{p_1}x = s^{p_2}x$ which is equivalent to $s^{p_1}x' < s^{p_2}x'$ or $s^{p_1}x' = s^{p_2}x'$ with $x \neq x'$ so that we can again reduce the problem to the case $r=h-1$.

As a simplification we will write the formulas $s^p x < x_1$ and $s^p x = x_1$ as $x < s^{-p}x_1$ and $x = s^{-p}x_1$. Thus the formulas $s^p x < s^{p_1}x_1$ and $s^p x = s^{p_2}x_1$ are equivalent to $x < s^{p_1 - p}x_1$ and $x = s^{p_2 - p}x_1$. Therefore the formula we are considering can be written as

$$\bigvee x (x < t_1 \wedge \cdots \wedge x < t_k \wedge u_1 < x \wedge \cdots \wedge u_l < x \wedge x = v_1 \wedge \cdots \wedge x = v_m)$$

where the terms t, u, v are of the form $s^p y$, p some integer.

If k or l is bigger than 1 we can reduce the problem to the case $r=h-1$ as before. We therefore need only consider the formula $\bigvee x(x<t_1 \wedge u_1 < x \wedge x = v_1 \wedge \cdots \wedge x = v_m)$ and this can be reduced to a quantifier free formula in a way similar to that which we used in I.

It follows, just as in I, that *$\mathscr{A}$ is complete for the language $\mathscr{L}$.*

III. Some commutative groups with discrete total orderings

We consider the language $\mathscr{L}$ which has, in addition to the binary relation symbol $=$, two constant symbols 0,1, a unary function symbol $-$, a binary function symbol $+$ and a unary relation symbol >0.

The terms $1+\cdots+1$ and $t+\cdots+t$ (1 and t repeated p times) will be written as p and pt, and the term $t_1+(-t_2)$ as t_1-t_2.

Let $\mathscr{A}$ be the set of the following formulas

(a) The axioms for a commutative group:

$$\bigwedge x \bigwedge y \bigwedge z((x+y)+z=x+(y+z))$$
$$\bigwedge x \bigwedge y(x+y=y+x)$$
$$\bigwedge x(x+0=x)$$
$$\bigwedge x(x-x=0).$$

(b) The axioms for a total ordering compatible with the group structure:

$$\bigwedge x \bigwedge y(x>0 \wedge y>0 \rightarrow x+y>0)$$
$$\bigwedge x \neg (x>0 \wedge -x>0)$$
$$\bigwedge x(x=0 \vee x>0 \vee -x>0).$$

(c) The axioms for a discrete ordering

$$\bigwedge x(x>0 \leftrightarrow (x=1 \vee x-1>0)).$$

It is clear (by induction on the length of t), that for each term t of $\mathscr{L}$ there are integers $a_1, \ldots, a_n, b \in \mathbf{Z}$ and variables $x_1, \ldots, x_n$ such that $t=a_1x_1+\cdots+a_nx_n+b$ is a consequence of $\mathscr{A}$. (In fact we only need the axioms of (a).)

We can show (see Exercise 2) that the set $\mathscr{A}$ does not allow the elimination of quantifiers in $\mathscr{L}$. Let $\mathscr{L}'$ be the language obtained from $\mathscr{L}$, by adding, for each integer $n>1$, the unary relation symbol $n|$ (read "n divides") and let $\mathscr{A}'$ be the set of formulas obtained by adding to $\mathscr{A}$ the formulas

(d) $$\bigwedge x(n|x \leftrightarrow \bigvee y(x=ny)) \quad \text{for each} \quad n>1$$

and

(e) $$\bigwedge x(n|x \vee n|x+1 \vee \cdots \vee n|x+n-1) \quad \text{for each} \quad n>1.$$

It is clear that each model of $\mathscr{A}$, that is each commutative group with a discrete total ordering, is also a model of (d), or, more precisely, given a model of $\mathscr{A}$, there is a unique value of $n|$ so that (d) is satisfied. On the other hand (e) is not a consequence of the set $(a)\cup(b)\cup(c)\cup(d)$. (We will write (a, b, c, d) for this set in future.) We can show (see Exercise 2) that (a, b, c, d) does not allow the elimination of quantifiers in $\mathscr{L}'$ but we will see that $(a, b, c, d, e)=\mathscr{A}'$ does allow it. To do this we consider a formula F of the form $\bigvee x(\alpha_1 \wedge \cdots \wedge \alpha_n)$ where each α_i is an atomic formula of $\mathscr{L}'$ or the negation of an atomic formula of $\mathscr{L}'$. Thus α_i is of one of the forms $t_1=t_2$ (which, by $\mathscr{A}'$, is equivalent to $t=0$ with $t=t_1-t_2$), $t\neq 0$, $t>0, \neg(t>0)$, $n|t$ or $\neg(n|t)$.

It follows from $\mathscr{A}'$ that $t\neq 0$ is equivalent to $t>0 \vee -t>0$, that $\neg(t>0)$ is equivalent to $t=0 \vee -t>0$ and that $\neg(n|t)$ is equivalent to $n|t+1 \vee \cdots \vee n|t+n-1$. Hence we can suppose that each α_i is of one of the forms $t=0$, $t>0$ or $n|t$.

Each term t can be written in the form $px+t'$ with $p\in\mathbf{Z}$ and t' a term which does not contain x. To make things clearer we will write $t_1>t_2$ for $t_1-t_2>0$.

Thus the formula F can be written in the form

$$\bigvee x(p_1x > t_1 \wedge \cdots \wedge p_kx > t_k \wedge q_1x = u_1 \wedge \cdots \wedge q_lx = u_l \wedge \\ \wedge n_1|r_1x - v_1 \wedge \cdots \wedge n_m|r_mx - v_m)$$

where the p, q, r are in $\mathbf{Z}$ and the t, u, v are terms which do not contain x.

It follows from $\mathscr{A}'$ that the formula $n_1|r_1x-v_1$ is equivalent to

$$(n_1|r_1x \wedge n_1|v_1) \vee (n_1|r_1x + 1 \wedge n_1|v_1 + 1) \vee \\ \vee \cdots \vee (n_1|r_1x + n_1 - 1 \wedge n_1|v_1 + n_1 - 1).$$

If we make this substitution in F and use the fact that $A\wedge(B\vee C)$ is equivalent to $(A\wedge B)\vee(A\wedge C)$ we can reduce the problem to that of considering a formula of the same form of F except that the v_i are integers (positive, negative or zero).

We put $h=|p_1|+\cdots+|p_k|+|q_1|+\cdots+|q_l|+n_1+\cdots+n_m+|r_1|+\cdots+|r_m|$. We proceed by recursion on h, which we will call the *rank* of F. Suppose that we have eliminated quantifiers for all formulas of rank less than h and that F is a formula of rank h.

If $k\geqslant 2$, F is equivalent to

$$(p_2t_1 \geqslant p_1t_2 \wedge \bigvee x(p_1x > t_1 \wedge p_3x > t_3 \wedge \cdots))\vee \\ \vee (p_1t_2 > p_2t_1 \wedge \bigvee x(p_2x > t_2 \wedge p_3x > t_3 \wedge \cdots))$$

and we are reduced to the case of a formula of rank $h-1$.

If $l \geqslant 2$ we note that $q_1 x = u_1 \wedge q_2 x = u_2$ is equivalent to $q_1 x = u_1 \wedge (q_2 - q_1)\, x = u_2 - u_1$. Thus with, say $|q_1| \leqslant |q_2|$, we have $|q_1| + |q_2 - q_1| < |q_1| + |q_2|$ and we can again reduce the problem to that of a formula of rank less than h.

If $k=1$ and $l=1$ the formula F can be written as

$$\bigvee x(px > t \wedge qx = u \wedge n_1 | r_1 x - v_1 \wedge \cdots \wedge n_m | r_m x - v_m)$$

and this is equivalent to

$$(pu > qt \wedge q|u \wedge qn_1 | r_1 u - v_1 q \wedge \cdots \wedge qn_m | r_m u - v_m q)$$

which is quantifier free.

If $k=0$ and $l=1$, F is equivalent to the same quantifier free formula except that we drop "$pu > qt$".

Suppose then that $k=1$ and $l=0$ (the case where $k=0$ and $l=0$ can be dealt with in the same way). F can be written

$$\bigvee x(px > t \wedge n_1 | r_1 x - v_1 \wedge \cdots \wedge n_m | r_m x - v_m).$$

If one of the n_i, say n_1, can be written as $n_1 = nn'$, where n and n' are coprime, $n_1 | r_1 x - v_1$ is equivalent to $n | r_1 x - v_1 \wedge n' | r_1 x - v_1$. Since $n + n' < n_1$ we are therefore reduced to a formula of rank less than h. Thus we can assume that all the n_i are of the form $\pi_i^{\rho_i}$, where π_i is a prime.

Let $a_1, \ldots, a_k$ be the integers in the interval $[0, n_1 - 1]$ such that $n_1 | ra_1 - v_1, \ldots, n_1 | ra_k - v_1$ (if any exist). It can easily be seen that the formula $n_1 | r_1 x - v_1$ is equivalent to $n_1 | x - a_1 \vee \cdots \vee n_1 | x - a_k$. Making this substitution in F we are reduced to the case of k formulas each of rank less than h.

Thus we can suppose that $r_1 = \cdots = r_m = 1$ and that F can be written

$$\bigvee x(px > t \wedge n_1 | x - v_1 \wedge \cdots \wedge n_m | x - v_m).$$

If, say, $n_1 = \pi^{\rho_1}$ and $n_2 = \pi^{\rho_2}$ with $\rho_1 \leqslant \rho_2$, the formula $n_1 | x - v_1 \wedge n_2 | x - v_2$ is equivalent to $n_1 | v_1 - v_2 \wedge n_2 | x - v_2$. Therefore we can assume that the n_i are of the form $\pi_i^{\rho_i}$, where the π_i are distinct primes.

Since the n_i are pairwise coprime there is some integer u in the interval $[0, n_1 \ldots n_m - 1]$ such that $n_1 | u - v_1, \ldots, n_m | u - v_m$ and we can deduce that F is equivalent to $\top$. For suppose that, for example, $p \geqslant 0$; then, for $t \geqslant 0$, $x = u + n_1 \ldots n_m t$ satisfies $px > t \wedge n_1 | x - v_1 \wedge \cdots \wedge n_m | x - v_m$ and for $t < 0$, $x = u$ satisfies it.

This completes our proof that $\mathscr{A}'$ allows the elimination of quantifiers in $\mathscr{L}'$.

As before, we see that if F is a closed formula, F' to which it is equivalent contains no free variables. The atomic formulas of F' are therefore $t=0$, $t>0$ and $n|t$, where t is a term of $\mathscr{L}'$ without any variables and so is an integer. Thus each of these atomic formulas is equivalent to $\top$ or $\bot$. Therefore *$\mathscr{A}'$ is complete for $\mathscr{L}'$.*

IV. Algebraically closed fields

The language $\mathscr{L}$ that we consider has two constant symbols 0, 1, a unary function symbol $-$, two binary function symbols $+$, $\times$ and no relation symbols other than $=$. (We write xy for $\times xy$ and $x+y$ for $+xy$.)

Let $\mathscr{A}$ be the set of the following formulas

(a) Axioms for a commutative group with respect to $+$:

$$\bigwedge x \bigwedge y \bigwedge z(x+(y+z)=(x+y+z))$$
$$\bigwedge x \bigwedge y(x+y=y+x)$$
$$\bigwedge x(x+0=x)$$
$$\bigwedge x(x+(-x)=0).$$

(b)

$$\bigwedge x \bigwedge y \bigwedge z(x(yz)=(xy)z)$$
$$\bigwedge x \bigwedge y(xy=yx)$$
$$\bigwedge x(x\cdot 1=x)$$
$$\bigwedge x \bigvee y(x=0 \vee xy=1)$$
$$\bigwedge x \bigwedge y \bigwedge z(x(y+z)=xy+xz)$$
$$0\neq 1.$$

It is clear that each model of (a, b) is a commutative field and that for each term t of $\mathscr{L}$ there is a polynomial $p(x_1, \ldots, x_n)$ with coefficients in **Z** such that $t=p(x_1, \ldots, x_n)$ is a consequence of (a, b).

(We write p for the term $1+\cdots+1$(1 repeated p times) and t^p for the term $t\times\cdots\times t$(t repeated p times).)

(c) For each $n>1$ the formula

$$\bigwedge x_0 \bigwedge x_1 \ldots \bigwedge x_{n-1} \bigvee x(x_0+x_1x+\cdots+x_{n-1}x^{n-1}+x^n=0).$$

Clearly each model of $\mathscr{A}=(a, b, c)$ is an algebraically closed field. We will see that $\mathscr{A}$ allows the elimination of quantifiers in $\mathscr{L}$. To show this we make use of

Lemma 3: *Let $p(x_1, \ldots, x_k, x)$ and $q(x_1, \ldots, x_k, x)$ be two terms of $\mathscr{L}$, i.e.*

two polynomials with coefficients in $\mathbf{Z}$. *Then there is a quantifier free formula* F *of* $\mathscr{L}$ *such that in each model of* (a, b), *i.e. in each commutative field* K, $\bar{F}$ *is the set of those* $(\xi_1, \ldots, \xi_k) \in K^k$ *such that* $p(\xi_1, \ldots, \xi_k, x)$ *divides* $q(\xi_1, \ldots, \xi_k, x)$.

PROOF: Let $p(x) = a_0 + a_1 x + \cdots + a_m x^m$ and $q(x) = b_0 + b_1 x + \cdots + b_n x^n$ where the a_i and b_j are polynomials in $x_1, \ldots, x_k$, with coefficients in $\mathbf{Z}$.

We obtain the desired formula F by recursion on $m+n$. Clearly for $m+n=0$ the formula we want is $a_0 \neq 0 \vee b_0 = 0$.

Now suppose we have found a formula F with the required property whenever $m+n<h$ and that the polynomials $p(x)$ and $q(x)$ are such that $m+n=h$.

If $n<m$ then, by our hypothesis, there is a formula F corresponding to the polynomials $p_1 = a_0 + a_1 x + \cdots + a_{m-1} x^{m-1}$ and $q(x)$. The formula we want is therefore

$$(a_m \neq 0 \wedge b_0 = b_1 = \cdots = b_n = 0) \vee (a_m = 0 \wedge F).$$

If $m \leqslant n$ we put $p_1 = a_0 + a_1 x + \cdots + a_{m-1} x^{m-1}$ and $q_1 = a_m q(x) - b_n x^{n-m} p(x)$, so q_1 is of degree less than n. By hypothesis there is a formula F corresponding to the pair of polynomials p_1, q and a formula G corresponding to the pair p, q_1. The formula we want is therefore

$$(a_m = 0 \wedge F) \vee (a_m \neq 0 \wedge G).$$

This completes the proof of the lemma.

We now consider a formula F of $\mathscr{L}$ of the form $\bigvee x(\alpha_1 \wedge \cdots \wedge \alpha_r)$, where each α_i is an atomic formula of $\mathscr{L}$ or the negation of an atomic formula of $\mathscr{L}$. Thus each α_i is of the form $t_1 = t_2$ or $t_1 \neq t_2$, and so is equivalent to a formula of the form $t=0$ or $t \neq 0$ (where $t = t_1 - t_2$). But $t_1 \neq 0 \wedge \cdots \wedge t_l \neq 0$ is equivalent to $t_1 \cdots t_l \neq 0$, so we can see that F can be written as $\bigvee x(t_1 = 0 \wedge \cdots \wedge t_k = 0 \wedge t \neq 0)$.

Each t_i is a polynomial in x whose coefficients are polynomials in the other variables with coefficients in $\mathbf{Z}$. Let the term of highest degree in t_i be $a_i x^{n_i}$. Clearly we can assume that no n_i is zero since if, for example, $n_1 = 0$, F is equivalent to $t_1 = 0 \wedge \bigvee x(t_2 = 0 \wedge \cdots \wedge t_k = 0 \wedge t \neq 0)$.

We now proceed by recursion on the sum of the n_i, which we will call the *rank* of F. If $k \geqslant 0$ and, say, $n_1 \geqslant n_2$, we put $t_1' = a_2 t_1 - a_1 x^{n_1 - n_2} t_2$ and $t_2' = t_2 - a_2 x^{n_2}$. Then t_1' is of degree less than n_1 and t_2' is of degree less than n_2. The formula F is equivalent to

$$(a_2 = 0 \wedge \bigvee x(t_1 = 0 \wedge t_2' = 0 \wedge \cdots \wedge t_k = 0 \wedge t \neq 0)) \vee$$
$$\vee (a_2 \neq 0 \wedge \bigvee x(t_1' = 0 \wedge t_2 = 0 \wedge \cdots \wedge t_k = 0 \wedge t \neq 0))$$

and so we are reduced to two formulas of lower rank.

If $k=1$ the formula F can be written $\bigvee x(t_1=0 \wedge t \neq 0)$. We know that in any algebraically closed field K, given two polynomials $p(x)$, $q(x)$ with one free variable x and coefficients in K, there is some x_0 in K such that $p(x_0)=0$ and $q(x_0) \neq 0$ if and only if p does not divide q^n, where n is the degree of p with respect to x. Hence if G is the quantifier free formula that, by Lemma 3, is associated with the pair t_1, t^n(n=degree t_1) the formula F is equivalent to $\neg G$ (that is, it has the same value as $\neg G$ in all algebraically closed fields).

If $k=0$ the formula F can be written $\bigvee x(t \neq 0)$. Let $t=a_0+a_1x+\cdots +a_nx^n$. Since all algebraically closed fields are infinite and each polynomial in a single variable which is not identically zero has only a finite number of roots we can see that F is equivalent to $a_0 \neq 0 \vee \cdots \vee a_n \neq 0$.

This completes the proof that $\mathscr{A}$ allows the elimination of quantifiers in $\mathscr{L}$.

We see, as before, that each closed formula of $\mathscr{L}$ is equivalent to a quantifier free formula whose atomic formulas are of the form $t=0$, where t is a term which does not contain any variables, and so of the form $n=0$ where $n \in \mathrm{N}$, the set of natural numbers. Now if $n>1$ neither $n=0$ nor $n \neq 0$ is a consequence of $\mathscr{A}$ because there are algebraically closed fields of characteristic p for $p=0$ or any prime number. Therefore $\mathscr{A}$ *is not complete* but it becomes so if we add any *one* of the formulas $p=0$ for p prime (axiom for a field of characteristic p) or the *set* of formulas $\{p \neq 0 : p \text{ prime}\}$ (axioms for a field of characteristic 0).

We have the following application of this result.

THEOREM 4: *If the polynomials $p_1, \ldots, p_k$ in the variables $x_1, \ldots, x_n$, with coefficients in the field K have a common zero in some extension field L of K, then they have a common zero which is algebraic over K.*

PROOF: Let Ω be the algebraic closure of K and let D_Ω be the diagram of Ω. The set $\mathscr{A}$ of axioms for an algebraically closed field allows the elimination of quantifiers and so, by Theorem 2, $\mathscr{A} \cup D_\Omega$ is complete.

Let $\mathscr{L}$ be the language of $\mathscr{A} \cup D_\Omega$. The formula

$$\bigvee x_1 \dots \bigvee x_n (p_1 = 0 \wedge \dots \wedge p_k = 0)$$

is a formula of $\mathscr{L}'$ which is satisfied in a model of $\mathscr{A} \cup D_\Omega$, namely the algebraic closure of L. Hence it is satisfied in all models of $\mathscr{A} \cup D_\Omega$ and, in particular, in Ω.

V. Real closed fields

The language $\mathscr{L}$ that we consider has two constant symbols 0, 1, one unary function symbol $-$, two binary function symbols $+$, $\times$, one unary relation symbol >0 and the binary relation symbol $=$.

Let $\mathscr{A}$ be the set of the following formulas

(*a*) The axioms for a commutative field (i.e. the sets (*a*) and (*b*) of IV).

(*b*)

$$\bigwedge x \bigwedge y (x > 0 \wedge y > 0 \to x + y > 0)$$
$$\bigwedge x (x = 0 \vee x > 0 \vee -x > 0)$$
$$\bigwedge x \neg (x > 0 \wedge -x > 0)$$
$$\bigwedge x \bigwedge y (x > 0 \wedge y > 0 \to xy > 0).$$

Each model of (*a*, *b*) is an ordered field.

(*c*)

$$\bigwedge x \bigvee y (x = y^2 \vee -x = y^2)$$
$$\bigwedge x_0 \bigwedge x_1 \dots \bigwedge x_{2n} \bigvee x (x_0 + x_1 x + \dots + x_{2n} x^{2n} + x^{2n+1} = 0)$$

for each $n \geqslant 1$.

The models of $\mathscr{A} = (a, b, c)$ are the real closed fields. (For the properties of such fields that we use here see, for example, B. L. van der Waerden, Modern Algebra.) We will show that $\mathscr{A}$ allows the elimination of quantifiers in $\mathscr{L}$.

For each term t there is, as before, a polynomial $p(x_1, \dots, x_n)$ with coefficients in $\mathbf{Z}$ such that $t = p(x_1, \dots, x_n)$ is a consequence of $\mathscr{A}$.

For simplicity we will write the formula $t - t' > 0$ as $t > t'$ or $t' < t$ and the formula $t < t' \wedge t' < t''$ as $t < t' < t''$. Each atomic formula F of $\mathscr{L}$ is equivalent to a formula of the form $p(x, x_1, \dots, x_n) = 0$ or $p(x, x_1, \dots, x_n) > 0$. Each quantifier free formula F is equivalent (in all models of $\mathscr{A}$) to a disjunction of formulas $p_1 = 0 \wedge \dots \wedge p_k = 0 \wedge q_1 > 0 \wedge \dots \wedge q_l > 0$. The *degree* in x of an equation $p_i = 0$ is the highest degree of x in p_i, and the degree of an inequality $q_j > 0$ is $1 +$ the highest degree of x in q_j. The degree of F itself is the maximum of the degrees of its atomic parts.

LEMMA 5: *For each quantifier free formula A of the form* $p_1=0\wedge\cdots\wedge p_k=0\wedge q_1>0\wedge\cdots\wedge q_l>0$, *where the* p_i, q_j *are polynomials in* $x, x_1, \ldots, x_n$, *there is a quantifier free formula B which is equivalent to A (in all models of* $\mathscr{A}$*) such that the degree of x in B is less than or equal to the least degree of x in the polynomials* p_i *(which we assume is not zero).*

PROOF: We prove the lemma by induction on the sum of the degrees of x in the p_i and q_j, which we will call the *rank* of A. Suppose that we have proved the lemma for all formulas of rank less than h and let $p_1=0\wedge\cdots\wedge p_k=0\wedge q_1>0\wedge\cdots\wedge q_l>0$ be a formula of rank h.

If $k\geqslant 2$, let $a_1x^{m_1}$ and $a_2x^{m_2}$ be the terms of highest degree in p_1 and p_2, and put $\pi_1=a_2p_1-a_1x^{m_1-m_2}$ (assuming $m_1\geqslant m_2$), and $\pi_2=p_2-a_2x^{m_2}$. Then the formula that we are considering is equivalent to

$$(a_2=0\wedge p_1=0\wedge \pi_2=0\wedge\cdots\wedge p_k=0\wedge q_1>0\wedge\cdots\wedge q_l>0)\vee$$
$$\vee(a_2\neq 0\wedge \pi_1=0\wedge p_2=0\wedge\cdots\wedge p_k=0\wedge q_1>0\wedge\cdots\wedge q_l>0)$$

and we are therefore reduced to the case of two formulas of rank less than h.

If $k=1$ the formula can be written $p=0\wedge q_1>0\wedge\cdots\wedge q_l>0$. If all the q_i are of degree in x less than the degree of x in p the formula itself satisfies the lemma. If not, say, for example, q_1 is of degree greater than p and let ax^m and bx^n be the terms of highest degree in p and q_1; so $m\leqslant n$. Put $P=p-ax^m$ and $Q=a^2q_1-abx^{n-m}p$. Then the formula is equivalent to

$$(a=0\wedge P=0\wedge q_1>0\wedge\cdots\wedge q_l>0)\vee$$
$$\vee(a\neq 0\wedge p=0\wedge Q>0\wedge q_2>0\wedge\cdots\wedge q_l>0)$$

and so we are again reduced to the case of two formulas of rank less than h.

If $k=0$ there is nothing to prove; so this completes the proof of the lemma.

THEOREM 6: *Let* $A(x, x_1, \ldots, x_n)$ *be a quantifier free formula of degree h in x. Let a, b be two variables other then* $x, x_1, \ldots, x_n$. *Then there is a quantifier free formula F whose variables are* $a, b, x_1, \ldots, x_n$, *whose degree in a and b is less than or equal to h, none of whose atomic formulas contains both a and b and such that*

$$F\leftrightarrow \bigvee x(a<x<b\wedge A(x,x_1,\ldots,x_n))$$

is a consequence of $\mathscr{A}\cup\{a<b\}$.

PROOF: The proof is by induction on the degree of x in A. If this degree is zero then A does not contain x. Therefore the formula $\bigvee x(a<x<b \wedge A)$ is equivalent to $A \wedge a<b$ and so the formula F that we want is A itself.

Suppose now that we have proved the Theorem for formulas of degree less than h and that the degree of x in A is h.

A is equivalent to a disjunction of formulas of the form $u_1 \wedge \cdots \wedge u_r$ where each u_i is an atomic formula or the negation of an atomic formula, and hence is of one of the forms $p=0, p\neq 0, p>0$ and $\neg(p>0)$. Since $p\neq 0$ is equivalent to $p>0 \vee -p>0$ and $\neg(p>0)$ is equivalent to $p=0 \vee -p>0$ we can assume that A is of the form $p_1=0 \wedge \cdots \wedge p_k=0 \wedge q_1>0 \wedge \cdots \wedge q_l>0$.

Lemma 5 shows that if $k\geqslant 2$, or if $k=1$ and one of the q_j is of degree in x greater than or equal to the degree in x of p_1 we can replace A by B; so we are reduced to a formula of lower degree and can therefore apply the induction hypothesis.

Thus we can assume that A is of one of the forms I: $p=0 \wedge q_1>0 \wedge \cdots \wedge q_l>0$, where the degree of q_j is less than the degree of p, so the degree of p equals the degree of A, which is h, or II: $q_1>0 \wedge \cdots \wedge q_l>0$.

We first consider A of degree h and form II. Let $G = \bigvee x(a<x<b \wedge q_1>0 \wedge \cdots \wedge q_l>0)$, the degree in x of $q_j (1\leqslant j\leqslant l)$ being $<h$. In any real closed field, G is true if and only if in some open interval (α, β) contained in (a, b) each q_j is strictly positive. The following set of conditions exhausts all possibilities:

$$G_0(a, b) = \bigwedge x[a < x < b \rightarrow (q_1 > 0 \wedge \cdots \wedge q_l > 0)]$$
$$G_i(a, b) = \bigvee u[a < u < b \wedge q_i(u) = 0 \wedge G_0(a, u)] \vee$$
$$\vee \bigvee v[a < v < b \wedge q_i(v) = 0 \wedge G_0(v, b)] \quad (1 \leqslant i \leqslant l)$$
$$H_{ij}(a, b) = \bigvee u \bigvee v[a < u < v < b \wedge q_i(u) = 0 \wedge$$
$$q_j(v) = 0 \wedge G_0(u, v)] \qquad (1 \leqslant i \leqslant l, 1 \leqslant j \leqslant l).$$

We shall reduce each of these cases by use of the induction hypothesis. In each model of $\mathscr{A}$,

$$G_0(a, b) \leftrightarrow [q_1(a) \geqslant 0 \wedge \cdots \wedge q_l(a) \geqslant 0 \wedge \neg \bigvee x(a < x < b \wedge q_1 = 0) \wedge$$
$$\wedge \cdots \neg \bigvee x(a < x < b \wedge q_l = 0)].$$

Since the degree of $q_j=0$ is $<h$, the induction hypothesis applies to each formula $\bigvee x(a<x<b \wedge q_j=0)$. So $G_0(a, b)$ is equivalent to a quantifier free formula of degree $<h$ in a and b, whose components are of the form

$K_r(a) \wedge L_r(b)$ $(1 \leqslant r \leqslant s)$. $G_i(a, b)$ is equivalent to the disjunction $(1 \leqslant r \leqslant s)$ of formulas

$$K_r(a) \wedge \bigvee u[a < u < b \wedge q_i(u) = 0 \wedge L_r(u)] \vee \\ L_r(b) \wedge \bigvee v[a < v < b \wedge q_i(v) = 0 \wedge K_r(v)];$$

to each component of $G_i(a, b)$ we can apply the induction hypothesis since the degree in u of $q_i(u)=0 \wedge L_r(u)$ and the degree in v of $q_i(v)=0 \wedge K_r(v)$ are all $<h$.

Finally $H_{ij}(a, b)$ is equivalent to the disjunction $(1 \leqslant r \leqslant s)$ of formulas

$$\bigvee u(a < u < b \wedge q_i(u) = 0 \wedge K_r(u) \wedge \\ \bigvee v[u < v < b \wedge q_j(v) = 0 \wedge L_r(v)]).$$

Since $q_i(v)=0 \wedge L_r(v)$ is of degree $<h$ in v, the induction hypothesis yields formulas $M_{jrt}(u) \wedge N_{jrt}(b)$ of degree $<h$ in u and b such that

$$\bigvee v[u < v < b \wedge q_j(v) = 0 \wedge L_r(v)] \leftrightarrow \bigvee_t [M_{jrt}(u) \wedge N_{jrt}(b)].$$

So $H_{ij}(a, b)$ is equivalent to the disjunction (over r and t) of

$$N_{jrt}(b) \wedge \bigvee u[a < u < b \wedge q_i(u) = 0 \wedge K_r(u) \wedge M_{jrt}(u)],$$

to which the induction hypothesis evidently applies. This concludes the reduction of formulas of form II and degree h.

By Lemma 5 we need only consider formulas A of the form $p=0 \wedge q_1>0 \wedge \cdots \wedge q_{l'}>0$ where the degree of p in x is h, and the degree of each $q_j (1 \leqslant j \leqslant l')$ is less than h. We shall reduce this case to formulas of degree $<h$, and to formulas of form II of degree h; the latter have just been dealt with.

A is evidently equivalent to $A_1 \vee A_2 \vee A_3$ where

$$A_1 \text{ is } p = 0 \wedge p' = 0 \wedge q_1 > 0 \wedge \cdots \wedge q_{l'} > 0,$$
$$A_2 \text{ is } p = 0 \wedge p' > 0 \wedge q_1 > 0 \wedge \cdots \wedge q_{l'} > 0,$$
$$A_3 \text{ is } p = 0 \wedge -p' > 0 \wedge q_1 > 0 \wedge \cdots \wedge q_{l'} > 0,$$

and p' denotes the derivative of p with respect to x.

A_1 represents the case where p has a multiple zero. Since the degree of p' in x is $<h$, by Lemma 5, A_1 is equivalent to a formula of degree $<h$ and the induction hypothesis applies.

$\bigvee x(a<x<b \wedge A_2)$ is true in a real closed field if and only if there is some open interval (α, β) contained in (a, b) in which all the $q_j (1 \leqslant j \leqslant l')$

and p' are strictly positive, and $p(\alpha)<0, p(\beta)>0$. Put $l=l'+1$ and $q_l=p'$. Using again the notation

$$G_0(a, b) = \bigwedge x\,[a < x < b \rightarrow (q_1 > 0 \wedge \cdots \wedge q_l > 0)],$$

we have: $\bigvee x(a<x<b \wedge A_2)$ is equivalent to the disjunction of the formulas

$$p(a) < 0 \wedge p(b) > 0 \wedge G_0(a, b),$$

$$p(a) < 0 \wedge \bigvee u\,[a < u < b \wedge q_i(u) = 0 \wedge p(u) > 0 \wedge G_0(a, u)] \vee$$
$$\vee\, p(b) > 0 \wedge \bigvee v\,[a < v < b \wedge q_i(v) = 0 \wedge - p(v) > 0 \wedge G_0^{-}(v,b)]$$
$$(1 \leqslant i \leqslant l),$$

$$\bigvee u \bigvee v\,[a < u < v < b \wedge q_i(u) = 0 \wedge q_j(v) = 0 \wedge$$
$$- p(u) > 0 \wedge p(v) > 0 \wedge G_0(u, v)] \quad (1 \leqslant i \leqslant l, 1 \leqslant j \leqslant l).$$

G_0 has already been treated. All the other formulas are patently of degree $<h$ because all the q are of degree $<h$.

A_3 is treated by interchanging p' and $-p'$, $p<0$ and $p>0$.

This completes the proof of Theorem 6.

THEOREM 7: *$\mathscr{A}$ allows the elimination of quantifiers in $\mathscr{L}$.*

PROOF: It is sufficient to prove the Theorem for a formula of the form $\bigvee x A(x, x_1, \ldots, x_n)$. We add to $\mathscr{L}$ the two constants u and $1/u$ and to $\mathscr{A}$ the axiom $u \cdot 1/u = 1$. By Theorem 6, the formula

$$\bigvee x\left(-1 < x < 1 \wedge A\left(x \cdot \frac{1}{u}, x_1, \ldots, x_n\right)\right)$$

is equivalent to a quantifier free formula Q. Each atomic formula of Q is of the form $p(x \cdot 1/u)=0$ or $p(x \cdot 1/u)>0$, and so, by the axiom $u \cdot 1/u=1$, of the form $p(x, u)=0$ or $p(x, u)>0$. Hence there is a quantifier free formula $R(z)$, where z is a variable of $\mathscr{L}$, such that $u \cdot 1/u = 1 \rightarrow \bigvee x(-1<x<1 \wedge A(x \cdot 1/u, x_1, \ldots, x_n))$ is equivalent to $R(u)$. Clearly in all models of $\mathscr{A}$ the two formulas $\bigvee x A(x, x_1, \ldots, x_n)$ and $\bigvee z(0<z<1 \wedge R(z))$ are equivalent. But, by Theorem 6, this last formula is equivalent to a quantifier free formula.

This completes the proof of Theorem 7.

In particular, we can deduce that *$\mathscr{A}$ is complete*, since the atomic formulas of $\mathscr{L}$ without variables are of the form $n=0$ and $n>0$, where $n \in \mathbf{Z}$. The first of these is equivalent to $\perp$ unless $n=0$, since all real closed fields are of characteristic zero, and the second to $\top$ or $\perp$.

VI. Separable Boolean rings

The language $\mathscr{L}$ that we consider has two constant symbols 0,1, two binary function symbols $+$, $\times$ and the binary relation symbol $=$. (As usual we write t_1+t_2 for $+t_1t_2$ and t_1t_2 for $\times t_1t_2$.)

Let $\mathscr{A}$ be the set of the following formulas

(*a*) Axioms for a commutative group with respect to $+$:

$$\bigwedge x \bigwedge y \bigwedge z(x+(y+z)=(x+y)+z)$$

$$\bigwedge x \bigwedge y(x+y=y+z)$$

$$\bigwedge x(x+0=x)$$

$$\bigwedge x \bigvee y(x+y=0).$$

(*b*)

$$\bigwedge x \bigwedge y \bigwedge z(x(yz)=(xy)z)$$

$$\bigwedge x(x\cdot 1=1\cdot x=x)$$

$$\bigwedge x \bigwedge y \bigwedge z(x(y+z)=xy+xz)$$

$$1\neq 0.$$

(*c*)

$$\bigwedge x(x^2=x).$$

(*a*) and (*b*) together make up the axioms for a ring with identity, (*a*), (*b*) and (*c*) those for a Boolean ring.

All Boolean rings are commutative and satisfy $\bigwedge x(2x=0)$; this follows because $(x+1)^2=x+1=x^2+2x+1$ and so $2x=0$, and also $(x+y)^2=x+y$, whence $xy+yx=0$ and so $xy=yx$.

If x, y are terms of $\mathscr{L}$ we will write $x\cup y$ for the term $x+y+xy$ and $x\subset y$ for the formula $xy=x$. Clearly the terms of $\mathscr{L}$ are polynomials $p(x_1, \ldots, x_n)$ which are of degree one in each of the variables $x_1, \ldots, x_n$ and in which all the coefficients are 0 or 1.

Let $F(x)$ be the formula $x\neq 0 \wedge \bigwedge y(y\subset x\rightarrow y=0 \vee y=x)$. The elements which satisfy this formula are called *atoms*.

We add to $\mathscr{L}$ an infinite sequence of unary relational symbols B, A_1, $A_2, \ldots, A_n, \ldots$, and to $\mathscr{A}$ the following set of formulas (in the notation of Chapter 2, p. 25):

(*d*) for each positive integer n the formula

$$\bigwedge x(A_nx\leftrightarrow \bigvee x_1 \ldots \bigvee x_n(\bigwedge_{1\leqslant i<j\leqslant n} x_i\neq x_j \wedge \bigwedge_{1\leqslant i\leqslant n}(F(x_i)\wedge x_i\subset x))),$$

$$\bigwedge x(Bx\leftrightarrow \bigwedge y(y\subset x\rightarrow A_1y)]).$$

It is clear that given any model of (*a*, *b*, *c*) we can define the values of $B, A_1, \ldots, A_n, \ldots$, in a unique way so as to satisfy the formulas of (*d*).

The elements which satisfy $A_n x$ are those which contain n distinct atoms. B is satisfied by those, possibly empty, elements all of whose subsets contain an atom and are called *atomic*.

We shall write $\mathscr{A}'$ for the set of formulas (a, b, c, d), and $\mathscr{A}' \vdash A$ for: A is a consequence of $\mathscr{A}'$, where A is a formula in the language $\mathscr{L}'$ of $\mathscr{A}'$.

We shall show that $\mathscr{A}'$ *together with the axiom*

$$\bigwedge x \bigvee y [y \subset x \wedge By \wedge \neg A_1(x+y)],$$

i.e., every element x is *separable* into disjoint parts such that one of them is atomic and the other contains no atoms, *allows elimination of quantifiers in its language* $\mathscr{L}'$. (The axiom follows from its particular case $\bigvee y\,[By \wedge \neg A_1(1+y)]$ in $\mathscr{A}$.)

Remarks. For an application, see Exercise 7. By extending the language further one obtains an elimination for arbitrary boolean rings, but the known methods are too long to be included here.

Note that for each term t of $\mathscr{L}'$ which contains x there are terms a and b not containing x such that $\mathscr{A}' \vdash t = ax+b$, and all atomic formulas are (equivalent in each model of $\mathscr{A}'$ to) $ax+b=0$, $B(ax+b)$, $A_n(ax+b)$ $(n \geqslant 1)$ for some terms a and b not containing x.

We collect simple distributive laws and simple properties of disjoint elements that are consequences of $\mathscr{A}'$.

LEMMA 8: (i) $(a_1 x=0 \wedge \cdots \wedge a_k x=0) \leftrightarrow (a_1 \cup \cdots \cup a_k)\cdot x=0$, (ii) $\neg A_1(x \cup y) \leftrightarrow (\neg A_1 x \wedge \neg A_1 y)$, (iii) $B(x \cup y) \leftrightarrow (Bx \wedge By)$.

PROOF: (i) follows by induction with respect to k. Evidently $(ax=0 \wedge bx=0) \to (a \cup b)x=0$. Suppose $(a \cup b)x$, i.e. $(a+b+ab)x, =0$; then

$$a(a+b+ab)x = (a^2+ab+a^2b)x = (a+ab)x = ax = 0,$$

and hence $(ax=0 \wedge bx=0) \leftrightarrow (a \cup b)x=0$. (ii) As in (i), one uses elementary properties of set theoretic union and intersection which hold formally for $\cup$, resp. for $\cdot$: $z \subset x \to z \subset x \cup y$, and $(zx) \cup (zy) = z(x \cup y)$, from which (ii) and (iii) follow.

LEMMA 9: (i) $x\cdot(1+x)=0$, (ii) $xy=0 \to x+y = x \cup y$ and, in particular, $x \cup (1+x) = 1$ (x is the complement of $1+x$), (iii) $xy=0 \to [x+y=0 \leftrightarrow (x=0 \wedge y=0)]$, (iv) *if* $G_i(x)$ *are formulas of* $\mathscr{L}'$ *then*

$$\bigwedge\!\!\!\bigwedge_{1 \leqslant i < j \leqslant n} (x_i x_j = 0) \to [\bigwedge\!\!\!\bigwedge_{1 \leqslant i \leqslant n} \bigvee u G_i(x_i u) \leftrightarrow \bigvee u \bigwedge\!\!\!\bigwedge_{1 \leqslant i \leqslant n} G_i(x_i u)].$$

PROOF: (i)-(iii) follow by computation.

$$\text{(iv)}\quad [\vee u \bigwedge_{1\leqslant i\leqslant n} G_i(x_i u)] \to \bigwedge_{1\leqslant i\leqslant n} \vee u G_i(x_i u)$$

is a theorem of predicate calculus. Put $w=\sum_i u_i x_i$; then

$$\bigwedge_{1\leqslant i<j\leqslant n} (x_i x_j = 0) \to u_i w = u_i x_i,$$

since $u_i u_j x_i=0$ for $j\neq i$, and $u_i^2 x_i = u_i x_i$. So

$$[\bigwedge_{1\leqslant i<j\leqslant n} G_i(x_i u_i)] \to G_j(u_j w)$$

for $1\leqslant j\leqslant n$, and hence (iv).

The first elimination result will concern *atoms*.

LEMMA 10: *Suppose neither a nor b contains x.* (i)-(v) *are consequences of* $\mathscr{A}'$ *and Fx where*

(i) $(ax+b=b \wedge ax=0) \vee (ax+b=b+x \wedge (1+a)x=0)$,

(ii) $(b+x=b\cup x \wedge bx=0) \vee (x\cup(b+x)=b \wedge (1+b)x=0)$,

(iii) $ax+b=0 \leftrightarrow [(ax=0 \wedge b=0) \vee ((1+a)x=0 \wedge x=b)]$,

$ax+b\neq 0 \leftrightarrow [(ax=0 \wedge b\neq 0) \vee ((1+a)x=0 \wedge x\neq b)]$,

(iv) $B(b+x) \leftrightarrow Bb$,

(v) for $n\geqslant 1$, $A_n(b+x) \leftrightarrow [(bx=0 \wedge A_{n-1}b) \vee$

$\vee ((1+b)x=0 \wedge A_{n+1}b)]$, where $A_0 b = \top$ by definition.

PROOF: (i) Since x is an atom, $ax=0 \vee ax=x$; $ax=x \leftrightarrow (1+a)x=0$. (ii) Again, x being an atom, $bx=0 \vee bx=x$; $bx=0 \to b+x=b\cup x$ by Lemma 9(ii); $bx=x \to x(b+x)=0$ and so, by Lemma 9 (ii), $x+(b+x)= x\cup(b+x),= b$ since $2x=0$. (iii) is clear. (iv) Note that $Fx\to Bx$; by (ii) and Lemma 8(iii), if $bx=0$, $B(b+x) \leftrightarrow (Bb \wedge Bx)$, hence $B(b+x)\leftrightarrow Bb$; similarly, if $x(b+x)=0$, $[Bx \wedge B(b+x)] \leftrightarrow Bb$, and so again $B(b+x)\leftrightarrow Bb$. (v) Note that $Fx \to A_1 x$ and $Fx \to x\neq 0$; if $bx=0$, $x\subset b+x$, and so if $A_{n-1}b$, $A_n(b+x)$; if $A_n(b+x)$, b contains at least $(n-1)$ atoms, x being one, and $\neg x\subset b$. Similarly, if $x\subset b$, $A_n(b+x) \leftrightarrow A_{n+1}b$.

COROLLARY 11: *If Fx then every formula* $(\neg)(ax+b=0)$ (i.e. every formula of the form $ax+b=0$ or $\neg(ax+b=0)$), $A_n(ax+b)$, $B(ax+b)$, *where a and b do not contain x, is equivalent to a disjunction of conjunctions of formulas not containing x and of equations of the form* $ax=0$, $x=b$, $x\neq c$.

THEOREM 12: *Let $G(x)$ be a quantifier free formula* of $\mathscr{L}'$. *Then* $\bigvee x[F(x)\wedge G(x)]$ *is equivalent to a quantifier free formula.*

PROOF: By Cor. 11, it is sufficient to consider $G(x): a_1x=0\wedge\cdots\wedge a_kx=0\wedge x=b_1\cdots\wedge x=b_l\wedge x\neq c_1\wedge\cdots\wedge x\neq c_m$.

If $x=b_i$ appears, $\bigvee x[G(x)\wedge F(x)]\leftrightarrow G(b_i)\wedge F(b_i)$; applying Lemma 8 (i) it is sufficient to consider

$$\bigvee x[F(x)\wedge ax=0\wedge x\neq c_1\wedge\cdots\wedge x\neq c_m].$$

By induction on m:

$$\bigvee x[F(x)\wedge ax=0\wedge \bigwedge_{1\leqslant i\leqslant m} x\neq c_i]$$

is equivalent to the disjunction of the following formulas:

(i) $\bigvee x(\neg[F(c_i)\wedge ac_i=0]\wedge F(x)\wedge ax=0\wedge \bigwedge_{j\neq i} x\neq c_j)\quad(1\leqslant j\leqslant m)$

(ii) $F(c_i)\wedge ac_i=0\wedge F(c_j)\wedge ac_j=0\wedge$
$c_i=c_j\wedge\bigvee x[F(x)=0\wedge ax=0\wedge\bigwedge_{j\neq i} x\neq c_j]\,(1\leqslant i<j\leqslant m)$

(iii) $\bigwedge_{1\leqslant i\leqslant n}[F(c_i)\wedge ac_i=0\wedge\bigwedge_{j\neq i} c_j\neq c_i]\wedge\bigvee x[F(x)\wedge$
$ax=0\wedge\bigwedge_{1\leqslant i\leqslant m} x\neq c_i]$.

We can apply the induction hypothesis to (i) and (ii), and (iii) is equivalent to

$$A_{m+1}(1+a)\wedge\bigwedge_{1\leqslant i\leqslant m}[F(c_i)\wedge ac_i=0\wedge\bigwedge_{j\neq i} c_j\neq c_i].$$

The Theorem just proved establishes elimination of quantifiers for formulas in which all quantifiers range over atoms. To treat the general case one uses the following construction of *disjoint cases*.

LEMMA 13: *Let $a_1,\ldots,a_n$ be terms of $\mathscr{L}'$ (and hence of $\mathscr{L}$) not containing x. Then there are terms $t_1,\ldots,t_N$, also not containing x, and subsets $I_1,\ldots,I_n$ of $\{1,\ldots,N\}$ such that*

$$\mathscr{A}\vdash t_it_j=0(1\leqslant i<j\leqslant N),\ \mathscr{A}\vdash a_r=\sum_{i\in I_r} t_i(r=1,\ldots,n).$$

PROOF by induction on n: If $u_1,\ldots,u_k$ satisfy the conditions of the lemma (on the t) for $a_2,\ldots,a_n$ then $a_1u_1,\ldots,a_1u_k,(1+a_1)u_1,\ldots,(1+a_1)u_k,$ $a_1(1+u_1+\ldots+u_k)$ satisfy the lemma.

COROLLARY 14: *Let $G(x)$ be a conjunction of formulas $H_r(a_r x+b_r)$ $(1 \leqslant r \leqslant n)$ where $H_r(z)$ is $\neg A_1(z)$ or $(\neg)$ $(z=0)$ or $(\neg) B(z)$. Then $G(x)$ is equivalent to a disjunction of conjunctions of formulas $H'(c_i x)$, $H'(c_i x+c_i)$, $H'(d_i)$ of the same type where c_i and d_i do not contain x, and such that, for distinct terms c_i, c_j, $\mathscr{A} \vdash c_i c_j=0$.*

PROOF: Note first that by Lemma 8 (ii) and (iii) and by Lemma 9 (ii), either $\mathscr{A}' \vdash xy=0 \rightarrow [H(x+y) \leftrightarrow (Hx \wedge Hy)]$ or $\mathscr{A}' \vdash xy=0 \rightarrow [H(x+y) \leftrightarrow (Hx \vee Hy)]$. By the lemma, if $t_1, \ldots, t_N$ correspond to $a_1, \ldots, a_n$, $b_1, \ldots, b_n$

$$a_r x + b_r = (x \cdot \sum_{i \in I_r} t_i) + \sum_{i \in J_r} t_i$$

for suitable subsets I_r, J_r of $\{1, 2, \ldots, N\}$. Hence

$$a_r x + b_r = (x+1) \sum_{i \in I_r \cap J_r} t_i + (x \cdot \sum_{i \in I_r - J_r} t_i) + \sum_{i \in J_r - I_r} t_i,$$

where, clearly, $I_r \cap J_r$, $I_r - J_r$, $J_r - I_r$ are pairwise disjoint.

So $H_r(a_r x+b_r)$ is either equivalent to

$$\bigwedge_{i \in I_r \cap J_r} H_r(t_i x + t_i) \wedge \bigwedge_{i \in I_r - J_r} H_r(t_i x) \wedge \bigwedge_{i \in J_r - I_r} H_r(t_i)$$

or to the formula obtained by replacing the conjunctions by disjunctions:

$$\bigvee_{i \in I_r \cap J_r} H_r(t_i x + t_i) \vee \bigvee_{i \in I_r - J_r} H_r(t_i x) \vee \bigvee_{i \in J_r - I_r} H_r(t_i).$$

Substituting these formulas for each $H_r(a_r x+b_r)$ in $G(x)$, and using distributivity of $\wedge$ over $\vee$, we obtain the desired result.

LEMMA 15: *$\bigvee x[H_1(a_1 x+b) \wedge \ldots \wedge H_n(a_n x+b_n)]$ is equivalent to a quantifier free formula (for H_i, $1 \leqslant i \leqslant n$, of the type considered in Corollary 14).*

PROOF: By Corollary 14 it is sufficient to consider the formulas

$$\bigvee x [K_1(a_1 x) \wedge \cdots \wedge K_m(a_m x)]$$

where each $K(z)$ is a conjunction of $\neg A_1 z$, $\neg A_1(1+z)$, $(\neg)(z=0)$, $(\neg)$ $(z=1)$, $(\neg)$ $B(z)$, $(\neg)$ $B(1+z)$, and for $i \neq j$, $\mathscr{A} \vdash a_i a_j=0$.

By Lemma 9 (iv) it is then sufficient to consider $\bigvee x K(ax)$.

We may suppose that neither $ax=0$ nor $ax+a=0$ is a component of the conjunction $K(ax)$, since if $ax=0$ or $ax+a=0$ is then $\bigvee x K(ax) \leftrightarrow K(0)$, respectively $\bigvee x K(ax) \leftrightarrow K(a)$ is a theorem. We may suppose that $ax \neq 0$ appears in $K(ax)$, since $K(ax) \leftrightarrow ([ax=0 \wedge K(ax)] \vee [ax \neq 0 \wedge K(ax))$; similarly $ax+a \neq 0$.

Note that $x \neq 0 \to (Bx \to A_1 x)$ and hence $x \neq 0 \to (\neg A_1 x \to \neg Bx)$. So $K(ax)$ is equivalent to a conjunction of $ax \neq 0 \wedge ax + a \neq 0$, and one of the following formulas: $\perp$ or

a) $\neg A_1(ax) \wedge \neg A_1(ax+a)$ (since if e.g. $B(ax)$ occurs the conjunction is contradictory, and $\neg B(ax)$ is redundant by above),

b) (i)$\neg A_1(ax) \wedge B(ax+a)$ or (ii)$\neg A_1(ax) \wedge \neg B(ax+a)$ and similarly with 'ax' and '$ax+a$' interchanged,

c) (i) $B(ax) \wedge B(ax+a)$, (ii) $B(ax) \wedge \neg B(ax+a)$ or $\neg B(ax) \wedge B(ax+a)$, (iii) $\neg B(ax) \wedge \neg B(ax+a)$.

In case (a) $\bigvee x K(ax) \leftrightarrow (a \neq 0 \wedge \neg A_1 a)$;$\to$ is evident. $\neg A_1 a \to \neg Fa$ and $(a \neq 0 \wedge \neg Fa) \to \bigvee x(x \neq 0 \wedge x \subset a \wedge x \neq a)$; so $\bigvee x(ax \neq 0 \wedge ax + a \neq 0)$, apply Lemma 8 (ii).

In case (b) (i) $\bigvee x K(ax) \leftrightarrow (A_1 a \wedge \neg Ba)$. By *separability*, if $A_1 a \wedge \neg Ba$ we have $b \subset a \wedge \neg A_1 b$, with $B(a+b)$; since $A_1 a$, $b \neq a$; since $\neg Ba$, $b \neq 0$. For (b) (ii), $\bigvee x K(ax) \leftrightarrow (\neg Ba \wedge a \neq 0)$. If $\neg Ba$, by *separability*, we have $b \neq 0$, $b \subset a$, $\neg A_1 b \wedge B(a+b)$ where $a+b$ is possibly$=0$. Since $\neg A_1 b \to Fb$, there is $c \neq 0$, $c \neq b$, $c \subset b$, and $\neg A_1 c$, $\neg A_1(c+b)$. Take $ax = c$, $ax + a = c + a$.

In case (c) (i) $\bigvee x K\ (ax) \leftrightarrow (Ba \wedge A_2 a)$. If $A_2 a$, there are at least two atoms one of which $=b$(with $b \subset a$), the other contained in $a+b$. By Lemma 8 (iii) and disjointness of b and $a+b$, $Bb \wedge B(a+b)$. (ii) $\bigvee x K(ax) \leftrightarrow (\neg Ba \wedge A_1 a)$. Since $A_1 a$, there is $b \subset a \wedge Fb$. Since $Fb \to Bb$, for $ax = a+b$, $B(ax+a)$, and since $\neg Ba$, $\neg B(ax)$. (iii) $\bigvee x K(ax) \leftrightarrow (\neg Ba \wedge a \neq 0)$. By *separability*, if $\neg Ba$, there is $b \subset a$, $\neg A_1 b \wedge B(a+b)$ with $b \neq 0$ (but possibly$=a$). Again, since $\neg A_1 b \to \neg Fb$, and $b \neq 0$ there is $c \subset b \wedge c \neq 0$, with $\neg A_1 c \wedge \neg A_1(b+c)$. Then $\neg Bc \wedge \neg B(a+c)$.

This takes care of all cases.

THEOREM 16: *Let $G(x)$ be a quantifier free formula of $\mathscr{L}'$. Then $\bigvee x G(x)$ is equivalent to a quantifier free formula of $\mathscr{L}'$ (in all separable Boolean rings).*

PROOF: By Theorem 1 it is sufficient to consider conjunctions $G(x)$ of atomic formulas and negations of such formulas. Writing

$E_n(x)$ (read: x contains *exactly n* atoms) for $A_n(x) \wedge \neg A_{n+1}(x)$ $(n \geqslant 1)$, $E_0(x)$ for $\neg A_1(x)$ we have

(i) $\neg A_n(x) \leftrightarrow [\neg A_1(x) \vee E_1(x) \vee \cdots \vee E_{n-1}(x)]$ $(n \geqslant 1)$.

Also, if y is a variable not occurring in $A_n(x)$, resp. $E_n(x)$, using the definition: $A_0(x) = \top$ in Lemma 10(v), we have

$$\text{(ii)} \quad A_n(x) \leftrightarrow \bigvee y[Fy \wedge y \subset x \wedge A_{n-1}(x+y)] \qquad (n \geqslant 1)$$
$$\text{(iii)} \quad E_n(x) \leftrightarrow \bigvee y[Fy \wedge y \subset x \wedge E_{n-1}(x+y)] \qquad (n \geqslant 1).$$

By (i) it is sufficient to consider $G(x)$ of the form $G'(x) \wedge G_1(x)$ where $G'(x)$ is of the type listed in Cor. 14 and $G_1(x)$ is a conjunction of *unnegated* atomic formulas $A_n(ax+b)$, $E_n(ax+b)$.

The *degree* of $G(x)$ in x is, by definition, the ordered pair (0, 0) if $G_1(x)$ is empty, and (h, k) if $h \geqslant 1$ is the length (i.e., number of conjuncts) of $G_1(x)$ and $G_1(x)$ is $C_k(ax+b) \wedge G_2(x)$ where $C_k(ax+b)$ is either $A_k(ax+b)$ or $E_k(ax+b)$ (the first conjunct in $G_1(x)$). For $k \geqslant 1$, the degree of $G_2(x)$ is $<(h, k)$ in the lexicographic ordering of pairs of integers.

Since this is a well-ordering we can use induction on the degree of $G(x)$.

If the degree is (0, 0) the Theorem reduces to Lemma 15.

If the degree is (h, k), $h \geqslant 1$, and y does not occur in $G(x)$, by (ii),

$$\bigvee xG(x) \leftrightarrow \bigvee x(G'(x) \wedge \bigvee y[Fy \wedge y \subset ax+b \wedge C_{k-1}(ax+b+y)] \wedge G_2(x))$$

and so,

$$\bigvee xG(x) \leftrightarrow \bigvee y[Fy \wedge \bigvee xH(x, y)]$$

where $H(x, y)$ is $G'(x) \wedge ayx+by+y=0 \wedge C_{k-1}(ax+y+b) \wedge G_2(x)$, since $y \subset ax+b \leftrightarrow ayx+(by+y)=0$.

The degree (in x) of H is less than (h, k). Since $ayx+by+y=0$ is of the type considered in Cor. 14, the degree of H is that of $C_{k-1}(ax+y+b) \wedge G_2(x)$. We have two cases. If $k>1$, the degree of H is $(h, k-1)$, and so $<(h, k)$; if $k=1$, the degree of H is that of G_2, and also $<(h, k)$. This proves the Theorem.

Exercises

1. Show that in Section II the use of the symbol s was necessary to ensure that we could eliminate quantifiers. To be more precise, we consider the language $\mathscr{L}$ which has the single binary relation symbol $<$ other than $=$ and we let $\mathscr{A}$ be the following set of formulas of $\mathscr{L}$

a) the axioms for a total ordering

b)

$$\bigwedge x \bigvee y \bigwedge z(x < z \leftrightarrow y = z \vee y < z)$$
$$\bigwedge x \bigvee y \bigwedge z(z < x \leftrightarrow y = z \vee z < y).$$

The models of $\mathscr{A}$ are the same as those of Section II, namely discretely ordered sets without first or last element, but $\mathscr{A}$ does not allow the elimination of quantifiers in $\mathscr{L}$.

Answer. We consider the model of $\mathscr{A}$ which is the ordered set $\mathbf{Z}$ of integers. If $D_{\mathbf{Z}}$ is the diagram of this model and if $\mathscr{A}$ allows the elimination of quantifiers the set $\mathscr{A} \cup D_{\mathbf{Z}}$ is complete. However if we add the number $\frac{1}{2}$ to this model we still have a model of $\mathscr{A} \cup D_{\mathbf{Z}}$, but the formula $\bigvee x(0<x<1)$ is not satisfied in the first model and is satisfied in the second. This shows that $\mathscr{A} \cup D_{\mathbf{Z}}$ is not complete and so $\mathscr{A}$ does not allow the elimination of quantifiers.

2. Let $\mathscr{L}$, $\mathscr{L}'$ be the languages of Section III. Let (*a*), (*b*), (*c*), (*d*) be the sets of axioms given in that section.

i) Show that the set (*a*, *b*, *c*) does not allow the elimination of quantifiers in $\mathscr{L}$.

ii) Show that the set (*a*, *b*, *c*, *d*) does not allow the elimination of quantifiers in $\mathscr{L}'$.

Answer. We consider the group $G=\mathbf{Z}\times\mathbf{Z}$ ordered as follows: $(a, b)>0$ if and only if either $a>0$ or $a=0$ and $b>0$. G is a model of (*a*, *b*, *c*) which contains $\mathscr{E}$ as a sub-model (identifying $(0, n)$ with n). Let $D_{\mathbf{Z}}$ be the diagram of $\mathbf{Z}$. Then $(a, b, c, d, D_{\mathbf{Z}})$ is not complete since the formula $\bigwedge x \bigvee y(x=2y \vee x+1=2y)$ is true in $\mathbf{Z}$ but not in G.

3. a) Let $\mathscr{A}$ be a countable set of formulas in a language with equality. Show that if $\mathscr{A}$ has an infinite normal model then for each infinite cardinal $\aleph$, $\mathscr{A}$ has a model of cardinal $\aleph$.

b) Prove that if $\mathscr{A}$ has only infinite models and for some infinite cardinal $\aleph$ all the models of $\mathscr{A}$ of cardinal $\aleph$ are isomorphic, that is if $\mathscr{A}$ is categorical for the class of realizations of cardinal $\aleph$, then $\mathscr{A}$ is complete.

c) Show that all countable models of the axioms of Section I, that is all countable densely ordered sets with first and last element, are isomorphic to the segment $[0, 1]$ of the set of dyadic numbers (rationals whose denominator is a power of 2). Deduce that these axioms are complete.

d) For this question we use the properties of transcendental bases of extensions of a field K (see BOURBAKI, Algèbre, Ch. 5).

Show that if Ω is an algebraically closed field and K and K' are algebraically closed extensions of Ω with transcendental bases of the same cardinal then K and K' are isomorphic.

Deduce that two algebraically closed fields of the same characteristic and of cardinal $2^{\aleph_0}$ are isomorphic and hence that the axioms for an algebraically closed field of characteristic p, where p is zero or a prime, are complete.

Answer.

a) We add to $\mathscr{L}$ a set C of constant symbols of cardinal $\aleph$. Let $\mathscr{B}$ be the set of all the formulas $a \neq b$ for distinct elements a, b of C. Every finite subset of $\mathscr{A} \cup \mathscr{B}$ has a model, namely the given infinite model of $\mathscr{A}$, and hence $\mathscr{A} \cup \mathscr{B}$ has a model. Let $\widehat{\mathscr{A}} = \{\hat{A} : A \in \mathscr{A}\}$, then $\widehat{\mathscr{A}} \cup \mathscr{B}$ has a canonical model which is clearly of cardinal $\aleph$.

b) Let F be a closed formula of $\mathscr{L}$ which is not a consequence of $\mathscr{A}$. Hence $\mathscr{A} \cup \{\neg F\}$ has a model and consequently a model of cardinal $\aleph$ since $\mathscr{A}$ has only infinite models. Since all models of $\mathscr{A}$ of cardinal $\aleph$ are isomorphic $\neg F$ is satisfied in all models of $\mathscr{A}$ of cardinal $\aleph$. Therefore $\neg F$ is a consequence of $\mathscr{A}$ since if $\mathscr{A} \cup \{F\}$ has any model it has a model of cardinal $\aleph$. It follows that $\mathscr{A}$ is complete.

c) Clearly every densely ordered set is infinite. Let $\{0, a_1, \ldots, a_n, \ldots\} \cup \{1\}$ be a countable densely ordered set whose first element is 0 and whose last element is 1.

We define an order preserving map ϕ of $\{0, a_1, \ldots, a_n, \ldots\} \cup \{1\}$ into the segment $[0, 1]$ of the dyadic numbers as follows.

Let $\phi(0)=0$, $\phi(1)=1$. Now suppose that $\phi(a_r)$ has been defined for $r \leqslant n$. Let b, c be the elements of $X_n = \{0, a_1, \ldots, a_n, 1\}$ such that a_{n+1} is immediately between b and c, i.e. such that $b < a_{n+1} < c$ and there is no element of X_n between b and c. Then we let $\phi(a_{n+1}) = \frac{1}{2}[\phi(b) + \phi(c)]$.

We show that each dyadic number in $[0, 1]$ is in the image of ϕ. For suppose not; let $(2q+1)/2^n$ be the first dyadic number in $[0, 1]$, with respect to the ordering given by $(2q+1)/2^n < (2q'+1)/2^{n'}$ if $n < n'$ or $n = n'$ and $q < q'$, which is not in the image of ϕ. Then $q/2^{n-1}$ and $(q+1)/2^{n-1}$ are in the image and are equal to $\phi(a_i)$ and $\phi(a_j)$ for some i, j. Let a_k be the first a which lies between a_i and a_j, then $\phi(a_k) = (2q+1)/2^n$. Therefore ϕ is an isomorphism and the proof is completed.

d) Let $\{b_i : i \in I\}$ and $\{b'_i : i \in I\}$ be two transcendental bases of K and K' over Ω. K is therefore algebraic over $\Omega(b_i)_{i \in I}$ and is therefore the algebraic closure of $\Omega(b_i)_{i \in I}$. Similarly K' is the algebraic closure of $\Omega(b'_i)_{i \in I}$. But $\Omega(b_i)_{i \in I}$ and $\Omega(b'_i)_{i \in I}$ are both isomorphic to the field of rational fractions $\Omega(X_i)_{i \in I}$ and hence their algebraic closures are isomorphic.

Let Ω_p be the algebraic closure of the prime field of characteristic p, thus Ω_p is countable. If the cardinal $\bar{\bar{I}}$ of I is greater than or equal to $\aleph_0$, the cardinal of the field of rational fractions $\Omega(X_i)_{i\in I}$ is equal to $\bar{\bar{I}}$ and hence also to that of its algebraic closure. Hence if K is an algebraically closed field of characteristic p and of cardinal $2^{\aleph_0}$ the transcendental base of K over Ω_p is of cardinal $2^{\aleph_0}$. Two algebraically closed fields of characteristic p and of cardinal $2^{\aleph_0}$ have therefore transcendental bases over Ω_p of the same cardinal and are therefore isomorphic. Since the axioms for an algebraically closed field of characteristic p have no finite models we need only use the result of b) with $\aleph=2^{\aleph_0}$ to see that these axioms are complete.

4 (Hilbert's nullstellensatz). Let K be a field and L an algebraically closed extension of K. If $p_1, \ldots, p_k$ are polynomials in the n variables $x_1, \ldots, x_n$ with coefficients in K which have no common root in L, then there are polynomials $q_1, \ldots, q_k$ in the n variables $x_1, \ldots, x_n$ with coefficients in K such that

$$\sum_{i=1}^{k} q_i p_i = 1 .$$

Answer. Let $\mathscr{A}$ be the set of axioms for an algebraically closed field and let D_K be the diagram of K. Then $\mathscr{A} \cup D_K$ is complete and has L as a model. Therefore $p_1, \ldots, p_k$ have no common root in any algebraically closed extension of K. Since any extension of K can be embedded in an algebraically closed extension of K it follows that $p_1, \ldots, p_k$ have no common root in any extension of K.

Let I be the ideal of $K[x_1, \ldots, x_n]$ generated by $p_1 \ldots, p_k$. If this ideal is not $K(x_1, \ldots, x_n)$ itself it can be extended to a maximal ideal J. The quotient $K[x_1, \ldots, x_n]/J$ is an extension of K in which $p_1, \ldots, p_k$ have a common root, namely the image of $\{x_1, \ldots, x_n\}$ under the canonical map of $K[x_1, \ldots, x_n]$ into the quotient. But this is impossible, hence $I= K[x_1, \ldots, x_n]$ and so $1 \in I$. This completes the proof.

5. a) We recall that any ordered field can be embedded in a real closed field (see Van der Waerden).

Show that if a polynomial $p(x_1, \ldots, x_n)$ with coefficients in an ordered field K is $\geqslant 0$ for all values of $x_1, \ldots, x_n$ in some real closed extension of K then the polynomial is $\geqslant 0$ for all values of $x_1, \ldots, x_n$ in any ordered extension of K.

b) A field L is said to be *real* if, for any $x_1, \ldots, x_n$ in L, $x_1^2 + \cdots + x_n^2 + 1 \neq 0$. We recall that any real field can be embedded in a real closed field and so can be ordered.

Let $a \in L$. Show that if a is not the sum of squares, $L(\sqrt{-a})$ is real. Deduce that there is an ordering of L in which $a < 0$.

c) Consider a real field K in which for each $a \in K$ either a or $-a$ is the sum of squares. Show that if the polynomial $p(x_1 \ldots, x_n)$ with coefficients in K is $\geqslant 0$ for all values of $x_1, \ldots, x_n$ in some real closed extension of K, then there are rational fractions $r_1, \ldots, r_k$ with coefficients in K such that $p = r_1^2 + \cdots + r_k^2$.

d) Let $p(x_1, \ldots, x_n)$ be a polynomial with coefficients in the field of rationals $\mathbf{Q}$, which is positive or zero for all values of $x_1, \ldots, x_n$ in $\mathbf{Q}$. Then there are rational fractions $r_1, \ldots, r_k$ with coefficients in $\mathbf{Q}$ such that $p = r_1^2 + \cdots + r_k^2$.

Answer.

a) Let D_K be the diagram of K and $\mathscr{A}$ the set of axioms for a real closed field. Then $\mathscr{A} \cup D_K$ is complete. Since the formula $\bigwedge x_1 \ldots \bigwedge x_n\ (p(x_1, \ldots, x_n) \geqslant 0)$ is satisfied in one model of $\mathscr{A} \cup D_K$ it is satisfied in all real closed fields containing K and hence in all ordered fields containing K since these can be embedded in real closed fields.

b) Each element of $L(\sqrt{-a})$ is of the form $\alpha + \beta\sqrt{-a}$ with $\alpha, \beta \in L$. If $1 + \sum_i (\alpha_i + \beta_i \sqrt{-a})^2 = 0$ then

$$1 + \sum_i \alpha_i^2 - a \sum_i \beta_i^2 = 0$$

and hence

$$a = \frac{1 + \sum_i \alpha_i^2}{\sum_i \beta_i^2} = \frac{1 + \sum_i \alpha_i^2}{(\sum_i \beta_i^2)^2} \times \sum_i \beta_i^2$$

and so a is a sum of squares, which is a contradiction.

c) It is clear that K can be ordered in only one way, that is, so that $a \geqslant 0$ if a is the sum of squares and $a < 0$ otherwises. Hence in all ordered fields containing K, $p(x_1, \ldots, x_n) \geqslant 0$. The field $K(X_1, \ldots, X_n)$ of rational fractions in n variables over K is a real field. Hence $p(X_1, \ldots, X_n)$, that is the value of the polynomial $p(x_1, \ldots, x_n)$ for $x_1 = X_1, \ldots, x_n = X_n$, where the X_i are the base elements of the field $K(X_1, \ldots, X_n)$, is greater than or equal to zero for all orderings of the field $K(X_1, \ldots, X_n)$ and hence it is the sum of squares of elements of this field.

d) If $p(x_1, ..., x_n) \geqslant 0$ for $x_1, ..., x_n \in \mathbf{Q}$, then since p is a continuous function, $p(x_1, ..., x_n) \geqslant 0$ for $x_1, ..., x_n \in \mathbf{R}$. So it is sufficient to note that on the one hand $\mathbf{R}$ is real closed and that on the other each positive element of $\mathbf{Q}$ is the sum of squares of elements of $\mathbf{Q}$ to obtain this result (ARTIN'S THEOREM).

6. a) Let $\mathscr{L}$ be the language described in Section III and let $\mathscr{L}'$ be the language obtained from $\mathscr{L}$ by adding a binary function symbol $\times$.

Show that there is no formula of $\mathscr{L}$, with three free variables, whose value in the standard realization (on $\mathbf{Z}$) of $\mathscr{L}$ is the set

$$\{(m, n, p) \in \mathbf{Z}^3 : m = np\}.$$

b) Let $\mathscr{A}$ be the set of formulas of $\mathscr{L}'$ which are satisfied by the standard realization of $\mathscr{L}$ (where $\times$ is interpreted as multiplication), and let $\mathscr{A}_1$ be the set of formulas obtained by substituting for $\times$ in $\mathscr{A}$ another binary function symbol $\times_1$ which is not in $\mathscr{L}'$. Show that the set $\mathscr{A} \cup \mathscr{A}_1$ has a model in which the values of $\times$ and $\times_1$ are different.

Answer.

a) Let $F(x, y, z)$ be a formula with the required property. Since the standard realization satisfies the axioms of Section III there is a quantifier free formula $G(x)$ with a single free variable such that $G(x)$ and $\bigvee y F(x, y, y)$ have the same value in the standard realization, this common value being the set of squares.

But we will show that for any quantifier free formula $H(x)$ of L with a single free variable, there are two positive integers N and p such that for integers $n \geqslant N$, $n \in \bar{H}$ if and only if $n+p \in \bar{H}$, where $\bar{H}$ is the value of $H(x)$ in the standard realization. This is obvious if H is atomic since then H is of one of the forms $ax+b=0$, $ax+b>0$ or $n|ax+b$ with $a, b \in \mathbf{Z}$. Also if H and H' have this property so too do $\neg H$ and $H \vee H'$. So it is true of all quantifier free formulas H.

We therefore have a contradiction since there are no positive integers N, p such that for all $n \geqslant N$, n is a square if and only if $n+p$ is one.

b) Suppose that in all models of $\mathscr{A} \cup \mathscr{A}_1$ the values of $\times$ and $\times_1$ are the same. Then the formula $\bigwedge a \bigwedge b (a \times b = a \times_1 b)$ is a consequence of $\mathscr{A} \cup \mathscr{A}_1$. Hence, by the Definability Theorem, there is a formula $F(a,b,c)$ of $\mathscr{L}$ such that $F(a, b, c) \leftrightarrow a = b \times c$ is a consequence of $\mathscr{A}$. Since $\mathscr{A}$ is satisfied in the standard realization of $\mathscr{L}$ the value of F in this realization is $\{(m, n, p) \in \mathbf{Z}^3 : m = np\}$ which contradicts the previous result.

7. (a) Let $\mathscr{L}$ be the language of Boolean rings, and $\mathscr{L}_1$ the language of fields of sets, i.e., $\mathscr{L}_1$ contains two monadic relation symbols I and P('I' for: individual, 'P' for: part) and a binary relation symbol ε; we shall write $x\varepsilon y$ for εxy.

For any set X, $X \neq \emptyset$, let $E \subset \mathfrak{P}(X)$ where $\emptyset \in E$, $X \in E$; for $x \in X$, $\{x\} \in E$, and E is closed under symmetric difference ($\dot{-}$) and intersection ($\cap$). Thus, if $\mathfrak{M} = \langle E, \emptyset, X, \dot{-}, \cap \rangle$ and $\mathfrak{M}_1 = \langle X \cup E, X, E, \in \rangle$ ($\in$ being the membership relation restricted to $X \times E$) then $\mathfrak{M}$ is a realisation of $\mathscr{L}$, $\mathfrak{M}_1$ of $\mathscr{L}_1$.

(i) Show that $\mathfrak{M}$ is an atomic Boolean ring, i.e. each $x \in E$ satisfies $B(x)$ in $\mathfrak{M}$.

(ii) For each formula A of $\mathscr{L}$ find a formula A_1 of $\mathscr{L}_1$ with the same free variables $x_1, \ldots, x_n$ such that, for all X and E as in (i), $(\bar{x}_1, \ldots, \bar{x}_n)$ satisfies A in $\mathfrak{M}$ if and only if $(\bar{x}_1, \ldots, \bar{x}_n)$ satisfies A_1 in $\mathfrak{M}_1$ and conversely.

(iii) Write

$$I_n(x) \quad \text{for} \quad Px \wedge \bigvee x_1 \ldots \bigvee x_n [x_1 \varepsilon x \wedge \cdots \wedge x_n \varepsilon x \wedge \bigwedge\!\!\!\bigwedge_{1 \leqslant i < j \leqslant n} (x_i \neq x_j)],$$

$P_0(x)$ for $\bigwedge u \neg (u \varepsilon x)$, $P_1(x)$ for $\bigwedge u (u \varepsilon x)$,

$$I'_n(x) \quad \text{for} \quad \bigvee x_1 \ldots \bigvee x_n [x_1 \not\varepsilon x \wedge \cdots \wedge x_n \not\varepsilon x \wedge \bigwedge\!\!\!\bigwedge_{1 \leqslant i < j \leqslant n} x_i \neq x_j].$$

Deduce from (ii) that for each formula $A(x)$ of $\mathscr{L}_1$ with a single free variable x there is a propositional combination $A^*(x)$ of $I(x)$, $I_n(x)$ $(n \geqslant 1)$, $I'_n(x)$, $P_0(x)$ and $P_1(x)$ such that, for all x and E, $\bar{A} = \bar{A}^*$ in $\mathfrak{M}_1$.

(b) Let $\langle X_1, R_1 \rangle (R_1 \subset X_1^2)$ be an ordering of the type of the rationals $\geqslant 0$ (under the usual ordering), and $\langle X_2, R_2 \rangle (R_2 \subset X_2^2)$ an ordering of the type of the negative integers, with $X_1 \cap X_2 = \emptyset$. Let $\langle X, R \rangle = \langle X_1 \cup X_2, R_1 \cup R_2 \cup X_1 \times X_2 \rangle$, i.e., the order type of the rationals $\geqslant 0$ followed by the negative integers.

Let E be the collection of finite unions of disjoint half open intervals in $\langle X, R \rangle$ under the order topology, i.e. of sets $\{x : (a, x) \in R, (x, b) \in R, x \neq b, a \in X, b \in X\}$.

(i) Show that $\mathfrak{M}_2 = \langle E, \emptyset, X, \dot{-}, \cap \rangle$ is a Boolean ring such that $\bar{x} \in E$ is atomic if and only if it consists of intervals all of whose end points are in X_2; and contains no atoms if all its intervals $\subset X_1$.

(ii) Show that X itself is not separable in $\mathfrak{M}_2$, but for any proper partition $\bar{x} \cup \bar{y}$ of X (i.e., $\bar{x} \in E$, $\bar{y} \in E$, $\bar{x} \cap \bar{y} = \emptyset$, $\bar{x} \neq 0$, $\bar{y} \neq 0$, $\bar{x} \cup \bar{y} = X$) either $\bar{x}$ or $\bar{y}$ is separable.

(iii) Deduce that the set of axioms a), b), c) does not permit elimination of quantifiers for the language $\mathscr{L}'$; similarly for a), b), c) and d) and the language $\mathscr{L}''$ where $\mathscr{L}''$ is obtained from $\mathscr{L}'$ by adding the monadic predicate symbol S, and d) is: $\bigwedge x(Sx \leftrightarrow \bigvee y[y \subset x \wedge By \wedge \neg A_1(x+y)]$.

Answer.

a) (i) It is clear that $\mathfrak{M}$ is a Boolean ring. Every element $\{x\}$, for $x \in X$, is an atom, and every $y \in E$ contains such an $\{x\}$ because y is a subset of X. So $\mathfrak{M}$ is atomic.

(ii) We "define" in a natural way the operations of $\mathfrak{M}$ in the language $\mathscr{L}'$ and the relations of $\mathfrak{M}_1$ in $\mathscr{L}$. Formally suppose $A \in \mathscr{L}$, A in prenex form, the quantifier free part written as a disjunction of conjunctions of the form $a \subset b$ and negations of such formulas ($a = b \leftrightarrow a \subset b \wedge b \subset a$). Let u be a variable not appearing in A; for each term a of $\mathscr{L}$ we find A_a of $\mathscr{L}_1$ such that $(\bar{u}, \bar{x}_1, \ldots, \bar{x}_n)$ satisfies A_a in $\mathfrak{M}_1$ if and only if $\{\bar{u}\} \subset \bar{a}$, where $\bar{a}$ is the value of a in $\mathfrak{M}$; since each $\bar{x}_i \subset X (1 \leqslant i \leqslant n)$, $\bar{x}_i$ satisfies $\bar{P}$ in $\mathfrak{M}_1$; if a is the symbol 0 or 1, $A_a = \bot$, resp. $= \top$; if $a = b \cdot c$, $a = b + c$, $A_a = A_b \wedge A_c$ resp. $\neg(A_b \wedge A_c) \wedge (A_b \vee A_c)$; $(a \subset b)_1 = Px_1 \wedge \cdots \wedge Px_n \wedge \bigwedge u (A_a u \rightarrow A_b u)$, $(\neg(a \subset b))_1 = Px_1 \wedge \cdots \wedge Px_n \wedge \bigvee u (A_a u \wedge \neg A_b u)$; $(A \wedge B)_1$ and $(A \vee B)_1$ are $A_1 \wedge B_1$, resp. $A_1 \vee B_1$; $(\bigwedge x_i A)_1 = \bigwedge x_i (Px_i \rightarrow A_1)$, $(\bigvee x_i A)_1 = \bigvee x_i (Px_i \wedge A_1)$. The first half of (ii) follows by induction on the length of A.

For the converse, given a formula A of $\mathscr{L}_1$ containing the free variables $x_1, \ldots, x_n$, we have to find a formula A' of $\mathscr{L}$ such that $(\bar{x}_1, \ldots, \bar{x}_n)$ satisfies $\bar{A}$ in $\mathfrak{M}_1$ if and only if $(\bar{x}_1', \ldots, \bar{x}_n')$ satisfies A' in $\mathfrak{M}$ where $\bar{x}_i = \bar{x}_i$ if $\bar{x}_i \in E$, and $\bar{x}_i' = \{\bar{x}_i\}$ if $\bar{x}_i \in X$ (identification of individuals with their unit sets). We put $(Ix)' = Fx$, $(Px)' = \top$, $(x \varepsilon y)' = Fx \wedge x \subset y$, $(\neg A)' = \neg(A')$, $(A \wedge B)' = A' \wedge B'$, $(A \vee B)' = A' \vee B'$, $(\bigwedge xA)'$ and $(\bigvee xA)'$ are $\bigvee xA$, resp. $\bigvee xA'$. The proof is evident.

(iii) Given $A(x)$ (with a single free variable x) of $\mathscr{L}_1$, consider $A'(x)$ of $\mathscr{L}$ constructed in (ii). By Section VI, since $\mathfrak{M}$ is an atomic Boolean ring, $A'(x)$ is equivalent to a propositional combination of $A_n x$, $x = 0$, $x = 1$, $A_n(1+x)$; by (ii), $A(x)$ is equivalent in $\mathfrak{M}_1$ to $\top$, $\bot$, $\bigwedge u \neg (u \varepsilon x)$, $\bigwedge u (u \varepsilon x)$ or: x is an individual, or x, resp. the complement of x contains at least, resp. at most n individuals.

(b) (i) It is clear that $\mathfrak{M}_2$ is a Boolean ring. The only atoms are the intervals with a single element since if $[a, b) \in E$ and $[c, d) \subset [a, b)$ also $[c, d) \in E$; so $[a, b)$ is an atom if and only if $a \in X_2$ and b is the successor of a. Since finite unions of atoms are atomic, if $\bar{x} \in E$ and $\bar{x}$ is a finite union of intervals with endpoints in X_2, then $\bar{x}$ is atomic. On the other hand, if $a, b \in X_1$, $[a, b)$ contains no atom because all its non empty parts are unions of intervals $[c, d)$ with end points in X_1. (ii) X, i.e. $\bar{1}$, is not separable, because X_2 has no first element and so the set theoretic union of the atomic elements of $\mathfrak{M}_2$, namely X_2, has no greatest lower bound in $\mathfrak{M}_2$. But if $X = \bar{x} \cup \bar{y}$, $\bar{x} \neq \emptyset$, $\bar{y} \neq \emptyset$ either $\bar{x}$ or $\bar{y}$, say $\bar{x}$, contains an interval $[a, b]$ with $a \in X_1$, $b \in X_2$; then $\bar{y}$ consists of a finite set of (disjoint) intervals $[a, b)$ with $a \in X_1 \wedge b \in X_1$ or $a \in X_2 \wedge b \in X_2$; the former contain no atoms, the latter are atomic.

(iii) Suppose a), b), c), d) permitted the elimination of quantifiers for $\mathscr{L}''$, in particular of the formula $F = \bigvee y[y \neq 0 \wedge y \neq 1 \wedge By \wedge \neg A_1(1+x)]$ of $\mathscr{L}'$ itself. It would be equivalent to a propositional combination of formulas $A_n 1$, $B_n 1$, $S1$ ($\neg A_n 0$, $B0$, $S0$ being consequences of a), b), c), d)). F is false in $\mathfrak{M}_2$ which also satisfies $A_n 1$ $(n \geqslant 1)$, $\neg B1$, $\neg S1$. But there are evidently Boolean rings which also satisfy $A_n 1$ $(n \geqslant 1)$, $\neg B1$, $\neg S1$ in which F is true, e.g. the Boolean ring constructed analogously to $\mathfrak{M}_2$, starting with the ordered sum of (X, R) and a disjoint copy of it in place of (X, R).

Chapter 5

PREDICATE CALCULUS WITH SEVERAL TYPES OF OBJECTS: THE HIERARCHY OF FINITE TYPES

The first part of this chapter and Exercises 1, 2 and 3 contain a second method, mentioned in the summary of Chapter 2, for developing first order predicate logic, including the reduction of the theory of functions to that of their graphs. The essential results are formulated and proved directly for languages with several types of variables which are common in mathematics. The use of such languages is in principle reducible to the use of languages with a single type of variable and unary predicates $M_i(x)$ for "x is of type i". However in practice these languages are useful because they allow simple formulations of certain results, for example, an improved version of the Interpolation Lemma, which will be useful in the next chapter. The method of constructing canonical models given in this chapter is in practice much more convenient for languages with several types of variables than that of Chapter 2. For the relation between these two methods see Exercise 2.

In the second part we study languages with several types of variables constructed as follows: one type for individuals, one for sets of individuals, one for families of such sets and so on for a finite number of steps. These languages are familiar from axiomatic mathematics where, for example, in the theory of groups, the elements of the given group constitute the individuals while the sub-groups are *sets* of such individuals (sets on which we take the restriction of the group operation). More generally, the languages considered here concern the finite levels in the structure or "hierarchy" of (simple) types. In Exercise 5 the cumulative type structure and its relation to the simple type structure are described.

In the class of realizations here considered (that of general models), the domain C_0 of the individual variables is arbitrary and the domains of the other variables are families of sets of the types 1, 2, ..., respectively, of the hierarchy having C_0 as base, and which satisfy certain closure conditions. The study of these general realizations can be reduced to the theory of Chapter 2 (by use of the axioms of extensionality). Two other classes of realizations are treated in the last chapter.

A *language $\mathscr{L}$ with k types of objects* is a language which consists of:
1) k infinite disjoint sets $V_{\mathscr{L}}^{(1)}, \ldots, V_{\mathscr{L}}^{(k)}$. The elements of $V_{\mathscr{L}}^{(i)} (1 \leqslant i \leqslant k)$, are called *variables of type i of $\mathscr{L}$*;
2) k disjoint sets $C_{\mathscr{L}}^{(1)}, \ldots, C_{\mathscr{L}}^{(k)}$. The elements of $C_{\mathscr{L}}^{(i)} (1 \leqslant i \leqslant k)$, are called *constant symbols of type i of $\mathscr{L}$*;

3) for each integer $n \geqslant 0$ a set $R_{\mathscr{L}}^{(n)}$, the elements of which are called *n-ary relational symbols* (with variables of arbitrary type);
4) for each sequence $(i_1, ..., i_n)$ of integers between 1 and k, a set $S_{\mathscr{L}}^{(i_1, ..., i_n)}$ the elements of which are called *relational symbols of type* $(i_1, ..., i_n)$, (or n-ary relational symbols the first variable of which is of type i_1, ..., and the n-th is of type i_n).

All these sets are assumed to be pairwise disjoint.

The *atomic formulas* of $\mathscr{L}$ are defined to be the sequences of one of the following forms
a) $R(\xi_1, ..., \xi_n)$, where R is an n-ary relation symbol, $(R \in R_{\mathscr{L}}^{(n)})$ and $\xi_1, ..., \xi_n$ are variables or constant symbols of $\mathscr{L}$ of arbitrary type, that is,

$$\xi_i \in \bigcup_{j=1}^{k} (C_{\mathscr{L}}^{(j)} \cup V_{\mathscr{L}}^{(j)}) \quad \text{for} \quad 1 \leqslant i \leqslant n;$$

b) $S(\xi_1^{(i_1)}, ..., \xi_n^{(i_n)})$ where S is a relation symbol of type $(i_1, ..., i_n)$, $(S \in S_{\mathscr{L}}^{(i_1, ..., i_n)})$, and $\xi_j^{(i_j)}$ is a variable or a constant symbol of $\mathscr{L}$ of type i_j, $1 \leqslant j \leqslant n$.

The set of atomic formulas of $\mathscr{L}$ is denoted by $\mathrm{At}_{\mathscr{L}}$.

The set $\mathscr{F}_{\mathscr{L}}$ of formulas of $\mathscr{L}$ is the set of function schemas built up with the atomic formulas of $\mathscr{L}$ as the 0-ary symbols, $\neg$ and $\bigvee x$ (where $x \in V_{\mathscr{L}}^{(1)} \cup \cdots \cup V_{\mathscr{L}}^{(k)}$) as the unary symbols and $\vee$ as the only binary symbol (see Chapter 0).

The abbreviations $\bigwedge x, \rightarrow, \leftrightarrow$ and $\wedge$ are defined just as in Chapter 2 as also are the notions of the *free variables* of a formula of $\mathscr{L}$ and of a *closed formula* of $\mathscr{L}$.

We define a *realization of the language $\mathscr{L}$ with k types of objects* to consist of
1) k non-empty sets $E_1, ..., E_k$. $E_i (1 \leqslant i \leqslant k)$ is called the *domain of type i* of the realization;
2) for each $i (1 \leqslant i \leqslant k)$, a map $c \rightarrow \bar{c}$ of $C_{\mathscr{L}}^{(i)}$ into E_i;
3) for each integer $n \geqslant 0$ a map $R \rightarrow \bar{R}$ of $R_{\mathscr{L}}^{(n)}$ into $\mathscr{P}((E_1 \cup \cdots \cup E_k)^n)$;
4) for each sequence $(i_1, ..., i_n)$ of integers between 1 and k a map $S \rightarrow \bar{S}$ of $S_{\mathscr{L}}^{(i_1, ..., i_n)}$ into $\mathscr{P}(E_{i_1} \times \cdots \times E_{i_n})$.

The value $\bar{F}$ of a formula F of $\mathscr{L}$ in this realization is a subset of $E_1^{V_{\mathscr{L}}(1)} \times \cdots \times E_k^{V_{\mathscr{L}}(k)}$ (that is, it is a set of sequences $(\delta_1, ..., \delta_k)$ where δ_i is a map of $V_{\mathscr{L}}^{(i)}$ into E_i, or alternatively since the sets $V_{\mathscr{L}}^{(i)}$ are pairwise disjoint, it is a set of maps δ of $\bigcup_{j=1}^{k} V_{\mathscr{L}}^{(j)}$ into $\bigcup_{j=1}^{k} E_j$ such that for $1 \leqslant j \leqslant k$, $\delta(V_{\mathscr{L}}^{(j)}) \subseteq E_j$). This set $\bar{F}$ is defined as follows:

If F is an atomic formula it is of the form $R(\xi_1^{(i_1)}, \ldots, \xi_n^{(i_n)})$ with $R \in R_{\mathscr{L}}^{(n)}$ or $R \in S_{\mathscr{L}}^{(i_1, \ldots, i_n)}$, where $\xi_1^{(i_1)}, \ldots, \xi_n^{(i_n)}$ are variables or constant symbols of types $i_1, \ldots, i_n$ respectively. In this case $\bar{F}$ is the set of those $\delta \in E_1^{V_{\mathscr{L}}(1)} \times \cdots \times E_k^{V_{\mathscr{L}}(k)}$ such that

$$(\delta'(\xi_1^{(i_1)}), \ldots, \delta'(\xi_n^{(i_n)})) \in \bar{R}$$

where $\delta'(\xi_j^{(i)}) = \delta(\xi_j^{(i)})$ if $\xi_j^{(i)}$ is a variable and $\delta'(\xi_j^{(i)}) = \overline{\xi_j^{(i)}}$ if $\xi_j^{(i)}$ is a constant symbol.

By the Theorem on Function Schemas (Theorem 0.3), if we put $\overline{F \vee G} = \bar{F} \cup \bar{G}$, $\overline{\neg F} = \complement \bar{F}$ and $\overline{\bigvee x F} =$ the projection of $\bar{F}$ along the variable x (that is the set of those $\delta \in E_1^{V_{\mathscr{L}}(1)} \times \cdots \times E_k^{V_{\mathscr{L}}(k)}$ such that there is some $\delta_1 \in \bar{F}$ which is equal to δ, except possibly at x), then $\bar{F}$ is defined for each formula F.

Just as in Chapter 2 we can see that the value of a closed formula F is either $E_1^{V_{\mathscr{L}}(1)} \times \cdots \times E_k^{V_{\mathscr{L}}(k)}$ or $\emptyset$. In the first case we say that F is *satisfied* by the given realization. If $\mathscr{A}$ is a set of closed formulas of $\mathscr{L}$ the formula F is a *consequence* of $\mathscr{A}$ and we write $\mathscr{A} \vdash F$ (as on p. 66), if every realization which satisfies $\mathscr{A}$ (that is, which satisfies each formula of $\mathscr{A}$) also satisfies F. A *theorem* of $\mathscr{L}$ is a formula whose closure is satisfied by each realization of $\mathscr{L}$.

The notion of a formula in *prenex normal form* or a *prenex formula* is defined as in Chapter 2. We can again show that each formula of $\mathscr{L}$ is equivalent to a prenex formula.

A realization of $\mathscr{L}$ is called a *canonical realization* if its domain of type i is $C_{\mathscr{L}}^{(i)}$, the set of constants of $\mathscr{L}$ of type i, for each i, $1 \leqslant i \leqslant k$, and if for each constant symbol c of $\mathscr{L}$, $\bar{c}$, the value of c in the realization, is c itself. Hence if one of the sets $C_{\mathscr{L}}^{(i)}$ is empty $\mathscr{L}$ does not have any canonical realization.

To each canonical realization of $\mathscr{L}$ there corresponds a realization of the propositional calculus on the closed atomic formulas of $\mathscr{L}$ defined as follows:

The value of $R(a_1^{(i_1)}, \ldots, a_n^{(i_n)})$, where R is an n-ary relation symbol or a relation symbol of type $(i_1, \ldots, i_n)$ and $a_1^{(i_1)}, \ldots, a_n^{(i_n)}$ are constant symbols of types $i_1, \ldots, i_n$, respectively, is 1 or 0 according as to whether or not $(a_1^{(i_1)}, \ldots, a_n^{(i_n)}) \in \bar{R}$.

Conversely each realization of the propositional calculus on the set of closed atomic formulas of $\mathscr{L}$ defines a canonical realization of $\mathscr{L}$. The following lemma can easily be proved by induction on the length of F.

LEMMA 1: *Let F be a closed quantifier free formula of $\mathscr{L}$. Then given any canonical realization of $\mathscr{L}$, F is satisfied by this realization if and only if it is satisfied by the corresponding realization of the propositional calculus on the set of closed atomic formulas of $\mathscr{L}$.*

Let $\{\Delta_n^{(i)}: 1 \leqslant i \leqslant k, n \text{ an integer } \geqslant 1\}$ be a family of disjoint sets each of the same cardinal as the set of formulas of $\mathscr{L}$, and each disjoint from $\mathscr{L}$ so that no finite sequence of variables or of other symbols of $\mathscr{L}$ belongs to $\Delta_n^{(i)}$. Let $\Delta^{(i)} = \bigcup_{n \geqslant 1} \Delta_n^{(i)}$ and let $\mathscr{L}_\Delta$ be the language which is obtained by adding to $\mathscr{L}$ each element of $\Delta^{(i)}$ as a constant symbol of type i. Thus the set of constant symbols of $\mathscr{L}_\Delta$ of type i is $C_{\mathscr{L}}^{(i)} \cup \Delta^{(i)}$.

$$\text{Let } \Delta_n = \bigcup_{1 \leqslant i \leqslant k} \Delta_n^{(i)} \quad \text{and} \quad \Delta = \bigcup_{n \geqslant 1} \Delta_n = \bigcup_{1 \leqslant i \leqslant k} \Delta^{(i)}.$$

For each $a \in \Delta^{(i)}$ the *rank* of a is the integer n such that $a \in \Delta_n^{(i)}$, the integer i, between 1 and k, being the type of a. The rank of a formula F of $\mathscr{L}_\Delta$ is the greatest rank of the elements of Δ which occur in it, or 0 if no elements of Δ occur in it, i.e., if F is a formula of $\mathscr{L}$.

We choose a variable $x^{(i)}$ of $\mathscr{L}$ of type i for each $i (1 \leqslant i \leqslant k)$, and we let $F_n^{(i)}$ be the set of formulas of $\mathscr{L}_\Delta$ of rank n which have $x^{(i)}$ as their only free variable. Clearly $F_n^{(i)}$ and $\Delta_{n+1}^{(i)}$ have the same cardinal, namely that of the set of formulas of $\mathscr{L}$. Hence for each pair (i, n), with $1 \leqslant i \leqslant k$ and n an integer $\geqslant 0$, there is a one-one map ε of $F_n^{(i)}$ onto $\Delta_{n+1}^{(i)}$. Therefore for each $a \in \Delta^{(i)}$ there is a unique formula, $A(x^{(i)})$, with $x^{(i)}$ as its only free variable, such that $a = \varepsilon(A(x^{(i)}))$. Further, the rank of $A(x^{(i)})$ is one less than the rank of a.

We let Ω_a be the formula

$$\bigvee x^{(i)} A(x^{(i)}) \rightarrow A(a)$$

where $a = \varepsilon(A(x^{(i)}))$.

We let

$$\Omega_n^{(i)} = \{\Omega_a : a \in \Delta_n^{(i)}\}$$
$$\Omega^{(i)} = \{\Omega_a : a \in \Delta^{(i)}\}$$
$$\Omega_n = \{\Omega_a : a \in \Delta_n\}$$

and

$$\Omega = \{\Omega_a : a \in \Delta\}.$$

Thus

$$\Omega = \bigcup_{n \geqslant 1} \Omega_n = \bigcup_{1 \leqslant i \leqslant k} \Omega^{(i)}.$$

PROPOSITION 2: *Each realization of $\mathscr{L}$ can be extended to $\mathscr{L}_\Delta$ so as to be a model of Ω.*

PROOF: Let $\mathfrak{M}$ be a realization of $\mathscr{L}$ with domains $E_1, \ldots, E_k$. We define the value $\bar{a}$ of $a \in \Delta$ by recursion on the rank of a.

Suppose that we have defined $\bar{b}$ for each $b \in \bigcup_{p<n} \Delta_p$ in such a way that $\Omega_1, \ldots, \Omega_{n-1}$ are all satisfied, and let $a \in \Delta_n$. The formula $A(x)$ such that $a = \varepsilon(A(x))$ is of rank $n-1$ and therefore has a value $\overline{A(x)}$ in the realization of $\mathscr{L} \cup \Delta_1 \cup \cdots \cup \Delta_{n-1}$ which has already been defined. If $\overline{A(x)}$ is not empty there is some $\alpha \in E_i$, where i is the type of a, such that $\alpha \in \overline{A(x)}$. We put $\bar{a} = \alpha$. If $\overline{A(x)}$ is empty we let $\bar{a}$ be an arbitrary element of E_i. In either case Ω_a, which is $\bigvee x A(x) \rightarrow A(a)$, is satisfied.

This completes the proof.

PROPOSITION 3: *For each model $\mathfrak{M}$ of Ω there is a canonical model $\mathfrak{M}_1$ which satisfies the same closed formulas of $\mathscr{L}_\Delta$ as $\mathfrak{M}$.*

PROOF: Let R be an n-ary relation symbol of $\mathscr{L}$ or a relation symbol of type $(i_1, \ldots, i_n)$ of $\mathscr{L}$, and let $\bar{R}_{\mathfrak{M}}$ be the value of R in the given realization $\mathfrak{M}$. We define $\bar{R}_{\mathfrak{M}_1}$, the value of R in the realization $\mathfrak{M}_1$ by $\bar{R}_{\mathfrak{M}_1} = \{(a_1, \ldots, a_n)$: the formula $R(a_1, \ldots, a_n)$ is satisfied in $\mathfrak{M}\}$. (If R is a relation symbol of type $(i_1, \ldots, i_n)$ then $a_1, \ldots, a_n$ are respectively of types $i_1, \ldots, i_n$ or else $R(a_1, \ldots, a_n)$ is not a formula of $\mathscr{L}_\Delta$.)

Now let F be a closed formula of $\mathscr{L}_\Delta$. We will show by induction on the length of F that F is satisfied by $\mathfrak{M}$ if and only if it is satisfied by $\mathfrak{M}_1$. This is obvious if F is atomic from the way that we have defined $\mathfrak{M}_1$.

Suppose that the result is true for all formulas of length less than h and that F is a closed formula of length h.

If F is $\neg G$, then by the induction hypothesis, G is satisfied, say, by both $\mathfrak{M}$ and $\mathfrak{M}_1$, hence F is satisfied by neither $\mathfrak{M}$ nor $\mathfrak{M}_1$. Conversely, if G is satisfied by neither $\mathfrak{M}$ nor $\mathfrak{M}_1$ then F is satisfied by them both; similarly if F is $G \vee H$.

If F is $\bigvee x G(x)$, suppose first that F is satisfied by $\mathfrak{M}$. Since $\mathfrak{M}$ is a model of Ω, $\mathfrak{M}$ satisfies $G(g)$ where $g = \varepsilon(G(x))$, because Ω contains the formula $\bigvee x G(x) \rightarrow G(g)$. Hence, by the induction hypothesis, $\mathfrak{M}_1$ satisfies $G(g)$ and so satisfies F. Suppose now that $\mathfrak{M}$ does not satisfy F. Then $\mathfrak{M}$ satisfies all the formulas $\neg G(a)$ where a is a constant symbol of $\mathscr{L}_\Delta$ of the same type as x. Therefore, by the induction hypothesis, $\mathfrak{M}_1$ also satisfies all these formulas. But the domain of $\mathfrak{M}_1$ of type i is the set of constant symbols of $\mathscr{L}_\Delta$ of type i and so $\mathfrak{M}_1$ satisfies $\bigwedge x \neg G(x)$, that is $\mathfrak{M}_1$ satisfies $\neg F$.

This completes the proof.

With each closed prenex formula F of $\mathscr{L}_\Delta$ we associate a set $\langle F\rangle$ of closed quantifier free formulas of $\mathscr{L}_\Delta$, and a subset $\Delta(F)$ of Δ, defined by recursion on the length of F as follows:
i) if F is quantifier free, $\langle F\rangle=\{F\}$ and $\Delta(F)=\emptyset$;
ii) if F is $\bigvee xG(x)$ then $\langle F\rangle=\langle G(g)\rangle$ and $\Delta(F)=\{g\}\cup\Delta(G(g))$ where $g=\varepsilon(G(x))$;
iii) if F is $\bigwedge xG(x)$ then $\langle F\rangle=\bigcup_a\langle G(a)\rangle$ and $\Delta(F)=\bigcup_a\Delta(G(a))$ where a ranges over all constants of $\mathscr{L}_\Delta$ of the same type as x.

Let $\Omega(F)=\{\Omega_a : a\in\Delta(F)\}$.

LEMMA 4: *Each canonical model of* $\langle F\rangle$ *satisfies* F *and each model of* $\{F\}\cup\Omega(F)$ *satisfies* $\langle F\rangle$ (or, for short, $F, \Omega(F)\vdash\langle F\rangle$).
PROOF: The proof is by induction on the length of F. The lemma is obvious if F is quantifier free since then $\langle F\rangle=\{F\}$.

Suppose that the lemma is true for all formulas of length less than h and that F is of length h.

If F is $\bigvee xG(x)$ and $\mathfrak{M}$ is a canonical model of $\langle F\rangle$, $\mathfrak{M}$ is a model of $\langle G(g)\rangle$ where $g=\varepsilon(G(x))$. By the induction hypothesis $\mathfrak{M}$ satisfies $G(g)$ and also F. Also, since Ω_g, i.e. $\bigvee xG(x)\rightarrow G(g)$, $\in\Omega(F)$, $\{F\}\cup\Omega(F)\vdash G(g)$; since $\Omega(G(g))\subset\Omega(F)$, and, by the induction hypothesis, $\{G(g)\}\cup\Omega(G(g))\vdash\langle G(g)\rangle$, we have $\{F\}\cup\Omega(F)\vdash\langle G(g)\rangle$, i.e. $\{F\}\cup\Omega(F)\vdash\langle F\rangle$.

If F is $\bigwedge xG(x)$ and $\mathfrak{M}$ is a canonical model of $\langle F\rangle$, $\mathfrak{M}$ is a model of $\bigcup\{\langle G(a)\rangle$: a is a constant symbol of $\mathscr{L}_\Delta$ of the same type as $x\}$. By the induction hypothesis $\mathfrak{M}$ satisfies each of the formulas $G(a)$ and so, since $\mathfrak{M}$ is a canonical model, $\mathfrak{M}$ satisfies $\bigwedge xG(x)$, i.e. F. By the induction hypothesis $G(a), \Omega(G(a))\vdash\langle G(a)\rangle$, and so, since $\Omega(F)\supset\Omega(G(a))$, also $G(a), \Omega(F)\vdash\langle G(a)\rangle$. Since, further, for each a, $F\vdash G(a)$, we have $F, \Omega(F)\vdash\langle G(a)\rangle$, i.e., $F, \Omega(F)\vdash\bigcup_a\langle G(a)\rangle$, and so $F, \Omega(F)\vdash\langle F\rangle$, as required.

THEOREM 5. THE FINITENESS THEOREM: *If each finite subset of a set* $\mathscr{A}$ *of closed formulas of* $\mathscr{L}$ *has a model, then* $\mathscr{A}$ *has a model.*
PROOF: We can assume that $\mathscr{A}$ contains only closed prenex formulas.

Let $\mathscr{B}=\bigcup\{\langle F\rangle : F\in\mathscr{A}\}$. Let $\mathscr{U}$ be an arbitrary finite subset of $\mathscr{B}$ so that $\mathscr{U}\subseteq\langle F_1\rangle\cup\cdots\cup\langle F_n\rangle$. Since, by hypothesis, $\{F_1, \ldots, F_n\}$ has a model, it follows from Proposition 2 that $\Omega\cup\{F_1, \ldots, F_n\}$ has a model and hence from Proposition 3, that $\Omega\cup\{F_1, \ldots, F_n\}$ has a canonical model. Since $\Omega(F)\subset\Omega$, by Lemma 4, Ω, $F_i\vdash\langle F_i\rangle$; so this canonical model satisfies

$\langle F_1\rangle\cup\cdots\cup\langle F_n\rangle$ and hence also $\mathscr{U}$. Thus every finite subset $\mathscr{U}$ of $\mathscr{B}$ has a canonical model and hence also a model in the sense of the propositional calculus on the closed atomic formulas of $\mathscr{L}_\Delta$, by Lemma 1. Hence, by the Finiteness Theorem for propositional calculus, $\mathscr{B}$ has a model in the sense of the propositional calculus, and therefore, by Lemma 1, $\mathscr{B}$ has a canonical model. By Lemma 4, since this canonical model satisfies $\langle F\rangle$ for each $F\in\mathscr{A}$, it also satisfies $\mathscr{A}$.

This completes the proof.

COROLLARY 6: *Let I be a totally ordered set and let $\{\mathscr{A}_i : i\in I\}$ be a family of sets of closed formulas of $\mathscr{L}_\Delta$ such that if $i, j\in I$ and $i<j$ then $\mathscr{A}_i\subseteq\mathscr{A}_j$. If each $\mathscr{A}_i$ has a model then so has $\mathscr{A}=\bigcup_{i\in I}\mathscr{A}_i$.*

PROOF: It is sufficient to show that each finite subset $\mathscr{A}_0=\{F_1, \ldots, F_n\}$ of $\mathscr{A}$ has a model. Suppose, say, that $F_j\in\mathscr{A}_{i_j}(1\leqslant j\leqslant n)$ and let i_k be the greatest element of $\{i_1, \ldots, i_n\}$. Then $\mathscr{A}_0\subseteq\mathscr{A}_{i_k}$, and so because $\mathscr{A}_{i_k}$ has a model so too does $\mathscr{A}_0$.

LEMMA 7: *If F and G are two closed prenex formulas of $\mathscr{L}_\Delta$ such that $\Delta(F)\cap\Delta(G)\neq\emptyset$, F and G contain the same relation symbols and variables and constants of the same types.*

PROOF: Let $b\in\Delta(F)\cap\Delta(G)$. Since $b\in\Delta, b=\varepsilon(B(x))$ for some formula $B(x)$ with a single free variable. We show, by induction on the length of F that $B(x)$ and F contain the same relation symbols and variables and constants of the same types.

F cannot be quantifier free or else $\Delta(F)$ would be empty. If F is $\bigvee xH(x)$ then since $b\in\Delta(F)$, $b\in\Delta(H(g))\cup\{g\}$ where $g=\varepsilon(H(x))$. If $b\in\Delta(H(g))$ then by our induction hypothesis, $H(g)$ and $B(x)$ contain the same relation symbols and variables and constants of the same types and hence so too do F and $B(x)$. If $b=g$ then $B(x)=H(x)$ because ε is one-one and so again F and $B(x)$ contain the same relation symbols and variables and constants of the same types.

If F is $\bigwedge xH(x)$ then since $b\in\Delta(F)$, $b\in\Delta(H(a))$ for some constant symbol a of the same type as x. By the induction hypothesis, $H(a)$ and $B(x)$ contain the same relation symbols and variables and constants of the same types and hence so too do F and $B(x)$.

Similarly it can be proved that G and $B(x)$ contain the same relation symbols and variables and constants of the same types and therefore so too do F and G.

THEOREM 8. THE INTERPOLATION LEMMA: *Let F and G be two closed formulas of $\mathscr{L}$ such that $F \wedge G$ does not have a model. Then there is a formula H of $\mathscr{L}$, whose relation symbols and types are common to F and G such that $F \to H$ and $G \to \neg H$ are both theorems.*

PROOF: Since $F \wedge G$ does not have a model, it follows from Lemma 4 that $\langle F \rangle \cup \langle G \rangle$ does not have a canonical model and so is inconsistent in the sense of the propositional calculus on the closed atomic formulas of $\mathscr{L}_\Delta$, by Lemma 1.

Therefore, by the Interpolation Lemma for the propositional calculus there is a closed quantifier free formula C of $\mathscr{L}_\Delta$, whose atomic formulas are common to $\langle F \rangle$ and $\langle G \rangle$ such that $\langle F \rangle \vdash C$ and $\langle G \rangle \vdash \neg C$. The relation symbols and types which occur in $\langle F \rangle$ are just those that appear in F as can be seen at once from the definition of $\langle F \rangle$. Similarly for G. Hence the relation symbols and types of C are common to F and G. By Lemma 4, $\Omega(F)$, $F \vdash C$ and $\Omega(G)$, $G \vdash \neg C$. If $\Delta(F) \cap \Delta(G) \neq \emptyset$, then, by Lemma 7, F and G contain the same relation symbols and the same types. In this case the Theorem is trivial since it is sufficient to put $H = F$. We can therefore assume that $\Delta(F) \cap \Delta(G) = \emptyset$.

By the Finiteness Theorem

$$\Omega_{a_1}, \dots, \Omega_{a_n}, F \vdash C, \tag{1}$$

$$\Omega_{b_1}, \dots, \Omega_{b_p}, G \vdash \neg C, \tag{2}$$

where $a_1, \dots, a_n$ are distinct elements of $\Delta(F)$ and $b_1, \dots, b_p$ are distinct elements of $\Delta(G)$. Because $\Delta(F) \cap \Delta(G) = \emptyset$, $a_i \neq b_j$ $(1 \leqslant i \leqslant n, 1 \leqslant j \leqslant p)$. Let a_n, say, be an element of greatest rank in the set $\{a_1, \dots, a_n, b_1, \dots, b_p\}$. Then $\Omega_{a_1}, \dots, \Omega_{a_{n-1}}, \Omega_{b_1}, \dots, \Omega_{b_p}$ do not contain a_n. Let $C_1(z)$ be the formula obtained from C by replacing a_n by a variable z of the same type not occurring in C. So $C = C_1(a_n)$ and hence $C \vdash \bigvee z C_1(z)$. Therefore

$$\Omega_{a_1}, \dots, \Omega_{a_n}, F \vdash \bigvee z C_1(z).$$

But $\Omega_{a_1}, \dots, \Omega_{a_{n-1}}, F, \bigvee z C_1(z)$ do not contain a_n. Also Ω_{a_n} can be written as $\bigvee x A(x) \to A(a_n)$ where $A(x)$ does not contain x_n. Therefore

$$\Omega_{a_1}, \dots, \Omega_{a_{n-1}}, \bigvee y [\bigvee x A(x) \to A(y)], F \vdash \bigvee z C_1(z)$$

that is, because $\bigvee y [\bigvee x A(x) \to A(y)]$ is a theorem,

$$\Omega_{a_1}, \dots, \Omega_{a_{n-1}}, F \vdash \bigvee z C_1(z). \tag{3}$$

On the other hand

$$\Omega_{b_1}, \dots, \Omega_{b_p}, G \vdash \neg C_1(a_n).$$

Since a_n does not occur in $\Omega_{b_1}, \ldots, \Omega_{b_p}, G$ we can therefore deduce that

$$\Omega_{b_1}, \ldots, \Omega_{b_p}, G \vdash \bigwedge z \neg C_1(z). \tag{4}$$

We can repeat this procedure starting from (3) and (4), instead of from (1) and (2) and so on. Thus we can eliminate one by one the formulas $\Omega_{a_i}, \Omega_{b_j} (1 \leqslant i \leqslant n, 1 \leqslant j \leqslant p)$. After $n+p$ steps we obtain a formula H which has the same relation symbols and types as C such that $F \vdash H$ and $G \vdash \neg H$.

This completes the proof.

The following two lemmas will be used in the next chapter.

Let $a \in \Delta$. Let θ_a be the intersection of all those subsets X of Ω which have the following properties

1) $\Omega_a \in X$,
2) if $b \in \Delta$ and b occurs in a formula of X then $\Omega_b \in X$.

θ_a is therefore the smallest subset of X which has these two properties.

LEMMA 9: *Let $a_1, \ldots, a_n$ be the elements of Δ, other than a, which occur in Ω_a. Then $\theta_a = \theta_{a_1} \cup \cdots \cup \theta_{a_n} \cup \{\Omega_a\}$.*

PROOF: Clearly $\theta_{a_1} \cup \cdots \cup \theta_{a_n} \cup \{\Omega_a\}$ has the properties 1) and 2) above and so contains θ_a.

Conversely θ_a contains $\theta_{a_i} (1 \leqslant i \leqslant n)$ and so θ_a has the two properties which define θ_{a_i}. Therefore $\theta_{a_i} \subseteq \theta_a$ and so $\theta_{a_1} \cup \cdots \cup \theta_{a_n} \cup \{\Omega_a\} \subseteq \theta_a$.

This completes the proof.

We deduce at once that *for each $a \in \Delta$, θ_a is a finite set of formulas of Ω*. This is obvious if $a \in \Omega_1$ because then $\theta_a = \{\Omega_a\}$, and if it is true for all a of rank less than n then the previous lemma shows that it is also true for all a of rank n.

LEMMA 10: *Let $H(a_1, \ldots, a_n)$ be a closed formula of $\mathscr{L}_\Delta$ containing no elements of Δ other than $a_1, \ldots, a_n$. If $\Omega \vdash H(a_1, \ldots, a_n)$ then $\theta_{a_1}, \ldots, \theta_{a_n} \vdash$ $\vdash H(a_1, \ldots, a_n)$.*

PROOF: Suppose $\Omega \vdash H(a_1, \ldots, a_n)$, then by the Finiteness Theorem there is some finite subset Ω' of Ω such that $\Omega' \vdash H(a_1, \ldots, a_n)$. Let Σ be the set of all those finite subsets of Ω which contain $\theta_{a_1}, \ldots, \theta_{a_n}$ and which have $H(a_1, \ldots, a_n)$ as a consequence. Σ is not empty and hence contains some set $\Omega_0 = \theta_{a_1} \cup \cdots \cup \theta_{a_n} \cup \{\Omega_{b_1}, \ldots, \Omega_{b_p}\}$, containing the smallest number of formulas. We will show that $p = 0$.

Suppose that $p \neq 0$ and let $b_1, \ldots, b_p$ be arranged in increasing order of rank. Let $B_p(x)$ be the formula such that $b_p = \varepsilon(B_p(x))$. Then $\theta_{a_1}, \ldots, \theta_{a_n}$, $\Omega_{b_1}, \ldots, \Omega_{b_{p-1}}, \bigvee x B_p(x) \to B_p(b_p) \vdash H(a_1, \ldots, a_n)$. b_p does not occur in θ_{a_i} $(1 \leqslant i \leqslant n)$ because if it did, by the definition of θ_{a_i} we would have $\Omega_{b_p} \in \theta_{a_i}$ and hence $\Omega_0 - \{\Omega_{b_p}\} \in \Sigma$, which contradicts the choice of Ω_0. Also b_p does not occur in any of $\Omega_{b_1}, \ldots, \Omega_{b_{p-1}}$ because if it did the rank of b_p would be less than the rank of one of the $b_j (1 \leqslant j \leqslant p)$. Finally b_p does not occur in $H(a_1, \ldots, a_n)$ which does not contain any symbols of Δ other than $a_1, \ldots, a_n$. Therefore

$$\theta_{a_1}, \ldots, \theta_{a_n}, \Omega_{b_1}, \ldots, \Omega_{b_{p-1}}, \bigvee y (\bigvee x B_p(x) \to B_p(y)) \vdash H(a_1, \ldots, a_n);$$

but $\bigvee y (\bigvee x B_p(x) \to B_p(y))$ is a theorem and so

$$\theta_{a_1}, \ldots, \theta_{a_n}, \Omega_{b_1}, \ldots, \Omega_{b_{p-1}} \vdash H(a_1, \ldots, a_n)$$

which again contradicts the choice of Ω_0.

This completes the proof.

PREDICATE CALCULUS WITH EQUALITY, WITH k TYPES OF OBJECTS

A language $\mathscr{L}$ with k types of objects is said to be *with equality* if there is a distinguished binary relation symbol E of $\mathscr{L}$ $(E \in R_{\mathscr{L}}^{(2)})$.

Let $\mathscr{L}$ be a language with equality and let ξ, η be two variables or constant symbols (of arbitrary types). The atomic formula $E(\xi, \eta)$ will be written $\xi = \eta$.

A realization of $\mathscr{L}$ with domains $U_1, \ldots, U_k$, is said to be *normal* if the value of E in this realization is the diagonal of $(U_1 \cup \cdots \cup U_k)^2$, that is the set of all pairs (u, u) for $u \in U_1 \cup \cdots \cup U_k$.

A closed formula F is said to be a *normal consequence* of a set $\mathscr{A}$ of closed formulas of $\mathscr{L}$ if each normal realization which satisfies $\mathscr{A}$ also satisfies F. If F is a normal consequence of $\mathscr{A}$ we write $\mathscr{A} \models F$, or where there can be no confusion $\mathscr{A} \vdash F$. A formula F of $\mathscr{L}$ is called a *normal theorem* if its closure is satisfied by all normal realizations of $\mathscr{L}$.

Let $\mathscr{E}_{\mathscr{L}}$ be the set of the following formulas of $\mathscr{L}$

1) $\bigwedge x^{(i)} (x^{(i)} = x^{(i)})$, for each integer $i (1 \leqslant i \leqslant k)$ where $x^{(i)}$ is a variable of type i;

2) $\bigwedge x_1^{(i_1)} \ldots \bigwedge x_n^{(i_n)} \bigwedge y_1^{(j_1)} \ldots \bigwedge y_n^{(j_n)}$

$$[(x_1^{(i_1)} = y_1^{(j_1)} \wedge \cdots \wedge x_n^{(i_n)} = y_n^{(j_n)}) \to (R(x_1^{(i_1)}, \ldots, x_n^{(i_n)}) \to R(y_1^{(j_1)}, \ldots, y_n^{(j_n)}))]$$

for each relation symbol $R \in R_{\mathscr{L}}^{(n)}$ (including E, when $n = 2$), and for each sequence $i_1, \ldots, i_n, j_1, \ldots, j_n$ of $2n$ integers between 1 and k, where $x_1^{(i_1)}, \ldots, x_n^{(i_n)}, y_1^{(j_1)} \ldots, y_n^{(j_n)}$ are variables which are of types $i_1, \ldots, i_n, j_1, \ldots, j_n$, respectively;

3) $\bigwedge x_1^{(i_1)} \ldots \bigwedge x_n^{(i_n)} \bigwedge y_1^{(i_1)} \ldots \bigwedge y_n^{(i_n)}$
$$[(x_1^{(i_1)} = y_1^{(i_1)} \wedge \cdots \wedge x_n^{(i_n)} = y_n^{(i_n)}) \rightarrow (S(x_1^{(i_1)}, \ldots, x_n^{(i_n)}) \rightarrow S(y_1^{(i_1)}, \ldots, y_n^{(i_n)}))],$$

for each relation symbol S of type $(i_1, \ldots, i_n)$ where $x_j^{(i)}, y_j^{(i)}$ are variables of type i.

The formulas of $\mathscr{E}_{\mathscr{L}}$ are called the *axioms of equality for* $\mathscr{L}$. Let $\mathfrak{M}$ be a model of $\mathscr{E}_{\mathscr{L}}$ with domains $U_1, \ldots, U_k$. $\mathscr{E}_{\mathscr{L}}$ contains the formulas

$$\bigwedge x_1^{(i_1)} \bigwedge x_2^{(i_2)} \bigwedge y_1^{(j_1)} \bigwedge y_2^{(j_2)}$$
$$[(x_1^{(i_1)} = y_1^{(j_1)} \wedge x_2^{(i_2)} = y_2^{(j_2)} \wedge x_1^{(i_1)} = x_2^{(i_2)}) \rightarrow y_1^{(j_1)} = y_2^{(j_2)}],$$

and so because $\mathfrak{M}$ satisfies these formulas $\bar{E}_{\mathfrak{M}}$, the value of E in $\mathfrak{M}$, is the graph of an equivalence relation on $U_1 \cup \cdots \cup U_k$.

Hence we can derive a normal realization $\mathfrak{M}'$ from $\mathfrak{M}$ as follows: the domains of $\mathfrak{M}'$ are the images of $U_1, \ldots, U_k$ under the canonical map of $U_1 \cup \cdots \cup U_k$ into $U_1 \cup \cdots \cup U_k / \bar{E}_{\mathfrak{M}}$. If c is a constant symbol of $\mathscr{L}$ with value $\bar{c}_{\mathfrak{M}}$ in $\mathfrak{M}$, then its value $\bar{c}_{\mathfrak{M}'}$ in $\mathfrak{M}'$ is the equivalence class of $\bar{c}_{\mathfrak{M}}$ under the relation $\bar{E}_{\mathfrak{M}}$.

If $\bar{R}$ is a relation symbol (an n-ary relation symbol or one of type $(i_1, \ldots, i_n)$) whose value in $\mathfrak{M}$ is $\bar{R}_{\mathfrak{M}}$, its value $\bar{R}_{\mathfrak{M}'}$ in $\mathfrak{M}'$ is defined to be the image of $\bar{R}_{\mathfrak{M}}$ under the canonical map of $U_1 \cup \cdots \cup U_k$ into $U_1 \cup \cdots \cup U_k / \bar{E}_{\mathfrak{M}}$.

Just as in Chapter 3 we can prove that for each formula A of $\mathscr{L}$ which has, respectively, the values $\bar{A}_{\mathfrak{M}}$ and $\bar{A}_{\mathfrak{M}'}$, in $\mathfrak{M}$ and $\mathfrak{M}'$, $\bar{A}_{\mathfrak{M}}$ is closed under the equivalence relation $\bar{E}_{\mathfrak{M}}$ and $\bar{A}_{\mathfrak{M}'}$ is the image of $\bar{A}_{\mathfrak{M}}$ under the canonical map of $U_1 \cup \cdots \cup U_k$ into $U_1 \cup \cdots \cup U_k / \bar{E}_{\mathfrak{M}}$.

In particular, if A is a closed formula of $\mathscr{L}$, A is satisfied in $\mathfrak{M}$ if and only if it is satisfied in $\mathfrak{M}'$.

PROPOSITION 11: *A closed formula F of $\mathscr{L}$ is a normal consequence of a set $\mathscr{A}$ of closed formulas of $\mathscr{L}$ if and only if it is a consequence of $\mathscr{A} \cup \mathscr{E}_{\mathscr{L}}$.*
PROOF: Suppose F is a consequence of $\mathscr{A} \cup \mathscr{E}_{\mathscr{L}}$. Every normal model of $\mathscr{A}$ satisfies $\mathscr{E}_{\mathscr{L}}$ and hence satisfies F. Therefore F is a normal consequence of $\mathscr{A}$.

Suppose F is not a consequence of $\mathscr{A} \cup \mathscr{E}_{\mathscr{L}}$. Then there is some model $\mathfrak{M}$ of $\mathscr{A} \cup \mathscr{E}_{\mathscr{L}} \cup \{\neg F\}$. The normal model $\mathfrak{M}'$ derived from $\mathfrak{M}$ satisfies

$\mathscr{A}$ but does not satisfy F. Hence F is not a normal consequence of $\mathscr{A}$.

The Finiteness Theorem for the predicate calculus with k types of objects, with equality, can be deduced from the Finiteness Theorem for predicate calculus without equality (Theorem 5) in the same way as in Chapter 3. For the record we state this result now.

THEOREM 12: *Let $\mathscr{A}$ be a set of closed formulas of the language $\mathscr{L}$ with equality such that every finite subset of $\mathscr{A}$ has a normal model, then $\mathscr{A}$ has a normal model.*

We also have an Interpolation Lemma for the predicate calculus with equality as follows:

THEOREM 13: *Let F and G be two closed formulas of the language $\mathscr{L}$ with equality such that $F \wedge G$ does not have a normal model. Then there is a closed formula H of $\mathscr{L}$ whose relation symbols, other than equality, and types are common to F and G, and such that $F \rightarrow H$ and $G \rightarrow \neg H$ are normal theorems.*

PROOF: Let $\mathscr{L}$ be the language of $F \wedge G$, $\mathscr{L}_1$ the language built up from the symbols and types which are in F but not in G, $\mathscr{L}_2$ the language built up from the symbols and types common to F and G and $\mathscr{L}_3$ the language built up from the symbols and types which are in G but not in F.

It will be sufficient to show that the set

$$\mathscr{A} = \{F, G, \mathscr{E}_{\mathscr{L}_1 \cup \mathscr{L}_2}, \mathscr{E}_{\mathscr{L}_2 \cup \mathscr{L}_3}\}$$

(by a natural misuse of language we write $\mathscr{E}_{\mathscr{L}}$ for the conjunction of the formulas of $\mathscr{E}_{\mathscr{L}}$) does not have a model. For suppose that we have proved this. Then by the Interpolation Lemma (Theorem 8) applied to the formulas $\mathscr{E}_{\mathscr{L}_1 \cup \mathscr{L}_2} \wedge F$, $\mathscr{E}_{\mathscr{L}_2 \cup \mathscr{L}_3} \wedge G$, there is a closed formula H of $\mathscr{L}_2$ such that $\mathscr{E}_{\mathscr{L}_1 \cup \mathscr{L}_2}, F \vdash H$ and $\mathscr{E}_{\mathscr{L}_2 \cup \mathscr{L}_3}, G \vdash \neg H$ and so $F \rightarrow H$ and $G \rightarrow \neg H$ are normal theorems.

Suppose then that $\mathfrak{M}$ is a model of $\mathscr{A}$. Let V_1 be the union of the domains of $\mathfrak{M}$ of types which are in $\mathscr{L}_1$, and let V_2, V_3 be defined similarly for $\mathscr{L}_2$ and $\mathscr{L}_3$. We define a model $\mathfrak{M}_1$ of $\mathscr{A}$ which has the same domains as $\mathfrak{M}$ as follows.

If R is an n-ary relation symbol of $\mathscr{L}(R \in R_{\mathscr{L}}^{(n)})$ which has the value $\bar{R}_{\mathfrak{M}}$ in $\mathfrak{M}$ then we let $\bar{R}_{\mathfrak{M}_1}$, the value of R in $\mathfrak{M}_1$, be defined by

$$\bar{R}_{\mathfrak{M}_1} = \{(u_1, \ldots, u_n) \in (V_1 \cup V_2 \cup V_3)^n : (u_1, \ldots, u_n) \in \bar{R}_{\mathfrak{M}} \text{ and } u_1, \ldots, u_n \text{ are all elements of } V_1 \cup V_2 \text{ or all elements of } V_2 \cup V_3\}.$$

If S is a relation symbol of $\mathscr{L}$ of type $(i_1, \ldots, i_n)$ which has the value

$\bar{S}_{\mathfrak{M}}$ in $\mathfrak{M}$ we put $\bar{S}_{\mathfrak{M}_1} = \bar{S}_{\mathfrak{M}}$. (Note that the types $i_1, \ldots, i_n$ which occur in S either all belong to $\mathscr{L}_1 \cup \mathscr{L}_2$ if S occurs in F or all belong to $\mathscr{L}_2 \cup \mathscr{L}_3$ if S occurs in G. Hence if $(u_1, \ldots, u_n) \in \bar{S}_{\mathfrak{M}_1}$, $u_1, \ldots, u_n$ either all belong to $V_1 \cup V_2$ or all belong to $V_2 \cup V_3$.) Clearly $\mathfrak{M}$ and $\mathfrak{M}_1$ satisfy the same formulas of $\mathscr{L}_1 \cup \mathscr{L}_2$ and of $\mathscr{L}_2 \cup \mathscr{L}_3$ and therefore $\mathfrak{M}_1$ is a model of $\mathscr{A}$.

We define an equivalence relation $\tilde{E}$ on $V_1 \cup V_2 \cup V_3$ as follows: $(x, y) \in \tilde{E}$ if and only if either

i) $(x, y) \in \bar{E}_{\mathfrak{M}_1}$, or

ii) $x \in V_1$, $y \in V_3$ and for some $z \in V_2$, $(x, z) \in \bar{E}_{\mathfrak{M}_1}$ and $(z, y) \in \bar{E}_{\mathfrak{M}_1}$, or

iii) $x \in V_3$, $y \in V_1$ and for some $z \in V_2$, $(x, z) \in \bar{E}_{\mathfrak{M}_1}$ and $(z, y) \in \bar{E}_{\mathfrak{M}_1}$.

It is clear that $\tilde{E}$ is reflexive and symmetric. On $V_1 \cup V_2$ it is identical with $\bar{E}_{\mathfrak{M}_1}$ and hence is an equivalence relation on $V_1 \cup V_2$ since $\mathfrak{M}_1$ satisfies $\mathscr{E}_{\mathscr{L}_1 \cup \mathscr{L}_2}$. Similarly, on $V_2 \cup V_3$ it is identical with $\bar{E}_{\mathfrak{M}_1}$ and hence is an equivalence relation on $V_2 \cup V_3$ since $\mathfrak{M}_1$ satisfies $\mathscr{E}_{\mathscr{L}_2 \cup \mathscr{L}_3}$.

Now suppose $(x, y) \in \tilde{E}$ and $(y, z) \in \tilde{E}$ with, say $x, z \in V_1$ and $y \in V_3$. Then, by definition there exist $u, v \in V_2$ such that $(x, u), (u, y), (y, v), (v, z) \in \bar{E}_{\mathfrak{M}_1}$. Since $\bar{E}_{\mathfrak{M}_1}$ is an equivalence relation on $V_2 \cup V_3$, $(u, v) \in E_{\mathfrak{M}_1}$ and therefore $(x, z) \in \bar{E}_{\mathfrak{M}_1}$ whence $(x, z) \in \tilde{E}$ because $x, z \in V_1$. Therefore $\tilde{E}$ is indeed an equivalence relation on V.

For each n-ary relation symbol R, $(R \in R_{\mathscr{L}}^{(n)})$, we define $\tilde{R}$ by

$$\tilde{R} = \{(u_1, \ldots, u_n) \in V^n\text{: there is } (v_1, \ldots, v_n) \in V^n \text{ with } (u_1, v_1), \ldots, (u_n, v_n) \in \tilde{E} \text{ and } (v_1, \ldots, v_n) \in \bar{R}_{\mathfrak{M}_1}\}.$$

For each relation symbol S of type $(i_1, \ldots, i_n)$ we put

$$\tilde{S} = \bar{S}_{\mathfrak{M}_1} = \bar{S}_{\mathfrak{M}}.$$

The values of $\tilde{E}$ and of the $\tilde{R}$ and $\tilde{S}$ define a realization $\tilde{\mathfrak{M}}$ of $\mathscr{L}$ which has the same domains as $\mathfrak{M}$ and $\mathfrak{M}_1$.

We show first that $\tilde{\mathfrak{M}}$ satisfies $\mathscr{E}_{\mathscr{L}}$. Suppose that $(u_1, \ldots, u_n) \in \tilde{R}$, where $R \in R_{\mathscr{L}}^{(n)}$, and that $(u_1, v_1), \ldots, (u_n, v_n) \in \tilde{E}$. Then, by the definition of $\tilde{R}$, there is $(u_1', \ldots, u_n') \in \bar{R}_{\mathfrak{M}_1}$ with $(u_1, u_1'), \ldots, (u_n, u_n') \in \tilde{E}$. But then (u_1', v_1), $\ldots, (u_n', v_n) \in \tilde{E}$ and so, by the definition of $\tilde{R}$, $(v_1, \ldots, v_n) \in \tilde{R}$. This shows that the axioms for equality which involve the relation symbol R are satisfied in $\tilde{\mathfrak{M}}$.

Now suppose that S is a relation symbol of type $(i_1, \ldots, i_n)$ of $\mathscr{L}$. If, say, S occurs in F then all the types $i_1, \ldots, i_n$ are in $\mathscr{L}_1 \cup \mathscr{L}_2$. Therefore the axiom of equality for S is satisfied in $\mathfrak{M}_1$ since $\mathfrak{M}_1$ satisfies $\mathscr{E}_{\mathscr{L}_1 \cup \mathscr{L}_2}$, and hence by $\tilde{\mathfrak{M}}$ because $\tilde{S} = \bar{S}_{\mathfrak{M}_1}$.

Therefore $\tilde{\mathfrak{M}}$ satisfies $\mathscr{E}_{\mathscr{L}}$.

Next we show that if $R \in R_{\mathscr{L}}^{(n)}$ and if $u_1, \ldots, u_n$ are all in $V_1 \cup V_2$ or all in $V_2 \cup V_3$ then

$$(u_1, \ldots, u_n) \in \tilde{R} \quad \text{if and only if} \quad (u_1, \ldots, u_n) \in \bar{R}_{\mathfrak{M}_1}. \tag{1}$$

Suppose $(u_1, \ldots, u_n) \in \bar{R}_{\mathfrak{M}_1}$, then certainly $(u_1, \ldots, u_n) \in \tilde{R}$. Conversely suppose that $(u_1, \ldots, u_n) \in \tilde{R}$ and $u_1, \ldots, u_n$ are all in $V_1 \cup V_2$. Then by the definition of $\tilde{R}$ there are $v_1, \ldots, v_n$ such that $(u_1, v_1), \ldots, (u_n, v_n) \in \tilde{E}$ and $(v_1, \ldots, v_n) \in \bar{R}_{\mathfrak{M}_1}$. It follows that $v_1, \ldots, v_n$ are either all in $V_1 \cup V_2$ or all in $V_2 \cup V_3$.

If $v_1, \ldots, v_n$ are all in $V_1 \cup V_2$, since $(u_i, v_i) \in \tilde{E}$ $(1 \leqslant i \leqslant n)$, $(u_i, v_i) \in \bar{E}_{\mathfrak{M}_1}$ and therefore, because $\mathfrak{M}_1$ satisfies $\mathscr{E}_{\mathscr{L}_1 \cup \mathscr{L}_2}$, $(u_1, \ldots, u_n) \in \bar{R}_{\mathfrak{M}_1}$.

Now suppose that $v_1, \ldots, v_n$ are all in $V_2 \cup V_3$. If $v_i \in V_3$ $(1 \leqslant i \leqslant n)$, as $(u_i, v_i) \in \tilde{E}$ there is some w_i (possibly $w_i = u_i$) in V_2 such that $(u_i, w_i) \in \bar{E}_{\mathfrak{M}_1}$ and $(w_i, v_i) \in \bar{E}_{\mathfrak{M}_1}$. If $v_i \in V_2$ we put $w_i = v_i$ and the same relations hold between u_i, v_i and w_i. Because $\mathfrak{M}_1$ satisfies $\mathscr{E}_{\mathscr{L}_2 \cup \mathscr{L}_3}$ and $(v_1, \ldots, v_n) \in \bar{R}_{\mathfrak{M}_1}$ it follows that $(w_1, \ldots, w_n) \in \bar{R}_{\mathfrak{M}_1}$. Hence because $\mathfrak{M}_1$ satisfies $\mathscr{E}_{\mathscr{L}_1 \cup \mathscr{L}_2}$ we can deduce that $(u_1, \ldots, u_n) \in \bar{R}_{\mathfrak{M}_1}$. This proves the result (1).

Therefore $\tilde{\mathfrak{M}}$ and $\mathfrak{M}_1$ satisfy the same formulas of $\mathscr{L}_1 \cup \mathscr{L}_2$ and of $\mathscr{L}_2 \cup \mathscr{L}_3$. Thus $\tilde{\mathfrak{M}}$ satisfies F and G. Since $\tilde{\mathfrak{M}}$ satisfies $\mathscr{E}_{\mathscr{L}}$, $\mathscr{E}_{\mathscr{L}} \cup \{F, G\}$ has a model and so, by Proposition 9, $F \wedge G$ has a normal model which contradicts our hypothesis.

This completes the proof of the Interpolation Lemma.

LANGUAGES WITH k TYPES OF OBJECTS, WITH EQUALITY, WHICH HAVE FUNCTION SYMBOLS

In this section we restrict ourselves to giving definitions and stating results. The proofs of these results can be found in Exercise 1.

A language $\mathscr{L}$ with k types of variables, with equality and with function symbols is a language which consists of

1) k infinite disjoint sets $V_{\mathscr{L}}^{(1)}, \ldots, V_{\mathscr{L}}^{(k)}$. The elements of $V_{\mathscr{L}}^{(i)}$ $(1 \leqslant i \leqslant k)$ are the variables of $\mathscr{L}$ of type i;

2) for each integer $n \geqslant 0$, a set $R_{\mathscr{L}}^{(n)}$ whose elements are called n-ary relation symbols (with variables of arbitrary type). We also assume that $R_{\mathscr{L}}^{(2)}$ is

not empty and that it contains a distinguished element E which is called the identity or equality symbol;
3) for each sequence $(i_1, \ldots, i_n)$ of integers between 1 and k, a set $S_{\mathscr{L}}^{(i_1, \ldots, i_n)}$ whose elements are called relation symbols of type $(i_1, \ldots, i_n)$;
4) for each sequence $(i, i_1, \ldots, i_n)$ $(n \geqslant 0)$ of integers between 1 and k, a set $F_{\mathscr{L}}^{(i, i_1, \ldots, i_n)}$ whose elements are called function symbols of type $(i, i_1, \ldots, i_n)$; $i_1, \ldots, i_n$ are called the argument types, i the value type.

We assume that these sets are pairwise disjoint. We define (see Exercise 1) the set $\mathscr{T}$ of terms of $\mathscr{L}$. $\mathscr{T}$ is divided into k disjoint sets $\mathscr{T}_1, \ldots, \mathscr{T}_k$. $\mathscr{T}_i (1 \leqslant i \leqslant k)$ is the set of terms of (value) type i of $\mathscr{L}$.

The atomic formulas of $\mathscr{L}$ are those which are of one of the following forms:

i) $R(t_1, \ldots, t_n)$ where $R \in R_{\mathscr{L}}^{(n)}$ and $t_1, \ldots, t_n$ are terms of arbitrary type. In particular $E(t_1, t_2)$ is an atomic formula which will be written as $t_1 = t_2$;

ii) $S(t_1^{(i_1)}, \ldots, t_n^{(i_n)})$ where S is a relation symbol of type $(i_1, \ldots, i_n)$ and $t_1^{(i_1)}, \ldots, t_n^{(i_n)}$ are terms of types $i_1, \ldots, i_n$ respectively.

The set of formulas of $\mathscr{L}$ is the set of function schemas built up with the atomic formulas as 0-ary symbols, $\neg$ and $\bigvee x$ (for each $x \in V_{\mathscr{L}}^{(1)} \cup \cdots \cup V_{\mathscr{L}}^{(k)}$) as unary symbols and $\vee$ as the only binary symbol.

We define a *normal realization* of $\mathscr{L}$ to consist of
1) k non-empty sets $U_1, \ldots, U_k$. The set $U_i (1 \leqslant i \leqslant k)$ is called the domain of the realization of type i;
2) for each integer $n \geqslant 0$, a map $R \to \bar{R}$ of $R_{\mathscr{L}}^{(n)}$ into $\mathscr{P}((U_1 \cup \cdots \cup U_k)^n)$. We insist that $\bar{E}$ is the identity relation on $U_1, \ldots, U_k$, that is the set of pairs (u, u) with $u \in U_1 \cup \cdots \cup U_k$;
3) for each sequence $(i_1, \ldots, i_n)$ of integers between 1 and k a map $S \to \bar{S}$ of $S_{\mathscr{L}}^{(i_1, \ldots, i_n)}$ into $\mathscr{P}(U_{i_1} \times \cdots \times U_{i_n})$;
4) for each sequence $(i, i_1, \ldots, i_n)$ of integers between 1 and k a map $f \to \bar{f}$ of $F_{\mathscr{L}}^{(i, i_1, \ldots, i_n)}$ into the set of maps of $U_{i_1} \times \cdots \times U_{i_n}$ into U_i.

Let δ be an element of $U_1^{V_{\mathscr{L}}^{(1)}} \times \cdots \times U_k^{V_{\mathscr{L}}^{(k)}}$, in other words δ is a map of $V_{\mathscr{L}}^{(1)} \cup \cdots \cup V_{\mathscr{L}}^{(k)}$ into $U_1 \cup \cdots \cup U_k$ such that $\delta(V_{\mathscr{L}}^{(i)}) \subseteq U_i$ for each $i (1 \leqslant i \leqslant k)$. Then δ can be extended in a natural way to a map, which we also denote by δ, of $\mathscr{T}$ into $U_1 \cup \cdots \cup U_k$ such that $\delta(\mathscr{T}_i) \subseteq U_i$ for each $i (1 \leqslant i \leqslant k)$.

The value $\bar{F}$ of a formula F in the realization of $\mathscr{L}$ we have just described is a sub-set of $U_1^{V_{\mathscr{L}}^{(1)}} \times \cdots \times U_k^{V_{\mathscr{L}}^{(k)}}$, which is defined by recursion on the length of F as follows:
a) if F is an atomic formula it can be written $R(t_1, \ldots, t_n)$ where $R \in R_{\mathscr{L}}^{(n)}$

or $R \in S_{\mathscr{L}}^{(i_1, \dots, i_n)}$. Then $\bar{F}$, the value of F is defined by

$$\bar{F} = \{\delta \in U_1^{V_{\mathscr{L}}^{(1)}} \times \cdots \times U_k^{V_{\mathscr{L}}^{(k)}} : (\delta(t_1), \dots, \delta(t_n)) \in \bar{R}\};$$

b) $\overline{F \vee G} = \bar{F} \cup \bar{G}$, $\overline{\neg F} = \mathrm{c}\bar{F}$.

$\overline{\bigvee xF}$ = the projection of $\bar{F}$ along the variable x, that is $\overline{\bigvee xF}$ is the set of those $\delta \in U_1^{V_{\mathscr{L}}^{(1)}} \times \cdots \times U_k^{V_{\mathscr{L}}^{(k)}}$ such that there is some $\delta_1 \in \bar{F}$ which is equal to δ for all variables of $\mathscr{L}$ except possibly x.

We can define the notions of a formula F being satisfied by a realization $\mathfrak{M}$ and of a closed formula F being a consequence of a set $\mathscr{A}$ of closed formulas in the same way as at the beginning of this chapter.

The Finiteness Theorem expressed as in Theorem 12, remains true for languages with function symbols.

The Interpolation Lemma can be stated as

THEOREM 14: *Let F and G be two closed formulas of a language $\mathscr{L}$ with k types of objects, with equality, which contains function symbols. If $F \wedge G$ does not have a normal model there is a closed formula H of $\mathscr{L}$ whose relation symbols (other than $=$), function symbols and types are common to F and G and such that $F \to H$ and $G \to \neg H$ are normal theorems.* (The *types of a formula* are, by definition, the types of the variables occurring in A and the value types of its function symbols.)

The proof of this result can be found in Exercise 1.

THE THEORY OF FINITE TYPES

Let $\mathfrak{T}$ be the smallest set which has the following properties:

1) $0 \in \mathfrak{T}$;

2) if $\tau_1, \dots, \tau_n \in \mathfrak{T}$ then the ordered n-tuple $(\tau_1, \dots, \tau_n)$ is also an element of $\mathfrak{T}$.

The elements of $\mathfrak{T}$ are called *types*. If τ is a type other than 0 there are types $\tau_1, \dots, \tau_n$ such that $\tau = (\tau_1, \dots, \tau_n)$, since the set of all types which have this property satisfies conditions 1) and 2) above. Clearly the integer n and the types $\tau_1, \dots, \tau_n$ are uniquely determined by the type τ.

Given a type τ there is an integer $N \geqslant 0$ which has the following property: each sequence $\tau_1, \dots, \tau_k$ of types other than 0 which is such that $\tau_k = \tau$ and, for $1 \leqslant i \leqslant k$, τ_i is one of the elements of the n-tuple making up τ_{i+1}, is of length $k \leqslant N$. This can be seen at once because the set of all types for which such an integer N exists satisfies the conditions 1) and 2) above. The *rank* of τ is the least integer N with this property. It follows that the rank of τ is the length of the longest sequence $\tau_1, \ldots, \tau_k$ of types other than 0 such that $\tau_k = \tau$ and, for $1 \leqslant i < k$, τ_i is one of the elements of the n-tuple making up τ_{i+1}.

Let $r(\tau)$ be the rank of the type τ which is not 0. We put $r(0)=0$. We have at once that if $\tau = (\tau_1, \ldots, \tau_n)$ then $r(\tau) = 1 + \sup \{r(\tau_1), \ldots, r(\tau_n)\}$.

Given a type τ we let $[\tau]$, also called the *transitive closure* of τ, be the smallest set with the following properties

1′) $\tau \in [\tau]$;

2′) if $\tau' = (\tau_1, \ldots, \tau_n) \in [\tau]$ then $\tau_1, \ldots, \tau_n$ are all elements of $[\tau]$.

We can deduce from this definition that if $\tau = (\tau_1, \ldots, \tau_n)$ then $[\tau] = [\tau_1] \cup \cdots \cup [\tau_n] \cup \{\tau\}$. For $[\tau]$ has the two properties defining $[\tau_i]$ $(1 \leqslant i \leqslant n)$ and so $[\tau_i] \subseteq [\tau]$ whence

$$[\tau_1] \cup \cdots \cup [\tau_n] \cup \{\tau\} \subseteq [\tau].$$

Conversely $[\tau_1] \cup \cdots \cup [\tau_n] \cup \{\tau\}$ has the two properties which define $[\tau]$ and hence this set contains $[\tau]$. It therefore follows that $[\tau]$ is a finite subset of $\mathfrak{T}$, since by the remarks above the set of those τ for which $[\tau]$ is a finite subset of $\mathfrak{T}$, has the properties 1) and 2) above and, being a subset of $\mathfrak{T}$, must therefore be identical with $\mathfrak{T}$.

LEMMA 15: *Each element of* $[\tau]$ *other than* τ *has rank less than that of* τ.
PROOF: This can be proved at once by induction on the rank of τ.

We define an order relation $\leqslant$ on $\mathfrak{T}$ by putting $\tau \leqslant \sigma$ if and only if $\tau \in [\sigma]$. Clearly $\tau \leqslant \tau$. If $\tau \leqslant \sigma$ and $\sigma \leqslant \tau$ then τ and σ are of equal rank, but $\tau \in [\sigma]$ and so $\tau = \sigma$. If $\sigma \leqslant \tau$ and $\tau \leqslant \upsilon$ it can easily be shown by induction on the rank of υ that $\sigma \leqslant \upsilon$. Hence $\leqslant$ is indeed an order relation on $\mathfrak{T}$.

We consider a language $\mathscr{L}$ with equality (in the sense of Chapter 3, so that $\mathscr{L}$ has just objects of one type) and the family of sets $\{V^\tau : \tau \in \mathfrak{T}$ and $\tau \neq 0\}$, where the sets V^τ are infinite, pairwise disjoint and disjoint from $\mathscr{L}$ and the set $\{\varepsilon_\tau : \tau \in \mathfrak{T}$ and $\tau \neq 0\}$, where the ε_τ are all different and are not elements of $\mathscr{L} \cup \bigcup_{\tau \neq 0} V^\tau$. Let V^0 be the set of variables of $\mathscr{L}$.

For each type τ we denote by $\mathscr{L}^\tau$ the language with several types of objects (in the sense which we have just explained) defined as follows:

The types of the objects of $\mathscr{L}^\tau$ are the types σ such that $\sigma \leqslant \tau$. The set of variables of type σ is V^σ.

The function symbols of $\mathscr{L}^\tau$ are the function symbols of $\mathscr{L}$ regarded as having arguments and values of type 0.

The relation symbols of $\mathscr{L}^\tau$ are

1) the relation symbols of $\mathscr{L}$, except for the equality symbol, considered as having all their variables of type 0, and the equality symbol of $\mathscr{L}^\tau$ is that of $\mathscr{L}$; and

2) the symbols ε_σ for $\sigma \neq 0$, $\sigma \leqslant \tau$. If $\sigma = (\sigma_1, \ldots, \sigma_n)$ then ε_σ is an $n+1$-ary relation symbol of type $(\sigma_1, \ldots, \sigma_n, \sigma)$.

The variables of type σ will be denoted by x^σ, y^σ etc.

Type 0 will also be called the type of the *individuals*; for instance, variables of type 0 will also be called *individual variables*. The type (0, 0, ..., 0) (a sequence of n zeros) will also be called type of *n-ary relations* (unary for $n=1$, binary for $n=2$). Type (0) will be called the type of sets of individuals, type ((0)) the type of sets of sets of individuals and so on.

If $\sigma = (\sigma_1, \ldots, \sigma_n)$ is a type $\leqslant \tau$, the formula

$$\varepsilon_\sigma (x_1^{\sigma_1}, \ldots, x_n^{\sigma_n}, x^\sigma)$$

which is an atomic formula of $\mathscr{L}^\tau$ will also be written as

$$(x_1^{\sigma_1}, \ldots, x_n^{\sigma_n})\, \varepsilon_\sigma\, x^\sigma$$

or as

$$(x_1^{\sigma_1}, \ldots, x_n^{\sigma_n})\, \varepsilon\, x^\sigma .$$

We call the language $\mathscr{L}^\tau$ *the language of order τ on $\mathscr{L}$*. The formulas of $\mathscr{L}^\tau$ are called *formulas of order τ of $\mathscr{L}$*. Since if $\tau \leqslant \tau'$ each formula of order τ is also a formula of order τ' in this case $\mathscr{L}^\tau \subseteq \mathscr{L}^{\tau'}$. The formulas of order 0 of $\mathscr{L}$ are the ordinary formulas of $\mathscr{L}$.

For each type τ we let $\mathscr{T}_\tau$ be the set of the following formulas of order τ

$$\bigwedge x^\alpha \bigwedge x^\beta (x^\alpha \neq x^\beta)\ \alpha, \beta \leqslant \tau, \alpha \neq \beta$$

$$\bigwedge x^\alpha \bigwedge y^\alpha (\bigwedge x_1^{\alpha_1} \ldots \bigwedge x_n^{\alpha_n} [(x_1^{\alpha_1}, \ldots, x_n^{\alpha_n})\, \varepsilon\, x^\alpha \leftrightarrow (x_1^{\sigma_1}, \ldots, x_n^{\sigma_n})\, \varepsilon\, y^\alpha] \rightarrow x^\alpha = y^\alpha)$$

for each type $\alpha \leqslant \tau$, with $\alpha = (\alpha_1, \ldots, \alpha_n)$. This formula is called the *Axiom of Extensionality of order α*.

A realization of order τ of $\mathscr{L}$ or a *τ-realization* is defined to be a normal realization of $\mathscr{L}^\tau$ which satisfies $\mathscr{T}_\tau$. Hence a realization of order 0 of $\mathscr{L}$ is a normal realization of $\mathscr{L}$ in the ordinary sense. The domains $E_\sigma (\sigma \leqslant \tau)$ of a realization of order τ of $\mathscr{L}$ are therefore disjoint. If $\sigma = (\sigma_1, \ldots, \sigma_n)$ and $a \in E_\sigma$, an element $(a_1, \ldots, a_n)$ of $E_{\sigma_1} \times \cdots \times E_{\sigma_n}$ such that $(a_1, \ldots, a_n, a) \in \bar{\varepsilon}_\sigma$, where $\bar{\varepsilon}_\sigma$ is the value of ε_σ in the given realization, is called a "member" of a in this realization. It follows from the Axioms of Extensionality that two elements a, b of E_σ which have the same "members" are identical.

Let $\mathfrak{M}_\tau$ be a realization of order τ of $\mathscr{L}$, that is, a model of $\mathscr{T}_\tau$ with domains $E_\sigma(\sigma \leqslant \tau)$. Clearly if $\tau' \leqslant \tau$ the restriction of $\mathfrak{M}_\tau$ to the language $\mathscr{L}^{\tau'}$ and to the domains $E_\sigma(\sigma \leqslant \tau')$ is a model of $\mathscr{T}_{\tau'}$, and so is a realization $\mathfrak{M}_{\tau'}$ of order τ' of $\mathscr{L}$.

$\mathfrak{M}_{\tau'}$ is said to be the realization of order τ' *induced* by $\mathfrak{M}_\tau$ and $\mathfrak{M}_\tau$ is said to be *built on* $\mathfrak{M}_{\tau'}$. In particular for $\tau'=0$, we can see that each realization of order τ induces an ordinary realization of $\mathscr{L}$ on which it is built.

THEOREM 16: *Let $\mathfrak{M}$ be a realization of order* 0 *of $\mathscr{L}$. There is a realization $\mathfrak{M}_\tau$ of order τ of $\mathscr{L}$ which is unique up to isomorphism and which is such that*

1) *$\mathfrak{M}_\tau$ is built on $\mathfrak{M}$;*

2) *each realization $\mathfrak{N}_\tau$ of order τ of $\mathscr{L}$ built on $\mathfrak{M}$ can be embedded in $\mathfrak{M}_\tau$ so as to preserve each element of $\mathfrak{M}$ and the $\bar{\varepsilon}_\sigma$ relations* (for $\sigma \leqslant \tau$).

$\mathfrak{M}_\tau$ is called the *principal realization of order* τ (or: *principal τ-realization*) *over* $\mathfrak{M}$.

PROOF: Let E_0 be the domain of $\mathfrak{M}$. We define the set E_σ, the domain of type σ of $\mathfrak{M}_\tau$ by recursion on the rank of σ as follows:

If $\sigma=(\sigma_1, \ldots, \sigma_n)$, E_σ is a set which is disjoint from all the previously defined E_α and of cardinal $2^{\mathfrak{m}}$ where $\mathfrak{m}$ is the cardinal of $E_{\sigma_1} \times \cdots \times E_{\sigma_n}$. Therefore there is a one-one map ϕ_σ of E_σ onto $\mathscr{P}(E_{\sigma_1} \times \cdots \times E_{\sigma_n})$. We let $\bar{\varepsilon}_\sigma$, the value of ε_σ in $\mathfrak{M}_\tau$ be defined by

$$\bar{\varepsilon}_\sigma = \{(a_1, \ldots, a_n, a) : a_1 \in E_{\sigma_1}, \ldots, a_n \in E_{\sigma_n} \quad \text{and} \quad (a_1, \ldots, a_n) \in \varphi_\sigma(a)\}.$$

Thus the "members" of $a \in E_\sigma$ in $\mathfrak{M}_\tau$ are the elements of $\phi_\sigma(a)$. Because ϕ_σ is a one-one map the Axiom of Extensionality of order σ is satisfied. We have therefore defined a realization $\mathfrak{M}_\tau$ of $\mathscr{L}$ of order τ, built on $\mathfrak{M}$ if we let the function symbols of $\mathscr{L}$ and the relation symbols other than the ε_σ have the same values as in $\mathfrak{M}$.

Let $\mathfrak{N}_\tau$ be a realization of order τ of $\mathscr{L}$, built on $\mathfrak{M}$ with domains $F_\sigma(\sigma \leqslant \tau)$. Therefore $E_0 = F_0$. We define by recursion on the rank of σ a one-one map i_σ of F_σ into E_σ as follows: i_0 is the identity map. If $\sigma=(\sigma_1, \ldots, \sigma_n)$ then for each $a \in F_\sigma$ let $\hat{a} = \{(a_1, \ldots, a_n) \in F_{\sigma_1} \times \cdots \times F_{\sigma_n} : (a_1, \ldots, a_n)$ is a "member" of a in $\mathfrak{N}_\tau\}$. By the Axiom of Extensionality of order σ the map $a \to \hat{a}$ is a one-one map of F_σ into $\mathscr{P}(F_{\sigma_1} \times \cdots \times F_{\sigma_n})$. From the one-one maps $i_{\sigma_1} : F_{\sigma_1} \to E_{\sigma_1}, \ldots, i_{\sigma_n} : F_{\sigma_n} \to E_{\sigma_n}$, which have already been defined we can derive a one-one map j of $\mathscr{P}(F_{\sigma_1} \times \cdots \times F_{\sigma_n})$ into $\mathscr{P}(E_{\sigma_1} \times \cdots \times E_{\sigma_n})$.

We then put $i_\sigma(a)=\phi_\sigma^{-1}\circ j(\hat{a})$. i_σ is certainly one-one since it is the composition of maps which are one-one. It follows from the definition that $(a_1, \ldots, a_n)$ is a "member" of a in $\mathfrak{N}_\tau$ if and only if $(i_{\sigma_1}(a_1), \ldots, i_{\sigma_n}(a_n))$ is a "member" of $i_\sigma(a)$ in $\mathfrak{M}_\tau$. Hence the set of maps $i_\sigma(\sigma \leqslant \tau)$ together make up an embedding of $\mathfrak{N}_\tau$ into $\mathfrak{M}_\tau$ which preserves $\mathfrak{M}$. Suppose now a realization $\mathfrak{N}_\tau$ satisfies the conditions established above for $\mathfrak{M}_\tau$. Then, in particular, $\mathfrak{M}_\tau$ can be embedded in $\mathfrak{N}_\tau$ by a mapping i preserving each element of $\mathfrak{M}$ and the relations $\bar{\varepsilon}_\sigma$ for $\sigma \leqslant \tau$. Suppose that σ, necessarily $\neq 0$, is a type of least rank for which i does not preserve $\bar{\varepsilon}_\sigma$. Since $\mathfrak{M}_\tau$ is embedded in $\mathfrak{N}_\tau$ there is an element a of F_σ which is not the image of any element of E_σ. Suppose $\sigma=(\sigma_1, \ldots, \sigma_n)$ and consider the "members" of a in $\mathfrak{N}_\tau$: they are n-tuples $(a_1, \ldots, a_n)$ where $a_1 \in F_{\sigma_1}, \ldots, a_n \in F_{\sigma_n}$. Since $\sigma_j < \sigma (1 \leqslant j \leqslant n)$, $i^{-1}(\{a_j\}) \neq \emptyset$; by construction of $\mathfrak{M}_\sigma$, there is a $b \in E_\sigma : b = \phi^{-1}\{(i^{-1}a_1, \ldots, i^{-1}a_n) : (a_1, \ldots, a_n)$ is a "member" of a in $\mathfrak{N}_\tau\}$. So a and $i(b)$ have the same "members" in $\mathfrak{N}_\tau$, yet are distinct. This contradicts the axiom of extensionality which $\mathfrak{N}_\tau$ is supposed to satisfy. Hence $\mathfrak{M}_\tau$ and $\mathfrak{N}_\tau$ are isomorphic, i.e., $\mathfrak{M}_\tau$ is unique, as required.

Remark. A non-principal realization on $\mathfrak{M}$ can in general be embedded in different ways in $\mathfrak{M}_\tau$; e.g. if $E=\{a, b\}$, $F_{(0)}=\{\{a\}\}$, $F_{((0))}=\{\{\{a\}\}\}$, the following map $F_{((0))} \to E_{(((0)))}$ is also an embedding: $a \to a$, $b \to b$; $\{a\} \to \{a\}$, $\{\{a\}\} \to \{\{a\}, \{b\}\}$ since $\{\{a\}, \{b\}\}$ has no "members" *in* $F_{(0)}$ other than $\{a\}$.

The embedding i of $\mathfrak{N}_\tau$ into $\mathfrak{M}_\tau$ defined in Theorem 16 is the *only* map j of $\bigcup \{F_\sigma : \sigma \leqslant \tau\}$ into $\bigcup \{E_\sigma : \sigma \leqslant \tau\}$ which satisfies the conditions:

(i) j preserves each element of $\mathfrak{M}$, and the $\bar{\varepsilon}_\sigma$-relations $(\sigma \leqslant \tau)$;

(ii) the image $j(\bigcup\{F_\sigma : \sigma \leqslant \tau\})$ is transitive in $\bigcup\{E_\sigma : \sigma \leqslant \tau\}$, where a subset S of $\bigcup\{E_\sigma : \sigma \leqslant \tau\}$ is called *transitive* whenever

$$a \in E_\sigma \wedge \sigma=(\sigma_1, \ldots, \sigma_n) \wedge (a_1, \ldots, a_n) \in \phi_\sigma a \Rightarrow (a_1 \in S \wedge \cdots \wedge a_n \in S).$$

The proof of uniqueness of $\mathfrak{M}_\tau$ itself given in Theorem 16 also applies here.

The embedding i of $\mathfrak{N}_\tau$ into $\mathfrak{M}_\tau$ will be called *canonical.*

Suppose now that the language $\mathscr{L}$ contains the single relation symbol $=$. A realization of $\mathscr{L}$ therefore consists of a non-empty set E, say. We denote by $\mathfrak{M}^\tau(E)$ the principal realization of order τ built on E. $\mathfrak{M}^\tau(E)$ is called the *hierarchy of simple types* $\leqslant \tau$ *on the set E*. It follows from the previous theorem that each realization $\mathfrak{N}^\tau(E)$ of order τ built on E can be canonically embedded in $\mathfrak{M}^\tau(E)$.

Let E, F be two non-empty sets such that $E \subseteq F$. Clearly each realization of order τ built on E, and, in particular, the principal realization $\mathfrak{M}^\tau(E)$, becomes a realization of order τ built on F if its domain of type 0 is extended to F, the domains of type $\sigma \leqslant \tau (\sigma \neq 0)$ being left unchanged. Hence there is a canonical embedding of $\mathfrak{M}^\tau(E)$ into $\mathfrak{M}^\tau(F)$ which is an extension of the identity map of E into F. Let $\mathfrak{R}^\tau(E)$ and $\mathfrak{R}^\tau(F)$ be two realizations of order τ built on E and F respectively. Then there are three canonical embeddings α, β, γ such that

$$\mathfrak{R}^\tau(E) \overset{\alpha}{\rightarrow} \mathfrak{M}^\tau(E) \overset{\beta}{\rightarrow} \mathfrak{M}^\tau(F)$$

$$\mathfrak{R}^\tau(F) \overset{\gamma}{\rightarrow} \mathfrak{M}^\tau(F).$$

$\mathfrak{R}^\tau(F)$ is said to be a *τ-extension* of $\mathfrak{R}^\tau(E)$ if and only if $\gamma\mathfrak{R}^\tau(F)$ is an extension (in the sense of realizations of the language $\mathscr{L}^\tau$) of $\beta\alpha\mathfrak{R}^\tau(E)$.

Now let E and F be two sets with a non-empty intersection, and let $\mathfrak{R}^\tau(E)$ and $\mathfrak{R}^\tau(F)$ be two realizations of order τ built on E and F respectively. Since $\mathfrak{M}^\tau(E \cap F)$ is the principal realization of order τ built on $E \cap F$ there are canonical embeddings α_1, β_1, α_2, β_2 such that

$$\mathfrak{R}^\tau(E) \overset{\alpha_1}{\rightarrow} \mathfrak{M}^\tau(E) \overset{\beta_1}{\leftarrow} \mathfrak{M}^\tau(E \cap F)$$

$$\mathfrak{R}^\tau(F) \overset{\alpha_2}{\rightarrow} \mathfrak{M}^\tau(F) \overset{\beta_2}{\leftarrow} \mathfrak{M}^\tau(E \cap F).$$

The *τ-intersection* of $\mathfrak{R}^\tau(E)$ and $\mathfrak{R}^\tau(F)$ is the realization $\mathfrak{R}^\tau(E \cap F)$ built on $E \cap F$ which is defined as follows: $\mathfrak{R}^\tau(E \cap F)$ is a sub-realization of $\mathfrak{M}^\tau(E \cap F)$ and if $\xi \in \mathfrak{M}^\tau(E \cap F)$ then $\xi \in \mathfrak{R}^\tau(E \cap F)$ if and only if $\beta_1 \xi \in \alpha_1 \mathfrak{R}^\tau(E)$ and $\beta_2 \xi \in \alpha_2 \mathfrak{R}^\tau(F)$.

These two definitions can easily be extended to the general case of a language $\mathscr{L}$ with a single type of variable. For suppose that $\mathfrak{M}$ is a realization of $\mathscr{L}$ with domain E. Then being given a realization of order τ built on $\mathfrak{M}$ is equivalent to being given $\mathfrak{M}$ and a realization $\mathfrak{R}^\tau(E)$ of order τ built on E. Thus given two realizations $\mathfrak{M}$ and $\mathfrak{N}$ of $\mathscr{L}$ with domains E and F respectively let $(\mathfrak{M}, \mathfrak{R}^\tau(E))$ and $(\mathfrak{N}, \mathfrak{R}^\tau(F))$ be two realizations of order τ of $\mathscr{L}$ built on $\mathfrak{M}$ and $\mathfrak{N}$ respectively. We say that $(\mathfrak{N}, \mathfrak{R}^\tau(F))$ is a *τ-extension* of $(\mathfrak{M}, \mathfrak{R}^\tau(E))$ if and only if $\mathfrak{N}$ is an extension of $\mathfrak{M}$ and $\mathfrak{R}^\tau(F)$ is a τ-extension of $\mathfrak{R}^\tau(E)$.

If $\mathfrak{M}$ and $\mathfrak{N}$ agree on the set $E \cap F$, which we suppose is not empty (that is to say if the values of the relation and function symbols of $\mathscr{L}$ in $\mathfrak{M}$ and $\mathfrak{N}$ agree on $E \cap F$) then $\mathfrak{M} \cap \mathfrak{N}$ is a realization of $\mathscr{L}$ with domain $E \cap F$. The τ-intersection of $(\mathfrak{M}, \mathfrak{R}^\tau(E))$ and $(\mathfrak{N}, \mathfrak{R}^\tau(F))$ is the realization of order τ of $\mathscr{L}$ built on $\mathfrak{M}\cap\mathfrak{N}$ which is given by the pair $(\mathfrak{M}\cap\mathfrak{N}, \mathfrak{R}^\tau(E\cap F))$ where $\mathfrak{R}^\tau(E\cap F)$ is the τ-intersection of $\mathfrak{R}^\tau(E)$ and $\mathfrak{R}^\tau(F)$.

Exercises

1. Languages with k types of objects which have function symbols.

i) Give a definition for the sets $\mathscr{T}_1, \ldots, \mathscr{T}_k$ of terms of $\mathscr{L}$, a language with k types of object which has function symbols. Prove that given any normal realization of $\mathscr{L}$ with domains $U_1, \ldots, U_k$, each element δ of $U_1^{V_{\mathscr{L}}^{(1)}} \times \cdots \times U_k^{V_{\mathscr{L}}^{(k)}}$ can be extended in a unique manner to a map $\hat{\delta}$ of $\mathscr{T}_i$ into U_i (for each i, $1 \leqslant i \leqslant k$) in such a way that

a) $\hat{\delta}(x^{(i)}) = \delta(x^{(i)})$ for each variable $x^{(i)}$, and

b) $\hat{\delta}(f(t_1, \ldots, t_n)) = \bar{f}(\hat{\delta}(t_1), \ldots, \hat{\delta}(t_n))$, for each function symbol f of type $(i, i_1, \ldots, i_n)$ and each sequence $t_1, \ldots, t_n$ of terms of types $i_1, \ldots, i_n$ respectively.

ii) Let $\mathscr{L}_0$ be the language with k types of objects, with equality, which does not have any function symbols, whose relation symbols are those of $\mathscr{L}$ together with a relation symbol S_f of type $(i, i_1, \ldots, i_n)$ for each function symbol f of type $(i, i_1, \ldots, i_n)$ of $\mathscr{L}$. We assume that the symbols S_f are all different and do not occur in $\mathscr{L}$.

There corresponds to each formula F of $\mathscr{L}_0$ a formula F^* of $\mathscr{L}$ which is obtained from F by substituting the atomic formula $x^{(i)} = f(x_1^{(i_1)}, \ldots, x_n^{(i_n)})$ for each occurrence of the atomic formula $S_f(x^{(i}, x_1^{(i_1)}, \ldots, x_n^{(i_n)})$ in F.

Show that for each formula Φ of $\mathscr{L}$ there is an equivalent formula of $\mathscr{L}$ which has the same relation symbols (except perhaps equality), and the same function symbols and free variables, and the same types as Φ and which is of the form F^*.

iii) Let $\mathscr{A}_0$ be the set of the following formulas of $\mathscr{L}_0$

$$\wedge x_1^{(i_1)} \ldots \wedge x_n^{(i_n)} \vee x^{(i)} [S_f(x^{(i)}, x_1^{(i_1)}, \ldots, x_n^{(i_n)})]$$

and

$$\wedge x_1^{(i_1)} \ldots \wedge x_n^{(i_n)} \wedge x^{(i)} \wedge y^{(i)} [S_f(x^{(i)}, x_1^{(i_1)}, \ldots, x_n^{(i_n)}) \wedge S_f(y^{(i)}, x_1^{(i_1)}, \ldots, x_n^{(i_n)}) \rightarrow x^{(i)} = y^{(i)}]$$

for each function symbol f (of type $(i, i_1, \ldots, i_n)$) of $\mathscr{L}$.

Establish a one-one correspondence between the normal models of $\mathscr{A}_0$ and the realizations of $\mathscr{L}$ such that if $\mathfrak{M}$ is a realization of $\mathscr{L}$ and $\mathfrak{M}_0$

is the corresponding model of $\mathscr{A}_0$, for each closed formula F of $\mathscr{L}_0$, F is satisfied by $\mathfrak{M}_0$ if and only if F^* is satisfied by $\mathfrak{M}$.

Deduce from this the Finiteness Theorem and the Interpolation Lemma for the language $\mathscr{L}$.

Answer.

i) Let Z be the set of function schemas built with the elements of $V_{\mathscr{L}}^{(1)} \cup \cdots \cup V_{\mathscr{L}}^{(k)}$ as 0-ary symbols, and the elements of $F_{\mathscr{L}}^{(i, i_1, \ldots, i_n)}$ as n-ary symbols, for each sequence $(i, i_1, \ldots, i_n)$ of integers between 1 and k.

An element ξ of Z is said to be of type i if $\xi \in V_{\mathscr{L}}^{(i)}$ or if ξ begins with a function symbol $f \in F_{\mathscr{L}}^{(i, i_1, \ldots, i_n)}$, that is with a function symbol whose values are of type i. Let Z_i be the set of schemas of type i. Then the Z_i are pairwise disjoint and $Z = Z_1 \cup \cdots \cup Z_k$.

We define a map J of Z into $\{0,1\}$ by recursion on the length of the elements as follows:

$J(x) = 1$, for each variable x of $\mathscr{L}$.

If $\xi \in Z$ and ξ is not a variable of $\mathscr{L}$, ξ can be written uniquely in the form $f(\xi_1, \ldots, \xi_n)$ where $f \in F_{\mathscr{L}}^{(i, i_1, \ldots, i_n)}$ and $\xi_1, \ldots, \xi_n \in Z$. We put $J(\xi) = 1$ if $J(\xi_1) = \cdots = J(\xi_n) = 1$ and $\xi_1, \ldots, \xi_n$ are of types $i_1, \ldots, i_n$, respectively. Otherwise $J(\xi) = 0$.

Then we define the set $\mathscr{T}$ of terms of $\mathscr{L}$ to be the set of elements $\xi \in Z$ such that $J(\xi) = 1$. The set $\mathscr{T}_i$ of terms (whose value is) of type i of $\mathscr{L}$ is $Z_i \cap \mathscr{T}$.

LEMMA: *t is a term of type i if and only if t is a variable of type i or $t = f(t_1, \ldots, t_n)$ with $f \in F_{\mathscr{L}}^{(i, i_1, \ldots, i_n)}$, where $t_1, \ldots, t_n$ are terms of types $i_1, \ldots, i_n$ respectively: $f, t_1, \ldots, t_n$ are uniquely determined in this latter case.*

PROOF: If $t \in \mathscr{T}_i$ then $t \in Z$ and so t is either a variable or can be written uniquely as $t = f(t_1, \ldots, t_n)$ with $f \in F_{\mathscr{L}}^{(i, i_1, \ldots, i_n)}$ and $t_1, \ldots, t_n \in Z$. Since $J(t) = 1$, $J(t_1) = \cdots = J(t_n) = 1$ and so $t_1, \ldots, t_n$ are of types $i_1, \ldots, i_n$, respectively.

Conversely, if $t_1, \ldots, t_n$ are terms of types $i_1, \ldots, i_n$ respectively, then $f(t_1, \ldots, t_n)$ is a term of type i because $J(f(t_1, \ldots, t_n)) = 1$.

Now let $\mathfrak{M}$ be a realization of $\mathscr{L}$ with domains $U_1, \ldots, U_k$. For each $f \in F_{\mathscr{L}}^{(i, i_1, \ldots, i_n)}$ let $\bar{f}$ be the value of f in $\mathfrak{M}$. $\bar{f}$ is a map of $U_{i_1} \times \cdots \times U_{i_n}$ into U_i. Suppose we are given a map δ such that, for each $i (1 \leqslant i \leqslant k)$, $\delta(V_{\mathscr{L}}^{(i)}) \subseteq U_i$. We define the extension $\hat{\delta}$ of δ to the set of terms by recursion on the length of the terms as follows: If $t = f(t_1, \ldots, t_n)$ is a term of type i, with $f \in F_{\mathscr{L}}^{(i, i_1, \ldots, i_n)}$, $t_1 \in T_{i_1}, \ldots, t_n \in T_{i_n}$, then $\hat{\delta}(t) = \bar{f}(\delta(t_1), \ldots, \delta(t_n))$.

It can be seen at once that this extension of δ is a map of $\mathscr{T}_i$ into U_i for each $i (1 \leqslant i \leqslant k)$ which has the required properties.

ii) Suppose that Φ is an atomic formula of $\mathscr{L}$ of the form $x^{(i)} = t^{(i)}$, where $x^{(i)}$ is a variable of type i, and $t^{(i)}$ is a term of type i. We will prove, by induction on the length of $t^{(i)}$ that it is equivalent to a formula of the form F^*.

This is obvious if $t^{(i)}$ is of length 1 because then it is either a variable or a constant symbol of type i. If $t^{(i)}$ is of length $h > 1$ then $t^{(i)} = f(t_1^{(i_1)}, \dots, t_n^{(i_n)})$, with $f \in F_{\mathscr{L}}^{(i, i_1, \dots, i_n)}$ and where $t_1^{(i_1)}, \dots, t_n^{(i_n)}$ are terms of types $i_1, \dots, i_n$ respectively. Then $x^{(i)} = t^{(i)}$ is equivalent to

$$\bigvee x_1^{(i_1)} \dots \bigvee x_n^{(i_n)} [x_1^{(i_1)} = t_1^{(i_1)} \wedge \cdots \wedge x_n^{(i_n)} = t_n^{(i_n)} \wedge x^{(i)} = f(x_1^{(i_1)}, \dots, x_n^{(i_n)})]$$

provided none of the variables $x_1^{(i_1)}, \dots, x_n^{(i_n)}$ occurs in any of the terms $t_1, \dots, t_n$. (An analogous restriction is tacitly understood throughout the present exercise.)

By hypothesis, $x_1^{(i_1)} = t_1^{(i_1)}, \dots, x_n^{(i_n)} = t_n^{(i_n)}$ are respectively equivalent to $F_1^*, \dots, F_n^*$. Thus $x^{(i)} = t^{(i)}$ is equivalent to

$$\bigvee x_1^{(i_1)} \dots \bigvee x_n^{(i_n)} [F_1^* \wedge \cdots \wedge F_n^* \wedge x^{(i)} = f(x_1^{(i_1)}, \dots, x_n^{(i_n)})]$$

that is, to F^*, where F is the following formula of $\mathscr{L}_0$, namely

$$\bigvee x_1^{(i_1)} \dots \bigvee x_n^{(i_n)} [F_1 \wedge \cdots \wedge F_n \wedge S_f(x^{(i)}, x_1^{(i_1)}, \dots, x_n^{(i_n)})].$$

Further, the function symbols and types which occur in the formula $x^{(i)} = t^{(i)}$ are those which occur in $x_1^{(i_1)} = t_1^{(i_1)}, \dots, x_n^{(i_n)} = t_n^{(i_n)}$, and $x^{(i)} = f(x_1^{(i_1)}, \dots, x_n^{(i_n)})$. By the induction hypothesis they are those which occur in $F_1^*, \dots, F_n^*, x^{(i)} = f(x_1^{(i_1)}, \dots, x_n^{(i_n)})$ and thus those which occur in F^*.

Now let Φ be an arbitrary atomic formula of $\mathscr{L}$. Φ is $R(t_1^{(i_1)}, \dots, t_n^{(i_n)})$, say, where R is an n-ary relation symbol ($R \in R_{\mathscr{L}}^{(n)}$ or $R \in S_{\mathscr{L}}^{(i_1, \dots, i_n)}$) and $t_1^{(i_1)}, \dots, t_n^{(i_n)}$ are terms of types $i_1, \dots, i_n$ respectively.

Then Φ is equivalent to

$$\bigvee x_1^{(i_1)} \dots \bigvee x_n^{(i_n)} [x_1^{(i_1)} = t_1^{(i_1)} \wedge \cdots \wedge x_n^{(i_n)} = t_n^{(i_n)} \wedge R(x_1^{(i_1)}, \dots, x_n^{(i_n)})].$$

Since $x_1^{(i_1)} = t_1^{(i_1)}, \dots, x_n^{(i_n)} = t_n^{(i_n)}$ are equivalent, respectively, to $F_1^*, \dots, F_n^*$, Φ is equivalent to F^* where F is the formula

$$\bigvee x_1^{(i_1)} \dots \bigvee x_n^{(i_n)} [F_1 \wedge \cdots \wedge F_n \wedge R(x_1^{(i_1)}, \dots, x_n^{(i_n)})].$$

The relation symbols (except perhaps equality), the function symbols, the free variables and the types which occur in F^* are clearly those of Φ.

It can now be easily proved, by induction on the length of Φ, that each formula Φ of $\mathscr{L}$ is equivalent to a formula F^*, which has the same relation and function symbols and the same types as Φ. Indeed if $\Phi = \Phi_1 \vee \Phi_2$ then, by the induction hypothesis, Φ_1 is equivalent to F_1^* and Φ_2 to F_2^*. Thus Φ is equivalent to $F_1^* \vee F_2^*$ which is equivalent to $(F_1 \vee F_2)^*$. A similar proof works if $\Phi = \neg \Phi_1$ or $\Phi = \bigvee x \Phi_1$.

iii) If $\mathfrak{M}_0$ is a normal model of $\mathscr{A}_0$ with domains $U_1, \ldots, U_k$ and f is a function symbol of $\mathscr{L}$ of type $(i, i_1, \ldots, i_n)$ then the value of S_f in $\mathfrak{M}_0$ is the graph of a map of $U_{i_1} \times \cdots \times U_{i_n}$ into U_i. Hence from $\mathfrak{M}_0$ we can derive a realization $\mathfrak{M}$ of $\mathscr{L}$ which has the same domains as $\mathfrak{M}_0$. Clearly each realization of $\mathscr{L}$ can be obtained in this way and a formula F of $\mathscr{L}_0$ is satisfied by $\mathfrak{M}_0$ if and only if F^* is satisfied by $\mathfrak{M}$.

Now let $\mathscr{B}$ be a set of closed formulas of $\mathscr{L}$ every finite subset of which has a model. By ii) we can assume that each formula of $\mathscr{B}$ is of the form F^* where F is a formula of $\mathscr{L}_0$. Let

$$\mathscr{B}_0 = \{F : F^* \in \mathscr{B}\}.$$

If $\{F_1, \ldots, F_n\}$ is a finite subset of $\mathscr{B}_0$, $\{F_1^*, \ldots, F_n^*\}$ has, by hypothesis, some model and so $\mathscr{A}_0 \cup \{F_1, \ldots, F_n\}$ has a model. Hence we can deduce from the Finiteness Theorem for the language $\mathscr{L}_0$ that $\mathscr{A} \cup \mathscr{B}_0$ has a model $\mathfrak{M}_0$. The realization $\mathfrak{M}$ of $\mathscr{L}$ which corresponds to $\mathfrak{M}_0$ satisfies $\mathscr{B}$. This proves that the Finiteness Theorem holds for the language $\mathscr{L}$.

Finally let F and G be two formulas of $\mathscr{L}$ such that $F \wedge G$ does not have a model. There are two formulas A, B of $\mathscr{L}_0$ such that A^* is equivalent to F and B^* is equivalent to G, and which have the same relation symbols (except possibly equality), the same function symbols and the same types as F, G respectively.

Let $\mathscr{A}_1$ be the set of those formulas of $\mathscr{A}_0$ which correspond to the function symbols which occur in A^* and let $\mathscr{A}_2$ be the set of those formulas of $\mathscr{A}_0$ corresponding to the function symbols which occur in B^*. The types which occur in $\mathscr{A}_1$ are those which occur in A^*, and those of $\mathscr{A}_2$ are the same as those which are in B^*.

Since $A^* \wedge B^*$ does not have a model, $\{A, B\} \cup \mathscr{A}_1 \cup \mathscr{A}_2$ does not have one either. Therefore by the Interpolation Lemma for the language $\mathscr{L}_0$ with equality, applied to the two formulas $\mathscr{A}_1 \wedge A$, $\mathscr{A}_2 \wedge B$ there is a formula H whose relation and function symbols and types are common to A and B which is such that

$$\mathscr{A}_1, A \vdash H \quad \text{and} \quad \mathscr{A}_2, B \vdash \neg H.$$

We can therefore deduce that $A^* \vdash H^*$ and $B^* \vdash \neg H^*$ and thus that $F \vdash H^*$ and $G \vdash \neg H^*$.

This proves the Interpolation Lemma for the language $\mathscr{L}$.

2. The relation between the methods of Chapters 2 and 5.

Let $\mathscr{L}$ be a language with a single type of variable without function symbols. We define $\mathscr{L}_A$ and Ω as described in this chapter. Let F be a formula of $\mathscr{L}$ and let $\hat{F}$ be the universal formula constructed from F in the way explained in Chapter 2. Thus the language of $\hat{F}$ is that of F augmented by a finite number of function symbols $\phi_1, \ldots, \phi_m$.

Define functions $f_1, \ldots, f_m$ on Δ which have the same number of arguments as $\phi_1, \ldots, \phi_m$, respectively, such that, for any canonical model $\mathfrak{M}$ of Ω, if $\mathfrak{M}$ is extended to a realization $\mathfrak{M}'$ of $\mathscr{L}(\hat{F})$ by giving ϕ_i the value $f_i(1 \leqslant i \leqslant m)$ then F and $\hat{F}$ have the same values in $\mathfrak{M}'$.

Answer. We assume that F is a (not necessarily closed) prenex formula of $\mathscr{L}$ and we define the set $\{f_1, \ldots, f_m\}$ by recursion on the number of quantifiers in F. If F is quantifier free $F = \hat{F}$ and there is nothing to prove.

If $F = \wedge x G(x, x_1, \ldots, x_n)$ then $\hat{F} = \wedge x \hat{G}$. Thus the function symbols $\phi_1, \ldots, \phi_m$ of $\hat{F}$ are those of $\hat{G}$ and we give them the values $f_1, \ldots, f_m$ which have already been defined for $\hat{G}$. Since, by hypothesis, G and $\hat{G}$ have the same value in $\mathfrak{M}'$ so too do F and $\hat{F}$.

If $F = \vee x G(x, x_1, \ldots, x_n)$, let $\phi_1, \ldots, \phi_m$ be the function symbols which occur in $\hat{G}$. Then

$$\hat{F} = \hat{G}(\phi x_1 \ldots x_n, x_1, \ldots, x_n)$$

where ϕ is a new n-ary function symbol. We give $\phi_1, \ldots, \phi_m$ the values $f_1, \ldots, f_m$ which have already been defined for $\hat{G}$ and we define f by

$$f(a_1, \ldots, a_n) = \varepsilon(G(x, a_1, \ldots, a_n))$$

for $a_1, \ldots, a_n \in \Delta$.

Then
$$(a_1, \ldots, a_n) \in \overline{\hat{F}} \Leftrightarrow (f(a_1, \ldots, a_n), a_1, \ldots, a_n) \in \overline{\hat{G}}$$
$$\Leftrightarrow (f(a_1, \ldots, a_n), a_1, \ldots, a_n) \in \bar{G}$$

since $\overline{\hat{G}} = \bar{G}$. Thus

$$(a_1, \ldots, a_n) \in \hat{F} \Leftrightarrow \mathfrak{M} \text{ satisfies } G(a, a_1, \ldots, a_n)$$

where $a = \varepsilon(G(x, a_1, \ldots, a_n))$. Therefore, because $\mathfrak{M}$ is a model of Ω

$$(a_1, \ldots, a_n) \in \hat{F} \Leftrightarrow \mathfrak{M} \text{ satisfies } \vee x G(x, a_1, \ldots, a_n)$$

and so $\overline{\hat{F}} = \bar{F}$.

3. Refinements of the Uniformity Theorem (for predicate calculus with several types of variables).

a) Show that if $\bigvee x_1 \ldots \bigvee x_n A$, where A is quantifier free, is a theorem then there is a sequence $(t_1^{(i)}, \ldots, t_n^{(i)})$ $(1 \leqslant i \leqslant p)$ of n-tuples of terms of the language of A such that $A_1 \vee \cdots \vee A_p$ is a theorem, where A_i is obtained by replacing x_j in A by $t_j^{(i)}$.

b) Deduce that if $\mathscr{U}'$ is a set of universal prenex formulas and E is an existential formula which is a consequence of $\mathscr{U}'$ then there is a quantifier free formula, A, such that $\mathscr{U}' \vdash A$ and $A \vdash E$.

c) Deduce from b) that if $\mathscr{U}$ is a set of universal formulas, U is a universal formula and $\mathscr{U} \vdash U \leftrightarrow E$ then there is a quantifier free formula B such that $\mathscr{U} \vdash U \leftrightarrow B$ and $\mathscr{U} \vdash B \leftrightarrow E$.

Answer.

a) We consider the canonical realizations of the language $\mathscr{L}$ of A. The domain of type p in such a realization is the set of all those terms of type p of $\mathscr{L}$ whose variables occur free in A. (If A does not contain any free variables or individual constants, we consider instead all the terms of type p of $\mathscr{L} \cup \{a\}$ where a is some given variable.) Since $\bigvee x_1 \ldots \bigvee x_n A$ is a theorem, the set of formulas $\{\neg A_1, \neg A_2, \ldots\}$ does not have a canonical model. Hence it follows from the Finiteness Theorem for propositional calculus that there is some integer q such that $\neg A_1 \wedge \cdots \wedge \neg A_q$ does not have a model and therefore $A_1 \vee \cdots \vee A_q$ is a theorem.

b) By the Finiteness Theorem there is a finite subset $\mathscr{U}_1$ of $\mathscr{U}'$ such that $\mathscr{U}_1 \vdash E$. The conjunction of the formulas of $\mathscr{U}_1$ is equivalent to a universal formula, say $\bigwedge y_1 \ldots \bigwedge y_r C$. Suppose that $E = \bigvee z_1 \ldots \bigvee z_s D$ (C and D are both quantifier free). Then $\bigvee y_1 \ldots \bigvee y_r \bigvee z_1 \ldots \bigvee z_s (\neg C \vee D)$ is a theorem. Therefore by (a) there is some formula of $\mathscr{L}$ of the form

$$\neg C_1 \vee \cdots \vee \neg C_q \vee D_1 \vee \cdots \vee D_q$$

which is a theorem. Let A be $D_1 \vee \cdots \vee D_q$. Since $\bigwedge y_1 \ldots \bigwedge y_r C \vdash C_1 \wedge \cdots \wedge C_q$ and $\mathscr{U}' \vdash \bigwedge y_1 \ldots \bigwedge y_r C$ it follows that $\mathscr{U}' \vdash D_1 \vee \cdots \vee D_q$. On the other hand since $D_i \vdash E$ for each $i (1 \leqslant i \leqslant q)$, $D_1 \vee \cdots \vee D_q \vdash E$.

c) It is enough to consider closed formulas U, the case of free variables being reduced to this one by use of constants not occurring in $\mathscr{U} \cup \{U\}$. Let $\mathscr{U}' = \mathscr{U} \cup \{U\}$. Then $\mathscr{U}' \vdash E$ and so by (b) there is a quantifier free formula B such that $\mathscr{U}' \vdash B$ and $B \vdash E$. Therefore $\mathscr{U} \vdash U \rightarrow B$, and so $\mathscr{U} \vdash U \leftrightarrow B$ and $\mathscr{U} \vdash B \leftrightarrow E$.

4. Refinements of the Interpolation Lemma (for a language $\mathscr{L}$ with several types of variables).

Let $U = \bigwedge x_1 \dots \bigwedge x_m A$ and $E = \bigvee y_1 \dots \bigvee y_n B$, where A and B are quantifier free formulas of $\mathscr{L}$, such that none of the variables y_i occurs in A and none of the variables x_i occurs in B.

a) Deduce from the Interpolation Lemma for the propositional calculus on the atomic formulas of $\mathscr{L}$ that if $E \to U$ is a theorem, there is a quantifier free formula C such that $E \to C$ and $C \to U$ are theorems.

b) Let F and G be two closed formulas of $\mathscr{L}$ such that $F \to G$ is a theorem. Deduce from the Interpolation Lemma (Theorem 8) that there is a formula H such that $\mathscr{L}(H) \subseteq \mathscr{L}(F) \cap \mathscr{L}(G)$ and both $F \to H$ and $H \to G$ are theorems.

c) Find two formulas F and G of a language with equality such that $F \to G$ is a thèorem, G does not contain $=$ but there is no formula H not containing $=$ such that $\mathscr{L}(H) \subseteq \mathscr{L}(F) \cap \mathscr{L}(G)$ and both $F \to G$ and $G \to H$ are theorems.

Answer.

a) Since $\vdash E \to U$, the formula $B \to A$ is a theorem in the sense of propositional calculus. Therefore there is a formula C built up from the atomic formulas common to A and B such that both $B \to C$ and $C \to A$ are theorems. C only contains variables which are common to A and B and so, in particular, C does not contain any of the variables x_i nor any of the variables y_j. It follows therefore that both $\bigvee y_1 \dots \bigvee y_n B \to C$ and $C \to \bigwedge x_1 \dots \bigwedge x_m A$ are theorems, which is the desired result. (On the other hand if A and B are arbitrary formulas of the predicate calculus such that $\vdash B \to A$, there is not necessarily a formula C containing only variables common to A and B such that $\vdash B \to C$ and $\vdash C \to A$; take, for example $A = \bigvee y R(y)$ and $B = R(x)$.)

b) Theorem 8 shows that there is a formula H which only contains relation symbols and types common to F and G such that $\vdash F \to H$ and $\vdash H \to G$; it leaves open the possibility that H contains a constant c which does not occur in F, say. Let u be a variable which does not occur in H and H' be the result of replacing c by u in H; then $\vdash F \to \bigwedge u H'$ and $\vdash \bigwedge u H' \to G$. Similarly if H contains a constant c which does not occur in G then $\vdash F \to \bigvee u H'$ and $\vdash \bigvee u H' \to G$. So in this way we can get rid of all the constants in H which do not occur in both F and G.

c) Let F be the formula $\bigwedge x \bigwedge y (x = y)$. If P is a unary relation symbol the formula $F \to (\bigwedge x P(x) \vee \bigwedge x \neg P(x))$ is a theorem. A formula H satisfying the conditions of c) would have to be either $\top$ or $\bot$, which is absurd.

5. We define the *pure* type of order n, denoted by n, for each integer $n \geqslant 0$, by recursion as follows: 0 is the type of individuals and $n+1=(n)$. If $n>0$ and $\sigma \in [n]$ then σ is also a pure type of order $m \leqslant n$, and ε_σ is a binary relation symbol. If $\mathscr{L}$ is a first order language with a single type of variable which does not contain the symbol ε, and $n>1$ we let $\mathscr{L}^n_\varepsilon$ be the language which is obtained from $\mathscr{L}$ by adding the binary relation symbol ε and types of variables $(1, 2, \ldots, n)$. (The language $\mathscr{L}^n$ is the language $\mathscr{L}^\tau$ described in this chapter for $\tau = n$.)

For each integer $n>0$, we denote by S_n (the axiom for the *hierarchy* of *simple pure types* $\leqslant n$), the conjunction of the following formulas of $\mathscr{L}^n$, where $i, j \leqslant n$ and the variables x, y, z are of types i, j, j respectively; for each pair (i, j):

$\bigwedge x \bigwedge y \neg (x=y)$ where $i<j$ (simple types),

$\bigwedge x \bigwedge y \neg (x \varepsilon y)$ where $j \neq i+1$, $\bigwedge y \bigwedge z [\bigwedge x (x \varepsilon y \leftrightarrow x \varepsilon z) \to y=z]$ where $j=i+1$ (axiom of extensionality).

We denote by $S_n^\emptyset$ the conjunction of S_n and the formulas $\bigwedge y \bigvee x (x \varepsilon y)$ for $i<n$ and $j=i+1$ (each empty set is of type 0).

We denote by C_n (the axiom for the *hierarchy of cumulative types* $\leqslant n$), the conjunction of the following formulas, where the variables x, y, z are of types i, j, k respectively; for each pair (i, j):

$\bigwedge x \bigwedge y \bigvee z (x \varepsilon y \to z=x)$ where $j \leqslant i$ and $j=k+1$,

$\bigwedge y [\bigwedge x [x \varepsilon y \to \bigvee z (z=x)] \to \bigvee x (x=y)]$ where $j=i+1$ and $i=k+1$,

$\bigwedge x \bigwedge y \neg (x \varepsilon y)$ where $j=0$,

$\bigwedge x \bigwedge y [\bigwedge z (z \varepsilon x \leftrightarrow z \varepsilon y) \to x=y]$ where $k+1=\max\{i, j\}$.

a) Show how to transform

(i) an n-realization of $\mathscr{L}^n$ into a model of S_n and conversely,

(ii) a model of $S_n^\emptyset$ into a model of C_n but not conversely.

b) (Ordered pairs of simple types.) For each pair (i, j) of integers find a formula M_{ij} containing three free variables of types i, j, k respectively, where $k=2+\max\{i, j\}$, such that $\bar{M}_{ij}$ is a one-one map of $E_i \times E_j$ into E_k, in any realization of $\mathscr{L}^n_\varepsilon (k \leqslant n)$ which satisfies C_n and the conjunction of the formulas $\bigwedge x \bigwedge y \bigvee z \bigwedge u [u \varepsilon z \leftrightarrow (u=x \vee u=y)]$ (existence of pairs), where x, y, u are of type r, z is of type $r+1 (\leqslant n)$ and $r<k$.

From this derive a one-one map of $E_{i_1} \times \cdots \times E_{i_p}$ into E_k where $k=$

$N_p\langle i_1, \ldots, i_p\rangle$ and N_p is defined by
$N_2\langle i_1, i_2\rangle = 2+\max\{i_1, i_2\}$ and
$N_{p+1}\langle i_1, \ldots, i_p, i_{p+1}\rangle = N_2\langle i_1, N_p\langle i_2, \ldots, i_{p+1}\rangle\rangle$.

c) (The reduction of finite types to pure types.) Let N be the function defined on the set of finite types with pure types as values given by

$$N(0) = 0,$$
$$N(\sigma) = 1 + N(\sigma_1) \quad \text{if} \quad \sigma = (\sigma_1),$$
$$N(\sigma) = 1 + N_n\langle N(\sigma_1), \ldots, N(\sigma_n)\rangle,$$

if $\sigma = (\sigma_1, \ldots, \sigma_n)$ and N_n is the function defined in b) above. For each finite type $\sigma = (\sigma_1, \ldots, \sigma_n)$ find a formula M_σ of $\mathscr{L}^{(\sigma, N(\sigma))}$ containing two free variables such that in each principal realization of $\mathscr{L}^\tau(\sigma \in [\tau], N(\sigma) \in [\tau])$, $\bar{M}_\sigma$ is a one-one map of the domain E_σ into $E_{N(\sigma)}$.

Answer.

a)(i) We take for $x\varepsilon y$ the disjunction of the following formulas of $\mathscr{L}^n$

$$\bigvee x_i \bigvee x_{i+1}(x = x_i \wedge y = x_{i+1} \wedge x_i \varepsilon_{i+1} x_{i+1})$$

where $0 < i+1 \leqslant n$ and x is a variable of type i.

If $E_0, \ldots, E_n$ are the domains of a realization of $\mathscr{L}^n$ then $(E_0, \ldots, E_n, \bar{\varepsilon})$ is a model of S_n. Conversely, given a model $(E_0, \ldots, E_n, \bar{\varepsilon})$ of S_n we can derive an n-realization of $\mathscr{L}^n$ by putting $x\varepsilon_{i+1} y = x\varepsilon y$ provided that x is a variable of type i and y a variable of type $i+1$.

(ii) Let $(E_0, \ldots, E_n, \bar{\varepsilon})$ be a model of S_n^θ. Let $E_0^c = E_0$, and for $m \leqslant n-1$ let $E_{m+1}^c = E_m^c \cup E_{m+1}$. Then for $i<j$, $E_i^c \subseteq E_j^c$. Also it follows from the axiom for simple types that for each $\bar{x} \in E_m^c (m \leqslant n)$ there is a unique integer i, which we will denote by $\mu(\bar{x})$ such that $\bar{x} \in E_i$. It follows from S_n^θ that if $\bar{x}\bar{\varepsilon}\bar{y}$ then $\mu(\bar{y}) = \mu(\bar{x})+1$ and also that if $\bar{x} \neq \bar{y}$ and either $\mu(\bar{x}) \neq 0$ or $\mu(\bar{y}) \neq 0$ then there is some $\bar{z}$ with $\mu(\bar{z}) < \max\{\mu(\bar{x}), \mu(\bar{y})\}$ such that $\bar{z}\bar{\varepsilon}\bar{x}$ if and only if $\neg\, \bar{z}\bar{\varepsilon}\bar{y}$. These facts show that $\mathfrak{M} = (E_0^c, \ldots, E_m^c, \bar{\varepsilon})$ is a model of C_n.

It should be noted that if $(E_0', \ldots, E_n', \bar{\varepsilon})$ is a model of C_n it is not necessarily the case that $(E_0', E_1' - E_0', \ldots, E_n' - E_{n-1}', \bar{\varepsilon})$ is a model of S_n. For example, let $n=2$, $E_0' = \{a\}$, $E_1' = \{a, \{a\}\}$ and $E_2' = \{a, \{a\}, \{a, \{a\}\}\}$; let $\bar{\varepsilon} = \in$. Then $E_1' - E_0' = \{\{a\}\}$ and $E_2' - E_1' = \{\{a, \{a\}\}\}$ and $\{a, \{a\}\}$ has an "element" which is in $E_1' - E_0'$ and one which is in E_0'. This contradicts the axiom $\bigwedge x \bigwedge y \neg (x\varepsilon y)$ of S_2, where x is a variable of type 0 and y is of type 2.

b) The desired map is obtained by modifying the usual representation of ordered pairs in set theory in such a way that the pairs are of *simple pure* types. Put $\{x\}^0 = x$ and $\{x\}^{n+1} = \{\{x\}^n\}$. If $\bar{x}_i \in E_i$ and $\bar{x}_j \in E_j$ we put $\langle \bar{x}_i, \bar{x}_j \rangle = \{\{\bar{x}_i\}^{m-i+1}, \{\{\bar{x}_j\}^{m-j}, \{\bar{x}_i\}^{m-i}\}\}$, where $m = \max\{i, j\}$. Clearly both $\{\bar{x}_i\}^{m-i+1}$ and $\{\{\bar{x}_j\}^{m-j}, \{\bar{x}_i\}^{m-i}\}$ are of type $m+1$ and so $\langle \bar{x}_i, \bar{x}_j \rangle$ is of type $m+2$. (Clearly, in general, there is no one-one map of $E_i \times E_i$ into E_{i+1}, for example if E_i is of cardinal 3 then card $(E_i \times E_i) = 9$, but card $(E_{i+1}) \leqslant 8$: this shows why the type of the ordered pair must exceed by at least 2 the types of its elements.)

This map can be defined in the language $\mathscr{L}^k_\varepsilon$ and in a uniform way for each realization of $\mathscr{L}^k_\varepsilon$, that is to say, by means of the same formula M_{ij}. If x_i, x_j, x_k are the variables of M_{ij}, the fact that M_{ij} defines a one-one map, that is that

$$\wedge x_i \wedge x_j \wedge x_k \wedge x'_k (M_{ij}(x_i, x_j, x_k) \wedge M_{ij}(x_i, x_j, x'_k) \rightarrow x_k = x'_k)$$

and

$$\wedge x_i \wedge x'_i \wedge x_j \wedge x'_j \wedge x_k (M_{ij}(x_i, x_j, x_k) \wedge \wedge M_{ij}(x'_i, x'_j, x_k) \rightarrow (x_i = x'_i \wedge x_j = x'_j))$$

is a consequence of the axiom of extensionality (for the formula M_{ij}). We need the axiom for the existence of pairs only to show that M_{ij} does define a map, i.e. that $\wedge x_i \wedge x_j \vee x_k M_{ij}(x_i, x_j, x_k)$.

The extension to ordered p-tuples can be carried out in the classical way.

c) We define the maps $\bar{M}_\sigma$ by recursion on the length of σ. If $\sigma = 0$, $\bar{M}_\sigma$ is the identity map, if $\sigma = (\sigma_1, \ldots, \sigma_n)$ and $\bar{x} \in E_\sigma$ then we put $\bar{M}_\sigma(\bar{x}) = \{\langle \bar{M}_{\sigma_1}(\bar{x}_1), \ldots, \bar{M}_{\sigma_n}(\bar{x}_n) \rangle : (\bar{x}_1, \ldots, \bar{x}_n) \bar{\varepsilon}_\sigma \bar{x}\}$. It can easily be seen that the types of the values of $\bar{M}_\sigma$ are those given by the function N. As in b) the fact that $\bar{M}_\sigma$ is one-one can be deduced from the axiom of extensionality. We do not analyse the conditions needed which ensure that $\bar{M}_\sigma$ is a map.

6. We adopt the notation established in the previous exercise. For each integer $n \geqslant 0$ we define, by recursion $\mathfrak{G}^n_f(E)$ (the set of *hereditarily finite sets* on E of cumulative type n), as follows:

$$\mathfrak{G}^0_f(E) = E$$

$\mathfrak{G}^{n+1}_f(E)$ is the union of $\mathfrak{G}^n_f(E)$ with the set of all *finite* subsets of $\mathfrak{G}^n_f(E)$.

Clearly the realization $\mathfrak{M}^n_f(E)$ of $\mathscr{L}^n_\varepsilon$ which has domains $\mathfrak{G}^0_f(E), \ldots, \mathfrak{G}^n_f(E)$ and in which $\bar{\varepsilon}$ is the restriction of the membership relation to

$\mathfrak{G}_f^n(E)$, is a model of C_n provided that no element of $\mathfrak{G}_f^n(E)$ is a member of any element of E. Similarly if $\mathfrak{G}^0(E)=E$ and $\mathfrak{G}^{m+1}(E)=\mathfrak{G}^m(E)\cup \mathscr{P}(\mathfrak{G}^m(E))$ (where $\mathscr{P}$ denotes the power set operation), then the realization $\mathfrak{M}^n(E)$ of $\mathscr{L}_\varepsilon^n$ which has domains $\mathfrak{G}^0(E), \ldots, \mathfrak{G}^n(E)$ and in which $\bar{\varepsilon}$ is the restriction of the membership relation to $\mathfrak{G}^n(E)$ is also a model of C_n.

a) Show that if no element of $\mathfrak{G}^n(E)$ is a member of any element of E then $\mathfrak{M}_f^n(E)$ is, up to isomorphism, the smallest n-model of C_n which has E as domain of type 0 and which satisfies the axioms

$$\bigwedge x \bigwedge y \bigvee z \bigwedge u\,[u\varepsilon z \leftrightarrow (u\varepsilon x \vee u = y)] \qquad (\Sigma)$$

where x, y, z, u are of types i, j, k, l respectively with $k=\max\{i, j+1\}$ and $l<k\leqslant n$. (Closure with respect to the operation $x\cup\{y\}$.)

b) Show that the formulas

$$\bigwedge x \bigwedge y \bigvee z \bigwedge u\,[u\varepsilon z \leftrightarrow (u\varepsilon x \wedge u \neq y)]$$

where x, y, z, u are of types i, j, k, l respectively with $k+1=l=\max\{i,j\}\leqslant n$ are not consequences of the axioms (Σ) of a) even though they are satisfied in $\mathfrak{M}_f^n(E)$.

c) Let $\mathfrak{M}_f^2=\mathfrak{M}_f^2(E)$ and $\mathfrak{M}^2=\mathfrak{M}^2(E)$. Let $\mathfrak{P}$ be the set of all those finite subsets of E which contain an even number of elements. Find three formulas P_1, P_2, P_3, each containing a single free variable of type 1 such that P_1 defines $\mathfrak{P}$ in both $\mathfrak{M}_f^2$ and $\mathfrak{M}^2$, P_2 defines $\mathfrak{P}$ in $\mathfrak{M}_f^2$ but not in $\mathfrak{M}^2$ and P_3 defines $\mathfrak{P}$ in $\mathfrak{M}^2$ but not in $\mathfrak{M}_f^2$.

Answer.

a) This can easily be proved by induction on n, using the fact that if $\bar{x}\in\mathfrak{G}_f^{m+1}(E)$ then $\bar{x}=\{\bar{y}_1, \ldots, \bar{y}_s\}$ with $\bar{y}_i\in\mathfrak{G}_f^m(1\leqslant i\leqslant s)$. Note that the hypothesis means this: the elements of E have no 'members' *in* $\mathfrak{G}^n(E)$, i.e., they are 'individuals' as far as $\mathfrak{G}^n(E)$ is concerned.

b) Let E be an infinite set. We obtain a realization of $\mathscr{L}_\varepsilon^n$ if we take $\{E\}\cup\mathfrak{G}_f^1(E)$ as the domain of type 1 and $\mathfrak{G}_f^m(\{E\}\cup\mathfrak{G}_f^1(E))$ as the domain of type $m+1$. This realization satisfies the axioms (Σ) of a), but $E-\{\bar{x}\}$ is not in the domain of type 1 for any $\bar{x}\in E$.

c) To make things clearer we will augment the language $\mathscr{L}_\varepsilon^2$ by adding the constant symbol $\emptyset$ of type 0, the unary function symbol $\{\}$ whose variable is of type 0 and value is of type 1 (we write $\{y\}$ for $\{\}y$) and the binary function symbols $\cup$, $-$ whose variables and values are of type 1 (we write $x\cup z$ for $\cup xz$ and $x-z$ for $-xz$).

These new function symbols are defined in $\mathfrak{M}_f^2$ and $\mathfrak{M}^2$ by the following axioms:

$$\bigwedge x[x = \emptyset \leftrightarrow \bigwedge y \neg (y\varepsilon x)],$$
$$\bigwedge x \bigwedge y[x = \{y\} \leftrightarrow \bigwedge u(u\varepsilon x \leftrightarrow u = y)]$$

where u is of type 0,

$$\bigwedge x \bigwedge z \bigwedge v[v = x \cup z \leftrightarrow \bigwedge y(y\varepsilon v \leftrightarrow [y\varepsilon x \vee y\varepsilon z])]$$
$$\bigwedge x \bigwedge z \bigwedge v[v = x - z \leftrightarrow \bigwedge y(y\varepsilon v \leftrightarrow [y\varepsilon x \wedge \neg y\varepsilon z])]$$

where v is of type 1.

By the axiom of extensionality a model $\mathfrak{M}$ of C_2 can be extended in at most one way to a model $\mathfrak{M}^+$ of the axioms in the augmented language above (and $\mathfrak{M}$ can be so extended if the corresponding existential axioms $\bigvee z \bigwedge y \neg (y\varepsilon x)$ etc. hold in $\mathfrak{M}$). It follows from this that we can eliminate the new symbols by using the following method (which works for all "explicitly defined" symbols; cf. Exercise 1(ii)).

With each formula A of the augmented language we associate a formula A^- of $\mathscr{L}_\varepsilon^2$ such that the value of A in $\mathfrak{M}^+$ is the same as the value of A^- in $\mathfrak{M}$. To do this it is sufficient to replace first each atomic formula $t\varepsilon t_1$ in A by a formula

$$\bigvee u \bigvee v(u = t \wedge v = t_1 \wedge u\varepsilon v)$$

where u and v are variables of the same types as t and t_1 which do not occur in A, and then replace the equations $u{=}t$ and $v{=}t_1$ by their definitions (as given by the axioms above).

We let P_1 be the formula of $\mathscr{L}_\varepsilon^2$ with free variable y of type 1 which is obtained by eliminating the new symbols from the formula

$$y = \emptyset \vee \bigwedge x[(y\varepsilon x \wedge \bigwedge u \bigwedge a \bigwedge b[(a \neq b \wedge a\varepsilon u \wedge b\varepsilon u \wedge u\varepsilon x) \rightarrow ((u - \{a\}) - \{b\})\,\varepsilon x]) \rightarrow \emptyset\varepsilon x].$$

Let A be a closed formula of $\mathscr{L}_\varepsilon^2$ which is true in $\mathfrak{M}^2$ but not in $\mathfrak{M}_f^2$. Then we let $P_2 = (\neg A \rightarrow P_1)$ and $P_3 = (A \rightarrow P_1)$. (Since E is infinite one such A is, for example, the formula of $\mathscr{L}_\varepsilon^2$ corresponding to the formula

$$\bigvee x[\emptyset\varepsilon x \wedge \bigwedge u \bigwedge a \bigwedge b(a \neq b \wedge \neg a\varepsilon u \wedge \neg b\varepsilon u \wedge u\varepsilon x) \rightarrow ((u \cup \{a\}) \cup \{b\})\varepsilon x].)$$

Finally we note that Dedekind's method for defining $\mathfrak{P}$ gives us the following formula for P_3:

$$\bigwedge x[(\emptyset\varepsilon x \wedge \bigwedge u \bigwedge a \bigwedge b[(a \neq b \wedge \neg a\varepsilon u \wedge \neg b\varepsilon u \wedge u\varepsilon x) \rightarrow ((u \cup \{a\}) \cup \{b\})\varepsilon x]) \rightarrow y\varepsilon x].$$

7. We use the notation which was established in the preceding exercise. In particular, x is a variable of type 2, y, u and w are of type 1 and a and b are of type 0.

We write $y \cap u$ for $y-(y-u)$.

a) Find formulas $N(y, u)$, $A(y, u, w)$, $S(y, u)$ of $\mathscr{L}_\varepsilon^2$ which define in $\mathfrak{M}_f^{(2)}$ and in $\mathfrak{M}^{(2)}$ the relations

i) $\bar{y}$ and $\bar{u}$ are finite sets of type 1 of the same cardinal ($\bar{\bar{y}}=\bar{\bar{u}}$),

ii) $\bar{\bar{y}}+\bar{\bar{u}}=\bar{\bar{w}}$,

and iii) $\bar{\bar{u}}=(\bar{\bar{y}})^2$, respectively.

b) Deduce from a) a correspondence which associates with each formula F of first order arithmetic (Chapter 3, Exercise 2) a formula F_ε of $\mathscr{L}_\varepsilon^2$ such that F is true in the standard model if and only if F_ε is true in $\mathfrak{M}_f^{(2)}$, and also if and only if F_ε is true in $\mathfrak{M}^{(2)}$.

Answer.

a) We write y_1 for $y-u$ and u_1 for $u-y$, so $y_1 \cap u_1=\emptyset$. Let y' and u' be variables of type 1; then we let $N(y, u)$ be the formula

$$\bigwedge x[(\emptyset \varepsilon x \wedge \bigwedge y \bigwedge u' \bigwedge a \bigvee b[(y' \subseteq y_1 \wedge u' \subseteq u_1 \wedge y' \cup u' \varepsilon x \wedge a \varepsilon y_1 \wedge \\ \wedge \neg\, a \varepsilon y') \rightarrow (b \varepsilon u_1 \wedge \neg\, b \varepsilon u' \wedge y' \cup \{a\} \cup u' \cup \{b\} \varepsilon x)]) \rightarrow y_1 \cup u_1 \varepsilon x].$$

It can be verified that $N(y, u)$ is satisfied if and only if $\bar{y}$ and $\bar{u}$ are finite and $\bar{\bar{y}}=\bar{\bar{u}}$.

ii) We take for $A(y, u, w)$

$$\bigvee y_1 \bigvee u_1 (y_1 \cap u_1 = \emptyset \wedge N(y, y_1) \wedge N(u, u_1) \wedge N(w, y_1 \cup u_1)).$$

Note that if $\bar{y}$ and $\bar{u}$ are finite $\bigvee y_1 \bigvee u_1 (y_1 \cap u_1=\emptyset \wedge N(y, y_1) \wedge N(u, u_1))$ is always satisfied.

iii) We use the fact that $(m+1)^2=m^2+2m+1$ and we take for $S(y, u)$ the formula

$$\bigvee y_1 \bigvee u_1 [y_1 \cap u_1 = \emptyset \wedge N(y, y_1) \wedge N(u, u_1) \wedge \bigwedge x(\emptyset \varepsilon x \wedge \\ \bigwedge y' \bigwedge u' \bigwedge a \{(y' \subseteq y_1 \wedge u' \subseteq u_1 \wedge y' \cup u' \varepsilon x \wedge a \varepsilon y_1 \wedge \neg\, a \varepsilon y') \rightarrow \\ \bigvee y'' \bigvee u'' [A(y', y', y'') \wedge A(u' \cup \{a\}, y'', u'') \wedge u'' \subseteq u_1]\} \rightarrow y_1 \cup u_1 \varepsilon x)].$$

b) Given the formula F we first replace the atomic formulas $y \cdot u=w$ by $(y+u)^2-(y-u)^2=w+w+w+w$ and then by

$$\bigvee y' [(y' + u = y \vee y' + y = u) \wedge (y + u)^2 = w + w + w + w]$$

and finally we replace $y = u$ by $N(y, u)$, $y + u = w$ by $A(y, u, w)$ and $y^2 = u$ by $S(y, u)$. The formula F' that is obtained in this way is true in $\mathfrak{M}_f^2$ with E infinite if and only if F is true in the standard model of arithmetic. If we restrict each variable of type 1, say y, by the condition $N(y, y)$ we obtain the desired formula F_ε. (A formal definition of "E is infinite" is $\bigwedge y \bigvee a(\neg a \varepsilon y)$ where y is of type 1 and a is of type 0.)

This exercise "reduces" arithmetic to the theory of the pure types 0,1,2.

We note that by using the elimination of quantifiers for atomic Boolean rings (Chapter 4, Exercise 7(a)(ii)) we can show that the theory of types 0 and 1, formulated in the language $\mathscr{L}_\varepsilon^1$ does not admit a similar reduction.

CHAPTER 6

DEFINABILITY

This chapter concerns certain relations which hold between the formulas of a language and their realizations, i.e. the sets defined by these formulas in the realizations of the language.

As we have already seen (e.g. Chapter 2, Exercise 5 on universal formulas in prenex normal form), the syntactic structure of a formula A can imply certain obvious relations between its realizations $\bar{A}_{\mathfrak{M}}$ in different models $\mathfrak{M}$; at least if the models considered are "comparable" in an obvious sense. Conversely one can ask the following question. If for all models $\mathfrak{M}$ of a set $\mathscr{A}$ of formulas, the realizations $\bar{A}_{\mathfrak{M}}$ have these relations between each other, is A then (equivalent in all models of $\mathscr{A}$ to) a formula of the syntactic structure in question? The two chief cases concern, first, formulas which are stable for extensions and, second, those which are invariant for so-called τ-realizations of theories of finite types which were introduced in the previous chapter.

In order to compare models which are not trivially "comparable" we investigate those objects which "occur" in all models of a set $\mathscr{A}$ of formulas, for examples, the rational numbers in all the commutative fields of characteristic zero. The concept which is necessary for a precise formulation is that of a structure being *rigidly contained* in all models of $\mathscr{A}$. The main result which we establish is that each element of such a structure can be defined by particularly simple formulas.

The last two theorems characterize those subsets of such a "common part" which are definable in all models of $\mathscr{A}$, two concepts of definability being treated. These characterizations take on an especially simple form when applied to models of the theory of types (Exercise 7). These two concepts of definability allow the generalization of a number of classical results on recursively enumerable sets of axioms to arbitrary sets of axioms. See KREISEL, Model-theoretic invariants: applications to recursive and hyperarithmetic operations, in: The Theory of Models (North-Holland Publ. Co., Amsterdam, 1965) pp. 190–205, and MOSTOWSKI, Representability of sets in formal systems, Proceedings of Symposia in Pure Mathematics, Vol. 5 (American Mathematical Society, 1962) pp. 29–48.

We consider languages $\mathscr{L}$ with equality and p types of variables. $\bar{A}_{\mathfrak{M}}$ is the value of the formula A in the realization $\mathfrak{M}$ of $\mathscr{L}$. If $\mathfrak{M}'$ is also a realization of $\mathscr{L}$ and $\mathfrak{M}'$ is an extension of $\mathfrak{M}$, then, by a natural abuse of language, we will use $\mathfrak{M} \cap \bar{A}_{\mathfrak{M}'}$ to denote the restriction of $\bar{A}_{\mathfrak{M}'}$ to $\mathfrak{M}$, that is, we write $\mathfrak{M} \cap \bar{A}_{\mathfrak{M}'}$ for $\bar{A}_{\mathfrak{M}'} \cap (E_1^{V_{\mathscr{L}}(1)} \times \cdots \times E_p^{V_{\mathscr{L}}(p)})$ where E_i is the domain of $\mathfrak{M}$ of type i.

Let $\mathscr{L}'$ be a language with equality which is of the same similarity class as $\mathscr{L}$, that is $\mathscr{L}'$ has also p types of variables and there is a 1-1 mapping of $V_{\mathscr{L}}, R_{\mathscr{L}}, S_{\mathscr{L}}, F_{\mathscr{L}}$ onto $V_{\mathscr{L}'}, R_{\mathscr{L}'}, S_{\mathscr{L}'}, F_{\mathscr{L}'}$ respectively which keeps the types of the variables and the types and numbers of arguments unaltered. We assume that $\mathscr{L}'$ is disjoint from $\mathscr{L}$. Then Ext $(\mathscr{L}, \mathscr{L}')$ is the set of the following formulas of $\mathscr{L} \cup \mathscr{L}'$

i) $\bigwedge x_j \bigvee x'_j (x_j = x'_j) \quad (1 \leqslant j \leqslant p) \quad x_j$ is of type j,

ii) $$\bigwedge x_1 \ldots \bigwedge x_n \bigwedge x'_1 \ldots \bigwedge x'_n [(x_1 = x'_1 \wedge \cdots \wedge x_n = x'_n) \rightarrow (R(x_1, \ldots, x_n) \rightarrow R'(x'_1, \ldots, x'_n))]$$

for all relational symbols R of $\mathscr{L}$ and all sequences $x_1, \ldots, x_n$ admissible for R,

iii) $$\bigwedge x_1 \ldots \bigwedge x_n \bigwedge x'_1 \ldots \bigwedge x'_n [(x_1 = x'_1 \wedge \cdots \wedge x_n = x'_n) \rightarrow f(x_1, \ldots, x_n) = f'(x'_1, \ldots, x'_n)]$$

for each function symbol f of $\mathscr{L}$ and all sequences $x_1, \ldots, x_n$ admissible for f.

LEMMA 1: *The realization $\mathfrak{M}'$ of $\mathscr{L}'$ is an extension of the realization $\mathfrak{M}$ of $\mathscr{L}$ if and only if the sum $\mathfrak{M} \oplus \mathfrak{M}'$ is a realization of $\mathscr{L} \cup \mathscr{L}'$ which satisfies* Ext$(\mathscr{L}, \mathscr{L}')$.

The formula A of $\mathscr{L}$ is called $(\mathscr{U}, \mathscr{A})$-*invariant* if for each model $\mathfrak{M}$ of $\mathscr{U}$ and each pair $\mathfrak{M}', \mathfrak{M}''$ of models of $\mathscr{A}$ such that $\mathfrak{M}', \mathfrak{M}''$ are extensions of $\mathfrak{M}$ we have $\mathfrak{M} \cap \bar{A}_{\mathfrak{M}'} = \mathfrak{M} \cap \bar{A}_{\mathfrak{M}''}$. (Note that, in general, $\bar{A}_{\mathfrak{M}} \neq \mathfrak{M} \cap \bar{A}_{\mathfrak{M}'}$ since $\mathfrak{M}$ is not assumed to be a model of $\mathscr{A}$; see Exercise 1(7).) (An application of the notion of $(\mathscr{U}, \mathscr{A})$-invariance is given in Exercise 1.)

Throughout this chapter, for any formula A of $\mathscr{L}$, A' will denote the image of A under the mapping above of $\mathscr{L}$ onto $\mathscr{L}'$.

Let $x_1, \ldots, x_n$ be the free variables of A; then we have

THEOREM 2. INVARIANCE THEOREM: *If A is $(\mathscr{U}, \mathscr{A})$-invariant there is a formula B such that*

$$\mathscr{A}' \cup \mathscr{U} \cup \mathrm{Ext}(\mathscr{L}, \mathscr{L}') \vdash \bigwedge x_1 \cdots \bigwedge x_n \bigwedge x'_1 \cdots \bigwedge x'_n [(x_1 = x'_1 \wedge \cdots \wedge x_n = x'_n) \rightarrow (A' \leftrightarrow B)].$$

PROOF: We add the constants $a_1, \ldots, a_n$, where a_i is of the same type as x_i, and introduce a language $\mathscr{L}''$ which is of the same similarity class as $\mathscr{L}$ and which is disjoint from $\mathscr{L}$ and $\mathscr{L}'$. Since A is $(\mathscr{U}, \mathscr{A})$-invariant the set

$$\mathscr{A}' \cup \mathscr{A}'' \cup \mathscr{U} \cup \operatorname{Ext}(\mathscr{L}, \mathscr{L}') \cup \operatorname{Ext}(\mathscr{L}, \mathscr{L}'') \cup \\ \cup \{A', \neg A'', a_1 = a_1' \wedge \cdots \wedge a_n = a_n' \wedge a_1 = a_1'' \wedge \cdots \wedge a_n = a_n''\}$$

does not have any model. Separating the languages $\mathscr{L}'$ and $\mathscr{L}''$ we therefore have that the set

$$[\mathscr{A}' \cup \mathscr{U} \cup \operatorname{Ext}(\mathscr{L}, \mathscr{L}') \cup \{A' \wedge a_1 = a_1' \wedge \cdots \wedge a_n = a_n'\}] \cup \\ \cup [\mathscr{A}'' \cup \mathscr{U} \cup \operatorname{Ext}(\mathscr{L}, \mathscr{L}'') \cup \{\neg A'' \wedge a_1 = a_1'' \wedge \cdots \wedge a_n = a_n''\}]$$

has no model. Therefore, by the Interpolation Lemma, there is a formula Y of $\mathscr{L} \cup \{a_1, \ldots, a_n\}$ such that

$$\mathscr{A}' \cup \mathscr{U} \cup \operatorname{Ext}(\mathscr{L}, \mathscr{L}') \cup \{a_1 = a_1' \wedge \cdots \wedge a_n = a_n'\} \vdash A' \rightarrow Y$$

and

$$\mathscr{A}'' \cup \mathscr{U} \cup \operatorname{Ext}(\mathscr{L}, \mathscr{L}'') \cup \{a_1 = a_1'' \wedge \cdots \wedge a_n = a_n''\} \vdash A'' \rightarrow \neg Y.$$

Thus if we replace a_i by x_i in Y for $1 \leqslant i \leqslant n$ we obtain a formula B such that, identifying the languages $\mathscr{L}'$ and $\mathscr{L}''$,

$$\mathscr{A}' \cup \mathscr{U} \cup \operatorname{Ext}(\mathscr{L}, \mathscr{L}') \vdash \bigwedge x_1 \ldots \bigwedge x_n \bigwedge x_1' \ldots \bigwedge x_n' \\ [(x_1 = x_1' \wedge \cdots \wedge x_n = x_n') \rightarrow (A' \leftrightarrow B)].$$

This completes the proof.

We recall that a formula A of the language $\mathscr{L}$ is said to be *existential* (*universal*) if it is in prenex normal form and all the quantifiers that occur in it are existential (universal) quantifiers.

The formula A is said to be *$\mathscr{A}$-stable for extensions* if for each pair $\mathfrak{M}$, $\mathfrak{M}'$ of models of $\mathscr{A}$ such that $\mathfrak{M}'$ is an extension of $\mathfrak{M}$ we have that $\bar{A}_{\mathfrak{M}} \subseteq \bar{A}_{\mathfrak{M}'} \cap \mathfrak{M}$. In particular, if A is a closed formula which is true in $\mathfrak{M}$ then it is also true in $\mathfrak{M}'$.

A is said to be *$\mathscr{A}$-stable for restrictions* if $\neg A$ is $\mathscr{A}$-stable for extensions.

Clearly, given any set of formulas $\mathscr{A}$, all existential formulas are $\mathscr{A}$-stable for extensions and all universal formulas are $\mathscr{A}$-stable for restrictions.

THEOREM 3: *Let $\mathscr{A}$ be a set of closed formulas of $\mathscr{L}$ and let A and B be two formulas of $\mathscr{L}$ such that, for each pair $\mathfrak{M}$, $\mathfrak{M}'$ of models of $\mathscr{A}$ with $\mathfrak{M}'$ an extension of $\mathfrak{M}$, we have $\bar{A}_{\mathfrak{M}'} \cap \mathfrak{M} \subseteq \bar{B}_{\mathfrak{M}}$. Then there is a universal formula*

U of $\mathscr{L}$ such that

$$\mathscr{A} \vdash A \rightarrow U \quad \text{and} \quad \mathscr{A} \vdash U \rightarrow B .$$

PROOF: (See also Exercise 2.) Let $\mathscr{L}'$ be the language obtained by adding to $\mathscr{L}$ a set V_c' of new constant symbols of the same cardinal as $\mathscr{L}$. Let A_1, B_1 be the two formulas of $\mathscr{L}'$ that are obtained by replacing each of the free variables of A and B by an element of V_c'. Let V_1 be the (possibly empty) set of the constants that we have used to form A_1 and B_1. Let $\mathscr{U}$ be the set of universal formulas of $\mathscr{L} \cup V_c'$ which are consequences of $\mathscr{A} \cup \{A_1\}$.

It will be sufficient to show that $\mathscr{A} \cup \mathscr{U} \cup \{\neg B_1\}$ does not have a model. For suppose that we have proved this. Then, by the Finiteness Theorem, there is a finite subset $\mathscr{U}_{\mathrm{F}}$ of $\mathscr{U}$ such that $\mathscr{A} \cup \mathscr{U}_{\mathrm{F}} \vdash B_1$ and so $\mathscr{A} \vdash U_{\mathrm{F}} \rightarrow B_1$, where U_{F} is the conjunction of the formulas in $\mathscr{U}_{\mathrm{F}}$. But U_{F} is equivalent to a universal formula and on the other hand by the definition of the set $\mathscr{U}$, $\mathscr{A} \vdash A \rightarrow U_{\mathrm{F}}$. Note also, by Chapter 2, Exercise 5, if a set of formulas of $\mathscr{L}$ has a model, it also has a model of the same cardinal as $\mathscr{L}$, and we need only consider such models.

Suppose that $\mathscr{A} \cup \mathscr{U} \cup \{\neg B_1\}$ has a model $\mathfrak{M}$ and let $\mathscr{D}'$ be the diagram of $\mathfrak{M}$ written with the symbols of V_c'. Then each model $\mathfrak{M}'$ of $\mathscr{A} \cup \mathscr{D}'$ is, up to isomorphism, an extension of $\mathfrak{M}$. Since B_1 is not satisfied in $\mathfrak{M}$, by the hypothesis of the Theorem, A_1 is not satisfied in $\mathfrak{M}'$, and so $\mathscr{A} \cup \mathscr{D}' \vdash \neg A_1$. Hence for some finite subset $\mathscr{D}_{\mathrm{F}}'$ of $\mathscr{D}'$, whose conjunction is D_{F}', say, $\mathscr{A} \cup \mathscr{D}_{\mathrm{F}}' \vdash \neg A_1$ and therefore $\mathscr{A} \vdash D_{\mathrm{F}}' \rightarrow \neg A_1$, or equivalently, $\mathscr{A} \vdash A_1 \rightarrow \neg D_{\mathrm{F}}'$.

Let D_{F}'' be the formula obtained by replacing the constants of $V_c' - V_1$ which occur in D_{F}' by variables, say $y_1, \ldots, y_n$, of $\mathscr{L}$. Then the universal formula $\bigwedge y_1 \ldots \bigwedge y_n \neg D_{\mathrm{F}}''$ of $\mathscr{L} \cup V_1$ is a consequence of $\mathscr{A} \cup \{A_1\}$ and so is in $\mathscr{U}_1$. This shows that $\mathscr{A} \cup \mathscr{U} \cup \mathscr{D}'$ does not have a model because $\bigwedge y_1 \ldots \bigwedge y_n \neg D_{\mathrm{F}}'' \rightarrow \neg D_{\mathrm{F}}'$ is a theorem. Therefore $\mathscr{A} \cup \mathscr{U} \cup \mathscr{D}' \cup \{\neg B_1\}$ does not have a model. But since $\mathfrak{M}$ was chosen arbitrarily this proves that $\mathscr{A} \cup \mathscr{U} \cup \{\neg B_1\}$ is inconsistent.

COROLLARY: *If the formula C is $\mathscr{A}$-stable there is an existential formula E such that $\mathscr{A} \vdash C \leftrightarrow E$.*

PROOF: If C is $\mathscr{A}$-stable $\neg C$ satisfies the hypothesis of Theorem 3 when $A = B = \neg C$.

The next Theorem and Exercises 3,4 treat the modifications of the notions of invariance and stability appropriate to τ-models (Chapter 5).

We use the notation of Chapter 5. If $\sigma, \sigma' \in [\tau]$, by a natural misuse of language, we will write $\sigma\in\sigma'$ if $\sigma'=(\sigma_1, \ldots, \sigma_n)$ and for some $i(1\leqslant i\leqslant n)$ $\sigma=\sigma_i$, and we will write $y_i^{\sigma_i}\varepsilon x^{\sigma'}$ for the formula (for $j\neq i$)

$$\ldots \bigvee y_j \ldots [(y_1^{\sigma_1}\ldots y_i^{\sigma_i}\ldots y_n^{\sigma_n})\, \varepsilon_{\sigma'} x^{\sigma'}].$$

Let the language $\mathscr{L}_1^\tau$ be of the same similarity type as $\mathscr{L}^\tau$.

LEMMA 4. *$\mathfrak{M}_1$ is a τ-extension of $\mathfrak{M}$ if and only if $\mathfrak{M}\oplus\mathfrak{M}_1$ is a τ-realization of the language $\mathscr{L}\cup\mathscr{L}_1$ which satisfies the set of formulas $\tau-\mathrm{Ext}(\mathscr{L}, \mathscr{L}_1)$, i.e., the set consisting of* $\mathrm{Ext}(\mathscr{L}, \mathscr{L}_1)$ *together with the formulas*

$$\bigwedge x^\sigma \bigwedge x_1^\sigma \bigwedge y_1^{\sigma'} \bigvee y^{\sigma'} x^\sigma = x_1^\sigma \wedge y_1^{\sigma'}\varepsilon_1 x_1^\sigma \to y^{\sigma'} = {}_1^{\sigma'}y$$

for all $\sigma, \sigma'\in[\tau]$.

We use the following notation. If $\sigma, \sigma'\in[\tau]$ we write $y^\sigma\varepsilon[x^{\sigma'}]$ (read, "y belongs to the transitive closure of x") for the disjunction of the formulas

$$y^\sigma\varepsilon x^{\sigma'} \quad \text{and} \quad \bigvee x_{i_1}\ldots\bigvee x_{i_{n_i}}(y^\sigma\varepsilon x_{i_1}\varepsilon\ldots\varepsilon x_{i_{n_i}}\varepsilon x^{\sigma'})$$

for each finite sequence $(i_1, \ldots, i_{n_i})$ which satisfies the condition that $\sigma\in\tau_{i_1}\in\ldots\in\tau_{i_{n_i}}\in\sigma'$, x_{i_j} being a variable of type τ_{i_j}.

A formula A with free variables $x_1, \ldots, x_n$ is said to be *$\mathscr{A}-\tau$-invariant* if, for each pair $\mathfrak{M}$, $\mathfrak{M}'$ of τ-models of $\mathscr{A}$ whose restrictions to $E_0\cap E_0'$ are equal, and for each n-tuple $(\bar{x}_1, \ldots, \bar{x}_n)$ belonging to the τ-intersection of $\mathfrak{M}$ and $\mathfrak{M}'$ either $(\bar{x}_1, \ldots, \bar{x}_n)\in\bar{A}$ in both models or in neither.

A prenex formula $Q_1y_1\ldots Q_ky_kB_1$, where B_1 is quantifier free is said to be *restricted* (to $[x_1^{\tau_1}], \ldots, [x_n^{\tau_n}]$) if B_1 is of the form

$$(y_{i_1}\varepsilon[t_{i_1}]\wedge\cdots\wedge y_{i_p}\varepsilon[t_{i_p}])\to(y_{j_1}\varepsilon[s_{j_1}]\wedge\cdots\wedge y_{j_q}\varepsilon[s_{j_q}]\wedge C)$$

where $i_1, \ldots, i_p$ are the indices of the universal quantifiers and $j_1, \ldots, j_q$ those of the existential quantifiers and the t_i and s_j are either individual constants or variables.

THEOREM 5: *A is $\mathscr{A}-\tau$-invariant if and only if there is a restricted formula B such that $\mathscr{A}\vdash(A\leftrightarrow B)$.*

PROOF: We consider the three languages: $\mathscr{L}_0$ which is the restriction of $\mathscr{L}^\tau$ to the types in $[\tau_1]\cup\cdots\cup[\tau_n]$, to which the n constant symbols $a_1^{\tau_1}, \ldots, a_n^{\tau_n}$ have been added; $\mathscr{L}_1$ is obtained by replacing ε in $\mathscr{L}$ by a new symbol ε_1 and each type of variable $x, y, \ldots$, by $x_1, y_1, \ldots$; $\mathscr{L}_2$ is obtained in the same way except that ε is replaced by ε_2 and the variables by $x_2, y_2\ldots$. We write $\tau'=(\tau_1, \ldots, \tau_n)$.

If A is $\mathscr{A}-\tau$-invariant

$$\mathscr{A}_1 \cup \mathscr{A}_2 \cup \tau' - \mathrm{Ext}(\mathscr{L}_0, \mathscr{L}_1) \cup \tau' - \mathrm{Ext}(\mathscr{L}_0, \mathscr{L}_2) \cup \cup \mathrm{TC}(a_1^{\tau_1}, \ldots, a_n^{\tau_n}) \vdash A_1(a_1, \ldots, a_n) \leftrightarrow A_2(a_1, \ldots, a_n)$$

where $\mathrm{TC}(a_1^{\tau_1}, \ldots, a_n^{\tau_n})$ is the set of formulas which expresses in the language $\mathscr{L}_0$ that each element belongs to the transitive closure of the union $a_1^{\tau_1} \cup \cdots \cup a_{\tau_n}^n$, i.e. for each $\sigma \in [\tau_1] \cup \cdots \cup [\tau_n]$, it contains the formula $\bigwedge y^\sigma (y^\sigma \varepsilon [a_1^{\tau_1}] \vee \cdots \vee y^\sigma \varepsilon [a_n^{\tau_n}])$.

Separating the different types of variables and applying the Interpolation Lemma we obtain a formula B' of the language $\mathscr{L}_0$ such that

$$\mathscr{A}_1 \cup \tau' - \mathrm{Ext}(\mathscr{L}_0, \mathscr{L}_1) \cup \mathrm{TC} \vdash A_1 \rightarrow B'$$

and

$$\mathscr{A}_2 \cup \tau' - \mathrm{Ext}(\mathscr{L}_0, \mathscr{L}_2) \cup \mathrm{TC} \vdash B' \rightarrow A_2 .$$

The set of formulas $\tau' - \mathrm{Ext}(\mathscr{L}_0, \mathscr{L}_1) \cup \mathrm{TC}$ is satisfied when ε is replaced by ε_1 and each variable x of $\mathscr{L}_0$ by $x_1 \varepsilon_1 [a_1^{\tau_1}] \vee \cdots \vee x_1 \varepsilon_1 [a_n^{\tau_n}]$. Hence B' has the desired form B.

Clearly all formulas B of this form are τ-invariant.

The theorems which follow are about classes of models which are not "comparable". (For simplicity, we consider languages without function symbols.)

The realization $\mathfrak{M}$ of the language $\mathscr{L}$ is said to be *rigidly contained* in $\mathfrak{M}'$ if there is a *unique* map ϕ' of the domains $E_1, \ldots, E_p$ of $\mathfrak{M}$ into $E_1' \cup \cdots \cup E_p'$ such that

$$\phi'(E_i) \subseteq E_i' \quad (1 \leqslant i \leqslant p);$$

for each constant c of $\mathscr{L}$, $\phi'(\bar{c}) = \bar{c}'$, and for each relational symbol R of $\mathscr{L}$ the image of $\bar{R}$ under ϕ' is that induced by $\bar{R}'$($\bar{c}'$, $\bar{R}'$ are respectively, the values of c and R in $\mathfrak{M}'$).

$\mathfrak{M}$ is said to be *rigidly contained* in the *class* of models of a set $\mathscr{A}$ of formulas of $\mathscr{L}$ if $\mathfrak{M}$ is rigidly contained in each model of $\mathscr{A}$. *We do not assume that $\mathfrak{M}$ is a model of $\mathscr{A}$.*

A formula A, with a single free variable x, is called a *definition in $\mathfrak{M}$ of the element a* ($a \in E_i$), if a is the only element which satisfies A, that is

$$\bar{A} = \overset{(1)}{E_1^{V_{\mathscr{L}}}} \times \cdots \times \overset{(i-1)}{E_{i-1}^{V_{\mathscr{L}}}} \times \langle x, a \rangle \times \overset{(i+1)}{E_{i+1}^{V_{\mathscr{L}}}} \times \cdots \times \overset{(p)}{E_p^{V_{\mathscr{L}}}} ,$$

by a natural misuse of language we will say $\bar{A} = \{a\}$.

Let $M = E_1 \cup \ldots \cup E_p$.

THEOREM 6: *If $\mathfrak{M}$ is rigidly contained in the class of all models of $\mathscr{A}$ then for each element a of the domain of $\mathfrak{M}$ there is an existential formula A_a of $\mathscr{L}$ such that*

(i) *A_a defines the element a in $\mathfrak{M}$ and, in each model $\mathfrak{M}'$ of $\mathscr{A}$, A_a defines $\phi'(a)$;*

(ii) *for each n-ary relation symbol R of $\mathscr{L}$ and for each n-tuple $(a_1, \ldots, a_n)$ of individuals of $\mathfrak{M}$, $(a_1, \ldots, a_n) \in \bar{R}$ if and only if*

$$\mathscr{A} \vdash \bigwedge x_1 \ldots \bigwedge x_n [(A_{a_1}(x_1) \wedge \cdots \wedge A_{a_n}(x_n)) \rightarrow R(x_1, \ldots, x_n)]$$

and $(a_1, \ldots, a_n) \notin \bar{R}$ if and only if

$$\mathscr{A} \vdash \bigwedge x_1 \ldots \bigwedge x_n [(A_{a_1}(x_1) \wedge \cdots \wedge A_{a_n}(x_n)) \rightarrow \neg R(x_1, \ldots, x_n)].$$

PROOF: We adjoin to the language $\mathscr{L}$ the constants c_a', $c_a''(a \in M)$, which are all distinct (and do not occur in $\mathscr{L}$). Let $\mathscr{D}'$, $\mathscr{D}''$ be the diagrams of $\mathfrak{M}$ written in terms of these constants. Then in each model $\mathfrak{M}'$ of $\mathscr{A}$ there is a unique way of satisfying $\mathscr{D}'$ because $\mathfrak{M}$ is rigidly contained in the class of all models of $\mathscr{A}$, namely by putting $\bar{c}_a' = \phi'(a)$ for each $a \in M$. Similarly for any model $\mathfrak{M}''$ of $\mathscr{A}$ there is a unique way of satisfying $\mathscr{D}''$, namely by putting $\bar{c}_a'' = \phi''(a)$ for each $a \in M$. Therefore $\mathscr{A} \cup \mathscr{D}' \cup \mathscr{D}'' \vdash c_a' = c_a''$. Hence, by the Finiteness Theorem, there are finite subsets $\mathscr{D}_1'$, $\mathscr{D}_2''$ of $\mathscr{D}'$ and $\mathscr{D}''$ such that $\mathscr{A} \cup \mathscr{D}_1' \cup \mathscr{D}_2'' \vdash c_a' = c_a''$. Let B_a be the conjunction of the formulas which are obtained when the constants of $\mathscr{D}_1'$, other than c_a', are replaced by variables $x_i (1 \leqslant i \leqslant h)$ and the constants of $\mathscr{D}_2''$ are replaced by variables $y_j (1 \leqslant j \leqslant k)$ and c_a is replaced by the variable x. If we put $A_a = \bigvee x_1 \ldots \bigvee x_h \bigvee y_1 \ldots \bigvee y_k B_a$ we have that $\bigvee x A_a(x)$ is a consequence of $\mathscr{A}$ since in any model $\mathfrak{M}'$ of $\mathscr{A}$, $\mathscr{D}_1' \cup \mathscr{D}_2''$ is satisfied by putting $\bar{c}_b' = \bar{c}_b'' = \phi'(b)$ for each b. The uniqueness of the element satisfying $A_a(x)$ is a consequence of the fact that $\mathscr{A} \cup \mathscr{D}_1' \cup \mathscr{D}_2'' \vdash c_a' = c_a''$. Thus we have proved (i).

The completeness result (ii) comes from the fact that $\phi'(\bar{R})$ is, by hypothesis, the value of R in $\mathfrak{M}'$.

COROLLARY: *Under the conditions of Theorem 6, if to $\mathscr{L}$ is added the set of constants c_a for $a \in M$, each model $\mathfrak{M}'$ of $\mathscr{A}$ can be extended in a unique way to a model of $\mathscr{A} \cup \mathscr{A}_1$, where $\mathscr{A}_1 = \{\bigwedge x (A_a(x) \leftrightarrow x = c_a) : a \in M\}$. In this model $\bar{c}_a = \phi'(a)$. In particular $\mathscr{A} \cup \mathscr{A}_1 \vdash \neg (c_a = c_b)$ for all pairs a, b of distinct elements of M.*

Let $\mathscr{L}$ be a language with k types of objects which contains an infinite set **C** of constants c (each having the same type $i(1 \leqslant i \leqslant k)$). A normal realization of $\mathscr{L}$ is called a **C**-*realization* if $\bar{c}=c$ for each $c \in \mathbf{C}$. A subset X of **C** is said to be *definable* in a **C**-realization $\mathfrak{M}$ of $\mathscr{L}$ if there is a formula $A(x, x_1, \ldots, x_n)$ where x is of type i, and elements $a_1, \ldots, a_n$ of M of the same types as $x_1, \ldots, x_n$ such that

$$X = \{a \in M : a \text{ is of type } i \text{ and } (a, a_1, \ldots, a_n) \in \bar{A}\}$$

and $\bar{A}$ is the value of $A(x, x_1, \ldots, x_n)$ in $\mathfrak{M}$.

Clearly if X is finite, say $X=\{c_1, \ldots, c_n\}$, then X is definable in all **C**-realizations by the formula

$$x = c_1 \vee \cdots \vee x = c_n .$$

We have the following converse result:

THEOREM 7: *If $\mathscr{A}$ is a set of closed formulas of $\mathscr{L}$ which has a* **C**-*model and X is definable in all* **C**-*models of $\mathscr{A}$, then X is finite.*

PROOF: We note first that a **C**-realization is, up to isomorphism, a realization in which the values of distinct elements of **C** are distinct. Therefore we assume that $\mathscr{A}$ contains all the formulas $c \neq c'$ for pairs (c, c') of distinct elements of **C**.

We construct the language $\mathscr{L}_\Delta$ and the set of formulas Ω in the way explained in Chapter 5. The cardinal of the set of those formulas of Ω which contain a single free variable, of type i, is equal to the cardinal of $\mathscr{L}_\Delta$. Hence there is an enumeration of this set in the form

$$\{A_j(x) : j < \operatorname{card}(\mathscr{L}_\Delta)\} .$$

$$\text{Let } \mathscr{A}_0^+ = \mathscr{A} \cup \Omega(\mathscr{A}) \quad \text{and for } \quad j > 0$$

1. $$\text{let } \mathscr{A}_j^+ = \bigcup_{h<j} \mathscr{A}_h^+ \cup \{(\varepsilon(A_j x) \neq c) : c \in \mathbf{C}\}$$

(where the map ε was defined on p. 83) if this set has a normal model, and

2. $$\mathscr{A}_j^+ = \bigcup_{h<j} \mathscr{A}_h^+ , \quad \text{otherwise.}$$

If case 2 applies, then by the Finiteness Theorem, there is a finite set $\{c_{n_1}, \ldots, c_{n_j}\}$ of elements of **C** such that

$$\Omega(\mathscr{A}) \cup \bigcup_{h<j} \mathscr{A}_h^+ \vdash \bigwedge x [A_j(x) \to (x = c_{n_1} \vee \cdots \vee x = c_{n_j})] .$$

By Corollary 5.6, if $\mathscr{A}$ has a model then $\bigcup\{\mathscr{A}_j^+ : j < \operatorname{card}(\mathscr{L}_\Delta)\}$ has a canonical model. In any such model, if j satisfies the first condition then $\bar{A}_j \nsubseteq \mathbf{C}$ and so $\bar{A}_j \neq X$ or A_j is empty, while if j satisfies the second condition $\bar{A}_j$ is finite.

This completes the proof.

A subset X of $\mathbf{C}$ is said to be *definable-on* $\mathbf{C}$ in a $\mathbf{C}$-realization $\mathfrak{M}$ of $\mathscr{L}$ if there is a formula $A(x, x_1, \ldots, x_n)$, where x is of type i, and there are elements $a_1, \ldots, a_n$ of M of the same types as $x_1, \ldots, x_n$, such that

$$X = \{c \in \mathbf{C} : (c, a_1, \ldots, a_n) \in \bar{A}\}.$$

Clearly X is definable-*on* $\mathbf{C}$ in all $\mathbf{C}$-realizations of a set $\mathscr{A}$ if there is a formula $A(x)$, with a single free variable, such that for all $c \in \mathbf{C}$

$$c \in X \quad \text{if and only if} \quad \mathscr{A} \vdash A(c)$$

and

$$c \notin X \quad \text{if and only if} \quad \mathscr{A} \vdash \neg A(c).$$

We have the following *partial* converse result (cf. Exercise 8 for a simplification in the case of denumerable languages and Exercise 9 for a counterexample to the full converse):

THEOREM 8: *Let $\mathscr{A}$ be a set of closed formulas of $\mathscr{L}$ which has a* $\mathbf{C}$*-model and let $c_1^*, c_2^*, \ldots$ be constants not in $\mathscr{L}$. If $X \subseteq \mathbf{C}$ is definable-on* $\mathbf{C}$ *in all* $\mathbf{C}$*-models of $\mathscr{A}$, then there is a formula $A(x, x_1, \ldots, x_n)$ of $\mathscr{L}$ and a family $\{F_j(x_1, \ldots, x_n) : j < \lambda\}$ of formulas of $\mathscr{L}$ such that* card $\lambda <$ card $\mathscr{L}$, card $\lambda \leqslant$ card $\mathbf{C}$, *the set*

$$\mathscr{A} \cup \{F_j(c_1^*, \ldots, c_n^*) : j < \lambda\}$$

has a model and for all $c \in \mathbf{C}$
$c \in X$ if and only if for some $j < \lambda$

$$\mathscr{A} \vdash \bigwedge x_1 \ldots \bigwedge x_n [F_j(x_1, \ldots, x_n) \rightarrow A(c, x_1, \ldots, x_n)]$$

and $c \notin X$ if and only if for some $j < \lambda$

$$\mathscr{A} \vdash \bigwedge x_1, \ldots, \bigwedge x_n [F_j(x_1, \ldots, x_n) \rightarrow \neg A(c, x_1, \ldots, x_n)].$$

(This theorem can also be deduced from a more general result about infinite formulas given in the next chapter.)

PROOF: We will show that if the conclusion of this Theorem does not hold then X is not definable in a certain class of canonical models. Let $\langle A_j(x) \rangle$

be an enumeration, possibly transfinite, of all the formulas of $\mathscr{L}_\Delta$ with a single free variable (of type i). Since each formula is a finite string of symbols and $\mathscr{L}_\Delta$ is infinite the set of these formulas has the same cardinal as $\mathscr{L}_\Delta$. We can assume therefore that $j<\text{card}(\mathscr{L}_\Delta)$.

Let $\mathscr{A}_0^+=\mathscr{A}$. For $j>0$ we consider the two cases:

1. For all $k\leqslant j$ the set of formulas

$$\{A_k(c):c\in\mathbf{C},\,c\in X\}\cup\{\neg\,A_k(c):c\in\mathbf{C},\,c\notin X\}$$

is not a consequence of $\bigcup_{h<k}\mathscr{A}_h^+\cup\Omega$

a) either there is a $c\in X$ such that $A_j(c)$ is not a consequence of $\bigcup_{h<j}\mathscr{A}_h^+\cup\Omega$; then let $c=c_j$ and put

$$\mathscr{A}_j^+=\bigcup_{h<j}\mathscr{A}_h^+\cup\{\neg\,A_j(c_j)\};$$

b) or there is no such c, and hence there is a $c\notin X$ such that $\neg\,A_j(c)$ is not a consequence of $\bigcup_{h<j}\mathscr{A}_h^+\cup\Omega$; let $c=c_j$ and put

$$\mathscr{A}_j^+=\bigcup_{h<j}\mathscr{A}_h^+\cup\{A_j(c_j)\}.$$

2. If case 1 does not apply we put $\mathscr{A}_j^+=\bigcup_{h<j}\mathscr{A}_h^+$.

By the Corollary to the Finiteness Theorem $\bigcup_j\mathscr{A}_j^+$ has a canonical model $\mathfrak{M}$. If case 1 applies then $X\neq\bar{A}_j\cap\mathbf{C}$ so if this case applies for all j, X is not definable-*on* $\mathbf{C}$ in $\mathfrak{M}$ since each element of $\mathfrak{M}$ has a name in $\mathscr{L}_\Delta$. Therefore there is some $\lambda<\text{card}(\mathscr{L}_\Delta)$ such that the set

$$\{A_\lambda(c):c\in\mathbf{C},\,c\in X\}\cup\{\neg\,A_\lambda(c):c\in\mathbf{C},\,c\notin X\}$$

is a consequence of $\Omega\cup\mathscr{A}\cup\{A_j'(c_j):j<\lambda\}$, where $A_j'=\neg\,A_j$ if 1a) applies and $A_j'=A_j$ if 1b) applies.

Therefore for each $c\in\mathbf{C}$, $\{A_\lambda(c):c\in X\}\cup\{\neg A_\lambda(c):c\notin X\}$ is a consequence of $\Omega\cup\mathscr{A}\cup\{A_j'(c_j):j\in I_c\}$ for some finite set I_c of ordinals less than λ. Let $c_1^*,\ldots,c_n^*$ be the elements of Δ which occur in A_λ and $a_1,\ldots,a_m$ those which occur in $\{A_j'(c_j):j\in I_c\}$. Then, by Lemma 5.10,

$$\{A_j'(c_j):j\in I_c\}\cup\mathscr{A}\cup\{\theta_{a_1}\wedge\cdots\wedge\theta_{a_m}\wedge\theta_{c^*_1}\wedge\cdots\wedge\theta_{c^*_n}\}$$
$$\vdash\{A_\lambda(c):c\in X\}\cup\{\neg\,A_\lambda(c):c\notin X\}.$$

Let A^c be the conjunction of the $A_j'(c_j)$ for $j\in I_c$, and let $F_c(c_1^*,\ldots,c_n^*)$

be obtained by replacing the elements of Δ, other than $c_1^*, \ldots, c_n^*$ in

$$\theta_{a_1} \wedge \cdots \wedge \theta_{a_n} \wedge \theta_{c^*_1} \wedge \cdots \wedge \theta_{c^*_n} \wedge A^c$$

by new variables and binding these by existential quantifiers. Then, for each c, either $\mathscr{A} \vdash (F_c \to A_\lambda(c))$ or $\mathscr{A} \vdash (F_c \to \neg A_\lambda(c))$. Clearly the cardinal of the set of formulas $\{F_c : c \in \mathbf{C}\} \leqslant \text{card } \mathbf{C}$; and it is bounded by the cardinal of the collection of finite subsets of $\{A_j'(c_j) : j < \lambda\} \cup \{\theta_a : a \in \Delta$, a occurs in $A_j'(c_j), j < \lambda\}$.

Exercises

1. We adopt the notation used in the Invariance Theorem. Prove the following results:

a) If A is a formula which is $(\mathscr{U}, \mathscr{A})$-invariant and if all universal (prenex) formulas which are consequences of $\mathscr{A}$ are also consequences of $\mathscr{U}$ then the formulas B and $\neg B$ (of the Invariance Theorem) are both $\mathscr{U}$-stable.

b) If the conditions of a) hold and $\mathscr{U}$ is a set of universal formulas then there is a quantifier free formula C such that $\mathscr{U} \vdash B \leftrightarrow C$ (see e)).

c) If $\mathscr{U}$ is the set of universal formulas which are consequences of $\mathscr{A}$ and if every existential formula is $(\mathscr{U}, \mathscr{A})$-invariant then for each formula A there is a quantifier free formula B such that $\mathscr{A} \vdash A \leftrightarrow B$.

d) Deduce from c) the following "algebraic" criteria for the elimination of quantifiers:

(i) for algebraically closed fields: if there is an algebraically closed field, which contains the commutative field C and in which the existential formula F is true, then F is true in the algebraic closure of C;

(ii) similarly for real closed fields, with C an ordered field.

e) Find a counter-example to the result b) if the requirement that $\mathscr{U}$ contains only universal formulas is omitted.

f) Find sets of axioms $\mathscr{A}$ and $\mathscr{U}$, and a formula A which is $(\mathscr{U}, \mathscr{A})$-, but not $(\mathscr{U}, \mathscr{U})$-invariant.

Answer.

a) By the Embedding Theorem, each model of $\mathscr{U}$ can be embedded in a model of $\mathscr{A}$. Suppose then that $\mathfrak{M}$ and $\mathfrak{M}_1$ are two models of $\mathscr{U}$, with $\mathfrak{M}_1$ an extension of $\mathfrak{M}$. Let $\mathfrak{M}'$ be an extension of $\mathfrak{M}_1$ which is a model of $\mathscr{A}$. If B is true in $\mathfrak{M}$, A is true in $\mathfrak{M}'$ since $\mathfrak{M}'$ is an extension of $\mathfrak{M}$

which is a model of $\mathscr{A}$. Consequently B is true in $\mathfrak{M}_1$ since $\mathfrak{M}'$ is also an extension of $\mathfrak{M}_1$. Similarly for $\neg B$.

b) By Theorem 3, there are existential formulas C_1 and C_2 such that $\mathscr{U} \vdash B \leftrightarrow C_1$ and $\mathscr{U} \vdash \neg B \leftrightarrow C_2$ since B and $\neg B$ are $\mathscr{U}$-stable. Hence, by the Finiteness Theorem, there is a finite subset $\mathscr{U}_1$ of $\mathscr{U}$ such that $\mathscr{U}_1 \vdash (C_1 \leftrightarrow \neg C_2)$. Let $C_1 = \bigvee x_1 \dots \bigvee x_n D_1$ and $C_2 = \bigvee y_1 \dots \bigvee y_l D_2$, where D_1 and D_2 are quantifier free, and let U_1, the conjunction of the formulas in $\mathscr{U}_1$, be $\bigwedge z_1 \dots \bigwedge z_m U$. Then the existential formula

$$\bigvee z_1 \dots \bigvee z_m \neg U \vee \bigvee x_1 \dots \bigvee x_n D_1 \vee \bigvee y_1 \dots \bigvee y_l D_2$$

is a theorem. Hence, by the Uniformity Theorem (Chapter 3), there is a sequence $s_1^{(i)}, \dots, s_n^{(i)}, t_1^{(i)}, \dots, t_l^{(i)}, u_1^{(i)}, \dots u_m^{(i)}, (1 \leqslant i \leqslant p)$ of terms such that

$$\underset{1 \leq i \leq p}{\mathrm{W}} \neg U(u_1^{(i)}, \dots, u_m^{(i)}) \vee \underset{1 \leq i \leq p}{\mathrm{W}} D_2(t_1^{(i)}, \dots, t_l^{(i)}) \vee \underset{1 \leq i \leq p}{\mathrm{W}} D_1(s_1^{(i)}, \dots, s_n^{(i)})$$

is a theorem of the propositional calculus. Let C be the disjunction $\underset{1 \leqslant i \leqslant p}{\mathrm{W}} D_1(s_1^{(i)}, \dots, s_n^{(i)})$, then $\mathscr{U} \vdash C \vee C_2$ and so $\mathscr{U} \vdash \neg C_2 \rightarrow C$. But $C \rightarrow C_1$ is a theorem and $\mathscr{U} \vdash C_1 \rightarrow C_2$ and therefore $\mathscr{U} \vdash C \leftrightarrow C_1$.

c) Since $\mathscr{A} \vdash \mathscr{U}$, we have, by b), that $\mathscr{A} \vdash B \leftrightarrow C$. However in order to be able to eliminate quantifiers it is sufficient that we can eliminate them from existential formulas (see Chapter 4).

d) (i) Let $\mathscr{A}$ be the set of axioms for an algebraically closed field (see Chapter 4, Section IV), and let $\mathscr{U}$ be the set of axioms for a commutative field. Clearly $\mathscr{A} \vdash \mathscr{U}$ and we know that every commutative field can be embedded in an algebraically closed field, namely its algebraic closure. Therefore the hypotheses of c) are satisfied.

(ii) Let $\mathscr{A}$ be the set of axioms for a real closed field (see Chapter 4, Section V) and let $\mathscr{U}$ be the set of axioms for an ordered field. (If in place of $\mathscr{U}$ we took the set $\mathscr{U}'$ of axioms for a real field, which are orderable fields, c) would apply but this would not give a useful criterion since there are existential formulas which are not $(\mathscr{U}', \mathscr{A})$-invariant.)

e) Let $\mathscr{L}$ be the language of Chapter 4, Exercise 2 and let $\mathscr{U}$ be the set of axioms (a, b, c, e) of Chapter 4, Section III. Then although $\mathscr{U} \vdash 2|x \leftrightarrow \neg(2|x+1)$ and $2|x$ is existential it is not equivalent to any quantifier free formula of $\mathscr{L}$.

f) Let $\mathscr{U}$ and $\mathscr{A}$ be as in d) (ii), and A true in all real closed fields, but not in all ordered fields, e.g. $A = \bigvee x(x^2 = 2)$. (This shows that one cannot take A itself for B in Theorem 2.)

2. We adopt the notation used in Theorem 3.
Prove Theorem 3 by using the Interpolation Lemma (Chapter 5).

Answer. Let $\mathrm{Ext}_1(\mathscr{L}, \mathscr{L}')$ be the conjunction of the universal formulas

$$\bigwedge x_1 \dots \bigwedge x_n \bigwedge x'_1 \dots \bigwedge x'_n$$
$$[(x_1 = x'_1 \wedge \cdots \wedge x_n = x'_n) \rightarrow (R(x_1, \dots, x_n) \leftrightarrow R'(x'_1, \dots, x'_n))]$$

for all n-ary relation symbols R of $\mathscr{L}$ and all admissible sequences $x_1, \dots, x_n$ for R, and the universal formulas

$$\bigwedge x_1 \dots \bigwedge x_n \bigwedge x'_1 \dots \bigwedge x'_n$$
$$[(x_1 = x'_1 \wedge \cdots \wedge x_n = x'_n) \rightarrow (f(x_1, \dots, x_n) = f'(x'_1, \dots, x'_n))]$$

for all n-ary function symbols f of $\mathscr{L}$ and all admissible sequences $x_1, \dots, x_n$ for f.

Suppose A and B together contain less than m free variables. Let $\mathscr{L}_1$ be the language obtained from $\mathscr{L}$ by adding the new individual constants $a_r (r < m)$ and $\mathscr{L}'_1$ be the language obtained from $\mathscr{L}'$ by adding the new constants $a'_r (r < m)$. Let A_1 and B_1 be the formulas of $\mathscr{L}_1$ obtained by substituting the constants a_r for the free variables in A and B. Let $\mathrm{Ext}_1(\mathscr{L}_1, \mathscr{L}'_1)$ be the formula $\mathrm{Ext}_1(\mathscr{L}, \mathscr{L}') \wedge a_1 = a'_1 \wedge \cdots \wedge a_m = a'_m$.

Let C be the formula

$$\bigwedge y_1 \bigvee y'_1 (y_1 = y'_1) \wedge \cdots \wedge \bigwedge y_p \bigvee y'_p (y_p = y'_p)$$

where y_j is a variable of type $j (1 \leqslant j \leqslant p)$.
By the hypothesis of Theorem 3,

$$\mathscr{A} \cup \mathscr{A}' \cup \{C \wedge \mathrm{Ext}_1(\mathscr{L}_1, \mathscr{L}'_1) \wedge A'_1\} \vdash B_1 .$$

Therefore, by the Finiteness Theorem, there are formulas A_{F}, A'_{F} which are finite conjunctions of formulas of $\mathscr{A}$ and $\mathscr{A}'$ such that

$$A'_{\mathrm{F}} \wedge A'_1 \wedge C \wedge \mathrm{Ext}(\mathscr{L}_1, \mathscr{L}'_1) \vdash A_{\mathrm{F}} \rightarrow B_1 .$$

As a consequence

$$\hat{A}'_{\mathrm{F}} \wedge \hat{A}'_1 \wedge \bigwedge y_1 (\phi_1(y_1) = y_1) \wedge \cdots \wedge \bigwedge y_p (\phi_p(y_p) = y_p) \wedge$$
$$\wedge \mathrm{Ext}(\mathscr{L}_1, \mathscr{L}'_1) \vdash (\neg \check{A}_{\mathrm{F}} \vee \check{B}_1)$$

in the notation of Chapter 3. We note that the function symbols of $\hat{A}'_F$, $\hat{A}'_1$ which do not occur in $\mathscr{L}_1 \cup \mathscr{L}'_1$ only have as arguments or values variables of the types of $\mathscr{L}'$ and those of $\neg \check{A}_F \vee \check{B}_1$ only those of $\mathscr{L}$. The function symbols $\phi_j (1 \leqslant j \leqslant p)$ have as arguments variables of the types of $\mathscr{L}$ and values of the types of $\mathscr{L}'$. Hence each term of $\hat{\mathscr{L}}'_1 \cup \check{\mathscr{L}}_1$ whose *value* is a type of $\mathscr{L}$ is also a term of $\mathscr{L}_1$.

There is a quantifier free formula V of $\check{\mathscr{L}}_1$ (see Exercise 3 of Chapter 5) such that

$$\text{(i)} \quad \hat{A}'_F \wedge \hat{A}'_1 \wedge \bigwedge y_1 (\phi_1(y_1) = y_1) \wedge \cdots \wedge \bigwedge y_p (\phi_p(y_p) = y_p) \wedge \wedge \operatorname{Ext}_1(\mathscr{L}_1, \mathscr{L}'_1) \vdash V$$

and

$$\text{(ii)} \quad V \vdash \neg \check{A}_F \vee \check{B}_1 .$$

Since V does not contain any symbols of $\hat{\mathscr{L}} - \mathscr{L}$ it follows from (i) that

$$\mathscr{A}' \cup \{A'_1 \wedge C \wedge \operatorname{Ext}_1(\mathscr{L}, \mathscr{L}'_1)\} \vdash V .$$

Identifying the languages $\mathscr{L}$ and $\mathscr{L}'$ we also have that $\mathscr{A} \vdash A_1 \rightarrow V$. Similarly $\mathscr{A} \vdash V \rightarrow B_1$. The proof is completed by eliminating the symbols of $\check{\mathscr{L}}_1 - \mathscr{L}_1$ in V by using universal quantifiers of $\mathscr{L}$.

3. We use the notation of the theory of types (Chapter 5).

The formula $A = Q_1 x_1 \ldots Q_m x_m A_1$ (A_1 quantifier-free) is called a *Σ-formula* if A_1 is of the form $(x_{i_1} \varepsilon t_1 \wedge \cdots \wedge x_{i_k} \varepsilon t_k) \rightarrow B$ where $i_1 < \cdots < i_k$ are the indices of the variables occurring in the universal quantifiers of A and where $t_j (1 \leqslant j \leqslant k)$ is either x_n for some $n < i_j$ or one of the constants of A_1 or a free variable of A. A Σ-formula is therefore an existential formula if one ignores each variable $x_j (j \leqslant m)$ which is restricted to a variable x_n with $n < j$, or to a constant of A_1 or a free variable of A.

a) Show that each Σ-formula is stable for τ-extensions.

b) Find a τ-realization $\mathfrak{M}$ and an extension $\mathfrak{N}$ of $\mathfrak{M}$ such that $\mathfrak{N}$ is a τ-realization, but not a τ-extension of $\mathfrak{M}$. Hence find a Σ-formula A which is not stable for all extensions of $\mathfrak{M}$.

c) Let $\mathscr{A}$ be a set of formulas such that if $\mathfrak{M}$ and $\mathfrak{M}'$ are τ-models of $\mathscr{A}$ and if the τ-intersection of $\mathfrak{M}$ and $\mathfrak{M}'$ is not empty then the latter is also a τ-model of $\mathscr{A}$. Show that if A and $\neg A$ are both $\mathscr{A}$-stable for τ-extensions then A is $\mathscr{A} - \tau$-invariant. Deduce that if C_1 and C_2 are two Σ-formulas such that $\mathscr{A} \vdash C_1 \leftrightarrow \neg C_2$ then C_1 and C_2 are $\mathscr{A} - \tau$-invariant.

Answer.

a) is obvious. (Note that the converse of a) is also true. But the proof which uses Lemma 4 and the method of Exercise 2 is complicated.)

b) Let $\tau=(0)$ and let $\mathscr{L}$ be the language with a single unary relation symbol P. We let $\mathfrak{M}$ be the realization of $\mathscr{L}$ given by $E_0=\{a\}$, $E_{(0)}=\{\{a\}\}$, $a\in\bar{P}$, where E_0 and $E_{(0)}$ are the domains of $\mathfrak{M}$.

Let $\mathfrak{N}$ be the extension of $\mathfrak{M}$ given by

$$U_0=\{a,b\},\quad a\neq b;\quad U_{(0)}=E_{(0)}$$
$$a\in\bar{P},\quad b\notin\bar{P},\quad a\bar{\varepsilon}\{a\}, b\bar{\varepsilon}\{a\},$$

where $\bar{\varepsilon}$ is the value of $\varepsilon_{(0)}$ in $\mathfrak{N}$.

If we take for A the formula $\bigvee x^{(0)}\bigwedge z(z\varepsilon x^{(0)}\rightarrow P(z))$, A is a Σ-formula which is satisfied in $\mathfrak{M}$ but not in $\mathfrak{N}$.

c) Let $\mathfrak{M}_0$ be the τ-intersection of $\mathfrak{M}$ and $\mathfrak{M}'$, and let $\bar{x}_i$ be in the domain of type τ_i of $\mathfrak{M}_0$, for $i\leqslant n$. Since $\mathfrak{M}$ is a τ-extension of $\mathfrak{M}_0$ either $(\bar{x}_1, \ldots, \bar{x}_n)$ satisfies A in both $\mathfrak{M}_0$ and in $\mathfrak{M}$ or in neither, and similarly for $\mathfrak{M}_0$ and $\mathfrak{M}'$. Hence A is $\mathscr{A}-\tau$-invariant. Since, by Exercise 3b) all Σ-formulas are stable for τ-extensions C_1 and C_2 are $\mathscr{A}$-stable. Since $\mathscr{A}\vdash(\neg C_1)\leftrightarrow C_2$, C_1 and $\neg C_1$ are both $\mathscr{A}$-stable for extensions, and hence $\mathscr{A}-\tau$-invariant.

4. We modify the notation of Theorem 5 and Exercise 3 as follows. We say that $\mathfrak{M}'$ is a (τ^0)-*extension* of $\mathfrak{M}$ if $\mathfrak{M}$ and $\mathfrak{M}'$ are τ-realizations, $\mathfrak{M}'$ is a τ-extension of $\mathfrak{M}$ and $E_0=E_0'$. A formula A is said to be $\mathscr{A}-(\tau^0)$-*invariant* if for each pair $\mathfrak{M}$, $\mathfrak{M}'$ of τ-models of $\mathscr{A}$ such that $E_0=E_0'$ and the restrictions of $\mathfrak{M}$, $\mathfrak{M}'$ to E_0 are equal we have that for each n-tuple $(\bar{x}_1, \ldots, \bar{x}_n)$ with $\bar{x}_i\in E_{\tau_i}\cap E'_{\tau_i}(1\leqslant i\leqslant n)$, $(\bar{x}_1, \ldots, \bar{x}_n)\in\bar{A}_{\mathfrak{M}}$ if and only if $(\bar{x}_1, \ldots, \bar{x}_n)\in\bar{A}_{\mathfrak{M}'}$. The notions of a $\Sigma-(\tau^0)$-formula and of a (τ^0)-restricted formula are obtained from those of a Σ-formula and of a restricted formula by dropping all restriction on the variables of type 0.

a) Show that A is $\mathscr{A}-(\tau^0)$-invariant if and only if there is a formula B which is (τ^0)-restricted to the free variables of A such that $\mathscr{A}\vdash A\leftrightarrow B$.

b) Let $\mathscr{A}$ be a set of closed formulas of $\mathscr{L}^\tau$ such that given any τ-model $\mathfrak{M}$ of $\mathscr{A}$ the principal extension of $\mathfrak{M}$ (see Chapter 5) is also a τ-model of $\mathscr{A}$. Show that if A and $\neg A$ are both $\mathscr{A}$-stable for (τ^0)-extensions they are also $\mathscr{A}-(\tau^0)$-invariant.

c) Find a counter-example to b) when "(τ^0)" is replaced by "τ".

Answer.

a) Let $x_1^{\tau_1}, \ldots, x_n^{\tau_n}$ be the free variables of A which are not of type 0. We introduce the languages $\mathscr{L}_0^\tau, \mathscr{L}_1^\tau, \mathscr{L}_2^\tau$ and the type τ', and add the constants $a_1^{\tau_1}, \ldots, a_n^{\tau_n}$ (as in Lemma 4) and we let $\mathrm{TC}_0(a_1^{\tau_1}, \ldots, a_n^{\tau_n})$, or just TC_0, be the conjunction of the formulas

$$\bigwedge y^\sigma (y^\sigma \varepsilon [a_1^{\tau_1}] \vee \cdots \vee y^\sigma \varepsilon [a_n^{\tau_n}]) \qquad \sigma \neq 0 .$$

Since A is (τ^0)-invariant we have

$$\begin{aligned}&\mathscr{A}_1 \cup \mathscr{A}_2 \cup \tau - \mathrm{Ext}(\mathscr{L}_0, \mathscr{L}_1) \cup \tau - \mathrm{Ext}(\mathscr{L}_0, \mathscr{L}_2) \cup \\ &\quad \cup \{\bigwedge x_1^0 \bigvee x^0 (x^0 = x_1^0), \bigwedge x_2^0 \bigvee x^0 (x^0 = x_2^0)\} \cup \mathrm{TC}_0 \vdash \\ &\quad A_1 (a_1^{\tau_1}, \ldots, a_n^{\tau_n}) \leftrightarrow A_2 (a_1^{\tau_1}, \ldots, a_n^{\tau_n}) .\end{aligned}$$

By the Interpolation Lemma we can find a formula B', of $\mathscr{L}_0$ such that

$$\mathscr{A}_1 \cup \tau - \mathrm{Ext}(\mathscr{L}_0, \mathscr{L}_1) \cup \{\bigwedge x_1^0 \bigvee x^0 (x^0 = x_1^0)\} \cup \mathrm{TC}_0 \vdash A_1 \leftrightarrow B' .$$

If we replace ε by ε_1 and all the variables x of $\mathscr{L}_0$ of type other than zero by $x_1 \varepsilon_1 [a_1^{\tau_1}] \vee \cdots \vee x_1 \varepsilon_1 [a_n^{\tau_n}]$, B' takes the desired form. The converse is obvious.

b) Let $\mathfrak{M}$ and $\mathfrak{M}'$ be two τ-models of $\mathscr{A}$ such that $E_0 = E_0'$ and the restrictions of $\mathfrak{M}$ and $\mathfrak{M}'$ to E_0 are equal. It follows that the principal extensions of $\mathfrak{M}$ and $\mathfrak{M}'$ are also equal. If $\mathfrak{M}_0$ is their common principal extension and if $\bar{x}_i (1 \leqslant i \leqslant n)$ belongs to their τ-intersection, $\bar{x}_i$ is also in the domain of type τ_i of $\mathfrak{M}_0$. Since $\mathfrak{M}_0$ is a (τ^0)-extension of $\mathfrak{M}$ and A and $\neg A$ are both $\mathscr{A} - (\tau^0)$-stable, $(\bar{x}_1, \ldots, \bar{x}_n) \in \bar{A}_{\mathfrak{M}}$ if and only if $(\bar{x}_1, \ldots, \bar{x}_n) \in \bar{A}_{\mathfrak{M}_0}$, a similar result holds for the pair $\mathfrak{M}', \mathfrak{M}_0$. Therefore A is $\mathscr{A} - (\tau^0)$-invariant.

c) Let $\mathscr{A}_1$ be the set of formulas of the first order language $\mathscr{L}$ such that there are two existential formulas A_1, A_2 containing the single variable x and $\mathscr{A}_1 \vdash A_1 \leftrightarrow \neg A_2$, but such that there is no quantifier free formula A' with $\mathscr{A}_1 \vdash A_1 \leftrightarrow A'$, as in Example 1(c). We consider the language $\mathscr{L}^{(0)}$ and we put

$$\mathscr{A} = \mathscr{A}_1 \cup \{\bigwedge x^{(0)} \bigwedge y^{(0)} [\bigwedge z^0 (z \varepsilon x \leftrightarrow z \varepsilon y) \rightarrow x = y]\} .$$

Clearly $\mathscr{A}$ satisfies the hypothesis of b). We put $A = \bigwedge x (x \varepsilon X \rightarrow A_1)$ where X is a variable of type (0). Since $A \vdash \neg A \leftrightarrow \bigvee x (x \varepsilon X \wedge A_2)$, A and $\neg A$ are $\mathscr{A}$-stable for τ-extensions. But A is not $\mathscr{A} - \tau$-invariant because there is no formula B restricted to $[X]$ such that $\mathscr{A} \vdash A \leftrightarrow B$. Indeed if there were such a formula B then by taking $\bar{X}=\{u\}$ and replacing all parts of B of the form $y\varepsilon X$ by $y=u$ we would obtain a quantifier free formula equivalent to A_1.

5. a) Show that

(i) the field of rational numbers is rigidly contained in all commutative fields of characteristic zero;

(ii) the field of complex rational numbers is contained but not rigidly contained in all closed algebraic fields of characteristic zero.

b) Let $\mathscr{L}$ be the language (of set theory) whose only relational symbol is ε. Let A be the conjunction of the formulas

$$\bigvee x \bigwedge y \neg (y\varepsilon x)$$
$$\bigwedge x \bigwedge y \bigvee z \bigwedge u [u\varepsilon z \leftrightarrow (u\varepsilon x \vee u = y)]$$
$$\bigwedge x \bigwedge y [\bigwedge z (z\varepsilon x \leftrightarrow z\varepsilon y) \rightarrow x = y].$$

Let $\mathscr{L}_1$ be the language which is obtained when the individual constant c and the ternary relation symbol R are added to $\mathscr{L}$. Put

$$B = \bigwedge y \neg (y\varepsilon c) \wedge [R(x, y, z) \leftrightarrow \bigwedge u [u\varepsilon z \leftrightarrow (u\varepsilon x \vee u = y)].$$

Show that

(i) no realization of $\mathscr{L}$ is rigidly contained in all models of A,

(ii) each model of A can be extended in a unique way to a model of B,

(iii) the realization of $\mathscr{L}_1$ whose set of individuals is the set C_ω of all hereditarily finite sets and in which $\bar{\varepsilon}$ is $\in \cap (C_\omega \times C_\omega)$, $\bar{c}$ is the empty set and $\bar{R}$ is the relation $\bar{z}=\bar{x}\cup\{\bar{y}\}$, is rigidly contained in all models of $A \wedge B$.

Answer.

a) (i) is obvious even if we drop the constants 0 and 1 of the language of fields. Using the notation of Theorem 5 we take as the formula $A_0(x, x_1)$ the formula $x_1+x=x_1$ and for $A_1(x, x_1)$ the formula $(x\cdot x_1=x_1 \wedge x\neq x_1)$.

(ii) the map $z\rightarrow\bar{z}$ where $\bar{z}$ is the conjugate of z shows that the field of complex rationals is not even rigidly contained in itself.

b) (i) A realization of $\mathscr{L}$, contained in all models of A, is $\langle C_\omega, \in \cap (C_\omega \times C_\omega)\rangle$. This is not even rigidly contained in itself since it is isomorphic to all subrealizations C_ω^a defined as follows. $a\in C_\omega$ and C_ω^a is the smallest class which contains a and is closed under the operation $(x, y)\rightarrow x\cup\{y\}$.

(ii) A implies the existence of the empty set and by the third axiom, the axiom of extensionality, this empty set is unique. Hence the value of

c is determined. Similarly, given a model of A, the axiom of extensionality determines the value of R.

(iii) This is obvious because each element of C_ω can be generated from the empty set by the operation $(x, y) \to x \cup \{y\}$.

6. Consider a first order language $\mathscr{L}$ with a single type of object, and the language $\mathscr{L}^\tau$ associated with it in Chapter 5. We will assume that $\mathscr{L}$ contains a set $\mathbf{C}$ of individual constants. Let $\mathscr{A}$ be a set of formulas of $\mathscr{L}$ which has a $\mathbf{C}$-model so that for each pair (c, c'), where c and c' are distinct elements of $\mathbf{C}$, $\mathscr{A} \vdash \neg c = c'$. If $\sigma \in [\tau]$, a set X^σ of the hierarchy of types built on $\mathbf{C}$ is said to *belong* to a realization $\mathfrak{N}^\tau$ of $\mathscr{A}^\tau$ if X^σ is the image of an element of $\mathfrak{N}^\tau$, of type σ, under the canonical map of $\mathfrak{N}^\tau$ into $\mathfrak{N}_0^\tau$, where $\mathfrak{N}_0^\tau$ is a $\mathbf{C}$-model isomorphic to the restriction of $\mathfrak{N}^\tau$ to the type 0, and where $\mathfrak{N}_0^\tau$ is the principal realization on $\mathfrak{N}_0$.

Show that if X^σ belongs to all $\mathbf{C}$-realizations of $\mathscr{A}$ then X^σ is hereditarily finite on $\mathbf{C}$.

Answer. The set X^0 of elements of type 0 which are in the transitive closure of X^σ is defined, in all models, by the disjunction of all the formulas

$$\bigvee x_1^{\tau_1} \ldots \bigvee x_r^{\tau_r} (x \varepsilon x_1^{\tau_1} \varepsilon \ldots \varepsilon x_r^{\tau_r} \varepsilon a^\sigma)$$

where $\tau_1, \ldots, \tau_r$ is a finite sequence such that $0 \in \tau_1 \in \cdots \in \tau_r$ (using the notation of Lemma 4). The constant a^σ denotes the set X^σ which, by hypothesis, belongs to all models of $\mathscr{A}$. By Theorem 7, X^0 is therefore finite and so X^σ is hereditarily finite.

7. If $\mathscr{A}$ is a countable set of closed formulas of the language $\mathscr{L}$ which has a $\mathbf{C}$-model and if $X \subseteq \mathbf{C}$ is definable-*on* $\mathbf{C}$ in all $\mathbf{C}$-models of $\mathscr{A}$, show that there is a closed formula B and a formula $A(x)$ with a single free variable x such that $\mathscr{A} \vdash B \to A(c)$ if $c \in X$ and $\mathscr{A} \vdash B \to \neg A(c)$ if $c \notin X$.

Answer. By Theorem 8 there is a *finite* family

$$\{F_j(x_1, \ldots, x_n) : j \leqslant N\}$$

of formulas, and a formula $A_1(x, x_1, \ldots, x_n)$ such that

$$\mathscr{A} \cup \{\bigvee x_1 \ \ldots \ \bigvee x_n (F_1 \wedge \cdots \wedge F_N)\}$$

has a model and

$$\mathscr{A} \vdash \bigwedge x_1 \dots \bigwedge x_n [(F_1 \wedge \dots \wedge F_N) \rightarrow A_1(c, x_1, \dots, x_n)] \quad \text{if} \quad c \in X$$

and

$$\mathscr{A} \vdash \bigwedge x_1 \dots \bigwedge x_n [(F_1 \wedge \dots \wedge F_N) \rightarrow \neg A_1(c, x_1, \dots, x_n) \quad \text{if} \quad c \notin X.$$

We take as the formula B the formula $\bigvee x_1 \dots \bigvee x_n (F_1 \wedge \dots \wedge F_N)$ and as $A(x)$ the formula $\bigvee x_1 \dots \bigvee x_n (F_1 \wedge \dots \wedge F_N \wedge A_1)$. If $c \in X$, $\mathscr{A} \vdash B \rightarrow A(c)$ and if $c \notin X$, $\mathscr{A} \vdash \neg A(c)$ and a fortiori $\mathscr{A} \vdash B \rightarrow \neg A(c)$.

8. Let $\mathscr{L}_0$ be the language of ordered fields and let $\mathscr{A}_0$ be the set of axioms for a real closed field (see Chapter 4, Section V). We consider a set $\mathbf{C}$ of constants of $\mathscr{L}_0$ which represent each rational number, and the language $\mathscr{L}$ obtained by adding these extra individual constants to $\mathscr{L}_0$ .Give counter-examples to the following statements.

a) If $\mathscr{A}$ is countable and $X \subseteq \mathbf{C}$ is definable-*on* $\mathbf{C}$ in all $\mathbf{C}$-models of $\mathscr{A}$, there is a formula $A(x)$ of $\mathscr{L}$ such that for all $c \in \mathbf{C}$, $\mathscr{A} \vdash A(c)$ if $c \in X$ and $\mathscr{A} \vdash \neg A(c)$ if $c \notin X$.

b) If X is definable-*on* $\mathbf{C}$ in all $\mathbf{C}$-models of $\mathscr{A}$ there is a closed formula B and a formula $A(x)$ such that $\mathscr{A} \cup \{B\}$ has a model and for all $c \in \mathbf{C}$, $\mathscr{A} \vdash B \rightarrow A(c)$ if $c \in X$ and $\mathscr{A} \vdash B \rightarrow \neg A(c)$ if $c \notin X$. (Obviously we do not assume that $\mathscr{A}$ is countable.)

Answer. We let X be a cut of the rationals which is not definable in the language $\mathscr{L}_0$. Such a cut certainly exists since there are uncountably many cuts of the rationals while the set of cuts definable in $\mathscr{L}_0$ is countable since $\mathscr{L}_0$ is countable. We are trying to find a set of axioms $\mathscr{A} \supseteq \mathscr{A}_0$ such that X is definable-*on* $\mathbf{C}$ in all models of $\mathscr{A}$.

a) We add to $\mathscr{L}_0$ the two individual constants u and v, and we let $\mathscr{A}_1 = \{c < u < c' \vee c < v < c' : c \in X, c' \in -X\}$. We put $\mathscr{A} = \mathscr{A}_0 \cup \mathscr{A}_1$. X is definable in each model of $\mathscr{A}$ either by the formula $x < u$ or by $x < v$. Suppose that $A(x)$ is a formula of $\mathscr{L}$ such that $\mathscr{A} \vdash \mathscr{A}(c)$ if $c \in X$ and otherwise $\mathscr{A} \vdash \neg A(c)$.

Since $A(x)$ is a formula of $\mathscr{L}$ there is a formula $B(x, y, z)$ of $\mathscr{L}_0$ such that $A(x) = B(x, u, v)$. Consider the models $\mathfrak{M}$ whose domain is the set $\mathbf{R}$ of real numbers with the usual ordering and which satisfy $\mathscr{A}$ (so that either $\bar{u}$ or $\bar{v}$ is the cut X). If $\bar{u} = X$, then $\bigvee y \bigwedge z B(c, y, z)$ is true in $\mathfrak{M}$ for $c \in X$; if $\bar{v} = X$ then $\neg \bigvee y \bigwedge z B(c, y, z)$ is true in $\mathfrak{M}$ for $c \notin X$. Since $\bigvee y \bigwedge z B(x, y, z)$ is a formula of $\mathscr{L}_0$ and $\mathscr{A}_0$ is complete, for each $c \in \mathbf{C}$

$\mathscr{A}_0 \vdash \bigvee y \bigwedge z B(c, y, z)$ if $c \in X$, and $\mathscr{A}_0 \vdash \neg \bigvee y \bigwedge z B(c, y, z)$ otherwise. This contradicts that X is not definable in $\mathscr{L}_0$.

b) We add to $\mathscr{L}_0$ the individual constants $u_\alpha (\alpha < \aleph_1)$ and consider an enumeration $c_1, \ldots, c_n, \ldots,$ of the elements of X. Let

$$\mathscr{A}_1 = \{u_\alpha < c : c \in \mathbf{C} - X, \alpha < \aleph_1\} \cup \{u_\alpha \neq u_\beta : \alpha < \beta < \aleph_1\} \cup$$
$$\cup \{(u_{\alpha 0} < u_{\alpha_1} < \cdots < u_{\alpha_j}) \to (c_j < u_{\alpha_j}) : \alpha_i < \aleph_1, i \leqslant j\}$$

for each integer j.

$\mathscr{A}_0 \cup \mathscr{A}_1$ has a model $\mathfrak{M}$ since every finite subset has a model. Further, X is definable in all models of $\mathscr{A}_0 \cup \mathscr{A}_1$ since in an uncountable totally ordered set at least one element has an infinite number of predecessors. If u_α is such an element, then $x < u_\alpha$ defines X *on* $\mathbf{C}$ in the model $\mathfrak{M}$.

To prove b), we suppose that $B_1, B_2(x)$ are two formulas of $\mathscr{L}$. There are therefore two formulas $C_1(x_0, \ldots, x_p)$ and $C_2(x, x_0, \ldots, x_p)$ of $\mathscr{L}_0$ such that $B_1 = C_1(u_{\alpha_0}, \ldots, u_{\alpha_p})$ and $B_2 = C_2(x, u_{\alpha_0}, \ldots, u_{\alpha_p})$. If for $c \in \mathbf{C} \cap X$, $\mathscr{A} \cup \mathscr{A}_1 \vdash B_1 \to B_2(c)$ and, for $c \in \mathbf{C} - X$, $\mathscr{A} \cup \mathscr{A}_1 \vdash B_1 \to \neg B_2(c)$ then because $\mathbf{C}$ is countable, there is a countable subset $\mathscr{A}'_1$ of $\mathscr{A}_1$ such that

$$\mathscr{A} \cup \mathscr{A}'_1 \vdash B_1 \to B_2(c) \quad \text{for} \quad c \in X$$

and

$$\mathscr{A} \cup \mathscr{A}'_1 \vdash B_1 \to \neg B_2(c) \quad \text{for} \quad c \notin X.$$

Let $u_{\alpha_n}(n = p+1, p+2, \ldots)$ be an enumeration of the constants which occur in $\mathscr{A}'_1$, but not in $B_1 \to B_2(c)$ and suppose that $\bar{u}_{\alpha_0} < \cdots < \bar{u}_{\alpha_p}$ in $\mathfrak{M}$.

We put $B^*(y, x_0, \ldots, x_p) = C_1(x_0, \ldots, x_p) \wedge c_0 < x_0 \wedge c_1 < x_1 \wedge \cdots \wedge c_p < x_p \wedge x_0 < x_1 < \cdots < x_p < y$. Since B_1 is true in $\mathfrak{M}$ and $\bar{u}_{\alpha_0} < \cdots < \bar{u}_{\alpha_p}$ the formula $\bigvee x_0 \cdots \bigvee x_p B^*(c, x_0, \ldots, x_p)$ of $\mathscr{L}_0$ is true in $\mathfrak{M}$ for all $c \in \mathbf{C} - X$. But X is not definable in $\mathscr{L}_0$ and hence there is some $c_k \in X$ such that $\bigvee x_0 \cdots \bigvee x_p B^*(c_k, x_0, \ldots, x_p)$ is true in $\mathfrak{M}$.

We can now deduce

(i) for each integer i, $\bigwedge x_0 \ldots \bigwedge x_p [B^*(c_k, x_0, \ldots, x_p) \to C_2(c_i, x_0, \ldots, x_p)]$ is true in $\mathfrak{M}$.

Since, by hypothesis, $\mathscr{A} \cup \mathscr{A}'_1 \vdash C_1(u_{\alpha_0}, \ldots, u_{\alpha_p}) \to C_2(c_i, u_{\alpha_0}, \ldots, u_{\alpha_p})$, it is sufficient to note that if $B^*(c_k, \bar{x}_0, \ldots, \bar{x}_p)$ is true in $\mathfrak{M}$, $\mathscr{A}_0 \cup \mathscr{A}'_1$ is satisfied in the model $\mathfrak{M}'$ obtained from $\mathfrak{M}$ as follows:

$$\bar{u}_{\alpha_i} = \bar{x}_i \qquad 1 \leqslant i \leqslant p$$

and for $\bar{u}_{\alpha_{p+1}}, \bar{u}_{\alpha_{p+2}} \ldots$ we take an increasing sequence of elements from the domain of $\mathfrak{M}$ such that $c_n < \bar{u}_{\alpha_m} < X$ for all $n < m$. Consequently $C_2(c_i, u_{\alpha_0}, \ldots, u_{\alpha_p})$ is true in $\mathfrak{M}'$ and $C_2(c_i, x_0, \ldots, x_p)$ is therefore true in $\mathfrak{M}$.

Similarly we have

(ii) for each $c \in \mathbf{C} - X$, the formula $\bigwedge x_0 \ldots \bigwedge x_p [B^*(c_k, x_0, \ldots, x_p) \rightarrow \neg C_2(c, x_0, \ldots, x_p)]$ is true in $\mathfrak{M}$.

By (i) and (ii) $\bigwedge x_0 \ldots \bigwedge x_p [B^*(c_k, x_0, \ldots, x_p) \rightarrow \neg C_2(x, x_0, \ldots, x_p)]$ defines X *on* $\mathbf{C}$ in $\mathfrak{M}$. But $\mathscr{A}_0$ is complete and so this formula defines X in all models of $\mathscr{A}_0$, which contradicts the choice of $\mathscr{A}_0$.

CHAPTER 7

PRINCIPAL MODELS: MODELS OF INFINITE FORMULAS

The first part of this chapter deals with an important class of realizations of the language with a finite number of types which was described in Chapter 5. These are the principal (or full) models, where the domain C_0 is arbitrary but where the domain of each of the other types of variable is made up of *all* the sets, of the corresponding type, of the type structure with base C_0. The first result reduces validity for principal realizations of languages of *finite* order to validity in the principal realizations of certain (appropriately chosen) *second* order languages. As stated in the summary of Chapter 3, second order validity cannot, in general, be reduced to first order validity. This follows from the results of Exercise 5 of Chapter 3 and Exercises 1 and 5 of this chapter. We give a certain class of second order formulas which are equivalent to infinite sets of first order formulas: this is the generalization of the embedding theorem which we also mentioned in the summary of Chapter 3.

The infinite systems of axioms just mentioned (and those of previous chapters) can be considered as infinite conjunctions of finite formulas. The second part of this chapter treats languages which contain other *infinitely long* expressions, in particular the formulas $\bigwedge x \bigvee A_i x (i \in I)$ where $\bigvee A_i$ denotes the infinite disjunction of the finite formulas $A_i (i \in I)$. Exercise 5 gives a list of common structures defined by such formulas. The main result is a simple characterization of the class of finite formulas which are valid in all models of a countable system of axioms $A^m (m = 1, 2, \ldots)$ of the form $\bigwedge x \bigvee_n B_n^m x (n = 1, 2, \ldots)$. This result does not extend directly to the uncountable case (see Exercise 4). For recent work on the (flourishing) subject of infinite formulas see the book: The Theory of Models (North-Holland Publ. Co., Amsterdam, 1965) particularly the papers by KARP, KEISLER and SCOTT.

The last two results of the preceding chapter are generalized to the languages here treated; they take an especially simple form in the case of models of the theory of types which satisfy the infinite formula $\bigwedge x \bigvee_n (x = c_n)$, that is, models whose domain C_0 is the set $\{c_0, c_1, \ldots\}$.

To state more delicate results on languages containing infinite formulas and their realizations, one needs notions from the theory of recursive functions of (infinite) ordinals; even the generalization of the Finiteness Theorem to the case of the formula $\bigwedge x \bigvee_n (x = c_n)$ above needs notions from the theory of hyperarithmeticity (recursion on recursive ordinals). This theory also provides an explanation of the special role played by negation and conjunction among all the propositional connectives with an infinite number of variables.

We consider the languages $\mathscr{L}^\tau$ of the theory of types which was described in Chapter 5. It follows from the last Theorem of that chapter that we can associate with each realization $\mathfrak{M}$ of $\mathscr{L}$ a realization $\mathfrak{M}_\tau$ of order τ of $\mathscr{L}$ called the *principal realization of order τ built on $\mathfrak{M}$*. This realization is unique up to isomorphism. In a principal realization the relation $\bar{\varepsilon}_\sigma$, $\sigma=(\sigma_1, \ldots, \sigma_n)$ on $E_{\sigma_1}\times\cdots\times E_{\sigma_n}\times E_\sigma$ is isomorphic to the membership relation on $E_{\sigma_1}\times\cdots\times E_{\sigma_n}\times\mathscr{P}(E_{\sigma_1}\times\cdots\times E_{\sigma_n})$. That is to say, for *each* subset X of $E_{\sigma_1}\times\cdots\times E_{\sigma_n}$ there is a unique element a of E whose "members" in the realization are the elements of X.

A formula of order τ whose closure is satisfied by each principal realization of order τ of $\mathscr{L}$ is called a *theorem of order τ of $\mathscr{L}$*.

We can assume, without loss of generality, that $\mathscr{L}$ does not contain any constant symbols. For suppose that $F(a_1, \ldots, a_n)$ is a formula which contains the constant symbols $a_1, \ldots, a_n$. Then $F(a_1, \ldots, a_n)$ is a theorem of order τ if and only if $F(x_1, \ldots, x_n)$ is one too where $x_1, \ldots, x_n$ are variables of the same types as $a_1, \ldots, a_n$, respectively, which do not occur in $F(a_1, \ldots, a_n)$.

Let $\mathscr{L}_0$ be the language which is obtained from $\mathscr{L}^\tau$ when we regard all the variables as being of the same type (and we keep all the relation symbols of $\mathscr{L}^\tau$). Let $\mathscr{L}^*$ be the language obtained from $\mathscr{L}_0$ by adding the new unary relation symbols T_σ for each $\sigma\leqslant\tau$. With each formula F of $\mathscr{L}^\tau$ we associate a formula F^* of $\mathscr{L}^*$, defined by recursion on the length of F as follows.

i) If $F(x_1^{\sigma_1}, \ldots, x_n^{\sigma_n})$ is atomic, then

$$F^* = F(x_1,\ldots,x_n) \wedge T_{\sigma_1}(x_1) \wedge\cdots\wedge T_{\sigma_n}(x_n).$$

ii) If $F(x_1^{\sigma_1}, \ldots, x_n^{\sigma_n})=\neg G(x_1^{\sigma_1}, \ldots, x_n^{\sigma_n})$, then

$$F^* = \neg G^*(x_1,\ldots,x_n) \wedge T_{\sigma_1}(x_1) \wedge\cdots\wedge T_{\sigma_n}(x_n).$$

iii) If $F(x_1^{\sigma_1}, \ldots, x_n^{\sigma_n})=G(x_1^{\sigma_1}, \ldots, x_n^{\sigma_n})\vee H(x_1^{\sigma_1}, \ldots, x_n^{\sigma_n})$, then

$$F^* = (G^* \vee H^*) \wedge T_{\sigma_1}(x_1) \wedge\cdots\wedge T_{\sigma_n}(x_n).$$

iv) If $F=\bigvee xG(x^\sigma, x_1^{\sigma_1}, \ldots, x_n^{\sigma_n})$, then

$$F^* = \bigvee x\left[T_\sigma(x) \wedge G^*(x, x_1,\ldots,x_n)\right].$$

The formulas of order (0) of $\mathscr{L}^*$ are formed with a new set of variables of type (0) whose elements we will write as X, Y, Z, ... and a new binary relation symbol which we will write e.

Let U be the conjunction of the following formulas of order (0) of $\mathscr{L}^*$:
(1) $\bigwedge x \neg [T_\sigma(x) \wedge T_{\sigma'}(x)]$ for each pair σ, σ' of distinct types $\leqslant \tau$.

(2) $$\bigwedge x_1 \dots \bigwedge x_n \bigwedge x [\varepsilon_\sigma(x_1, \dots, x_n, x) \rightarrow T_{\sigma_1}(x_1) \wedge \cdots \wedge T_{\sigma_n}(x_n) \wedge T_\sigma(x)],$$

for each $\sigma = (\sigma_1, \dots, \sigma_n) \leqslant \tau$.

(3) $$\bigwedge x \bigwedge y [\bigwedge x_1 \dots \bigwedge x_n [\varepsilon_\sigma(x_1, \dots, x_n, x) \leftrightarrow \varepsilon_\sigma(x_1, \dots, x_n, y)] \rightarrow x = y],$$

for each $\sigma = (\sigma_1 \dots, \sigma_n) \leqslant \tau$.

(4) $$\bigwedge x_1 \dots \bigwedge x_n \bigvee y [T_{\sigma_1}(x_1) \wedge \cdots \wedge T_{\sigma_n}(x_n) \rightarrow [T_\sigma(y) \wedge \varepsilon_\sigma(x_1, \dots, x_n, y) \wedge \bigwedge u_1 \dots \bigwedge u_n (\varepsilon_\sigma(u_1, \dots, u_n, y) \rightarrow x_1 = u_1 \wedge \cdots \wedge x_n = u_n)]],$$

for each $\sigma = (\sigma_1, \dots, \sigma_n) \leqslant \tau$.

(5) $$\bigwedge X [\bigwedge x (x \varepsilon X \rightarrow T_\sigma(x)) \rightarrow \bigvee y [T_\sigma(y) \wedge \bigwedge x_1 \dots \bigwedge x_n [\varepsilon_\sigma(x_1, \dots, x_n, y) \leftrightarrow \bigvee z (z \varepsilon X \wedge \varepsilon_\sigma(x_1, \dots, x_n, z))]]],$$

for each $\sigma \leqslant \tau$.

Of the formulas above only those of (5) are of order (0), the others are all of order 0.

THEOREM 1: *Let F be a closed formula of $\mathscr{L}$ of order τ. Then F is a theorem of order τ if and only if $U \rightarrow F^*$ is a theorem of order* (0) *of $\mathscr{L}^*$.*
PROOF: Let $\mathfrak{M}^*$ be a model of (1, 2, 3) with domain E^*. From $\mathfrak{M}^*$ we can derive a realization $\mathfrak{M}_\tau$ of order τ of $\mathscr{L}$, whose domain of type σ is $\bar{T}_\sigma$, the value of T_σ in $\mathfrak{M}^*$, by giving the relation symbols of $\mathscr{L}^\tau$ the values which they have in $\mathfrak{M}^*$. By (1) the domains of $\mathfrak{M}_\tau$ are disjoint and by (2) and (3) $\mathfrak{M}_\tau$ satisfies the axioms of extensionality.

Each realization $\mathfrak{M}_\tau$ of order τ of $\mathscr{L}$ can be obtained in this way from a model $\mathfrak{M}^*$ of (1, 2, 3): if $E_\sigma (\sigma \leqslant \tau)$ are the domains of $\mathfrak{M}_\tau$ we let the domain E^* of $\mathfrak{M}^*$ be $\bigcup_{\sigma \leqslant \tau} E_\sigma$ and we define the value of T_σ in $\mathfrak{M}^*$ by $\bar{T}_\sigma = E_\sigma$. The other relation symbols of $\mathscr{L}^*$ are symbols of $\mathscr{L}^\tau$; they are given the same value in $\mathfrak{M}^*$ as they have in $\mathfrak{M}_\tau$. It can be seen at once that $\mathfrak{M}^*$ satisfies (1, 2, 3) since $\mathfrak{M}$ satisfies the axioms $\mathscr{T}_\tau$ on p. 97.

Let F be a formula of $\mathscr{L}^\tau$. It can easily be shown, by induction on the length of F, that the values of F and F^* in the two associated realizations of $\mathscr{L}^\tau$ and $\mathscr{L}^*$ are equal.

Now let $\mathfrak{M}^*$ be a principal model of U whose set of individuals (domain of type 0) is E^*. We will show that the realization $\mathfrak{M}_\tau$ of order τ of $\mathscr{L}$ which is associated with it is also a principal realization. To do this it will be sufficient to prove that the relation $\bar{\varepsilon}_\sigma$ on $\bar{T}_{\sigma_1} \times \cdots \times \bar{T}_{\sigma_n} \times \bar{T}_\sigma$ (where $\sigma = (\sigma_1, \ldots, \sigma_n)$ and $\bar{\varepsilon}_\sigma, \bar{T}_{\sigma_1}, \ldots, \bar{T}_{\sigma_n}$ are the values of $\varepsilon_\sigma, T_{\sigma_1}, \ldots, T_{\sigma_n}$ in $\mathfrak{M}^*$), is isomorphic to the membership relation on $\bar{T}_{\sigma_1} \times \cdots \times \bar{T}_{\sigma_n} \times \mathscr{P}(\bar{T}_{\sigma_1} \times \cdots \times \bar{T}_{\sigma_n})$, and hence that for each subset K of $\bar{T}_{\sigma_1} \times \cdots \times \bar{T}_{\sigma_n}$ there is some a in $\bar{T}_\sigma$ whose "members" in $\mathfrak{M}_\tau$ are the elements of K.

Let $(a_1, \ldots, a_n)$ be an arbitrary element of K. By (4) there is an element $\phi(a_1, \ldots, a_n)$ of $\bar{T}_\sigma$ whose only "member" in $\mathfrak{M}_\tau$ is $(a_1, \ldots, a_n)$. Because $\mathfrak{M}^*$ is a principal realization there is an element X of the domain of type (0) of $\mathfrak{M}^*$ whose "members" in $\mathfrak{M}_\tau$ are the elements $\phi(a_1, \ldots, a_n)$ for $(a_1, \ldots, a_n) \in K$. Therefore, by (5), there is some $y \in \bar{T}_\sigma$ whose "members" in $\mathfrak{M}_\tau$ are the elements $(a_1, \ldots, a_n)$ of K.

Each principal realization $\mathfrak{M}_\tau$ of $\mathscr{L}$ can be obtained in this way since it is sufficient to define the realization $\mathfrak{M}^*$ of order 0 as above. Then, as we have already seen, $\mathfrak{M}^*$ satisfies (1, 2, 3). $\mathfrak{M}^*$ also satisfies (4) since because $\mathfrak{M}$ is principal if $\sigma = (\sigma_1, \ldots, \sigma_n) \leqslant \tau$ and if $a_1 \in E_{\sigma_1}, \ldots, a_n \in E_{\sigma_n}$, then there is some $a \in E_\sigma$ whose only "member" in $\mathfrak{M}_\tau$ is $(a_1, \ldots, a_n)$. We take for $\mathfrak{M}^*$ the principal realization of order (0) built on the realization thus obtained, and it is obvious that $\mathfrak{M}^*$ satisfies (5).

Now let F be a closed formula of $\mathscr{L}^\tau$. If F is not a theorem of order τ there is a principal realization $\mathfrak{M}_\tau$ of order τ of $\mathscr{L}$ which does not satisfy F. In the principal model $\mathfrak{M}^*$ of U associated with $\mathfrak{M}_\tau$, F^* is not satisfied. Therefore $U \rightarrow F^*$ is not a theorem of order (0) of $\mathscr{L}^*$.

If $U \rightarrow F^*$ is not a theorem of order (0) of $\mathscr{L}^*$ there is a principal model $\mathfrak{M}^*$ of U which does not satisfy F^*. The realization $\mathfrak{M}_\tau$ of order τ of $\mathscr{L}$ associated with $\mathfrak{M}^*$ is principal and does not satisfy F. Therefore F is not a theorem of order τ.

This completes the proof of Theorem 1.

Warning. According to the conventions of Chapter 5, the formulas of ordinary predicate calculus (Chapter 2) are of order 0 by p. 97, and those of the language $\mathscr{L}^*$ above are of order 1 by Exercise 5. In the present chapter we shall use the more usual terms: 'first order' and 'second order' (and, generally, nth order if the variables occurring in the formula F considered have types of *rank* strictly less than n in the sense of p. 96, i.e., the type of the realization $\bar{F}$ of F has rank $\leqslant n$).

THE REDUCTION OF A CLASS OF SECOND ORDER FORMULAS

Let A be a formula of $\mathscr{L}^\tau$ whose free variables, say, $x_1, \ldots, x_n$ are either of the type of individuals or of the type of relations between individuals, i.e. of type $\sigma=(\sigma_1, \ldots, \sigma_n)$ where each $\sigma_j=0$ (we denote this type by (p)). Let $\mathscr{L}_m(m \leqslant n)$ be the first order language which is obtained by adding to $\mathscr{L}$ the symbols $s_i(i \leqslant m)$ which do not occur in $\mathscr{L}$, where s_i is of the same type as x_i. To make things clearer we will write c_i' for s_i if x_i is of type 0, and R_i' (a p_i-ary relation symbol) for s_i if x_i is of type (p_i). Each realization $\mathfrak{M}_m$ of $\mathscr{L}_m$ induces a realization $\mathfrak{M}$ of $\mathscr{L}$, namely the restriction of $\mathfrak{M}_m$ to the language $\mathscr{L}$. In fact $\mathfrak{M}_m=\mathfrak{M} \cup \{\bar{s}_i : i \leqslant m\}$, where $\bar{s}_i$ is an element of the domain of $\mathfrak{M}$ if $s_i=c_i'$, and an element of the domain $E_{(p_i)}$ of $\mathfrak{M}_\tau$ of type (p_i) if $s_i=R_i'$: in this case $\bar{s}_i \in E_{(p_i)}$ because *each* subset of E^{p_i} is in the domain of type (p_i) of the principal model.

We say that A is *reducible* to the class $\mathscr{A}$ of formulas of $\mathscr{L}_m$ if for each realization $\mathfrak{M} \cup \{\bar{s}_i : i \leqslant m\}$, $\{\bar{s}_i : i \leqslant m\}$ satisfies A in $\mathfrak{M}_\tau$ if and only if $\mathfrak{M}_m$ satisfies each formula of $\mathscr{A}$.

LEMMA 2: *Each formula* $\bigwedge x_{i+1} \ldots \bigwedge x_n A_n$ *of* $\mathscr{L}^\tau$, *where* A_n *is quantifier free is reducible to a (single) universal prenex formula* A_i^0 *of* $\mathscr{L}_i$ *and each formula of* $\mathscr{L}_n$ *is reducible to a (single) formula of* $\mathscr{L}^\tau$ (A_n^0 is called the *canonical translation of* A_n).

PROOF: Since A_n is quantifier free it is a propositional formula built up from the atomic formulas of $\mathscr{L}$ and the formulas $(t_1, \ldots, t_{p_i})\, \varepsilon_{(p_i)}\, x_i$ $(1 \leqslant i \leqslant n$, x_i is of type $(p_i))$. A_n^0 is the formula which is obtained from A_n by first replacing x_i by c_i' if x_i is of type 0 and then replacing $(t_1, \ldots, t_{p_i})$ $\varepsilon_{(p_i)}\, x_i$ by $R_i'(t_1, \ldots, t_{p_i})$. Clearly each atomic formula B of A_n is reducible to B_n^0 and the propositional connectives preserve reducibility. Conversely, each quantifier free formula of $\mathscr{L}_n$ is reducible to the formula of $\mathscr{L}^\tau$ which is obtained by first replacing each occurrence of c_i' by x_i and then replacing $R_i'(t_1, \ldots, t_{p_i})$ by $(t_1, \ldots, t_{p_i})\, \varepsilon_{(p_i)}\, x_i$. The quantifiers of $\mathscr{L}_n$ preserve reducibility since the (individual) variables range over the same domain in $\mathfrak{M}$ as in $\mathfrak{M}_n$.

Now suppose that $\bigwedge x_{i+2} \ldots \bigwedge x_n A_n$ is reducible to A_{i+1}^0; thus $\mathfrak{M} \cup \{\bar{s}_j : j \leqslant i\}$ satisfies $\bigwedge x_{i+1} \ldots \bigwedge x_n A_n$ if and only if for *each* value $\bar{s}_{i+1}^*$ of s_{i+1} in $\mathfrak{M}$ of the same type as x_{i+1}, $\mathfrak{M} \cup \{\bar{s}_j : j \leqslant i\} \cup \{s_{i+1}^*\}$ satisfies A_{i+1}^0.

We now consider the two cases:

1. x_{i+1} is of type 0 and so $s_{i+1}=c_{i+1}'$. In this case $\bigwedge x_{i+1} \ldots \bigwedge x_n A_n$

is equivalent to $\bigwedge x'_{i+1} A'_{i+1}$ where A'_{i+1} is obtained from A_{i+1} by replacing c'_{i+1} by x'_{i+1}. Clearly, $\bigwedge x'_{i+1} A'_{i+1}$ is a universal prenex formula of $\mathscr{L}_i$.

2. x_{i+1} is of type (p_i). Let $A'_{i+1} = \bigwedge u_1 \dots \bigwedge u_l X_1$, where X_1 is quantifier free. Let T be the set of terms which occur in X_1 and let $\bar{u}_1, \dots, \bar{u}_l$ be elements of E_0. Clearly, if there is some $\bar{R}'_{i+1}$ such that the realization $\mathfrak{M}' = \mathfrak{M} \cup \{\bar{s}_j : j \leqslant i\} \cup \{\bar{R}'_{i+1}, \bar{u}_1, \dots, \bar{u}_l\}$ satisfies $\neg X_1$, then the restriction of $\mathfrak{M}'$ to the finite set $\{\bar{t} : t \in T\}$ also satisfies $\neg X_1$. Let X_2 be the conjunction of all the formulas $t_1 = t'_1 \wedge \cdots \wedge t_q = t'_q \wedge S(t_1, \dots, t_q) \to S(t'_1, \dots, t'_q)$, for each q-ary relation symbol S of $\mathscr{L}_{i+1}$ and each $2q$-tuple $(t_1, \dots, t_q, t'_1, \dots, t'_q)$ of terms of T. Let $D_1, \dots, D_r$ be a list of all the diagrams on T in the language $\mathscr{L}_i$. If X_3 is the disjunction of the formulas $D_s (1 \leqslant s \leqslant r)$ such that the formula $X_2 \wedge \neg X_1 \wedge D_s$ is inconsistent then the formula we are looking for is $\bigwedge u_1 \dots \bigwedge u_l X_3$; for suppose that the realization $\mathfrak{M}' = \mathfrak{M} \cup \{\bar{s}_j : j \leqslant i\}$ satisfies this formula. Then for each l-tuple $(\bar{u}_1, \dots, \bar{u}_l)$, $\mathfrak{M}'$ satisfies one of the diagrams D_s and so there is no $\bar{R}'_{i+1}$ such that $\mathfrak{M} \cup \{\bar{s}_j : j \leqslant i\} \cup \{\bar{R}'_{i+1}\}$ satisfies $\bigvee u_1 \dots \bigvee u_l \neg X_1$.

In the opposite case, there are $\bar{u}_1, \dots, \bar{u}_l$ such that $\mathfrak{M} \cup \{\bar{s}_j : j \leqslant i\}$ satisfies X_3 and therefore there is a diagram D_s such that $X_2 \wedge \neg X_1 \wedge D_s$ has a model. In other words there is some $\bar{R}'_{i+1}$ such that $\{\bar{s}_j : j \leqslant i\} \cup \{\bar{R}'_{i+1}, \bar{u}_1, \dots, \bar{u}_l\}$ satisfies $\neg X_1$.

Theorem 3: *Let $A = Q_1 x_1 \dots Q_n x_n A_n$ be a closed prenex formula of $\mathscr{L}^\tau$ where A_n is quantifier free and if $Q_i = \bigvee$, x_i is of type (p_i) while if $Q_i = \bigwedge$ then x_i is either of type* 0 *or of type (p_i). Then A is reducible to a set $\mathscr{A}$ of closed universal prenex formulas of $\mathscr{L}$. That is, $\mathfrak{M}_\tau$ is a model of A if and only if $\mathfrak{M}$ is a model of $\mathscr{A}$.*

Proof: The proof is by induction on the number, n, of quantifiers in A. Let $A_i = Q_{i+1} x_{i+1} \cdots Q_n x_n A_n$. We will show that A_i is reducible to a set $\mathscr{A}_i$ of universal prenex formulas of $\mathscr{L}_i$.

By Lemma 2, A_n is reducible to a set $\mathscr{A}_n$ of universal prenex formulas of $\mathscr{L}_n$ (and this set reduces to a single formula). Now suppose that A_{i+1} is reducible to the set $\mathscr{A}_{i+1}$ of formulas of $\mathscr{L}_{i+1}$.

If $Q_{i+1} = \bigvee$, x_{i+1} is of type (p_i) and therefore $\{\bar{s}_j : j \leqslant i\}$ satisfies A_i in $\mathfrak{M}_\tau$ if and only if there is some $\bar{s}^*_{i+1} \in E_{(p_i)}$ such that $\{\bar{s}_j : j \leqslant i\} \cup \{\bar{s}^*_{i+1}\}$ satisfies A_{i+1}. And, by our induction hypothesis, this is equivalent to the existence of some s^*_{i+1} such that $\mathfrak{M} \cup \{\bar{s}_j : j \leqslant i\} \cup \{\bar{s}^*_{i+1}\}$ satisfies all the formulas of $\mathscr{A}_{i+1}$. Now by the Embedding Theorem (of Chapter 3) the realization

$\mathfrak{M} \cup \{\bar{s}_j : j \leqslant i\}$ can be embedded in a model of $\mathscr{A}_{i+1}$ if and only if it satisfies the set $\mathscr{A}_i$ of universal formulas of $\mathscr{L}_i$ which are consequences of $\mathscr{A}_{i+1}$. It follows, therefore, that A_i is reducible to this set $\mathscr{A}_i$.

If $Q_{i+1} = \wedge$, then by the induction hypothesis, $\{\bar{s}_j : j \leqslant i\}$ satisfies A_i in $\mathfrak{M}_\tau$ if and only if for each $\bar{s}^*_{i+1}$ in $\mathfrak{M}_\tau$, of the same type as x_{i+1}, the realization $\mathfrak{M} \cup \{\bar{s}_j ; j \leqslant i\} \cup \{\bar{s}^*_{i+1}\}$ satisfies A^0_{i+1}. It is now sufficient to apply Lemma 2 to obtain the desired result.

For a generalization of this Theorem, see Exercise 2.

Infinite formulas which define finitary relations

Let $\{A_i : i \in I\}$ be a family of formulas of $\mathscr{L}$ whose free variables are among $x_1, \ldots, x_p$. Let $\mathfrak{M}$ be a realization of $\mathscr{L}$ and let $\bar{A}_i$ be the value of A_i in $\mathfrak{M}$. $\mathfrak{M}$ is said to satisfy the infinite formula $\vee x_1 \ldots \vee x_p \bigwedge_i A_i$ if and only if $\bigcap_{i \in I} \bar{A}_i \neq \emptyset$. If $\bigcap_{i \in I} A_i = \emptyset$ then we say that $\mathfrak{M}$ satisfies the infinite formula $\wedge x_1 \ldots \wedge x_p \bigvee_i \neg A_i$ which is called the negation of the first infinite formula. In what follows we do not discuss general iterations of the propositional operations we have just mentioned (infinite conjunction $\bigwedge$, infinite disjunction $\bigvee$ and negation). The two types of formula we have described here are sufficient to define several classes of structures which cannot be defined by any set of finite first order formulas (see Exercise 5).

We will consider languages with several types of variables. Suppose that $\mathscr{L}$ is a language with equality and that $\mathfrak{M}$ is a model of $\mathscr{E}_{\mathscr{L}}$, and $\mathfrak{M}'$ is the normal realization derived from it by taking a quotient realization. We have already seen that $\mathfrak{M}$ and $\mathfrak{M}'$ satisfy the same closed formulas of $\mathscr{L}$. In fact we will now show that they satisfy the same infinite formulas of $\mathscr{L}$ as well. Suppose that $\vee x_1 \ldots \vee x_p \bigwedge_i A_i(x_1, \ldots, x_p)$ is an infinite formula and let $\bar{A}_i$ and $\bar{\bar{A}}_i$ be the values of $A_i(x_1, \ldots, x_p)$ in $\mathfrak{M}$ and $\mathfrak{M}'$ respectively. Since $\bar{A}_i$ is closed with respect to the equivalence relation $\bar{E}$, it follows that $\bar{\bar{A}}_i = \bar{A}_i / \bar{B}$. Therefore $\bigcap_{i \in I} \bar{\bar{A}}_i = \bigcap_{i \in I} \bar{A}_i / \bar{E}$ and hence $\bigcap_{i \in I} \bar{\bar{A}}_i$ and $\bigcap_{i \in I} \bar{A}_i$ are either both empty or both non-empty.

Lemma 4: *Let $\mathscr{A}$ be a consistent set of finite closed formulas of $\mathscr{L}$ and let $\{\mathscr{A}_i : i < \lambda\}$ be a family of sets of finite closed formulas of $\mathscr{L}$. If each model of $\mathscr{A}$ satisfies one of the sets $\mathscr{A}_i$, there is a set $\mathscr{B}$ of finite closed formulas of $\mathscr{L}$ and an ordinal $j \leqslant \lambda$ such that* $\operatorname{card}(\mathscr{B}) < \operatorname{card}(\lambda)$, $\operatorname{card}(\mathscr{B}) \leqslant \operatorname{card}(\mathscr{L})$, *$\mathscr{A} \cup \mathscr{B}$ is consistent and $\mathscr{A}_j$ is a consequence of $\mathscr{A} \cup \mathscr{B}$.*

Proof: We use the Corollary to the Finiteness Theorem (Chapter 5).

Clearly we can assume that λ is a cardinal. Let $\mathscr{A}_0^+ = \mathscr{A}$. For $j>0$ there are two cases to consider.

1. There is some $k \leqslant j$ such that $\mathscr{A}_k$ is a consequence of $\bigcup_{i<k} \mathscr{A}_i^+$. In this case we put $\mathscr{A}_j^+ = \bigcup_{i<j} \mathscr{A}_i^+$. So in this case $\mathscr{A}_j^+ = \mathscr{A}_k^+$ for all $j \geqslant k$.

2. If there is no such $k \leqslant j$ we put

$$\mathscr{A}_j^+ = \bigcup_{i<j} \mathscr{A}_i^+ \cup \{\neg A_j^*\}$$

where $A_j^* \in \mathscr{A}_j$ and is not a consequence of $\bigcup_{i<j} \mathscr{A}_i^+$.

There is a $j_0 < \lambda$ such that the first case applies; for, if not $\bigcup_{j<\lambda} \mathscr{A}_j^+$ and hence $\mathscr{A}$, would have a model which does not satisfy any $\mathscr{A}_j$ because it satisfies no A_j^*. We let $\mathscr{B} = \{\neg A_i^* : i < j_0\}$. So $\mathscr{B}$ has cardinal $<\lambda$, and $\leqslant$ card $(\mathscr{L})$ since the number of formulas of $\mathscr{L}$ is the same as the cardinal of $\mathscr{L}$ (there are more than card$(\mathscr{L})$ *sets* of formulas of $\mathscr{L}$, which are not equivalent).

THEOREM 5: *Let J be a set of infinite formulas of a language $\mathscr{L}$, with equality, of the form $\bigvee x_1 \ldots \bigvee x_n \mathop{\mathbb{\Lambda}}_\lambda A_\lambda^j(x_1, \ldots, x_n)$ where $\lambda < \Lambda = \text{card}(\mathscr{L})$. Let $\mathscr{A}$ be a set of formulas of $\mathscr{L}$ which has a normal model and such that each normal model of $\mathscr{A}$ satisfies one of the infinite formulas of J. Then there is an infinite formula of J, say $\bigvee x_1 \ldots \bigvee x_n \mathop{\mathbb{\Lambda}}_\lambda A_\lambda(x_1, \ldots, x_n)$, and a family $\{F_i(x_1, \ldots, x_n) : i \in I\}$ of formulas such that* card$(I) <$ card$(J) \times$ card $(\mathscr{L})$, card$(I) \leqslant$ card$(\mathscr{L})$, $\mathscr{A} \cup \{\bigvee x_1 \ldots \bigvee x_n \mathop{\mathbb{\Lambda}}_i F_i(x_1, \ldots, x_n)\}$ *has a normal model and for all $\lambda < \Lambda$ there is some $i \in I$ such that*

$$\mathscr{A} \vdash \bigwedge x_1 \ldots \bigwedge x_n (F_i \to A_\lambda).$$

PROOF: We will use the notion of a *canonical model* which we discussed in Chapter 5. Since we are concerned with a language with equality we will assume that $\mathscr{E}_{\mathscr{L}} \subseteq \mathscr{A}$. Then each model of $\mathscr{A}$, normal or otherwise, satisfies one of the infinite formulas of J and hence satisfies one of the sets $\{A_\lambda^j(a_1, \ldots, a_n) : \lambda < \Lambda\}$ for $a_1, \ldots, a_n \in \Delta$ of the same types as $x_1, \ldots, x_n$. This family of sets has cardinal $=$ card$(J) \times$ card$(\mathscr{L})$. By Lemma 4, there is a family $\{B_i : i \in I\}$ of formulas of $\mathscr{L}_\Delta$ such that card$(I) \leqslant$ card$(\mathscr{L})$ and card$(I) <$ card$(J) \times$ card$(\mathscr{L})$ and a set $\{A_\lambda^j(a_1, \ldots, a_n) : \lambda < \Lambda\}$ such that $\mathscr{A} \cup \Omega \cup \{B_i : i \in I\}$ has a model and has $A_\lambda^j(a_1, \ldots, a_n)$ as a consequence for each $\lambda < \Lambda$.

Thus for each $\lambda < \Lambda$ there is a finite subset of $\{B_i : i \in I\}$, whose conjunction we will denote by B_λ, and a finite subset of $\mathscr{A}$, whose conjunction we will denote by A_λ, such that

$$\Omega \vdash (A_\lambda \wedge B_\lambda) \rightarrow A^j_\lambda(a_1, \ldots, a_n).$$

If $b_1, \ldots, b_p$ are the elements of Δ which occur in B_λ we have therefore by Lemma 5.10 that

$$\theta_{a_1} \wedge \cdots \wedge \theta_{a_n} \wedge \theta_{b_1} \wedge \cdots \wedge \theta_{b_p} \vdash A_\lambda \wedge B_\lambda \rightarrow A^j_\lambda(a_1, \ldots, a_n)$$

and so

$$A_\lambda \vdash (\theta_{a_1} \wedge \cdots \wedge \theta_{a_n} \wedge \cdots \wedge \theta_{b_1} \wedge \cdots \wedge \theta_{b_p} \wedge B_\lambda) \rightarrow A^j_\lambda(a_1, \ldots, a_n).$$

As in Theorem 6.8 (p. 124) we eliminate the elements of Δ other than $a_1, \ldots, a_n$ that occur in $\theta_{a_1} \wedge \ldots \wedge \theta_{a_n} \wedge \theta_{b_1} \wedge \ldots \wedge \theta_{b_p} \wedge B_\lambda$, by existential quantification, and we denote the resulting formula by $F_\lambda(a_1, \ldots, a_n)$. The formulas F_λ make up a set whose cardinal is less than or equal to that of the set of finite subsets of I. The family of the $F_\lambda(a_1, \ldots, a_n)$ has therefore the desired properties.

COROLLARY: *If, in the statement of this Theorem, $\mathscr{L}$ and J are assumed to be countable (thus $\Lambda = \omega$) then there is a* finite *formula $B(x_1, \ldots, x_n)$ such that $\mathscr{A} \cup \{\bigvee x_1 \ldots \bigvee x_n B(x_1, \ldots, x_n)\}$ has a normal model and for each integer p,*

$$\mathscr{A} \vdash \bigwedge x_1 \ldots \bigwedge x_n [B(x_1, \ldots, x_n) \rightarrow A_p(x_1, \ldots, x_n)].$$

COUNTABLE LANGUAGES: COUNTABLE SETS OF INFINITE FORMULAS

The sets of variables, relation symbols and constant symbols of the languages that we now consider will all be assumed to be countable.

THEOREM 6: *Let $\mathscr{A}$ be a set of closed finite formulas of $\mathscr{L}$ and let J be a countable set of infinite formulas of the sort $\bigwedge x_1 \ldots \bigwedge x_p \, \mathrm{W}_n \, A^j_n(x_1, \ldots, x_p)$ $(j = 1, 2, \ldots; p = p(j))$. The set of finite formulas of $\mathscr{L}$ which are satisfied by all models of $\mathscr{A} \cup J$ is the smallest set $\mathscr{A}^J$ of finite formulas of $\mathscr{L}$ such that:*

i) *for each finite closed formula G of $\mathscr{L}$ if $\mathscr{A}^J \vdash G$ then $G \in \mathscr{A}^J$, and*

ii) *for each formula $G(x_1, \ldots, x_p)$ and for each integer j, if for all n*

$$\mathscr{A}^J \vdash \bigwedge x_1 \ldots \bigwedge x_p [A^j_n(x_1, \ldots, x_p) \rightarrow G(x_1, \ldots, x_p)]$$

then $\bigwedge x_1 \ldots \bigwedge x_p G(x_1, \ldots, x_p) \in \mathscr{A}^J$.

(This result would be false if J were not countable, see Exercise 3.)

PROOF: Clearly the set of formulas which are satisfied by all models of $\mathscr{A} \cup J$ contains $\mathscr{A}^J$.

Conversely, suppose that F is a formula which is satisfied by all models of $\mathscr{A} \cup J$. If $\mathscr{A}^J \cup \{\neg F\}$ has no normal model, F is a normal consequence of $\mathscr{A}^J$ and so $F \in \mathscr{A}^J$. If $\mathscr{A}^J \cup \{\neg F\}$ has a normal model, then, by hypothesis, any such model satisfies the negation of one of the formulas of J, say, $\bigvee x_1 \ldots \bigvee x_p \bigwedge\!\!\!\bigwedge_n \neg A_n^{j_0}(x_1, \ldots, x_p)$. By Theorem 5 there is a formula $G(x, \ldots, x_p)$ such that $\mathscr{A}^J \cup \{\neg F, \bigvee x_1 \ldots \bigvee x_p G(x_1, \ldots, x_p)\}$ has a normal model and such that for each integer n

$$\mathscr{A}^J \cup \{\neg F\} \vdash \bigwedge x_1 \ldots \bigwedge x_p [G(x_1, \ldots, x_p) \to \neg A_n^{j_0}(x_1, \ldots, x_p)]$$

and consequently

$$\mathscr{A}^J \cup \{\neg F\} \vdash \bigwedge x_1 \ldots \bigwedge x_p [A_n^{j_0}(x_1, \ldots, x_p) \to \neg G(x_1, \ldots, x_p)].$$

In this case

$$\mathscr{A}^J \vdash \bigwedge x_1 \ldots \bigwedge x_p [A_n^{j_0}(x_1, \ldots, x_p) \to (F \vee \neg G(x_1, \ldots, x_p))].$$

By hypothesis $\bigwedge x_1 \ldots \bigwedge x_p [F \vee \neg G(x_1, \ldots, x_p)] \in \mathscr{A}^J$. Since F is a closed formula, $F \vee \bigwedge x_1 \ldots \bigwedge x_p \neg G(x_1, \ldots, x_p)$ is a consequence of $\mathscr{A}^J$ and so is an element of $\mathscr{A}^J$. Therefore $\mathscr{A}^J \cup \{\neg F, \bigvee x_1 \ldots \bigvee x_p G(x_1, \ldots, x_p)\}$ does not have a model. It follows that $\mathscr{A}^J \cup \{\neg F\}$ does not have a model and so $\mathscr{A}^J \vdash F$.

COROLLARY: *$\mathscr{A} \cup J$ has a model if and only if $\mathscr{A}^J$ has a model.*
PROOF: If $\mathscr{A} \cup J$ has a model this model is also a model of $\mathscr{A}^J$. If $\mathscr{A} \cup J$ does not have a model the finite formula $\perp$ is satisfied by all models of $\mathscr{A} \cup J$. Therefore $\perp \in \mathscr{A}^J$ and so $\mathscr{A}^J$ does not have a model.

Exercises

1. a) Find second order formulas whose classes of principal models are, respectively,

(i) the well-ordered sets,

(ii) the well-ordered sets of order type ω,

(iii) the complete ordered sets,

(iv) the dense complete ordered sets without first or last element with a countable subset (of the domain) which is dense in the domain.

b) Show that the classes (ii) and (iv) above contain, up to isomorphism, a single element.

Answer. Let $\mathscr{L}$ be the first order language with equality which has a single binary relation symbol $<$. Let X, Y, Z be variables of type (0) and let U be a variable of type (0, 0). The rank of each of these variables is 1. Let O be the formula of $\mathscr{L}$ which is the conjunction of the axioms for a total ordering.

a) (i) the formula $O \wedge \bigwedge X \bigwedge x(X(x) \rightarrow \bigvee y[X(y) \wedge \bigwedge z(z<y \rightarrow \neg X(z))])$ of $\mathscr{L}^{(0)}$, which we will denote by B, expresses the fact that each non-empty set X ($\bigvee x X(x)$) has a first element, that is, that $<$ is a well-ordering. (Compare this with the result of Exercise 7 of Chapter 3.)

(ii) $B \wedge \bigwedge x[\bigwedge z \neg(z<x) \vee \bigvee y \bigwedge z(z<x \leftrightarrow (z=y \vee z<y))]$ is the required formula.

(iii) The formula

$$\bigwedge x \bigwedge y((X(x) \wedge y < x) \rightarrow X(y)) \wedge \bigvee x(X(x)) \wedge \bigvee x \neg(X(x)) \wedge \\ \wedge \bigwedge x \bigvee y(X(x) \rightarrow (x < y \wedge X(y)))$$

which we denote by $C(X)$ expresses the fact that X is a cut open at the right. The complete orders are the models of the formula

$$O \wedge \bigwedge X \bigvee x \bigwedge y[C(X) \rightarrow (X(y) \leftrightarrow y < x)]$$

which we denote by *Com*.

(iv) Let $D(Y)$ be the formula

$$\bigwedge x \bigwedge y(x < y \rightarrow \bigvee z(x < z \wedge z < y \wedge Y(z))).$$

$D(Y)$ expresses the fact that Y is a dense subset of the domain. Let $W(Z)$ be the formula of $\mathscr{L}^{(0)}$ which expresses the fact that the restriction of $<$ to Z is a well-ordering of order type ω, and let $I(U, Y, Z)$ be the formula which says that U is the graph of an isomorphism between Y and Z, namely the formula

$$\bigwedge x \bigvee y \bigwedge z[Y(x) \rightarrow (Z(y) \wedge [U(x, z) \leftrightarrow y = z])] \\ \wedge \bigwedge y \bigvee x \bigwedge z[Z(y) \rightarrow (Y(x) \wedge [U(z, y) \leftrightarrow x = z])] \\ \wedge \bigwedge x \bigwedge y[U(x, y) \rightarrow (Y(x) \wedge Z(y))].$$

Then the desired formula is

$$\bigwedge x \bigvee y(y < x) \wedge \bigwedge x \bigvee y(x < y) \wedge O \wedge Com \wedge \\ \wedge \bigvee Y \bigvee Z \bigvee U[D(Y) \wedge W(Z) \wedge I(U, Y, Z)].$$

b) Clearly the well-orderings of order type ω are all isomorphic to the natural ordering of the positive integers. By Exercise 3 of Chapter 4, all countable dense orderings without first or last element are isomorphic to the natural ordering of the rational numbers. It follows that each element of the class (iv) is isomorphic to the natural ordering of the continuum.

2. Let $\mathscr{L}'_m$ be the language which is obtained by adding to the language $\mathscr{L}$ for each $i \leqslant m$, either an individual constant $c_i(i \in I)$ or a p_i-ary relation symbol $R_i(i \in R)$ or a $(p_i - 1)$-ary function symbol $f_i(i \in F)$. Suppose that $F = \{n_1, \ldots, n_k\}$ with $n_i < n_{i+1}$ for $i < k$. Let $\mathscr{L}_m$ be the language obtained from $\mathscr{L}'_m$ by replacing, for each $i \in F, f_i$ by a new p_i-ary relation symbol R_i. For $j \leqslant k$ let $q_j = p_{n_j}$ and let F_j be the formula

$$\bigwedge u_1 \ldots \bigwedge u_{q_j - 1} \bigvee u_{q_j} \bigwedge w \left[R_{n_j}(u_1, \ldots, w) \leftrightarrow w = u_{q_j} \right].$$

a) For each quantifier free formula A' of $\mathscr{L}'_m$ find a universal prenex formula A_0 of $\mathscr{L}_m$ such that for each realization $\mathfrak{M}$ of $\mathscr{L}$, for each sequence $\bar{c}'_i$ of elements of the domain E_0 of $\mathfrak{M}(i \in I)$, $\bar{R}'_i \subseteq E^{p_i}(i \in R)$, $\bar{f}'_i : E_0^{p_i - 1} \to E_0(i \in F)$, $\bar{R}'_i \subseteq E^{p_i}$ and $\bar{R}'$ the graph of $\bar{f}_i(i \in F)$, $\mathfrak{M} \cup \{\bar{c}'_i : i \in I\} \cup \{\bar{R}'_i : i \in R\} \cup \{\bar{f}'_i : i \in F\}$ is a model of A' if and only if the realization $\mathfrak{M} \cup \{\bar{c}'_i : i \in I\} \cup \{\bar{R}'_i : i \in R \cup F\}$ satisfies A_0.

b) Let A' be a quantifier free formula of $\mathscr{L}'_n$, A_0 the corresponding formula of $\mathscr{L}_n$ as in a) and let A_n be the translation of $F_1 \wedge \cdots \wedge F_k \to A_0$ in $\mathscr{L}^\tau$ given by Lemma 2. Show that $Q_1 x_1 \ldots Q_n x_n A_n$ is reducible to a class of universal prenex formulas of $\mathscr{L}$.

c) $\mathscr{L}$ is a language with a single unary relation symbol P. Show that there is no set $\mathscr{A}$ of formulas of $\mathscr{L}$ such that the realization $\langle E, \bar{P} \rangle$ can be extended to a realization $\langle E, \bar{P}, \bar{f} \rangle$ which satisfies

$$\bigwedge x [f(f(x)) = x \wedge (P(x) \leftrightarrow \neg P(f(x)))]$$

if and only if $\langle E, \bar{P} \rangle$ satisfies $\mathscr{A}$.

d) deduce from c) that there is a closed formula $\bigvee x_1 \bigwedge x_2 \bigvee x_3 \bigwedge x_4 A$ of $\mathscr{L}^{(0,0)}$, where A is quantifier free and x_1 is of type $(0, 0)$, x_2, x_3, x_4 of type 0, which is not reducible to any set of formulas of $\mathscr{L}$.

Answer.

a) Let T be the smallest class of terms of $\mathscr{L}'_m$ which contains all the terms which occur in A' and such that $t_1, \ldots, t_{p_i - 1} \in T$ if $f_i(t_1, \ldots, t_{p_i - 1}) \in T$

$(i=n_1,\ldots,n_k)$. For each term $t\in T$ the *degree* of a constant is 0 and the *degree* of $t=1+\max\{\text{degree}(t_j):j<p_i\}$, if $t=f_i(t_1,\ldots,t_{p_i-1})$.

If t is of degree greater than zero, let y_t be an individual variable which does not occur in A' and let $y_t\neq y_{t'}$ if $t\neq t'$. We arrange the y_t according to the degree of t. For each $t=f_i(t_1,\ldots,t_{p_i-1})$ $(t\in T)$ let R_t be the formula $R_i(t_1^*,\ldots,t_{p_i-1}^*,y_t)$ where $t_j^*=y_{t_j}$ if t_j has degree >0 and $t_j^*=t_j$ otherwise. Let B be the conjunction of all the formulas R_t for $t\in T$ of degree >0. The desired formula is

$$\wedge y_{t_1}\cdots\wedge y_{t_s}(B\to A^1)$$

where $t_1,\ldots,t_s$ are the terms of degree >0 which are in T and A^1 is the formula which is obtained by replacing each such t in A' by y_t.

b) Let $A_i=Q_{i+1}x_{i+1}\cdots Q_nx_n[(F_j\wedge\cdots\wedge F_k)\to A]$, where $n_j\geqslant i+1$ and $n_{j-1}<i$. We will show that A_i is *reducible* to a set $\mathscr{A}_i$ of universal prenex formulas of $\mathscr{L}_i$ (in the following sense: if

$$\mathfrak{M}_i=\mathfrak{M}\cup\{\bar{c}_h':h\leqslant i,\,h\in I\}\cup\{\bar{R}_h':h\leqslant i,\,h\in R\}\cup\{\bar{f}_h':h\leqslant i,\,h\in F\}$$

then $\mathfrak{M}_i$ is a model of $\mathscr{A}_i$ if and only if

$$\mathfrak{M}\cup\{\bar{c}_h':h\leqslant i,\,h\in I\}\cup\{\bar{R}_h':h\in R\cup F,\,h\leqslant i\}$$

satisfies A_i, where for $h\in F$, $\bar{R}_h'$ is the graph of $\bar{f}_h'$).

If $i=n$ the result is a consequence of Lemma 2 and a).

Suppose that A_{i+1} is reducible to the class $\mathscr{A}_{i+1}$ of universal prenex formulas of $\mathscr{L}_{i+1}$. If $i+1\neq n_j$ we apply the Embedding Theorem (for languages with function symbols).

If $i+1=n_j$, $Q_{i+1}=\wedge$; let the formula $X\in\mathscr{A}_{i+1}$ be $\wedge u_1\ldots\wedge u_lX_1$ where X_1 is quantifier free. Let T be the set of terms built up from the terms which occur in X (as in a)). With each $t\in T$ we associate the term t^* defined by recursion on the degree of t as follows: If the degree of t is 0 then $t^*=t$. If $t=f_{n_h}(t_1,\ldots,t_q)$, where $q=p_{n_h}-1$ and $h\neq j$, then $t^*=f_{n_h}(t_1^*,\ldots,t_q^*)$ and if $h=j$ then $t^*=y_t$, where y_t is a variable which does not occur in X and we assume that if $t\neq t'$ then $y_t\neq y_{t'}$. Let $\bar{u}_1,\ldots,\bar{u}_l$ be elements of the domain of $\mathfrak{M}$. Now if the function $\bar{f}_{i+1}$ is such that $\mathfrak{M}_i\cup\{\bar{f}_{i+1},\bar{u}_1,\ldots,\bar{u}_l\}$ satisfies $\neg X_1$ the same is also true for any function $\bar{f}_{i+1}^*$ taking the same values as $\bar{f}_{i+1}$ on $\{\bar{t}:t\in T\}$. Let X_1^* be the formula which is obtained from X_1 by replacing t by t^* and let X_2 be the conjunction of all the formulas

$$(t_1^*=s_1^*\wedge\cdots\wedge t_q^*=s_q^*)\to y_t=y_s$$

where $s, t \in T$, $t = f_{i+1}(t_1, \ldots, t_q)$ and $s = f_{i+1}(s_1, \ldots, s_q)$ and $q = p_{i+1} - 1$. There is an $\bar{f}_{i+1}$ such that $\mathfrak{M}_i \cup \{\bar{f}_{i+1}\}$ satisfies X_1 if and only if $\mathfrak{M}_i$ satisfies

$$\bigwedge y_{t_1} \ldots \bigwedge y_{t_r} (X_2 \to X_1^*)$$

where $y_{t_1}, \ldots, y_{t_r}$ is a list of the new variables we have introduced.

c) $\langle E, \bar{P} \rangle$, with $\bar{P} \subseteq E$ can be extended to a model of

$$\bigwedge x [f(f(x)) = x \wedge P(x) \leftrightarrow \neg P(f(x))]$$

if and only if $\bar{P}$ and $E - \bar{P}$ have the same cardinal. By the results on the elimination of quantifiers (Chapter 4, Exercise 7) for each closed formula X of $\mathscr{L}$, X is either true in each realization in which $\bar{P}$ and $E - \bar{P}$ are both infinite or X is false in all such realizations. We take E_0 uncountable, $\bar{P}_0$ countable, E_1 countable (and infinite) and $\bar{P}_1$ and $E_1 - \bar{P}_1$ both countable: then, for any $\mathscr{A}$, either both $\langle E_0, \bar{P}_0 \rangle$ and $\langle E_1, \bar{P}_1 \rangle$ are models of $\mathscr{A}$ or neither; but $\langle E_1, \bar{P}_1 \rangle$ satisfies the formula above, and $\langle E_0, \bar{P}_0 \rangle$ does not.

d) $\langle E, \bar{P} \rangle$ can be extended to a model of

$$\bigwedge x [f(f(x)) = x \wedge P(x) \leftrightarrow \neg P(f(x))]$$

if and only if it can be extended to a model of

$$\bigwedge x \bigvee y \bigwedge z [(B(x, z) \leftrightarrow z = y) \wedge B(y, x) \wedge (P(x) \leftrightarrow \neg P(y))].$$

The desired formula is now obtained by applying Lemma 2.

3. a) Let $\mathscr{A}$ be a set of finite formulas of $\mathscr{L}$ and J a set of infinite formulas of the sort $\bigwedge x_1 \ldots \bigwedge x_p \, \mathrm{W}_n \, A_n(x_1, \ldots, x_p)$. Let $\mathscr{A}^J$ be the set of formulas defined in the statement of Theorem 6. Show that $F \in \mathscr{A}^J$ if and only if there is a countable subset $\mathscr{A}_1$ of $\mathscr{A}$ and a countable subset J_1 of J such that $F \in \mathscr{A}_1^{J_1}$. (Clearly we are not assuming that $\mathscr{A}$ is countable.)

b) Let $\mathscr{L}$ be the language with a single type of variable defined as follows. $C_{\mathscr{L}} = \mathbf{N}$; $R_{\mathscr{L}}^{(1)} = \{R_\xi : \xi \in \mathscr{P}(\mathbf{N})\} \cup \{R\}$ where R is (an arbitrary set which is) neither in $\mathbf{N}$ nor in $R_{\mathscr{L}}^{(1)}$. Let $\mathscr{A}$ be the set of the following formulas of $\mathscr{L}$

$$\{R_\xi(n) : n \in \xi, \; \xi \in \mathscr{P}(\mathbf{N})\}$$
$$\{\neg R_\xi(n) : n \notin \xi, \; \xi \in \mathscr{P}(\mathbf{N})$$
$$\{\bigvee x (R(x) \leftrightarrow \neg R_\xi(x)) : \xi \in \mathscr{P}(\mathbf{N})\}$$

and let $J = \{\bigwedge x \, \mathrm{W}_n \, (x = n)\}$.

Show that $\mathscr{A} \cup J$ does not have a model, but that each countable subset of $\mathscr{A} \cup J$ has a model. Deduce that $\mathscr{A}^J$ has a model.

c) Suppose that $\mathscr{L}$ is the language defined as follows:

$$C_{\mathscr{L}} = \mathbf{N},\ R^{(1)}_{\mathscr{L}} = \{R\}.$$

Let $\mathscr{A} = \emptyset$ and let J be the uncountable set

$$\{\bigwedge x \, \mathrm{W}_n (x = n)\} \cup \{\mathrm{W}_n (\neg)^{\xi_n} R(n) : \xi \in \mathscr{P}(\mathbf{N})\}$$

where $(\neg)^{\xi_n}$ is $\neg$ if $n \in \xi$ and $\neg\neg$ if $n \notin \xi$.

Show that $\mathscr{A} \cup J$ does not have a model but that each countable subset of it does have one.

Answer.

a) It is sufficient to show that the closure conditions which we imposed on the set $\mathscr{A}^J$ are also satisfied by the smallest set $\mathscr{A}^c$ of finite formulas of $\mathscr{L}$ such that

(i) $\mathscr{A} \subseteq \mathscr{A}^c$,

(ii) for each closed formula G of $\mathscr{L}$ if $\mathscr{A}^c \vdash G$ then $G \in \mathscr{A}^c$,

(iii) for each j and for each formula $G(x_1, \ldots, x_p)$ $(p = p(j))$, if there is a countable subset $\mathscr{A}_0 \cup J_0$ of $\mathscr{A} \cup J$ such that for each n

$$\bigwedge x_1 \ldots \bigwedge x_p (A^j_n(x_1, \ldots, x_p) \to G(x_1, \ldots, x_p))$$

is satisfied in all models of $\mathscr{A}_0 \cup J_0$ then $\bigwedge x_1 \ldots \bigwedge x_p G(x_1, \ldots, x_p) \in \mathscr{A}^c$. This is because if for each n there is some countable set $\mathscr{A}_n \cup J_n$ such that $\mathscr{A}_n \cup J_n \vdash \bigwedge x_1 \ldots \bigwedge x_p (A^j_n(x_1, \ldots, x_p) \to G(x_1, \ldots, x_p))$ then we can take for $\mathscr{A}_0$ the countable set $\bigcup_n (\mathscr{A}_n \cup J_n)$.

b) and c) are obvious when we take into account the fact that in any model of $\bigwedge x \, \mathrm{W}_n (x = n)$ the value of R can only be one of the sets $\{n : n \in \xi\}$ for some $\xi \in \mathscr{P}(\mathbf{N})$.

4. Let $\mathscr{L}$ be a countable language with equality and with k types of variables, such that $\mathbf{N} \subseteq C^{(1)}_{\mathscr{L}}$, i.e. such that the natural numbers are constant symbols of type 1 of $\mathscr{L}$. A normal realization of $\mathscr{L}$ with domains $U_1, \ldots, U_k$ is called an *ω-realization* if and only if $U_1 = \mathbf{N}$ and $\bar{n} = n$ for each $n \in \mathbf{N}$, where $\bar{n}$ is the value of n in the realization. Let $\mathscr{A}$ be a set of closed formulas of $\mathscr{L}$ which contains the formula $n \neq n'$ for each pair (n, n') of distinct natural numbers.

a) Show that the set of formulas which are satisfied by all ω-models of $\mathscr{A}$ is the smallest set $\mathscr{A}^\omega$ of formulas of $\mathscr{L}$ such that

(i) $\mathscr{A} \subseteq \mathscr{A}^\omega$,

(ii) for each closed formula F of $\mathscr{L}$ if $\mathscr{A}^\omega \vdash F$ then $F \in \mathscr{A}^\omega$, and

(iii) for each formula $G(x)$ of $\mathscr{L}$, if for each non-negative integer n, $\mathscr{A}^\omega \vdash G(n)$ then $\bigwedge x G(x) \in \mathscr{A}^\omega$.

b) Use Theorem 5 to show that if $X \subseteq \mathbf{N}$ is definable (see Chapter 6) in all ω-models of $\mathscr{A}$ then there are two formulas F and $G(x)$, where x is of type 1, such that for each $p \in \mathbf{N}$,

$$p \in X \quad \text{if and only if} \quad \mathscr{A}^\omega \cup \{F\} \vdash G(p)$$

and

$$p \notin X \quad \text{if and only if} \quad \mathscr{A}^\omega \cup \{F\} \vdash \neg G(p).$$

c) Show that a) is false if the restriction to countable languages is dropped.

Answer.

a) A normal realization of $\mathscr{L}$ is an ω-realization if and only if it satisfies the infinite formula $\bigwedge x \, \mathrm{W}_n \, (x=n)$. We can therefore apply Theorem 6.

b) We first remark that in an ω-realization of $\mathscr{L}$ a subset X of $\mathbf{N}$ is definable if and only if it is definable-*on* $\mathbf{N}$ (since $\mathbf{N}$ is the domain of type 1 of such a realization).

For each formula $A(x, x_1, \ldots, x_n)$ and each integer p let $A_p(x_1, \ldots, x_n) = A(p, x_1, \ldots, x_n)$ if $p \in X$ and $\neg A(p, x_1, \ldots, x_n)$ if $p \notin X$.

Since X is definable in all ω-models of $\mathscr{A}$ each such ω-model satisfies one of the infinite formulas

$$\bigvee x_1 \ldots \bigvee x_n \, \underset{p}{\mathbb{M}} \, A_p(x_1, \ldots, x_n)$$

for some formula $A(x, x_1, \ldots, x_n)$ of $\mathscr{L}$. Thus each model of $\mathscr{A}$ satisfies either one of these formulas or the formula $\bigvee x \, \mathbb{M}_p \, (x \neq p)$, where x is of type 1, and each model of $\mathscr{A}^\omega$ satisfies one of these infinite formulas, say, $\bigvee x_1 \ldots \bigvee x_n \mathbb{M}_p A_p(x_1, \ldots, x_n)$. By the Corollary to Theorem 5 there is a formula $B(x_1, \ldots, x_n)$ such that $\mathscr{A}^\omega \cup \{\bigvee x_1 \ldots \bigvee x_n B(x_1, \ldots, x_n)\}$ is consistent and $\mathscr{A}^\omega \vdash \bigwedge x_1 \ldots \bigwedge x_n [B(x_1, \ldots, x_n) \to A_p(x_1, \ldots, x_n)]$ for each integer p. We obtain the desired result by taking $\bigvee x_1 \ldots \bigvee x_n B(x_1, \ldots, x_n)$ for F and $\bigvee x_1 \ldots \bigvee x_n [B(x_1, \ldots, x_n) \to A(x, x_1, \ldots, x_n)]$ for $G(x)$. (This could also be proved by using the method of Theorem 6.8.)

c) The answer is given by b) of the previous exercise because $J = \{ \bigwedge x$

$\mathrm{W}_n(x=n)\}$ that is because the set $\mathscr{A}$ defined there does not have any ω-models but $\mathscr{A}^\omega$ is consistent.

5. a) Using infinite formulas define the following classes of structures
(i) Archimedean ordered fields,
(ii) groups generated by p elements $a_1, \ldots, a_p$,
(iii) hereditarily finite sets of type $\leqslant\tau$.

b) Show that each of the above classes is the class of models of a single second order formula but that none is the class of models of a set of finite first order formulas.

Answer.

a) (i) Let $\mathscr{L}$ be the language of ordered fields. We add to the set $\mathscr{A}$ of axioms for such fields the formula $\bigwedge x\, \mathrm{W}_n\, (x<\sigma_n)$, where σ_1 is 1 and σ_{n+1} is the term σ_n+1.

(ii) Let $\mathscr{L}$ be the language of groups. We add to the set $\mathscr{A}$ of axioms for a group the formula

$$\bigwedge x \mathop{\mathrm{W}}_n (x = s_n)$$

where $\{s_n : n\in \mathbf{N}\}$ is an enumeration of all the terms of the form

$$a_1^{p_{11}} \ldots a_p^{p_{1p}} \ldots a_1^{p_{n1}} \ldots a_p^{p_{np}}$$

where each $p_{ij}(1\leqslant i\leqslant n,\ 1\leqslant j\leqslant p)$ is $+1$, -1 or 0.

(iii) Let $\mathscr{L}$ be the language with the single binary relation symbol $=$. We construct the language $\mathscr{L}^\tau$ as in Chapter 5. We take as our set of axioms the set of axioms for the Theory of Types and, for each $\sigma<[\tau]$ with $\sigma=(\sigma_1, \ldots, \sigma_n)$, the formula

$$\bigwedge x^\sigma \mathop{\mathrm{W}}_n E_n(x)$$

where $E_n(x)$ is the formula

$$\bigwedge x_1^{\sigma_1} \ldots \bigwedge x_{n+1}^{\sigma_1} \ldots \bigwedge x_1^{\sigma_p} \ldots \bigwedge x_{n+1}^{\sigma_p} \Big[\mathop{\mathrm{M}}_{1\leqslant r\leqslant n+1} (x_r^{\sigma_1}, \ldots, x_r^{\sigma_p}\, \varepsilon_\sigma x) \to \mathop{\mathrm{W}}_{1\leqslant i<j\leqslant n+1} (x_i^{\sigma_1} = x_j^{\sigma_1} \wedge \cdots \wedge x_i^{\sigma_p} = x_j^{\sigma_p})$$

and x is a variable of type σ.

b) Clearly (see Exercise 1 of Chapter 3) none of these classes is the class of models of a set of finite first order formulas. This can be seen if in case (i) we refer to Exercise 7 of Chapter 3; in case (ii) we add a new constant a and the axioms $s_1\neq a, \ldots, s_n\neq a, \ldots$; and in case (iii) we add a constant $a^{(0)}$ of type (0), the constants $c_1, c_2, \ldots,$ of type 0 and the axioms $c_n \varepsilon_{(0)} a^{(0)}$ for $n=1, 2, \ldots,$ and $c_m \neq c_n$ for each pair of distinct integers (m, n).

On the other hand each infinite formula of a) is equivalent to a single finite second order formula as follows:

We consider two cases where (the second order variable) X ranges over α) the class of all subsets of the domain of the realisation considered, β) the family of all its finite subsets (see Chapter 5, Exercise 6 b)). We use the notation bottom of p. 137.

(i) We write A for $\bigwedge X([zeX \wedge \bigwedge y(y+1eX \rightarrow yeX)] \rightarrow 1eX)$ and B for $\bigvee X[(1eX \wedge \bigwedge y[(y<z \wedge yeX) \rightarrow y+1eX]) \rightarrow zex]$.

In both cases $\mathbf{W}_n(z=\sigma_n) \rightarrow A$ holds.

In case α) one also has $A \rightarrow \mathbf{W}_n(z=\sigma_n)$ and in case β) $B \rightarrow \mathbf{W}_n(z=\sigma_n)$. Hence, in both cases

$$(A \wedge B) \leftrightarrow \underset{n}{\mathbf{M}}(z = \sigma_n),$$

since $\bigwedge zB$ holds in case α). Since $\mathbf{W}_n(x<\sigma_n)$ is equivalent to

$$\bigvee z[x < z \wedge \underset{n}{\mathbf{M}}(z = \sigma_n)],$$

we have in α) and β)

$$\bigvee z(x < z \wedge A \wedge B) \leftrightarrow \underset{n}{\mathbf{W}}(x < \sigma_n).$$

(ii) We only consider case α); the modification needed in case β) is analogous to that treated in (i).

$$\underset{n}{\mathbf{W}}(x = s_n) \leftrightarrow \bigwedge X[(xeX \wedge \bigwedge y[(ya_1eX \vee ya_1^{-1}eX \vee \cdots \vee ya_peX \vee ya_p^{-1}eX) \rightarrow yeX]) \rightarrow 1eX].$$

(iii) We write $y=z\cup(z_1, \ldots, z_p)$ (where y and z are variables of type σ, $\sigma=(\sigma_1, \ldots, \sigma_p)$ and $z_1, \ldots, z_p$ are variables of type $\sigma_1, \ldots, \sigma_p$ respectively) for

$$\bigwedge x_1^{\sigma_1} \ldots \bigwedge x_p^{\sigma_p}((x_1, \ldots, x_p)\varepsilon_\sigma y \leftrightarrow [(x_1, \ldots, x_p)\varepsilon_\sigma z \vee (x_1 = z_1 \wedge \cdots \wedge x_p = z_p)]).$$

Then, in case (α), if x is a variable of type σ,

$$\underset{n}{\mathbf{W}} E_n x \leftrightarrow \bigwedge X([xeX \wedge \bigwedge y \bigwedge z \bigwedge z_1 \ldots \bigwedge z_p([yeX \wedge y = z \cup (z_1, \ldots, z_p)] \rightarrow (zeX \wedge z_1eX \cdots \wedge z_peX))] \rightarrow \emptyset eX).$$

Appendix I

THE AXIOMATIC METHOD

The general nature of this method is usually described as follows. Instead of assertions about abstract properties of *specific* objects and concepts (such as space, material point, probability, etc.), one considers statements of the following form: given *any* collection of objects (whose nature is not otherwise specified) and given any set of relations between these objects, if the relations satisfy certain logical conditions (called axioms) then they also satisfy certain other logical conditions (called theorems of the given axiomatic theory). In different branches of ordinary mathematics a small number of particular axiomatic systems have been isolated and studied. Thereby a good deal of mathematics has been built up in a systematic and comprehensible way. But one has not been interested in *arbitrary* axiomatic systems or even in general *classes* of axiomatic systems. Thus the experience of "ordinary" mathematics provides no reason for supposing that there are useful results about general classes of axiomatic systems which would contribute to the effective use of the axiomatic method.

We shall now give some applications of a study of general classes of axiomatic systems, mainly – though not exclusively – of axioms expressed in *first order predicate logic*, a notion which is defined precisely in Chapters 1 and 2. Broadly speaking, this language can be characterized by saying that its formulas express properties of relations defined on a domain E and that in the definitions of these properties the quantifiers range only over the elements of E and not, say, over the subsets of E. For example, the fact that a relation is an order relation can be expressed by a first order formula but not the fact that it is a well-ordering. Or again, the fact that a structure is a group (that is to say, that the relation $a \cdot b = c$ satisfies the group axioms) can be expressed by a first order formula. Similarly the property of being a commutative group is of first order. However the fact that a group can be ordered is not expressed by a first order formula since this is the property that "there is an ordering of E

compatible with the group structure" or, in other words, "there is a *subset* of E^2 such that ...". Nevertheless the property of being an orderable group is equivalent to a certain *infinite* set of first order conditions. Finally, the properties of being a group having a finite number of generators and of being a countable group are not equivalent to any set, even infinite, of first order conditions.

Thus because of the exclusion of higher order quantifiers the class of axiomatic systems for which these general results hold does not include all of mathematics. One can make up for this, at least partially, by use of infinite systems of axioms. By considering structures which satisfy an infinite set of conditions a whole class of problems can be covered which are *formulated* in higher order terms but which can be *reduced* to problems about infinite sets of first order conditions. Examples of this are given in Chapters 1–3, mainly in Exercises. The most useful results, all connected with one another, are these:

1. The Finiteness Theorem. This says that if a first order formula A holds in all those structures which satisfy a set $\mathscr{A}$ of first order formulas, then there is some finite subset $\mathscr{A}_1$ of $\mathscr{A}$ which implies A.

2. The Method of Constants (Chapter 3, Exercise 2). This generalizes the well-known algebraic principle for introducing transcendental elements (where a structure containing an element ξ satisfying $p_n(\xi)\neq 0$ for all n is derived from a structure which contains, for each n, a ξ_n satisfying $p_i(\xi_n)\neq 0$ for all $i\leqslant n$).

3. The Embedding Theorem. This gives a condition which is both necessary and sufficient for a structure to be embeddable in a model of a given set $\mathscr{A}$ of axioms. (The results about groups mentioned above are immediate consequences of 1 and 3.)

Using these theorems we can simplify several known results which deal with the passage from finite subsystems to a whole system. They also lead to first order (equational) conditions for embeddability. But probably their chief interest is the way they make the general nature of a problem clear by separating what is general and what is particular. Thus at first sight it may seem remarkable that there is an algebraic condition, that is, a first order condition, necessary and sufficient for the existence of an ordering of a field compatible with the field operations (namely, $x_1^2+\cdots+x_n^2+1\neq 0$, for $n=1, 2, \ldots$). This *general* result is an immediate consequence of 3 above; only to decide points of detail is it necessary to look carefully at the conditions obtained, for example, to show that this set of conditions cannot be replaced by any finite set. We remark in passing that there is an interesting theory which relates the usual algebraic properties of certain classes of structures to the *syntactic* form of the axioms defining these classes. Thus the group axioms are all equational, the axioms for a field contain Boolean combinations of equations (conditional equations) such as $x=0 \vee x \cdot x^{-1}=e$; the axioms for a real closed field all take the form of a string of universal quantifiers followed by a string of existential quantifiers followed by a Boolean combination of equations. This theory enables us to answer such questions as 'Why can we express the fact that a field can be ordered by a set of inequations but not by a set of equations?'. The answer is that if a set of equations is satisfied by a given structure it is satisfied by each homomorphic image of an arbitrary substructure of this structure. Thus if a set of equations is satisfied by the field of rational numbers it is also satisfied by the field of integers modulo 2, but the field of rationals can be ordered while that of the integers modulo 2 cannot. A very elementary example of this theory is given in Exercise 8 of Chapter 3 which provides a useful condition for an axiomatic theory to possess a free model. For recent developments see ABRAHAM ROBINSON, Introduction to Model Theory and to the Metamathematics of Algebra (North-Holland Publ. Co., Amsterdam, 1963). (Chapter 6 of the present book explains the methods used in this theory.)

In Chapter 4 there is a more specific use of the notion of a first order formula. This use enables us to exploit the full force of certain particular constructions. For example, the algebraic theory of resultants leads to an equational condition on the coefficients of two polynomials which is necessary and sufficient for them to have a common root. But this same construction provides much more, namely, an analogous set of conditions for an arbitrary formula in the theory of algebraically closed fields! A similar but more interesting case is that of real closed fields. A long time ago Sturm showed that a polynomial vanishes in a closed segment $[a, b]$ if and only if certain polynomial inequalities (the terms of which are rational combinations of a, b and the coefficients of the given polynomial) are satisfied. Artin and Schreier showed that this result depends only on the axioms for a real closed field. Once we have the notion of a first order formula it is natural to try to extend this result to *all* first order formulas of the theory of fields. This problem was mentioned in passing by Herbrand and completely settled by Tarski who proved that *each* first order formula of this theory is equivalent to a Boolean combination of equations and inequalities. In particular, a formula without free variables is either true in all real closed fields or false in them all. Thus although it is obvious that not all real closed fields are isomorphic they are nevertheless all equivalent with respect to first order formulas which are built up from polynomial equations and inequalities. A proof of Artin's Theorem on the representation of non-negative forms as sums of squares of rational functions follows almost immediately from this result. This is done as an exercise in Chapter 4.

If $\mathscr{A}$ is a set of axioms all of whose models are equivalent with respect to first order formulas expressible in the language of $\mathscr{A}$, then $\mathscr{A}$ is said to be *complete*. MORLEY (Categoricity in Power, Trans. Amer. Math. Soc. **114** (1965) 514–538) has recently constructed a remarkable theory of the models of complete sets. This theory is closely parallel to Cantor's theory of closed subsets of the real line. The closed subsets which we most naturally think of are all very special. If they are not themselves perfect their first or second derivatives are perfect (possibly empty). However, for each countable ordinal α there is a closed set whose α-th derivative is not perfect. In a similar way the ordinals which, in Morley's theory, correspond to the complete sets of axioms which have turned up in other branches of mathematics are all finite, although for each countable ordinal α there is a (countable) complete set whose corresponding ordinal is α.

It follows from the Finiteness Theorem that each set of first order axioms which has an infinite model has models of different infinite cardinals (which are therefore not isomorphic). Historically, the first – and the best known – systems of axioms, for example, Peano's axioms for arithmetic and Dedekind's for the continuum, were introduced to characterize uniquely certain infinite structures. If we look at these systems more closely we see that their intended interpretation does not take into account all the general models, but only some of them. In other words it is not only the meaning of the logical symbols that is laid down, but also that of certain other symbols. In particular, in certain classical systems of axioms "set variables" occur and the models considered are those in which these variables range over the set of *all* sub-sets (of the set which we earlier denoted by E). Languages which contain such set variables are called *higher order* languages and the particular models just described are called *principal* models, where a language is said to be of order n if it contains variables over $\mathfrak{P}^i(E)$ for each $i<n$, with $\mathfrak{P}^0(E)=E$, $\mathfrak{P}^{i+1}(E)=\mathfrak{P}[\mathfrak{P}^i(E)]$, $\mathfrak{P}$ denoting the power set operation. The axiom systems of Peano and

Dedekind are of second order. Some isolated results, for example, the reduction of validity of order n (n finite, $n>2$) to second order validity, can be found in Chapter 7, but most of the general results about first order systems cannot be extended to the higher order case. We define an intermediate class of models, the *ω-models*, by requiring that the value of one of the unary relation symbols be the set of natural numbers and the value of one of the binary relation symbols be the successor relation. We constantly meet classes of such structures in everyday mathematics, for example, vector spaces over the field of rationals; in contrast, the class of vector spaces over an arbitrary (not fixed) field is just the class of all models (without any restriction) of a set of first order axioms. In Chapter 7 some results about general models are extended to ω-models; only, we often have to require that the sets of axioms be at most countably infinite. Much more on the subject of ω-models (and, more generally, of models defined by infinitely long formulas) can be found in the references cited in the summary of Chapter 6.

The "negative" results about non-categoricity (with respect to first order axioms) do have a "positive" side, namely, the existence of non-principal models (which in Exercise 3 of Chapter 2 are also called non-standard models). Quite recently these models have been used to create Non-standard Analysis. This recent work differs from other attempts at doing Analysis on a non-Archimedean field K by bringing in the set of "integers *of* K" (which satisfy the axioms of arithmetic considered). The existence of non-principal models implies the existence of non-Archimedean fields which contain such (non-Archimedean) "integers" as well as non-Archimedean "real numbers" (for example, in a Taylor series $\sum a_n x^n$, the variable n ranges over all the integers of K and not just over the standard ones). This genuine Infinitesimal Analysis is expounded in ABRAHAM ROBINSON, Non-standard Analysis (North-Holland Publ. Co., Amsterdam, 1966).

The applications described so far are applications in the strict sense of the word in that the methods given in the main text enable us to answer questions which are explicitly formulated in ordinary mathematical language. It remains to consider what, in the long run, is the most fruitful rôle of new ideas, namely, the possibility of formulating questions that we have in mind but which we cannot express precisely in ordinary mathematical language (besides possible applications to less common branches of mathematics). In this connection probably the most striking example is the theory of uniformly definable sets, explained in Chapter 6, which is illustrated by the following simple questions. Consider the commutative fields of characteristic zero; they all contain a sub-field isomorphic to the field of rationals. So we can ask:

1. Which first order formulas $A(x)$ define the same set of rationals in all these fields, i.e. are satisfied by the same rationals in each of these fields?

2. Which first order formulas $A(x)$, satisfied *only* by rationals, define the same set of rationals in all these fields?

3. Which sets of rationals can be defined in this way?

4. Which sets of rationals can be defined in each commutative field of characteristic zero by a first order formula which may depend on the field?

Complete answers to these questions follow as corollaries to quite general theorems about arbitrary sets of axioms. Questions 3 and 4 are equivalent; this provides a new and powerful uniformity condition. The answer to question 2 is that they are (some of the) first order formulas which define finite sets only. In other words we cannot hope to distinguish the rationals by one and the same first order formula in all fields. In fact there is a commutative field of characteristic zero in which the rationals cannot be distinguished by any first order condition (or as an algebraist would put it, they are not algebraically definable). One need only reflect for a moment to see that these questions are only interesting if arbitrary first order formulas A are considered and not just equations or Boolean combinations of equations. Obviously this is another reason why the above questions have never been dealt with in the literature of "ordinary" mathematics.

This work on definable sets in general models also extends to the ω-models described above. It provides an example of an application of model theory to two other branches of logic not dealt with in this book, namely, the theory of recursive sets and that of hyperarithmetic sets. This application is based on the following facts. On the one hand the basic notions of recursion theory are those of *finite set* (of natural numbers) and of *recursive set*; on the other hand, the sets which are uniformly definable in the usual axiomatic systems for arithmetic are just the finite sets, if definability is taken in the sense of 2 above, or if it is taken in the sense of 1 above, just the recursive sets. Thus we can generalize recursion theory in two directions, either by replacing the usual axioms for arithmetic by other axioms or by replacing the class of general models by some other class of models such as the ω-models mentioned above.

APPENDIX II

FOUNDATIONS OF MATHEMATICS

INTRODUCTION.

Foundational studies are concerned with describing and analysing so-called "intuitive" or "informal" mathematics, i.e., mathematics as understood by ordinary working mathematicians.

In the descriptive part of the subject, informal mathematics is reformulated in a formal language (e.g. that of set theory). Compared with the language of informal mathematics such formal languages have a very restricted vocabulary and a perfectly exact grammar, with a consequent increase in precision and freedom from inessential features. Contrary to current views discussed at the end of the introduction, this reformulation is only a tool in the study of foundations; depending essentially, as does any description of an intuitively understood subject, on our conception of the objects described: it is only from this point of view, i.e., that of meaning, that the formal language expresses correctly the assertions of informal mathematics, since, from the point of view of external form, formal and informal language have (fortunately!) very little in common. It should also be noted that the increased precision brought about by formalization, though very useful for technical development, is hardly of any use for resolving difficulties arising from defects in the original concepts (indeed on the contrary, it is by reflecting on informal concepts that we are led to a good formalization). For example, in the well known "crises" (see Part A, Section 1, below) the contradictions arose from principles (axioms, rules of inference) which were quite explicit, so that the difficulties were not due to any lack of formal precision; the problem was rather to distinguish amongst various formally precise principles those which were valid.

Foundational studies proper are concerned with just this kind of question which may require considerations quite different in character from those of ordinary mathematics. In particular, in foundations we try to find (a theoretical framework permitting the formulation of) good reasons *for* the basic principles accepted in mathematical practice, while the latter is only concerned with derivations *from* these principles. The methods used in a deeper analysis of mathematical practice often lead to an extension of our theoretical understanding. A particularly important example is the search for new axioms, which is nothing more than a continuation of the process which led to the discovery of the currently accepted principles.

The preceding considerations show that the methods used in foundations will necessarily go beyond those of mathematical practice: the discovery of the new concepts and methods needed may involve distinctly philosophical considerations, and in particular, one's conception of the nature of mathematics. If (1) one holds the view that intuitive mathematics is essentially concerned with certain (abstract) objects, one will be led to a "realist" theory of these basic objects: in such a system of foundations the meaning of intuitive statements is analysed in terms of this theory and the rules of reasoning are deduced from the laws obeyed by the basic objects. Realist foundations are thus analogous to theoretical physics which explains ordinary physical phenomena in terms of fundamental constituents of the physical world (elementary particles in the current theory). But if, (2), one holds the view that the essence of intuitive mathematics consists in proof or, more specifically, the various kinds of proof, one will be led to an "idealist" system of foundations, which refers to mathematical activity itself. An example of (1) will be found in Part A below dealing with *set-theoretic semantic foundations* (in this case the interpretations of the formulas are the "realizations" of Chapters 2 and 7); and examples of (2) in Part B which sketches *combinatorial syntactic foundations* (a rather narrow view of mathematical activity is involved here). For defects of both foundations, see Part B, Section 4.

Two particular difficulties in foundations deserve mention (though they arise in any attempt at a general, theoretical understanding). Firstly, in order to decide between two rival views, it is essential to adopt a detached standpoint. If one accepts one view, either consciously or unconsciously, there is a real danger of not taking the other one seriously! For a realist, an idealist appears to ignore the fundamental objects and to be lost in minor distinctions (analogous perhaps to the difference between observations made by the naked eye and with the aid of a microscope – a distinction to which no physical importance is ascribed). Conversely, an idealist will find it ridiculous to derive the rules of intuitive reasoning from the properties of abstract objects which, for him, have a very dubious status, or, at least, are hardly essential to mathematics. Secondly, if the viewpoints are of long standing and have consequently survived examination at any rate in respect of their consequences for elementary mathematics, considerable further development of informal mathematics may be needed in order to provide some criterion for deciding between them (such a criterion would be analogous to an *experimentum crucis* in physics). It goes without saying that an already quite highly developed technical apparatus may be necessary even for formulating a theoretical viewpoint, and the development of this is one of the principal tasks of mathematical logic.

As to the possibility of applying foundational studies to informal mathematics, the position is similar to that for any other theoretical analysis. In Appendix I some applications of semantic analysis are given. Syntactic methods have found applications in connection with computers; this is hardly surprising since one of the basic ideas behind this kind of analysis is that mathematical reasoning is capable of being mechanised. In fact we can say that there is no doubt about the usefulness in principle of foundational studies.

In practice the following situation sometimes arises. If some question, say in number theory, is formally undecided by the basic axioms accepted in mathematical practice, its solution may require assistance from foundational studies: in the first instance, in order to establish its undecidability and secondly in order to find new axioms (there are examples of these possibilities in Part A, Section 3). But at the present time the situation both in arithmetic and analysis is confused: on the one hand we do not *know* of any questions which are seriously studied by working mathematicians and which are also independent of the currently accepted axioms (see Part B, Section 1(c)); on the other hand mathematicians ignorant of foundational methods are not likely to find any (just as it is unlikely that anyone would notice group theoretic aspects of arithmetic unless he already knows what a group is).

Foundational studies and the problem of error

One of the standard problems of philosophy is that of determining how one might eliminate possible error from naive experience. The foundational considerations of the present study are only slightly relevant to this purpose (and, in particular, formalization itself is quite irrelevant). We cannot rule out the possibility that there may be defects in the basic concepts; but the two commonly cited examples of erroneous naive ideas are hardly conclusive, namely the paradoxes of set theory (Part A, Section 2) and the existence in arithmetic of formally undecidable propositions (Part A, Section 3). In point of fact, the objections raised by mathematicians to the introduction of the idea of set (at that time called "class") are notorious, as well as the efforts made to show that mathematical reasoning (even in elementary geometry!) is not capable of being mechanised. If anything, the naive attitude was excessively conservative.

POSITIVISM: AN ANTI-PHILOSOPHICAL DOCTRINE

According to this doctrine, which currently enjoys a certain vogue, foundational studies should be confined to their descriptive role; the traditional problems of foundations are ignored rather than resolved on the ground that they lack precision. We have already observed certain fundamental disadvantages of such a restriction at the beginning of this introduction, and they will be considered in greater detail in Part A, Section 4 (c) in connection with semantic foundations and in Part B, Section 4 in connection with combinatorial foundations. But it will be useful to make certain general observations about this doctrine at this point.

The restriction imposed by this doctrine on what is held to be precise (or meaningful) requires that statements be formulated in what are called "positivist" or "operational" terms, which in mathematics reduce to "formal". This requirement, in turn, derives its plausibility from the discovery (Part A, Section 4(a)) that elementary logical reasoning (i.e. of first order) is, if not formal (mechanical), at any rate capable of being formalized (mechanized). Prior to this discovery the positivist doctrine had no real foothold in mathematics.

It should be observed right away that the intuitive notion of logical consequence is involved in the very statement of this discovery since it asserts the equivalence of logical consequence and a certain purely formal relation; i.e., having *accepted* the notion of logical consequence, one *proves* that there is a formally precise definition of it. But positivists go further: having formulated (quite correctly) a criterion for formal precision, they conclude (wrongly) that this criterion defines the limits of mathematical thought. However, experience in foundations as well as in informal mathematics shows the contrary to be the case. Competent mathematicians come to unanimous and quite definite conclusions about questions that are not expressed with formal precision such as e.g. whether or not an axiom is valid for a certain intuitive concept (see Part A, Section 2(c), Part B, Section 2(c)), or whether a definition is satisfactory (e.g. for the length of a curve). Sometimes it is claimed that such questions do not form part of mathematics – a particularly curious view since, on the one hand, it is not stated to what discipline they do belong and, on the other hand, mathematicians do in fact concern themselves with just such questions. Since mathematicians find themselves in agreement on such questions (this is a point of fact which positivists simply ignore) there does not seem to be any reason why they should be dubbed as subjective. To summarize: the empirical facts throw doubt on the necessity, and consequently, in the long run, the fertility of the restrictions imposed by positivism but they do not put in question the significance and good sense of at any rate the majority of foundational problems (though the exceptions often attract the greatest attention).

Positivism does seem to have a certain pragmatic value. In connection with research, Appendix I describes certain useful consequences of the reduction of an abstract concept to a formal one, namely of "validity in all mathematical structures" to "formal consequence" [for the case of elementary (first order) reasoning]. In addition we remarked earlier that the theory of foundations may not be of any particular use in particular branches of informal mathematics, at any rate at any given moment. As to the position of foundational studies in mathematical education, they turn out to attract two distinct groups of students; those who have a definite gift for philosophy and those who are particularly bad at it (and, perhaps consequently, fascinated by it). The former will not be seduced by the positivist view and the latter will be consoled by a justification bad as it may be of their lack of philosophical talent. Naturally, they will not be led to look, say, for new basic axioms, but, in any case, they would not have found any; and, after all, it is quite possible to devote oneself to technical problems, i.e., problems already formulated in the language of mathematical practice. This is true even in mathematical logic e.g. in the parts of the subject dealt with in this book. What is lost in this way is, however, the most fruitful feature of mathematical logic, namely its specifically logical aspect; in particular, the problems and conjectures that follow from the different views of the nature of mathematics and its foundations, which, used properly, are fruitful even for the technical development of mathematics.

Part A

SET THEORETIC SEMANTIC FOUNDATIONS

The reader will recall from the preface that passages in square brackets presuppose some technical knowledge of mathematical logic. Comments in small print concern points of detail of either philosophical or mathematical interest.

Summary

Section 1 analyzes the "adequacy conditions" satisfied by the familiar reduction of classical mathematical structures to set theory, and the weaker conditions involved when intuitive logical consequence or the intuitive structure of the ordinals are reduced to set theory [the latter reduction is formulated in terms of *realizations* in a wider sense than that of Chapters 2 and 7].

Section 2 (a) distinguishes between several concepts involved in the "naive" idea of set, and Section 2 (b) describes one of them, the so-called cumulative type structure, called s.c.t. [cf. also Exercise 5 of Chapter 5]. Section 2 (c) derives Zermelo's axioms for this notion, both in first order and second order form; for an informal distinction between languages of different order cf. Appendix I [and for a precise one, cf. Chapter 7].

Section 2 (d) first gives simple examples of assertions which are true for s.c.t., but not consequences of Zermelo's axioms either in first or second order form. Finally, it gives a true arithmetic proposition which is not a consequence of the first order theory. This is a particular case of Gödel's incompleteness theorem, which holds for a wide class of axiomatic systems. (Its general formulation is not given because it requires an analysis of the notion of formal system, which in turn needs the notions of recursion theory, a part of logic not treated in the present book. But the details of Section 2 (d) are not superseded by the general theorem because they would be needed to verify that Zermelo's axioms are covered by it.) A distinction between Gödel's incompleteness result and other independence results is formulated in terms of second-order consequence.

Section 3 gives some other assertions valid for the s.c.t. and not derivable from Zermelo's axioms. It discusses so-called axioms of infinity, which assert the existence of sets of high (transfinite) type and their implications for assertions about sets of finite type, in particular the natural numbers, or sets of lowest infinite type, such as the real numbers.

Section 4 contains some technical information needed in Part B, Section 4 for the examination of philosophic views. Theorem 5 of Section 4 (a), a refinement of

Gödel's completeness theorem, gives a *mathematical* justification for the choice of the usual rules of first-order logical deduction, and Section 4 (b), for comparison, contains some further facts about second-order logical consequence. Section 4 (c) disposes of a well-known view which tries to combine a set theoretic semantic foundation with a privileged position of first-order consequence and/or with the idea that the notion of set is *defined* by the usual axioms.

The basic notions are: *set*, the *membership* relation (between sets), and the "logical" operations (on sets) of *union*, *complementation*, and *projection*. "Semantic" is used because the foundations described in the present section accept set theoretic terminology as meaningful, and not only as a "façon de parler" in need of further critical analysis: the practical significance of this distinction is specially important in Sections 2 and 3 below.

1. How does one analyze intuitive mathematics in these basic terms?

In other words: what does one mean by the reduction of (intuitive) mathematics to set theory?

In this reduction each mathematical structure is conceived as a *set*, itself an ordered n-tuple of sets consisting of a collection (universe) and relations on it; such sets are called *realizations* [cf. Chapters 2 and 7]. In particular, in arithmetic, the basic realization has the collection $\mathbf{N}$ of natural numbers as its universe, with the successor relation on $\mathbf{N} \times \mathbf{N}$; in analysis, it is the realization whose universe is the collection $\mathbf{R}$ of real numbers with the order relation on $\mathbf{R} \times \mathbf{R}$, and a denumerable dense subset $\mathbf{Q}$ of $\mathbf{R}$ (other structures can then be defined in analysis, such as geometry: the collection E_3 of points in 3 dimensions, with a partial order on E_3^3 (betweenness) and a metric).

To each mathematical structure $\mathfrak{S}$ is associated a *language* (the "language of $\mathfrak{S}$"). Roughly speaking, the language refers only to the structure and not to the nature of the objects in its universe (and so has meaning for structures whose universe consists of arbitrary kinds of objects; sometimes such a language is called: purely logical). In particular, if two structures are isomorphic they satisfy corresponding assertions in the languages of these structures. An example of such a language consists of all formulae built up from symbols $R_1, \ldots, R_k$ for the relations of $\mathfrak{S}$, universal and existential quantifiers, negation, conjunction[1]; see Appendix I for an in-

[1] The notation of the main text is used.
$\rightarrow$: implies (usually denoted by: $\Rightarrow$) $\wedge$: and (&), $\bigwedge$: for all ($\forall$)
$\neg$: not $\vee$: or, $\bigvee$: there is ($\exists$).

formal description of this language, the so-called predicate calculus of first order whose relation symbols have the same number of arguments as the relations of $\mathfrak{S}$. [Of course, if $\mathscr{L}_{\mathfrak{S}}$ is the first-order language of $\mathfrak{S}$, $\mathscr{L}^{\tau}_{\mathfrak{S}}$ of Chapter 7 is also a purely logical language: the difference is that to understand an assertion in $\mathscr{L}_{\mathfrak{S}}$, one need only know the structure $\mathfrak{S}$ itself and understand the logical operations of union, complementation, projection; to understand an assertion in $\mathscr{L}^{\tau}_{\mathfrak{S}}$, one must also know the hierarchy of types built up on the universe of $\mathfrak{S}$ up to type τ.]

If A is a formula in the language of $\mathfrak{S}$ whose free variables are $x_1, \ldots, x_n$, we shall denote by $\bar{A}$ the set of n-tuples of the universe of $\mathfrak{S}$ which satisfy A (in $\mathfrak{S}$).

The *reduction* of a structure $\mathfrak{S}$ to set theory is expressed by means of an *adequate* axiomatization, which consists of an axiom (or set of axioms) $\mathscr{A}_{\mathfrak{S}}$ satisfying the following conditions.

$\mathscr{A}_{\mathfrak{S}}$ is purely "logical" [formulated in the language of predicate calculus, Chapter 2 or Chapter 7].

$\mathfrak{S}$ satisfies $\mathscr{A}_{\mathfrak{S}}$ and hence: there exists a structure that satisfies $\mathscr{A}_{\mathfrak{S}}$, for short: $E^{\mathscr{A}\mathfrak{S}}$.

All structures that satisfy $\mathscr{A}_{\mathfrak{S}}$ are isomorphic (and, hence, isomorphic to $\mathfrak{S}$), for short: $U^{\mathscr{A}\mathfrak{S}}$.

All intuitive properties of $\mathfrak{S}$ can be expressed or defined in terms of those explicitly mentioned in $\mathscr{A}_{\mathfrak{S}}$ [precisely: defined in terms of the first or higher order language of $\mathscr{A}_{\mathfrak{S}}$], for short: $X^{\mathscr{A}\mathfrak{S}}$.

All assertions about $\mathfrak{S}$ that can be proved intuitively follow logically from $\mathscr{A}_{\mathfrak{S}}$: for short: $D^{\mathscr{A}\mathfrak{S}}$.

The reduction to set theory involves also a (set theoretic) reduction of the notion of intuitive logical consequence: a formula A in a given language is called *set theoretic consequence* of a set $\mathscr{A}$ of formulae (of the same language) if it is satisfied by every realization in the sense of p. 166 that satisfies all formulas of $\mathscr{A}$.

Discussion. (i) The notion of logical consequence used in the formulation of $D^{\mathscr{A}\mathfrak{S}}$ is the notion of consequence understood in ordinary mathematical reasoning[2]. Note that

[2] For instance, in Bourbaki rules of inference are given in the first chapter but never referred to afterwards, in contrast to definitions of mathematical structures, e.g. groups. Thus knowledge of these mathematical notions is needed for understanding the deductions, knowledge of the rules is not. Not surprisingly, since the rules of the first chapter were obtained by analysing the meaning of logical operations (Theorem 5 below), and it is knowledge of this meaning which permits one to follow the deductions.

if A is an intuitive consequence of $\mathscr{A}$ all realizations, in a *wider* sense of the word, that satisfy $\mathscr{A}$ also satisfy A: see p. 169 for one such extension. But for formulas of first order the two notions of consequence coincide (Theorem 5 of Section 4 below).

(ii) The difference between "$\mathfrak{S}$ satisfies A" where A is formulated in the language of $\mathfrak{S}$, and "A is consequence of $\mathscr{A}_{\mathfrak{S}}$" is, of course, that in the latter case, A is true in *all* structures that satisfy $\mathscr{A}_{\mathfrak{S}}$; in other words, only those properties of $\mathfrak{S}$ that are explicitly formulated in $\mathscr{A}_{\mathfrak{S}}$ are needed to conclude A. If $U^{\mathscr{A}\mathfrak{S}}$ happens to hold, by the fundamental property of logical languages, "$\mathfrak{S}$ satisfies A" if and only if "A is consequence of $\mathscr{A}_{\mathfrak{S}}$", A being purely logical.

(iii) [By Chapter 7, Exercise 1] there are axioms $\mathscr{A}_{\mathfrak{S}}$ for the principal intuitive structures studied in the 19th century (arithmetic, analysis) satisfying $E^{\mathscr{A}\mathfrak{S}}$ and $U^{\mathscr{A}\mathfrak{S}}$ [where, since $\mathfrak{S}$ is infinite, $\mathscr{A}_{\mathfrak{S}}$ must be a higher order formula to satisfy $U^{\mathscr{A}\mathfrak{S}}$].

(iv) Note that both $E^{\mathscr{A}\mathfrak{S}}$ and $U^{\mathscr{A}\mathfrak{S}}$ are formulated in the language of set theory (namely: the first order language $\mathscr{L}_E$) whose only relation symbol is $\in$, with variables ranging over sets and $\in$ denoting the membership relation. For the classical structures $\mathfrak{S}$, both $E^{\mathscr{A}\mathfrak{S}}$ and $U^{\mathscr{A}\mathfrak{S}}$ are derived from familiar properties of the basic set theoretic notions.

(v) In contrast, the verification of $X^{\mathscr{A}\mathfrak{S}}$ and $D^{\mathscr{A}\mathfrak{S}}$ requires a *case study* such as given in *Principia Mathematica*. Clearly $X^{\mathscr{A}\mathfrak{S}}$ depends on what is regarded as mathematically significant about $\mathfrak{S}$; for example, in the case of arithmetic, $X^{\mathscr{A}\mathfrak{S}}$ requires that addition and multiplication and other "arithmetical" functions be expressed in terms of the operations mentioned in $\mathscr{A}_{\mathfrak{S}}$, namely, the successor; but not necessarily "empirical" properties such as the number of electrons emitted by a particular atom between times n and $n+1$ for $n=0, 1, \ldots$.

(vi) If $U^{\mathscr{A}\mathfrak{S}}$ and $X^{\mathscr{A}\mathfrak{S}}$ are satisfied, clearly so is $D^{\mathscr{A}\mathfrak{S}}$, by the fundamental invariance under isomorphism of assertions formulated in a purely logical language. But even if $U^{\mathscr{A}\mathfrak{S}}$ is not satisfied, a case study may show that, in actual practice, $D^{\mathscr{A}\mathfrak{S}}$ holds in the sense that all assertions about $\mathfrak{S}$ that *have* been proved, follow logically from $\mathscr{A}_{\mathfrak{S}}$. (This possibility is actually realized at the present time even by certain *first* order axioms for arithmetic, cf. Part B.)

(vii) We remark in passing that the condition $U^{\mathscr{A}\mathfrak{S}}$ is appropriate for pure mathematics. But in applications, two abstractly isomorphic structures may not be equally effective; for instance, a structure $\mathfrak{S}'$ isomorphic to arithmetic, i.e., another notational system for the natural numbers, would be bad for counting if we could not effectively decide the successor relation in $\mathfrak{S}'$.

Warning. The adequacy conditions above have been established for the classical structures (iv), but not for the basic structure $\mathfrak{F}$ ($\mathfrak{F}$ for: fundamental) consisting of all sets with the *membership* relation, or the intuitive structure consisting of all *ordinals with the order relation.*

Indeed, if $\mathscr{A}_{\mathfrak{F}}$ is an axiomatization of $\mathfrak{F}$, $E^{\mathscr{A}\mathfrak{F}}$ asserts that there is a realization satisfying $A_{\mathfrak{F}}$ whose universe is a *set.* If $U^{\mathscr{A}\mathfrak{F}}$ were also satisfied, there would be a set in 1–1 correspondence with the collection of all sets.

ELEMENTARY RESULTS ON THE INTUITIVE NOTION OF ORDINAL

To formulate results we need the wider notion of realization mentioned above, which we explain for the particular language $\mathscr{L}_E$ of set theory, to which are added the predicate symbol O of one variable, and the predicate symbol P of two variables. The variables are not required to range over a *set*, but may range over *all* sets.

The realization of a predicate symbol is again not required to be a set, but may be a property of sets in the case of O or of pairs of sets in the case of P.

The extended notion of realization is well illustrated by the following analogous situation: In the present paragraph we shall confine ourselves to the structure $\mathfrak{f}$ of all hereditarily finite sets built up from a collection of individuals [cf. Chapter 5, Example 6]. This structure does not permit an adequate axiomatization $\mathscr{A}_{\mathbf{N}}$ of the structure $\mathbf{N}$ of arithmetic, since a realization in $\mathfrak{f}$ has necessarily a finite universe. We extend the notion of realization as follows: we consider $\mathscr{L}_E$ with the two relation symbols N and S with one, resp. two arguments, and the *following structure as a generalized realization*: the universe is that of $\mathfrak{f}$, $\in$ is membership restricted to finite sets, $\overline{N(x)}$ is the property (of sets) of being a natural number, i.e.,

$$x = \emptyset \vee \bigwedge y\,[\bigwedge z\,(z \cup \{z\} \in y) \to z \in y) \to (x \in y \to \emptyset \in y)]$$

and $S(x, y)$ is the relation: y is the successor of x, i.e., $y = x \cup \{x\}$, short for: $\bigwedge z\,[z \in y \leftrightarrow (z = x \vee z \in x)]$.

In the extended realization, the variables take (finite) sets as values, but their range is not finite.

Returning now to the general case [and using the language $\mathscr{L}_E^{(0,0)}$ (Chapter 5) extended by O and P], we require that each ordinal be a set and that the structure $\langle \bar{O}, \bar{P} \rangle$ of the ordinals with the order relation satisfy the following conditions:

(i) $\bar{P}$ is a strict ordering of $\bar{O}$, i.e.,
$\bigwedge x \bigwedge y\,[Pxy \leftrightarrow (Ox \wedge Oy \wedge x \neq y \wedge \neg Pyx)]$.

(ii) Every initial segment of $\bar{O}$ is a well-ordered set, i.e.,

$$\bigwedge x(Ox \to \bigvee y \bigvee z[\bigwedge u(u \in y \leftrightarrow Pux) \wedge \bigwedge u(u \in z \leftrightarrow \bigvee s \bigvee t[u = (s, t) \wedge s \in y \wedge t \in y \wedge Pst]) \wedge We(y, z)])$$

where (s, t) denotes the ordered pair and $We\,(y, z)$ means that $\bar{y}$ is well founded with respect to $\bar{z}$, i.e., if X is a variable over collections of sets [of type (0), as in Chapter 7, Example 1],

$$\bigwedge X \bigwedge v[(v \in y \wedge Xv) \to \bigvee w(w \in y \wedge Xw \wedge \bigwedge w'[(Xw' \wedge w' \in y \wedge w' \neq w) \to (w, w') \in z])].$$

(iii) Every pair of sets $\langle\bar{y}, \bar{z}\rangle$ where $\bar{z}$ well orders $\bar{y}$, is isomorphic to some initial segment of $\bar{O}$ ordered by $\bar{P}$.

These axioms are sufficient to determine $\langle\bar{O}, \bar{P}\rangle$ uniquely (just as Peano's axioms determine the structure of arithmetic). There are formulas of $\mathscr{L}_E$ which define $\bar{O}$ and $\bar{P}$ explicitly so as to satisfy the conditions (i)-(iii) above (just as the property of being a natural number and the successor relation were defined above).

For further information on ordinals and on the notation below, see e.g. HAUSDORFF, Set Theory (Chelsea Publ. Co., N.Y., 1957).

The following notation will be used in the Exercises below.

$x=0$ for $\bigwedge u \neg u \in x$; $x=y\cup\{z\}$ for $\bigwedge w[w\in x \leftrightarrow (w\in y \vee w=z)]$; $x=\{y\}$, $\{x, y\}$, (y, z) for $x=0\cup\{y\}$, $\{y\}\cup\{z\}$, resp. $\{\{y\}, \{y, z\}\}$ (ordered pair).

$x=(y, z, w)$ for $x=((y, z), w)$ (ordered triples).

$\text{Func}(x)$ for $\bigwedge z(z\in x \leftrightarrow \bigvee vw[z=(v, w)]) \wedge \bigwedge uvw([(u, v)\in x \wedge (u, w)\in x] \rightarrow v=w)$ (x is the graph of a function).

$\text{Dom}(y, x)$ for $\bigwedge u(u\in y \rightarrow \bigvee v[(u, v)\in x])$ (y is the domain of x).

For each numeral 1, 2, 3, …, one writes $1=\{0\}$, $2=\{1\}$ (since $1\cup\{1\}=\{1\}$), $3=2\cup\{2\}$…; cf. the definition of the natural numbers, p. 169.

$\text{Sf}(x)$ (finite sequence, i.e., a function whose domain is a natural number >0) for $\text{Func}(x)\wedge \bigvee y[N(y)\wedge \text{Dom}(y, x)\wedge y\neq 0]$, where N is as on p. 169.

$x=\text{Sub}(y, z, v)$ (x is the result of substituting v for z in the finite sequence y) for

$Sf(x)\wedge \text{Sf}(y)\wedge \bigwedge uw[(u, w)\in x \leftrightarrow ([(u, w)\in y \wedge w\neq z] \vee [(u, z)\in y \wedge w=v])]$.

$x+y=z$ (addition) [Chapter 5, Example 7].

$u=\widehat{yz}$ for the concatenation of y and z, i.e., $\text{Sf}(y)\wedge\text{Sf}(z)\wedge \bigwedge u[u\in x \leftrightarrow$ $\leftrightarrow (u\in y \vee \bigvee vwr[\text{Dom}(v, y)\wedge (w, r)\in z \wedge (w+v, r)=u])]$.

$x=\hat{y}$ for the accumulation of a finite sequence of finite sequences, i.e., $\text{Sf}(x)\wedge \text{Sf}(y)\wedge \bigvee w[\text{Dom}(w, x)\wedge \text{Dom}(w, y)]\wedge \bigwedge uv[(u, v)\in y \rightarrow \text{Sf}(v)]\wedge$ $\wedge \bigwedge u[(0, u)\in x \rightarrow (0, u)\in y]\wedge \bigwedge uvw\{[(u, v)\in x \wedge (u\cup\{u\}, w)\in y] \rightarrow (u\cup\{u\}, vw)\in x\}$.

2. How does one find laws for the basic set theoretical notions?

(Conceptual analysis of $\mathfrak{F}$.) Whatever sophisticated theoretical analysis may later be given, the discovery of such laws presents itself naively as follows:

One chooses a language, in particular $\mathscr{L}_E$ above, *and sets down asser-*

tions which are true for the realization (in the wider sense above) *in which the variables range over all sets and* $\in$ *is the membership relation.*

The *selection* actually made among such true assertions is to some extent determined by the "needs" of contemporary mathematics, for example one sets down the properties of $\mathfrak{F}$ which are actually used in establishing $E^{\mathscr{A}\mathfrak{S}}$ of $U^{\mathscr{A}\mathfrak{S}}$ for the classical structures $\mathfrak{S}$. But one also formulates more general principles of which these properties are special cases (cf. footnote 3 below).

Now, mathematicians sometimes ask (specializing Pilate): what is truth (for sets)? and (just as Pilate) do not wait for an answer. The interest of further analysis is undeniable: in fact, the whole of Part B will be devoted to *one* further analysis of this question. But here we shall accept the notion of set theoretic truth (which anyway is a corollary to accepting the basic set theoretic notions as meaningful) and see what one gets from it. In terms of this notion the problem of giving a foundation or a justification for axioms takes the following quite natural form:

Speaking generally, axioms are set theoretically justified if one has a (precise) concept which satisfies the axioms in the wider sense of realization. In particular, $\mathscr{A}_{\mathfrak{S}}$ is justified if $E^{\mathscr{A}\mathfrak{S}}$ is true.

The formal derivation of $E^{\mathscr{A}\mathfrak{S}}$ from traditional axioms of set theory provides then such a justification if we have at least one precise concept of set which satisfies these axioms. Sections 2 (b) and (c) are devoted to this point.

(a) THE NEED FOR DISTINCTIONS. Long before the set theoretic paradoxes led to sophisticated restrictions on definitions (Poincaré's predicativity) or on methods of proof (Brouwer's constructivity) there was *earlier* criticism of the notion of set because of certain ambiguities. Such criticism is not fatal because it is met by making necessary distinctions; however, at the time it was justified because the notion of set was introduced as a crude mixture containing at least 3 different elements: Sets were considered:

(i) as mere analogues of finite collections (a notion which was supposed to be understood) satisfying more or less the same laws;

(ii) as arbitrary subcollections of a *given* collection; this occurs throughout mathematics (sets *of* integers, or sets *of* points; the collection of integers and the collection of points (real numbers) being taken to be well defined);

(iii) as an abstraction from the more general notion of *property*, a set being the collection of objects which have a given property. (Since properties defined in different ways may be satisfied by precisely the same objects, the notion of set is here conceived as an invariant of properties.)

There is little use in mathematics itself of properties for which we have no *a priori* bound on the kinds of objects which satisfy them: but both in logic and in everyday language, such properties are used widely. An instance is the property of being non-empty (which, incidentally, applies to itself); or the property of being blue: for, even if it has such a bound, we use this property without any clear idea of the class of all blue things (past, present, or future). The possible interest of such properties for mathematics is taken up at the end of this paragraph.

Flagrant errors (contradictions) are rare in mathematical uses of the notion of set, because in any particular deduction *one* of the notions is tacitly understood. But the distinctions are essential for analyzing the errors known as paradoxes, where several precisely formulated principles (axioms, rules of inference) lead to contradictions, though each of them is plausible. More exactly, each of the principles is valid for *one* notion of set in the crude mixture, but none of the notions satisfies all these principles. Such errors are particularly disagreeable because (by what has just been said), unlike a computational error, they cannot be uniquely *located.* It is clear that the distinctions mentioned are needed for the very statement of such an analysis.

Example (comprehension axiom). If P is a property of elements *of* a given set a, one forms the set, in sense (ii), of all $x \in a$ which satisfy P, i.e.,

$$\bigwedge a \bigvee x \bigwedge y \left[y \in x \leftrightarrow (y \in a \wedge Py) \right]. \tag{*}$$

Sometimes a is understood tacitly, when

$$\bigvee x \bigwedge y (y \in x \leftrightarrow Py) \tag{**}$$

is valid, e.g., in analysis where a is the set of integers, y a numerical variable, and x a variable over sets of integers. [More generally, as in the theory of types (Chapter 5), if y is a type τ, x a type (τ) variable, a being now the collection of all objects of type τ.]

Russell noticed, actually so long after the notion of set was introduced into mathematics that the naive doubts about possible ambiguities had been almost forgotten, that (**) is contradictory if the tacit understanding is ignored [i.e., if the type distinction is removed] and ordinary logical rules are applied. In particular, if $y \notin y$ is put for Py and if any x satisfies $\bigwedge y (y \in x \leftrightarrow y \notin y)$, then also $x \in x \leftrightarrow x \notin x$, which is a contradiction.

For the notion of set (ii), (**) is not at all plausible, and certainly not evident. For the notion (iii), with $y \in x$ being interpreted as: the property

y has the property x, (**) is indeed evident provided the *most general* kind of property is considered, including properties which are not everywhere defined. Only in this case the familiar formal laws of logic [which hold for the interpretation of the logical symbols in Chapter 1] cannot be expected to be valid, for instance: Either A (is defined and) true or A (is defined and) false. So, for the notion (iii), we should accept the property x which applies to a property y if and only if y does not apply to itself, but this property x is not defined for the argument x.

Clearly Russell's paradox, or any of the others, affects the notion of set in sense (ii) no more than it affects, for instance, the notion of hereditarily finite set (built up from the empty set). Here it is obviously false that for each P there is a *finite* set x such that $\bigwedge y(y \in x \leftrightarrow Py)$ with y ranging over *finite* sets. An immediate counter example is provided by the properties Py:$y=y$, or: y is a natural number of p. 169 (or, of course, $y \notin y$!). On the other hand, (*) is clearly valid when all variables range over the hereditarily finite sets. Nevertheless, there exists a *contemporary problem of the paradoxes*:

Is the notion (iii) precise enough to permit a theory as rich as that of (ii) given in (b) below? In particular, what are its logical laws? And if it is rich, is it important for mathematical practice or only for foundations?

Discussion (relating the present section to some general points in the Introduction). The distinctions (i)–(iii) above constitute an example of *informal precision.* The discussion of the comprehension axiom illustrates how informal distinctions are used to find correct axioms, such as (*). The reader will have observed that the explicit formulation of (*) did not somehow drop from heaven as a means of clarifying the basic notion of set, but was the result of informal analysis, i.e., of the distinction between (ii) and (iii). As to (**), its explicit formulation certainly helped to show that the original crude mixture of notions was imprecise, but again the informal discussion of (iii) was necessary to show why (**) was plausible at all. Quite generally, explicit formulation (formalization) may help one to see when one's ideas are wrong, but it is, at best, an auxiliary towards getting them right.

The step from the informal distinctions (and, generally, from reflection on the meaning of a concept) to the formulation of formal axioms is called an *informal derivation.* The reader should review, in the light of actual informal derivations such as those above and in (b) and (c) below, the positivist doctrine (mentioned at the end of the Introduction), which considers informal derivations either as unreliable or as irrelevant to mathematics.

Note, finally, that the choice *between* different notions which an informal analysis has isolated need not be haphazard. Thus, at least for a "realistic" theory of foundations, considerations of *definability* give a (partial) criterion for which of two sets of notions is (more) *fundamental*: The set X is more fundamental than Y if Y can be defined from X, but not conversely. Thus the notion of set (ii) is more fundamental than that of finite set because the latter can be defined, even in $\mathscr{L}_E$, from the former, but not conversely.

It is plausible that, if the notion of set (iii) turns out to be precise on further study, it is more fundamental than (ii).

It must of course not be assumed that the notions which are fundamental for a realistic theory are particularly easy for us to grasp.

(b) Existence of a precise notion of set (ii) (i.e., set *of* something, satisfying (*)). Quite soon after the publication of Russell's paradox, both Russell and Zermelo formulated the precise notion of set, called *type theory*.

Zermelo's version, the so-called cumulative type structure (s.c.t.) [cf. Chapter 5, Example 5] is this:

C_0 is some collection of individuals, i.e., objects which have no members (C_0 possibly empty);

$C_{\alpha+1} = C_\alpha \cup \mathfrak{P}(C_\alpha)$, i.e., the union of C_α and of the collection of all its parts; and for limit numbers α, $C_\alpha = \bigcup_{\beta<\alpha} C_\beta$.

Equivalently, for

$$\alpha \neq 0: C_\alpha = \bigcup_{\beta<\alpha} C_\beta \cup \mathfrak{P}(C_\beta).$$

So, besides the basic (logical) operations on sets, we have here the *additional* operation $\mathfrak{P}$ and its *iteration* (to transfinite α if a transfinite ordinal α is assumed).

Let $\in_\alpha$ be the membership relation restricted to C_α.

The formula (**), sometimes called: unrestricted comprehension axiom, is *evidently false* in the structure $\langle C_\alpha, \in_\alpha \rangle$ for each α, i.e., when the variables in (**) are taken to range over C_α, e.g., if $P(y)$ is $y = y$ since $C_\alpha \notin C_\alpha$. The form (*) is *evidently true* for each α. For if $a \in C_\alpha$, take $x = \{y : y \in a$ and $P(y)$ is true in $\langle C_\alpha, \in_\alpha \rangle\}$; so, if $\alpha = \beta + 1$ then $y \in a \Rightarrow y \in C_\beta$ and since *all* subsets of $C_\beta \in C_{\beta+1}$, $x \in C_{\beta+1}$, i.e., $x \in C_\alpha$; if α is a limit number, and $a \in C_\alpha$, $a \in C_\beta$ (for some $\beta < \alpha$) and so again $x \in C_\alpha$.

Zermelo formulated laws, given in (c) below, which are not only the basis for all familiar axiomatic systems of set theory, but easily recognized to be satisfied by $\langle C_\alpha, \in_\alpha \rangle$ for all limit ordinals α: so, unless one has theoretical or empirical reasons against naive judgement, in particular against s.c.t., the precise notion of set above is a foundation for these axioms (particularly since only small α such as $\omega + \omega$, need be assumed).

(c) ZERMELO'S AXIOMS. The reader should verify as he reads them that they are satisfied in each $\langle C_\alpha, \in_\alpha \rangle$, α limit number.

1. Extensionality (*each* α):

$$\bigwedge xyz([z \in x \wedge \bigwedge u(u \in x \leftrightarrow u \in y)] \rightarrow x = y).$$

(If $C_0 = \emptyset$, even $\bigwedge xy[\bigwedge u(u \in x \leftrightarrow u \in y) \rightarrow x = y]$ holds.)

2. Power set (limit numbers α). If $z \subset x$ means: $\bigwedge u(u \in z \rightarrow u \in x)$

$$\bigwedge x \bigvee y \bigwedge z(z \in y \leftrightarrow z \subset x) \text{ (since } x \in C_\beta \Rightarrow y \in C_{\beta+1}).$$

[3. $$\bigwedge a \bigwedge X \bigvee x \bigwedge y[y \in x \leftrightarrow (y \in a \wedge X(y))]$$

where $\mathscr{L}_E$ is extended by *second* order variables X as in Chapter 7: This is needed to express (*) in its intended form; of course it is satisfied by $\langle C_\alpha, \in_\alpha \rangle$ for each $\alpha > 0$. Also basic results, like Theorem 1 below, are proved most simply for this form. However, current systems usually formulate *first order schemata* instead of 3, restricted to X which are explicitly defined by (finite) formulas of $\mathscr{L}_E$.]

3*. For each formula $A(y, x_1, \ldots, x_n)$ not containing the variable x:

$$\bigwedge x_1 \ldots \bigwedge x_n \bigvee x \bigwedge y(y \in x \leftrightarrow [y \in a \wedge A(y, x_1, \ldots, x_n)]).$$

4. Pairs: $\bigwedge x_1 x_2 \bigvee x \bigwedge y[y \in x \leftrightarrow (y = x_1 \vee y = x_2)]$ (limit α).

5. Union: $\bigwedge z \bigvee x \bigwedge y [y \in x \leftrightarrow \bigvee u(y \in u \wedge u \in z)]$ (all $\alpha > 0$).

Since each structure $\langle C_\alpha, \in_\alpha \rangle$ is built up by a transfinite iteration from individuals, the $\in$ relation is *well founded*. This is expressed by the so-called axiom of regularity:

[6. $$\bigwedge X \bigwedge a[X(a) \rightarrow \bigvee x \bigwedge y\{X(x) \wedge [X(y) \rightarrow y \notin x]\}].$$

Remark. The reader may verify that each structure that satisfies the axioms 1–6 is isomorphic to some $\langle C_\alpha, \in_\alpha \rangle$.

Once again, if one restricts oneself to first order axioms, one takes as schema the following consequences of 6:]

6*. For each formula $A(x)$

$$\bigwedge a[A(a) \rightarrow \bigvee x \bigwedge y\{A(x) \wedge [A(y) \rightarrow y \notin x]\}].$$

The axioms 1, 2, 4, 5, [3, 6, and consequently] 3*, 6* are satisfied by $\langle C_\omega, \in_\omega \rangle$ with $C_0 = \emptyset$ (the hereditarily finite sets). This is excluded by the

7. Axiom of infinity: $\bigvee x I_1(x)$ where $I_1(x)$ is

$$\bigvee y \bigwedge z(y \in x \wedge [z \in x \rightarrow \bigvee u(u \in x \wedge \bigwedge w[w \in u \leftrightarrow (w \in z \vee w \subset z)])]).$$

This is satisfied by $\langle C_\alpha, \in_\alpha \rangle$ for all $\alpha > \omega$ (hence: infinity, i.e., types of infinite ordinal) and all C_0; take $y = \emptyset$, and $u = z \cup \mathfrak{P}(z)$. Thus 1,2,4,5,7, [3, 6, and consequently] 3*, 6* are satisfied by $\langle C_\alpha, \in_\alpha \rangle$ for each limit number $\alpha > \omega$.

The systems [1, 2, 3, 4, 5]; 1, 2, 3*, 4, 5; [1, 2, 3, 4, 5, 7]; 1, 2, 3*, 4, 5, 7 will be denoted by $[\mathscr{A}_-]$, $\mathscr{A}^*_-$, $[\mathscr{A}]$, resp. $\mathscr{A}^*$.

EXERCISE 1: We use the notation of p. 170. For each formula $A(x)$ not containing the variable y, let $\bigvee ! x A(x)$ denote the formula $\bigvee x \bigwedge y [A(y) \leftrightarrow x = y]$ (read: there exists exactly one x satisfying A). Verify that
a) $\bigwedge yz \bigvee ! x (x = y \cup \{z\})$ follows from axioms 1 and 4,
b) for each triple of numerals n, m, p either $n + m = p$ is a consequence of $\mathscr{A}^*_-$ or $n + m \neq p$ is a consequence of $\mathscr{A}^*_-$.

$$\bigwedge yzv \{\mathrm{Sf}(y) \rightarrow \bigvee ! x [x = \mathrm{Sub}(y, z, v)]\},$$
$$\bigwedge yz \{[\mathrm{Sf}(y) \wedge \mathrm{Sf}(z)] \rightarrow \bigvee ! x [\mathrm{Sf}(x) \wedge s = \widehat{yz}]\},$$
$$\bigwedge y \{\mathrm{Sf}(y) \rightarrow \bigvee ! x [\mathrm{Sf}(x) \wedge x = \widehat{y}]\}$$

are consequences of $\mathscr{A}^*_-$.

Show also that $\bigwedge x ([\mathrm{Sf}(x) \wedge N(x)] \rightarrow \mathrm{Dom}(1, x))$ is consequence of 1 and 4.

[(a)–(c) show that the function symbols introduced p. 170 can be eliminated in the sense of Exercises 1 and 6 of Chapter 5.]

(d) DO ZERMELO'S AXIOMS AXIOMATIZE S.C.T. IN THE SENSE OF SECTION 1? By p. 168, $[U^{\mathscr{A}}$ and hence$]$ $U^{\mathscr{A}^*}$ is not satisfied, since, if $X \in C_\alpha$, $\overline{\overline{X}} < \overline{\overline{C}}_\alpha$.

The results below will show that [neither $X^{\mathscr{A}}$ nor $D^{\mathscr{A}}$ and hence] neither $X^{\mathscr{A}^*}$ nor $D^{\mathscr{A}^*}$ is satisfied, relative to the intuitive s.c.t. In fact $D^{\mathscr{A}^*}$ is violated in the strong form that $E^{\mathscr{A}^*}$ is not consequence of $\mathscr{A}^*$ [and $E^{\mathscr{A}}$ is not consequence of $\mathscr{A}$]; i.e., one cannot prove by use of the principles $\mathscr{A}^*$ that $\mathscr{A}^*$ has a model at all!

The results before Theorem 4 are technically very simple. They not only give insight into the general state of affairs, but illustrate how useful it is technically to use the interpretation of [$\mathscr{A}$ and] $\mathscr{A}^*$ by $\langle C_{\omega+\omega}, \in_{\omega+\omega} \rangle$.

[THEOREM 1: *$E^{\mathscr{A}}$, $E^{\mathscr{A}_-}$ are not (even) second order consequences of $\mathscr{A}$, $\mathscr{A}_-$ respectively* (even if 6 is added).

PROOF (by cardinality): Let $\mathfrak{M} = \langle C_{\omega+\omega}, \in_{\omega+\omega} \rangle$, $\mathfrak{M}_- = \langle C_\omega, \in_\omega \rangle$ both with $C_0 = \emptyset$. Then $\mathfrak{M}$, $\mathfrak{M}_-$ are the least models of $\mathscr{A}$, $\mathscr{A}_-$ resp., and so, in particular, every model of $\mathscr{A}$ has cardinal $\geqslant \sum \aleph^{(n)}$ where $\aleph^{(0)} = \aleph_0$,

$\aleph^{(n+1)} = 2^{\aleph^{(n)}}$, and every model of $\mathscr{A}_-$ is infinite. Since every element of $\mathfrak{M}_-$ is finite, $E^{\mathscr{A}_-}$ is false in $\mathfrak{M}_-$. Since every element of $\mathfrak{M}$ has cardinal $\leqslant \aleph^{(n)}$ for some n, $E^{\mathscr{A}}$ is false in $\mathfrak{M}$. Since further both $\mathfrak{M}$ and $\mathfrak{M}_-$ satisfy 6, Theorem 1 follows.

Recall that, in contrast, for the classical structures $\mathfrak{S}$, $E^{\mathscr{A}\mathfrak{S}}$ and $U^{\mathscr{A}\mathfrak{S}}$ are consequences even of $\mathscr{A}^*$!

The general idea of the proof will be repeated in Theorem 3 for $\mathscr{A}^*_-$ because the general reader is not assumed to know what the second order systems $\mathscr{A}_-$ and $\mathscr{A}$ are!.]

An obvious *first* failure of $D^{\mathscr{A}^*}$ [$D^{\mathscr{A}}$] is that Zermelo's axioms say nothing about the possibility of continuing $\langle C_\alpha, \in_\alpha \rangle$ beyond $\alpha = \omega + \omega$ [implicit in Theorem 1]. More formally, we have *non-saturation*:

THEOREM 2: *Let I_2 be the formula*

$$\bigvee y \bigwedge z \{y \in x \wedge I_1(y) \wedge [z \in x \rightarrow \bigvee u(u \in x \wedge \bigwedge v[v \in u \leftrightarrow (v \subset z \vee v \in z)]\},$$

where $I_1(y)$ is as in Axiom 7. Then neither I_2 nor $\neg\, I_2$ is a consequence of $\mathscr{A}^*$ even if 6* *is added.* (I_2 implies that there are sets of type $\omega + \omega$.)

[Note that though I_2 is a first order formula it is not (even) a second order consequence of $\mathscr{A}$.]

For Zermelo's Axioms are satisfied both in $\langle C_{\omega+\omega}, \in_{\omega+\omega} \rangle$ and in $\langle C_{\omega+\omega+\omega}, \in_{\omega+\omega+\omega} \rangle$; $\neg I_2$ is satisfied in the former, I_2 in the latter. In other words, Zermelo's Axioms are not saturated, i.e., they leave I_2 formally undecided.

[This simple result generalizes. Suppose (i) the axioms $\mathscr{F}$ are satisfied by the full s.c.t. and also by $\langle C_\alpha, \in_\alpha \rangle$ (e.g., $\alpha = \omega + \omega$ if $\mathscr{F} = \mathscr{A}$), and (ii) the formula A_α of $\mathscr{L}_E$ *defines* the property $x = C_\alpha$ in each $\langle C_\beta, \in_\beta \rangle$, i.e., C_α is the only object, if any, that satisfies A_α in the realization $\langle C_\beta, \in_\beta \rangle$ of $\mathscr{L}_E$. Then $\bigvee x A_\alpha$ is undecided by $\mathscr{F}$. Below more elementary assertions will be shown to be undecided by $\mathscr{A}^*$.]

THEOREM 3: *$E^{\mathscr{A}^*_-}$ is not a consequence of $\mathscr{A}^*_-$ even if* 6* *is added.* [This is the weakening of Theorem 1 mentioned above.]

PROOF: $\langle C_\omega, \in_\omega \rangle$ with $C_0 = \emptyset$ is the minimal model of $\mathscr{A}^*_-$. Since it is infinite but contains no infinite element, $E^{\mathscr{A}^*_-}$ is false in $\langle C_\omega, \in_\omega \rangle$, $E^{\mathscr{A}^*_-}$ expressing that there is a structure ($\in C_\omega$) which is a model of $\mathscr{A}^*_-$. Actually every model of 2, 4, 5 is infinite provided there is e.g. a null set, i.e., provided some special case of 3* is satisfied such as $y \in y \wedge y \notin y$ for $A(y)$ in 3*.

Theorem 3, but not its proof, is generalized in Gödel's *incompleteness* theorem.

THEOREM 4: *$E^{\mathscr{A}^*}$ is not consequence of $\mathscr{A}^*$.*

Remarks. (i) The proof of Theorem 4 generalizes to a large class of axioms other than $\mathscr{A}^*$, but the reader should consider the particular case of the set of axioms $\mathscr{A}_T = \{A : A \text{ is true in s.c.t.}\}$, for set theoretic formulas A. Evidently the resulting axiom system is saturated; what the proof of the Theorem shows is that $\mathscr{A}_T$ cannot be defined in set theoretic language in the precise sense of Corollary 1 below.

(ii) Particularly in Lemmas 4 and 5, one indicates only briefly that the conclusions of certain simple arguments [when formulated in $\mathscr{L}_E$] are consequences of $\mathscr{A}^*$. Once one knows that *some* true statements are not consequences of $\mathscr{A}^*$ (e.g. $E^{\mathscr{A}^*}$ itself!), one may doubt these indications. Without checking them, one has the following result: *either* Theorem 4 is true *or* $D^{\mathscr{A}^*}$ is false because these simple intuitive arguments are not logical consequences of $\mathscr{A}^*$; *or*, finally, $X^{\mathscr{A}^*}$ is false as in (i) above. For the applications below, these weaker conclusions are enough.

(iii) Formulas, and, more generally, all syntactic objects [cf. Chapter 0] are themselves considered to be sets, in particular ordered sequences of symbols and the symbols *are* sets: if this could not be done, $X^{\mathscr{A}^*}$ would be violated! Each symbol s is supposed to be *defined* by a formula of $\mathscr{A}^*$, i.e., a formula with a single free variable x such that s is the only object that satisfies the formula in s.c.t. We shall write $\boxed{x, s}$ for this formula. N.B. In Lemmas 1 and 2 below, all that is needed of $\boxed{x, s}$, and more generally of the so-called canonical definitions $\boxed{x, A}$ of other syntactic objects A, is that A be defined by it in s.c.t. But if one wants simple syntactic properties to be *consequences* of $\mathscr{A}^*$, the choice of canonical definitions becomes important; e.g., for $\boxed{x, \emptyset} = \bigwedge y \neg y \in x$ (definition of the empty set), $\bigvee x \boxed{x, \emptyset}$ is a consequence of $\mathscr{A}^*$. But suppose (for closed P) $\bar{P}$ is true but P not a consequence of $\mathscr{A}^*$; then $P \wedge \boxed{x, \emptyset}$ also defines $\emptyset$ in s.c.t., but $\bigvee x(P \wedge \boxed{x, \emptyset})$ is not consequence of $\mathscr{A}^*$.

The reason why objects are defined by means of formulas, and not by means of terms is, of course, that $\mathscr{L}_E$ does not contain function symbols, in contrast, e.g., to the basic language $\mathscr{L}_C$ of Part B below. The difference is not essential [in the following precise sense.

For each formula A of $\mathscr{L}_E$ and each formula B with the free variable x, we may introduce constants $\ulcorner A \urcorner$ and $\ulcorner B(\ulcorner A \urcorner) \urcorner$ together with the axioms: $\bigvee x\,(x = \ulcorner A \urcorner \wedge \boxed{x, A})$, $\bigvee y\,(y = \ulcorner B(\ulcorner A \urcorner) \urcorner \wedge \boxed{y, \bigvee x\,(B \wedge \boxed{x, A})})$; then the set $\overline{\ulcorner A \urcorner}$ *is* the formula A, and $\overline{\ulcorner B(\ulcorner A \urcorner) \urcorner}$ *is* the formula of $\mathscr{L}_E$ which expresses $\overline{B(\ulcorner A \urcorner)}$, i.e., the assertion that the formula A has the property $\bar{B}$. This notation shortens the statement of the lemmas below. The reader familiar with Exercises 1 and 6 of Chapter 5 will know how to eliminate these constants.]

(iv) An unusual feature of the proof is that relations between formulas and their meanings are treated, while in most mathematics, throughout any proof, one either talks only about the formal expressions (e.g., in numerical arithmetic) or, more usually, only about their meanings. We shall apply here the convention of p. 167 (with s.c.t. as the structure $\mathfrak{S}$): a bar over an expression A means the realization of A in s.c.t., in particular, if A is a closed formula, $\bar{A}$ means that A is satisfied in s.c.t.

[In most of the principal text, formulas are used to denote their realizations; of course, an exception is the definition of the notion of realization itself, e.g., at the beginning of Chapter 2, which involves the *relation* considered here. This will be taken up in Exercise 4 below.]

Another consequence of the unusual feature here considered is that certain purely formal conventions implicit in the ordinary use of symbols will have to be made explicit (some of them affect the very statement of the present theorem).

First, each of the expressions A, or Ax, or $A(x)$ is used to denote the same sequence of symbols of $\mathscr{L}_E$ [cf. Chapter 2, p. 18], $A(x)$ being useful when one wants to indicate that A contains the variable (denoted by) x and that $A(t)$ is obtained from A by substituting the expression (denoted by) t for x. [It is clear that the definition of substitution is simplest if the free variables of the formulas considered do not have bound occurrences.]

Second, since the assertion $E^{\mathscr{A}^*}$ refers to the language $\mathscr{L}_E$, $\mathscr{A}^*$ being a set of formulas of $\mathscr{L}_E$, Theorem 4 becomes specific only if a definite choice of symbols in $\mathscr{L}_E$ is made, for instance, as follows:

The relation symbols denoted by $=$ and $\in$ *are* the integer 0, respectively 1, i.e., the empty set and its unit set;

the logical symbols, denoted by $\neg$, $\vee$, $\bigvee$ are 2, 3, 4;

and the variables, sometimes denoted by $v_0, v_1, v_2, \ldots$ are 5, 6, 7, ...;

thus v_n denotes the integer $n+5$.

There are two main reasons for this choice. First, the proof below requires in any case a collection of symbols such that each has a canonical definition in $\mathscr{L}_E$ (for details and further conditions, cf. the relation $\overline{\text{Def}}$ after Exercise 2); it would not be sufficient to take an arbitrary collection. Second, by choosing the symbols among objects in C_ω, we obtain a formula undecided by $\mathscr{A}^*$ which refers only to C_ω, i.e., to the hereditarily finite sets.

The careful reader will notice that the language $\mathscr{L}_E$ need not be a structure in the narrow sense, i.e., a *set*. Specifically [by working directly with $\bar{D}$ instead of $\bar{V}$ after Lemma 3] the proof below establishes Theorem 4 uniformly for $\mathscr{A}^*_-$ as well as for $\mathscr{A}^*$; the reason why Theorem 4 is stated for the latter is, of course, because Theorem 3 provides already an (*ad hoc*) argument for the former.

EXERCISE 2. By reference to the definitions given on pp. 169–170 show that

(i) the integer n is the only object (of s.c.t.) which satisfies the formula E_n whose only free variable is v_{4n}, where

$$E_0 \text{ is } \neg \bigvee v_2 (v_2 \in v_0)$$
$$E_{n+1} \text{ is } \bigvee v_{4n} (E_n \wedge \bigwedge v_{4n+6} [v_{4n+6} \in v_{4n+4} \leftrightarrow (v_{4n+6} = v_{4n} \vee v_{4n+6} \in v_{4n})]);$$

(ii) the finite sequence $\langle n_0, \ldots, n_{k-1} \rangle$ of integers is the only object ($\bar{s}$) which satisfies

$$\bigvee x_0 \ldots \bigvee x_{k-1} \bigvee y_0 \ldots \bigvee y_k [E_{n_0}(x_0) \wedge \cdots \wedge E_{n_{k-1}}(x_{k-1}) \wedge E_0(y_0) \wedge \cdots \wedge E_k(y_k) \wedge \mathrm{Sf}(s) \wedge \mathrm{Dom}(y_k, s) \wedge (y_0, x_0) \in s \wedge \cdots \wedge (y_{k-1}, x_{k-1}) \in s].$$

Since every formula of $\mathscr{L}_E$ *is* a finite sequence of integers, Exercise 2 provides a schema for associating a *canonical definition* for every formula of $\mathscr{L}_E$. This definition is in turn a finite sequence of integers, and so one sees easily that there is a formula $\mathrm{Def}(y, x)$ of $\mathscr{L}_E$ which defines in s.c.t. the following relation:

x is a finite sequence of integers and y is the formula of $\mathscr{L}_E$ that defines x canonically (according to the schema of Exercise 2).

In other words, if $\bar{x}$ is a given formula A, and $\overline{\mathrm{Def}(y, x)}$ is true, then $\bar{y}$ is the formula $\boxed{s, A}$.

[Though the idea of the construction of Def is quite simple, the reader familiar with Chapters 0 and 2 should note certain conventions tacitly assumed in the formulation of Exercise 2.

(a) Since $\mathscr{L}_E$ contains no brackets, E_0 is more properly written: $\neg \bigvee v_2 \in v_2 v_0$, because it is the sequence $\langle 2, 4, 7, 1, 7, 5 \rangle$.

(b) The formulas E_n are such that the free variable v_{4n} has no bound occurrences. This will simplify the definition of substitution below. In order to ensure that the definitions E_n of the natural numbers do not use up the total supply of variables, we have used only the variables 5, 7, 9, ….

(c) In the construction of a canonical definition for $\langle n_0, ..., n_{k-1}\rangle$ it is of course assumed that the $x_0, ..., x_{k-1}, y_1, ..., y_k$ denote distinct variables, i.e., different integers > 4, which do not occur in the formulas E_i, E_{n_j} $(0 \leqslant i \leqslant k, 0 \leqslant j < k)$ nor in the formulas (abbreviated by): $(y_j, x_j) \in s$, Sf (s), Dom (y_k, s). In particular, in view of the canonical choice of definitions for integers, all the x and y must be $> m$, where $m = 4 \max(k, n_0, ..., n_{k-1})$. Also, they must be different from the bound variables which occur in the formulas Sf, Dom (which variables are denoted by u, v, w, r on p. 170). And finally, s must be different from all the variables mentioned. We shall suppose that neither v_1 nor v_3 occurs in any canonical definition (cf. Lemma 1).]

Capital letters will mean formulas in the language $\mathscr{L}_E$ of $\mathscr{A}^*$: they are not themselves symbols of $\mathscr{L}_E$. The variables x and y are arbitrary, but fixed [more precisely, they are different from all variables in canonical definitions, and consistent with the rule that free variables have no bound occurrences; adopting the canonical definitions of Example 2, one may take v_1 and v_3 for x and y].

LEMMA 1: *For any A with the single free variable x, there is a (closed) A_1 such that $A_1 \leftrightarrow \bigvee x\,(\boxed{x, A} \wedge \neg A)$ is true in s.c.t.; i.e., the syntactic object A_1 does not have the property $\bar{A}$.* (Actually, this is a consequence of $\mathscr{A}^*$.)

PROOF: Obtain first a formula S with variables x and y whose realization $\bar{\mathrm{S}}$ is the following relation between syntactic objects ($\bar{x} = A, \bar{y} = A'$): $\{A, A' : y$ is the only free variable of A and $A' = \bigvee y(\boxed{y, A} \wedge A)\}$.

To get S, give first a recursive definition of A' according to the length of A, by use of the notations on p. 170 and Exercise 1, and then convert recursive definitions into explicit set theoretic ones [Chapter 6, Exercise 7].

If now $H = \bigvee x(\mathrm{S} \wedge \neg A)$, the formula $\bigvee y(\boxed{y, H} \wedge H)$ can be taken for A_1. For $\bar{A}_1$ means that the (only) object which satisfies $\bar{H}$ is in fact the formal object H itself; but, since $\bar{H} = \overline{\bigvee x(\mathrm{S} \wedge \neg A)}$, the object H' in the relation $\bar{\mathrm{S}}$ to H, satisfies $\overline{\neg A}$. This object is A_1 itself.

(This construction is Gödel's variant of Cantor's diagonal argument.)

[EXERCISE 3: *Definition of the formula* S (x, y) *in Lemma 1.*

Form (x): x is a formula of $\mathscr{L}_E$ (where, as mentioned above, free variables nowhere have bound occurrences). Starting with the recursive (implicit) definition of the class of formulas of $\mathscr{L}_E$, one obtains an expression Form (x) which can be proved in $\underline{\mathscr{A}^*}$ to satisfy the implicit definition; cf. Exercise 6 of Chapter 5. (If one uses Dedekind's method, the proof requires $\mathscr{A}^*$.)

Vl(v, x): v is the only free variable of the formula x, and v has only free occurrences in x:

$\mathrm{Form}(x) \wedge \mathrm{Od}(v) \wedge \bigwedge u\,[(u,4)\in x \rightarrow (u \cup \{u\}, v) \notin x] \wedge$
$\bigwedge u \bigwedge w\,([\mathrm{Od}(u) \wedge u \neq v \wedge (w,u)\in x] \rightarrow \bigvee y\,[y\in w \wedge (y,4)\in x \wedge (y \cup \{y\}, u)\in x])$,

where $\mathrm{Od}(v)$ stands for $\bigvee q\,[N(q) \wedge v = q+q+5]$ in the notation of p. 170.

(Since v is a variable it is an odd integer > 4, i.e., $\mathrm{Od}(v)$; since v has only free occurrences it is nowhere preceded by a quantifier, i.e., by 4; and since v is the only free variable, every other variable, i.e., every other integer > 4 n the sequence x, has its first occurrence preceded by 4.)

S (x, y): x is a formula whose sole free variable is the second variable chosen above, e.g., v_3 ($= 7$), i.e., Vl $(x, 7)$; by Exercise 2, x has a canonical definition, say x_1, i.e., Def (x, x_1), with a sole free variable, say w, i.e., Vl (x_1, w). Take a variable p which occurs neither in x nor in x_1, say the first such variable and let its definition be F (p, x, x_1), i.e.,

$\mathrm{Od}(p) \wedge \bigwedge u\,[(u,p)\notin x \wedge (u,p)\notin x_1] \wedge \bigwedge u\,([u\in p \wedge \mathrm{Od}(u)] \rightarrow \bigvee v\,[(v,u)\in x \vee (v,u)\in x_1])$.

Substitute p for 7 in x, and for w in x_1 to get x', respectively x'_1, i.e., $x' = \mathrm{Sub}(x, 7, p)$, $x'_1 = \mathrm{Sub}(x_1, w, p)$, and

$$y = 4\frown p\frown 3\frown x'_1\frown x',$$

i.e., S (y, x) is

$\mathrm{Vl}(x,7) \wedge \bigvee x_1 w p x' x'_1\,[\mathrm{Def}(x, x_1) \wedge \mathrm{Vl}(x_1, w) \wedge \mathrm{F}(p, x, x_1) \wedge$
$x' = \mathrm{Sub}(x, 7, p) \wedge x'_1 = \mathrm{Sub}(x_1, w, p) \wedge y = 4\frown p\frown 3\frown x'_1\frown x']$.

This completes the definition of S.]

Corollary 1: Lemma 1 is enough to show that $X^{\mathscr{A}}$ is false (and, in fact $X^{\mathscr{A}_{\mathfrak{F}}}$ is false for any $\mathscr{A}_{\mathfrak{F}}$ in the language of set theory). For, the set

$$t = \{A_1 : A_1 \text{ is closed and } \bar{A}_1 \text{ is true (in s.c.t.)}\}$$

is not the realization of *any* formula A (if $t = \bar{A}$, the A_1 of Lemma 1 gives a contradiction). This was observed by Tarski.

But, if *truth of A* cannot be defined, and (set theoretic) consequence can [and was in Chapters 2,7], see [also] p. 167, one expects

Lemma 2: *If $\bar{V}$ (V with single free variable x) is the set of consequences of $\mathscr{A}^*$, there is a V_1 such that $\bar{V}_1$ is true, but V_1 not consequence of $\mathscr{A}^*$.*

Proof: By Lemma 1, there is a V_1 such that $V_1 \leftrightarrow \bigvee x(\boxed{x, V_1} \wedge \neg V)$is true, i.e., $\bar{V}_1$ is true, if and only if it is not a consequence of $\mathscr{A}^*$. But since all consequences of $\mathscr{A}^*$ are true (in s.c.t.), Lemma 2 is proved. (Evidently, one does not need here that *all* consequences of $\mathscr{A}^*$ be true, but only those of 'form' V_1.)

[N.B. The lemma applies equally to higher order consequence, in particular to the second order axioms in (c) because the only assumption is that the consequence relation be definable in the realization s.c.t. of $\mathscr{L}_E$. So it gives another non-saturation result for the second order system.]

COROLLARY 2: V_1 is not decided by $\mathscr{A}^*$, i.e., neither V_1 nor $\neg V_1$ is consequence of $\mathscr{A}^*$.

[EXERCISE 4: (i) Find a formula $\mathrm{Sat}(a, e, s, y)$ of $\mathscr{L}_E$ which defines the following relation $\overline{\mathrm{Sat}}$:

$\bar{e} \subset \bar{a} \times \bar{a}$, $\bar{y}$ is a formula of $\mathscr{L}_E$, $\bar{s} = \{(v_i, \xi_i) : v_i$ is a free variable of $\bar{y}$, and $\xi_i \in \bar{a}\}$, and the ξ satisfy $\bar{y}$ in the realization (a, e) of $\mathscr{L}_E$ in the sense of Chapter 2.

(ii) Deduce a definition $\mathrm{Sat}_0(a, e, y)$ of the relation:

$\bar{e} \subset \bar{a} \times \bar{a}$, $\bar{y}$ is a closed formula of $\mathscr{L}_E$, and $(\bar{a}, \bar{e})$ is a model of $\bar{y}$.

(iii) Find a formula $Z(y)$ which defines the property:

$\bar{y}$ is a formula of $\mathscr{L}_E$ and $\bar{y}$ is an axiom of Zermelo's set theory.

(iv) Show that $\bar{V}$ is defined by

$$\bigwedge ae(\bigwedge y[Z(y) \to \mathrm{Sat}_0(a, e, y)] \to \mathrm{Sat}_0(a, e, x)).$$

Note that, for a *given* closed formula A of $\mathscr{L}_E$, not containing the variables a and e, the relation: (a, e) *satisfies* A, is defined simply by restricting the quantifiers of A to a, and replacing each atomic formula $x \in y$ in A by $(x, y) \in e$. Exercise 4 is needed because $\mathscr{A}^*$ contains infinitely many formulas, and, more important, because $\bar{x} \in \bar{V}$ has to be defined for variable $\bar{x}$.]

Discussion of Lemma 2. Whether the non-saturation result of Lemma 2 is an improvement over Theorem 2 will depend on closer inspection of the *form* of V_1. For optimal results we shall try to find as simple a formula D as possible whose realization $= \bar{V}$, i.e., whose realization $\bar{D}$ is also the set of consequences of $\mathscr{A}^*$.

The principal properties of the formula D will be described here; but the proof (in particular, of $\bar{D} = \bar{V}$) and even the precise formulation of D need the work of Chapter 2.

(i) The formula D is obtained as follows. Lemma 3 provides "rules of inference" like those mentioned in footnote 2, and shows that the set of formulas of $\mathscr{L}_E$ deducible from $\mathscr{A}^*$ by means of these rules is $\bar{V}$. Further, the rules can be "expressed" in $\mathscr{L}_E$ itself in the sense that there exists a formula $\mathrm{Dem}(y, x)$ of $\mathscr{L}_E$ such that $\overline{\mathrm{Dem}}$ is the relation:

$\bar{y}$ is a deduction of $\bar{x}$ from $\mathscr{A}^*$ according to the rules (where $\bar{y}$ is a finite sequence of formulas of $\mathscr{L}_E$, and $\bar{x}$ a formula of $\mathscr{L}_E$).

Thus, $D(x)$ is $\bigvee y\, \mathrm{Dem}(y, x)$.

(ii) D is more elementary than V in the sense that the quantifiers of D are restricted to C_ω (when $\mathscr{L}_E$, i.e., its symbols, are defined as in Exercises 1, 2, 3) while certain quantifiers of V are not restricted to any set (according to the definition of set theoretic consequence on p. 167 [or in Chapter 2]).

(iii) Actually, the elementary character of D mentioned in (ii) is best expressed in terms of the basic notions of Part B; specifically, the sketch of these notions in Part B, Section 0 makes clear that the rules given in Lemma 3 are combinatorial, i.e., "purely formal". Consequently, if a formula $\in \bar{D}$, this fact can be verified in a combinatorial manner [cf. the remark after Lemma 3].

(iv) Lemmas (iv) and (v) show that $E^{\mathscr{A}^*} \to D_1$ is a consequence of $\mathscr{A}^*$, where D_1 is obtained from D as A_1 is obtained from A in Lemma 1. Since, by Lemma 2, D_1 is *not* a consequence of $\mathscr{A}^*$, Theorem 4 follows.

[LEMMA 3: $\bar{V}$ *(of Lemma 2) is* $\bar{D}$ *where* $\bar{D} = \overline{\bigvee y\, \mathrm{Dem}}$ (Dem *containing the variables y and x*) *and* $\overline{\mathrm{Dem}}$ *is the following relation, again between syntactic objects*:

$\{\langle B; A_1, A_2\rangle, A$: B *is the conjunction of some finite subset of* $\mathscr{A}^*$,
A_2 *is the prenex form of* $B \to A$ *given on p.* 19, *Chapter* 2,
A_1 *is a propositional identity of the form*
$F(t_1^1, \dots, t_m^1) \vee \dots \vee F(t_1^n, \dots, t_m^n)$,
where $\check{A}_2$ *is* $\bigvee x_1 \dots \bigvee x_m F$, *as on p.* 22, *Chapter* 2.

PROOF. By the finiteness theorem, if A is a consequence of $\mathscr{A}^*$, it is a consequence of some finite subset B of $\mathscr{A}^*$, and then $B \to A$ is valid. Apply now Chapter 2, pp. 23–24.

Note, if V is the (official) definition of validity (= true in all realizations, including of course infinite ones) the simplification achieved by Lemma 3 is this. To verify that a formula is in $\bar{V}$ one would have to 'look' at all realizations, to verify that it is in $\bar{D}$, one only has to look at finite configurations $\langle B, A_1, A_2\rangle$ and check the conditions above. Intuitively it is clear that *if* $A \in \bar{D}$ then this fact can be verified by finitely many trials. This fact can itself be formulated in set theoretic language; the formulation depends of course on the *choice* of the formula D, and hence of Dem. What is needed is a choice for which the formulation is a *consequence* of $\mathscr{A}^*$. If one did not find such a Dem, one would apply Remark (ii) above!

LEMMA 4. *Let* $D_A = \bigvee x(\boxed{x, A} \wedge D)$ *where A is a closed formula of* $\mathscr{L}_E$, *i.e. A does not contain free variables. Then*

$$D_A \to \bigvee x(\boxed{x, D_A} \wedge D)$$

is a consequence of $\mathscr{A}^*$. (Actually the lemma is needed for a particular A only.)

Before sketching the proof we remark that $A \to \overline{\bigvee x(\boxed{x, A} \wedge D)}$ is *not* true (in s.c.t.) for all (closed) A; e.g. it is not true if $\bar{A}$ is true, but A is not consequence of $\mathscr{A}^*$! By Lemmas 2 and 3 an example of such a formula A is D_1 above. So the lemma to be proved depends essentially on the *form* of D_A. What will be used first is this: for proper choice of Dem (in fact, for the obvious choice of Dem) and canonical definitions of any finite sequence of symbols $\langle \bar{b}, \bar{a}_1, \bar{a}_2 \rangle$ and A in the language $\mathscr{L}_E$, if $\langle\langle \bar{b}, \bar{a}_1, \bar{a}_2 \rangle, A \rangle \in \overline{\text{Dem}}$ then the formula $\bigvee x \bigvee y(\boxed{x, A} \wedge \boxed{y, \langle \bar{b}, \bar{a}_1, \bar{a}_2 \rangle} \wedge \text{Dem})$ can in fact be formally derived in $\mathscr{A}^*$. This is implicit in saying that elementary combinatorial mathematics can be formalized in the axiomatic system $\mathscr{A}^*$: for, as pointed out after Lemma 3, the verification of the hypothesis $\langle\langle \bar{b}, \bar{a}_1, \bar{a}_2 \rangle, A \rangle \in \overline{\text{Dem}}$ proceeds by checking a finite number of purely combinatorial conditions, and this process is mimicked in a formal derivation from $\mathscr{A}^*$. Next, if $\bigvee x \bigvee y(\boxed{x, A} \wedge \boxed{y, \langle \bar{b}, \bar{a}_1, \bar{a}_2 \rangle} \wedge \wedge \text{Dem})$ (with explicitly given y!) is a consequence of $\mathscr{A}^*$ so is $\bigvee x(\boxed{x, A} \wedge \bigvee y \,\text{Dem})$.

The final step is to show that the argument just sketched can itself be formalized in $\mathscr{A}^*$, i.e. that the assertion with *variables* for formulas b, a_1, a_2 and given A:

$$\bigvee x \bigvee y(\boxed{x, A} \wedge y = (b, a_1, a_2) \wedge \text{Dem}) \to \bigvee x \bigvee y\, [x = F(b, a_1, a_2) \wedge \text{Dem}]$$

is a consequence of $\mathscr{A}^*$ where $F(b, a_1, a_2)$ is a canonical definition of the function which associates to each triple $(\bar{b}, \bar{a}_1, \bar{a}_2)$ the formula $\bigvee x \bigvee y(\boxed{x, A} \wedge \boxed{y, \langle \bar{b}, \bar{a}_1, \bar{a}_2 \rangle} \wedge \wedge \text{Dem})$. Hence also

$$\mathscr{A}^* \vdash \bigvee x \bigvee y(\boxed{x, A} \wedge y = (b, a_1, a_2) \wedge \text{Dem}) \to \bigvee x \bigvee y(\boxed{x, D_A} \wedge \text{Dem}).$$

Since the variables b, a, a_1 do not occur in the conclusion,

$$\mathscr{A}^* \vdash \bigvee x \bigvee y(\boxed{x, A} \vee \text{Dem}) \to \bigvee x(\boxed{x, D_A} \wedge D),$$

as required.

The detailed verification of this goes back to the canonical definitions used; the nature of the problem is probably sufficiently clear from the discussion after Remark (iii) on p. 178.

LEMMA 5: *Suppose D satisfies Lemma 4 and, if $A \leftrightarrow B$ is consequence of $\mathscr{A}^*$, so is $\bigvee x(\boxed{x, A} \wedge D) \leftrightarrow \bigvee x(\boxed{x, B} \wedge D)$. Then if D_1 is the formula obtained in Lemma 2 when V is replaced by D then $(E^{\mathscr{A}^*} \to D_1)$ is a consequence of $\mathscr{A}^*$.*

What one uses is the contrapositive of Lemma 4: if a simple 'universal' formula like D_1 ($\bar{D}_1$ means: D_1 is not consequence of $\mathscr{A}^*$) is a consequence of $\mathscr{A}^*$ then D_1 holds (provided of course $\mathscr{A}^*$ is not contradictory). Formally, by cases according to whether D_1 is a consequence of $\mathscr{A}^*$:

(i) $\bigvee x(\boxed{x, D_1} \wedge \neg D) \to D_1$ by Lemma 1 without hypothesis; note that $\bigvee x(\boxed{x, D_1})$ is a consequence of $\mathscr{A}^*$.

(ii) If $\overline{E^{\mathscr{A}^*}}$ is true and D_1 is a consequence of $\mathscr{A}^*$, then $\neg D_1$ is not.

But if in Lemma 4 we take $A = \neg D_1$, then $D_A \leftrightarrow \neg D_1$, $\bigvee x(\boxed{x, \neg D_1} \wedge D) \leftrightarrow \bigvee x$

($\boxed{x, A}$ $\wedge$ D) are consequences of $\mathscr{A}^*$, and so $\neg \bigvee x(\boxed{x, \neg D_1} \wedge D) \rightarrow \neg\neg D_1$. So, without hypothesis, $E^{\mathscr{A}^*} \rightarrow D_1$ is consequence of $\mathscr{A}^*$.

COROLLARY: Theorem 4 follows because, by Lemma 2, D_1 is not consequence of $\mathscr{A}^*$.]

Discussion of Theorem 4. [$\mathscr{A}$ and hence] $\mathscr{A}^*$ fails to characterise s.c.t. in the sense of Section 1 because [$\mathscr{A}$ and hence] $\mathscr{A}^*$ is satisfied by $\langle C_\alpha, \in_\alpha \rangle$ for all limit numbers $\alpha > \omega$, and so [$U^{\mathscr{A}}$ and hence] $U^{\mathscr{A}^*}$ is false.

Further, $D^{\mathscr{A}^*}$ [and even $D^{\mathscr{A}}$] is not satisfied with respect to intuitive reasoning about sets of sufficiently high type, as shown by Theorem 2.

As far as intuitive reasoning about finite sets is concerned, $D^{\mathscr{A}^*}$ is not satisfied because $E^{\mathscr{A}^*}$ is equivalent to a combinatorial assertion by Lemma 3 and $\mathscr{A}^*$ does not decide $E^{\mathscr{A}^*}$, by Theorem 4.

A subject of general interest is the difference between Theorem 4 and the better known independence results, for instance in geometry. The *obvious* difference is of course that $\mathscr{A}^*$ is intended to formulate properties of a particular intuitive notion, namely that of *set* in sense (ii), p. 171, while the axioms of geometry, at least nowadays, are usually intended as a purely hypothetical deductive system. But a more mathematical formulation of this difference can also be given by use of the notion of second order consequence in Chapter 7.

[Note that, by the Remark on p. 175 after Axiom 6, the structure $(\bar{N}, \bar{S})$, p. 169, of the integers is uniquely determined by the axioms $\mathscr{A}$; so either $E^{\mathscr{A}^*}$ is a consequence of $\mathscr{A}$ or else $\neg E^{\mathscr{A}^*}$ – and, in fact, it is $E^{\mathscr{A}^*}$. In other words, the independence of $E^{\mathscr{A}^*}$ depends essentially on replacing the Axiom 3 by the schema 3*. In contrast, for instance the independence of the parallel axiom has nothing to do with the corresponding step in geometry. Specifically, consider the axioms of Pasch or Hilbert whose basic notions are: Points; the relation of congruence $C(a, b, c, d)$: the segment ab is congruent to the segment cd; and the (ternary) relation: a is between b and c, i.e. a, b, c are collinear and a is between the two others. All the axioms are of first order, except the so-called axiom of continuity (Dedekind cut). Sometimes one replaces this axiom by a first order schema exactly as one replaced 3 above by the schema 3*; in other words, instead of considering arbitrary cuts, one considers only those defined by formulas in the language above. But the *axiom of parallels is independent of the axiom of continuity of second order and not only of the first order schema.*]

$X^{\mathscr{A}^*}$ fails completely by Corollary 1. [This reason is that $\mathscr{L}_E$ uses *arbitrary* finite formulas, but not infinite ones: thus the set t of Corollary 1 is defined by

$$(\boxed{x, A_1} \wedge A_1) \vee (\boxed{x, A_2} \wedge A_2) \vee \cdots$$

cf. infinite formulas of Chapter 7, where $A_1, A_2, \ldots$ is an enumeration of the formulas of $\mathscr{L}_E$.]

Against these "negative" results there is the interesting positive corollary of Theorems 2 and 4: a purely combinatorial statement such as $E^{\mathscr{A}^*}$ which is undecided by $\mathscr{A}^*$, is a consequence of $\mathscr{A}^* \cup \{I_2\}$.

Naively, the inadequacies above are not surprising just because the adequacy of the axiomatizations in Section 1 for the classical structures *was* surprising. The shock comes because one has forgotten the original surprise [but cf. Section (c) for other views]. The situation is naturally compared with two well known cases in the history of mathematics: the irrationality of $\sqrt{2}$ showed that the system of rationals was inadequate for Euclidean geometry, and not, of course, that Euclidean constructions must be rejected; or $2^{\aleph_0} \times 2^{\aleph_0} = 2^{\aleph_0}$ showed that the notion of 1–1 correspondence was inadequate for analysing the intuitive concept of dimension and not that this concept is mathematically insignificant. But the real test of the theoretical value of the set theoretic concepts is to look at the development of their theory.

3. Improving the existing theory $\mathscr{A}^*[\mathscr{A}]$

Still accepting the s.c.t., we shall consider two directions of research, namely (a) the addition, (b) the elimination of axioms.

(a) In investigating s.c.t., one may follow the usual mathematical method employed in the study of particular structures (natural numbers, real numbers etc.), where, as one says, all legitimate methods are used. From this point of view the formulation of the axioms of Section 2(c) is only a beginning, and the process which led to them is to be continued. The results of Section 2(d) show that there is something to be done even if one confines oneself to questions formulated in the language of set theory because not all such questions are decided by $\mathscr{A}^*[\mathscr{A}]$. In short, addition of axioms is required.

(i) By Theorem 2, axioms are needed to express the existence of high types (so-called: axioms of infinity). One of them is the *replacement* axiom which ensures that for every well ordering $\langle a, a_1\rangle$ $(a_1 \subset a^2)$ in C_α there is a C_β where β is the ordinal of $\langle a, a_1\rangle$.
[In second order form:

$$\bigwedge X \bigwedge a [(\bigwedge x \in a) \bigvee ! y X (\langle x, y\rangle) \rightarrow \bigvee z \bigwedge u (u \in z \leftrightarrow \bigvee x [u \in a \wedge X(\langle x, u\rangle)])].$$

The general problems involved in formulating such axioms are discussed in: GÖDEL, What is Cantor's continuum problem; Amer. Math. Monthly **54** (1947) 515–525.

(ii) A special defect of [first order systems such as] $\mathscr{A}^*$, in particular 3*, is that $C_{\alpha+1}$ is intended to comprise *all* subsets of C_α, but 3* 'mentions' only those explicitly definable in set theoretic language; in particular, t of Corollary 1 (Section 2) which is in $C_{\omega+1}$, is not included. This t is 'essentially' defined in terms of the basic notions here considered, but a more radical improvement may well require the use of new primitive notions; cf. Corollary 5, Section 4 below.

[Closer inspection suggests that the defect (i) is theoretically more important than (ii): (ii) concerns only the *basic* operation of the power set construction, while (i) deals with the number of *iterations* of the step, a much more difficult matter conceptually. More formally, in (i) we have an inadequacy of both first and second order formulations of axioms for set theory, in (ii) only of first order systems. In any case (for second order consequence as defined in Chapter 7), every assertion of the form:

the formula A is a second order consequence of B,

is formulated in the first order language $\mathscr{L}_E$ (with s.c.t. as realization of $\mathscr{L}_E$): so, finding reasons for such an assertion reduces to finding (possibly new) axioms formulated in $\mathscr{L}_E$. Similarly, in the case of infinite formulas A, at least with quantifiers of bounded type, the realization $\bar{A}$ can be generally defined by an expression of $\mathscr{L}_E$. For more information concerning the relations between (i) and (ii), consult GÖDEL's Remarks on problems in mathematics, in: The Undecidable, ed. M. Davis (N.Y., 1965) pp. 84–88]. Naturally, the actual discovery of new axioms is sometimes easier via (ii).

Remark on axioms of infinity and traditional mathematics. Axioms of infinity are not only of interest in their own right, but because of their possible use in deriving conclusions about sets of low type, e.g. the use of the axiom I_2 in the discussion of Theorem 4 for deriving the purely *arithmetic* assertion D_1 [i.e. of an assertion which, expressed in $\mathscr{L}_E$, has all its quantifiers restricted to $\langle C_\omega, \in_\omega \rangle$]. (Evidently the *truth* of $\bar{D}_1$ does not "depend" on the existence of $\langle C_{\omega+\omega+1}, \in_{\omega+\omega+1} \rangle$, but its *evidence* may do so!) This situation is parallel to the use of analytic methods in number theory where functions of complex variables, i.e. objects of $\langle C_{\omega+2}, \in_{\omega+2} \rangle$, are considered, and theorems about them are used to obtain arithmetic consequences. Two differences are to be noted. First, as will be discussed in more detail in Part B, p. 205, the use of functions of a complex variable can be eliminated in *existing* proofs of analytic number theory in the precise (logical) sense that the theorems in question are also consequences of $\mathscr{A}^*_-$ of Section 2(d) (practically, the proofs from $\mathscr{A}^*_-$ are less easy to follow because complex functions have to be replaced by explicitly defined rational approximations). In contrast, D_1 is not consequence of $\mathscr{A}^*$, and so certainly not of $\mathscr{A}^*_-$. Second, speaking informally, D_1 has a primarily metamathematical, not arithmetic "interest"; more specifically, it is not known whether some of the open questions *familiar* from number theory are decided by suitable axioms of infinity.

(b) As to the *elimination* of axioms from $\mathscr{A}^*$, its interest for set theoretic semantic foundations is not too different in kind from the interest of ordinary axiomatic studies. Thus in mathematical practice, one wants a reduced set of axioms to be satisfied by an important mathematical structure that does not satisfy the original axioms. So, if $\mathscr{A}^*$ were to be reduced to $\mathscr{A}_1$ one would want $\mathscr{A}_1$ to be satisfied by an important concept (e.g. of set) which does not satisfy $\mathscr{A}^*$; but to be *foundationally* significant this concept would have to be basic, i.e. not in turn defined in terms of s.c.t.; on the contrary, by the criteria in Section 2(a) on fundamental notions (for a "realistic" foundation!), s.c.t. should be definable from this new concept[3].

No such basic notion is known at present. (The general notion of property, i.e. set in sense (iii) of Section 2(a), was mentioned as a possible basic notion for foundations, but its logic has not been studied enough to be discussed here.)

N.B. It will be seen below that the possibility of eliminating systematically some axioms of $\mathscr{A}^*$ from proofs actually occurring in certain branches of mathematical practice is important for the (non set theoretic) foundations of mathematics described in Part B.

[4. Historical notes; additional information on intuitive validity

We consider a language $\mathscr{L}$ of the predicate calculus with a finite num-

[3] The reader should note here the cavalier treatment of the axioms of set theory in Bourbaki's exposition (cf. their treatment of rules of inference, observed in footnote 2). The set theoretic axioms which intervene in particular deductions are rarely mentioned and little attempt is made to eliminate formally unnecessary ones, very much in contrast to all their efforts of eliminating unnecessary hypotheses in theorems about e.g. topological structures. Bourbaki's practice is perfectly consistent with the general principles on elimination of axioms formulated above if something like *set of s.c.t.* is tacitly understood and no independent basic notion is known. (The practice would be hopelessly unscientific if one were seriously interested in an 'empirical' justification of the kind considered in footnote 4 below: for, if all arguments in practice only use a subset $\mathscr{A}_1$ of the set theoretic axioms $\mathscr{A}^*$, experience would at best justify $\mathscr{A}_1$ and not $\mathscr{A}^*$.)

ber of relation and function symbols, and we denote by Val^1, Val^2, ... the sets of formulae of $\mathscr{L}$, $\mathscr{L}^2$, ... which are intuitively valid, by $\bar{V}^1$, $\bar{V}^2$, ... those valid in the sense of Chapters 2 and 7.

(a) SOME SET THEORETIC RESULTS, i.e. results formulated in $\mathscr{L}_E$ (as always with the realization s.c.t.) which help to establish relations between the set theoretically defined notions $\bar{V}^i$ and the primitive intuitive notions Val^i.

$\overline{\mathrm{Dem}}_0$ (cf. Lemma 3) will denote the relation $\langle A_1, A\rangle$ where A is a prenex formula of $\mathscr{L}$, $\breve{A}$ is $\bigvee x_1 \ldots \bigvee x_m F$ and A_1 is a propositional identity of the form $F(t_1^1, \ldots, t_m^1) \vee \cdots \vee F(t_1^n, \ldots, t_m^n)$; Chapter 2, p. 23: A_1 is a deduction of A from the empty set $\emptyset$. Put $\bar{D}_0 = \bigvee y\, \overline{\mathrm{Dem}_0}$.

I. $\bar{V}^1 \subset \bar{D}_0$. This set theoretic result is proved in Chapter 2, often called: Completeness of the rules of deduction of Lemma 3 for $\bar{V}^1$.

From the facts in footnote 2 concerning the notion of validity implicit in mathematical practice, follow two properties of the intuitive notion of logical validity:

II. $\mathrm{Val}^i \subset \bar{V}^i$, and III. $\bar{D}_0 \subset \mathrm{Val}^1$.

THEOREM 5: $\mathrm{Val}^1 = \bar{D}_0 = \bar{V}^1$.
Immediate from I, II and III.

COROLLARY 5: $\bar{D}_0 \subset \bar{V}^1$ follows from II and III without use of I, i.e. without use of Lemma 3.

NB. $\bar{D}_0 \subset \bar{V}^1$ is thus a set theoretic assertion here derived by use of the primitive notion Val^1. This use is inessential because $\bar{D}_0 \subset \bar{V}^1$ can also be derived from purely set theoretic principles, in particular from $\mathscr{A}^*_=$: in other words, the condition $D^{\mathscr{A}^*_=}$ of Section 1 is satisfied at least with respect to this particular proof involving Val^1. However, the corollary may serve as an example of the possible use of intuitive logical notions for deriving (new) axioms for sets.

Historically, the first formal rules for logical validity of first order formulas (somewhat different from Dem_0) were formulated by Frege; the analogue to II was also evident. However (the analogue to) $\mathrm{Val}^1 \subset \bar{D}_0$ was only suspected, and not proved until 50 years later, by Gödel.

Concerning a possible extension of Theorem 5 to higher order formulae: we do not know at present a convincing proof of $\mathrm{Val}^2 = \bar{V}^2$, and, as discussed in the next paragraph, we have no positive results about generalizing $\bar{D}_0 = \bar{V}^1$ (the other half of Theorem 5). – To see that this state of affairs does not by itself cast doubt on the significance of Val^2, compare, e.g., our present evidence for $\mathrm{Val}^2 = \bar{V}^2$ with that for $\mathrm{Val}^1 = \bar{V}^1$ before Gödel's proof. First, in both cases, whenever in actual practice one recognizes that a formula belongs to $\bar{V}^1 \cup \bar{V}^2$, one also recognizes that it is intuitively valid; and conversely. Second, for many $A \in \mathscr{L}^2$ we do not know whether $A \notin \bar{V}^2$ or $A \in \bar{V}^2$; but no more can we effectively decide for an arbitrary $A \in \mathscr{L}$, even *after* the proof of Theorem 5, whether $A \in \bar{V}^1$ or $A \notin \bar{V}^1$ (or, equivalently, whether $A \in \mathrm{Val}^1$ or $A \notin \mathrm{Val}^1$).

(b) More facts about $\bar{V}^1$ and $\bar{V}^2$. Examples 1 and 7 of Chapter 7 show that the finiteness theorem does not hold for second order consequence, and not even for infinite first order formulas (though, by the summary to Chapter 6, a generalization is known for countably infinite formulas).

More detailed information can be stated by using the notion of validity in $\langle C_\alpha, \in_\alpha \rangle$: we write V^i_α for the set of formulas in $\mathscr{L}^i$ which are true in all realizations of $\mathscr{L}$ which belong to C_α. Evidently, $V^i_\alpha \supset V^i_\beta$ if $\alpha < \beta$.

(i) For $\alpha > \omega$, $\bar{V}^1 = V^1_\alpha$ (Chapter 2, Exercise 2). In contrast:

(i′) Except for $\mathscr{L}$ containing only monadic relation symbols, $V^1_\omega \neq V^1_{\omega+1}$. (The assertion: every total ordering has a first element, $\in V^1_\omega$, being true in all finite structures, but $\notin V^1_{\omega+1}$.)

(ii) For $\mathscr{L} = \mathscr{L}_E$, for instance: $V^2_{\omega+\omega+1} \neq V^2_{\omega+\omega}$, because $\mathscr{A}$ has a model in $\langle C_{\omega+\omega+1}, \in_{\omega+\omega+1} \rangle$, but not in $\langle C_{\omega+\omega}, \in_{\omega+\omega} \rangle$.

More generally, suppose $I \in \mathscr{L}^2_E$, e.g. an axiom of infinity, is such that $\mathscr{A} \cup \{I\}$ has a model in C_{α_I+1}, but not in C_{α_I}: then $V^2_{\alpha_I+1} \neq V^2_{\alpha_I}$. Clearly, there is a bound α_E for all such α_I, namely the least upper bound of: $\{\alpha_I : I \in \mathscr{L}^2_I;\ \alpha_I = 0 \text{ if } I \in \bar{V}^2, \text{ and, if } I \notin \bar{V}^2, \alpha_I \text{ is the least } \alpha : I \notin V^2_\alpha\}$. So α_E is the analogue to ω in (i): but little is known about the size of α_E.

(iii) Concerning a possible analogue, say D^2, to D_0 recall that *one* essential respect in which D_0 is simpler than V^1 is that all quantifiers in D_0 are restricted to range over $\langle C_\omega, \in_\omega \rangle$, which, by (i′), contrasts with V^1. So one may ask whether $\bar{V}^2$ has a definition D^2 in which all quantifiers are restricted to $\langle C_{\alpha_E}, \in_{\alpha_E} \rangle$; nothing is known about this. (It is likely that a smooth theory of second order formulas will include infinitely long expressions.)

As in Chapter 6, the phrase "restricted to $\langle C_\alpha, \in_\alpha \rangle$" means that each quantifier x occurs in the form $\bigvee x\, (T_\alpha x \wedge$ or $\bigwedge x\, (T_\alpha x \rightarrow$, where the formula $T_\alpha x$ is a definition of C_α in the realization s.c.t.; the *canonical* definitions T have the further property that T_α defines C_α in *each* realization $\langle C_\beta, \in_\beta \rangle$ of $\mathscr{L}_E$ with $\beta \geqq \alpha$ (cf. Chapter 5, Exercise 4).

Quite trivially one has the following:

negative result: *If* $\langle C_\alpha, \in_\alpha \rangle$ *is the only model up to isomorphism of the formula* $A_\alpha \in \mathscr{L}_E^2$ *then* $\bar{V}^2 \neq \bar{D}^2$ *for any* $D \in \mathscr{L}_E$ *with all quantifiers restricted to* $\langle C_\alpha, \in_\alpha \rangle$.

This is an immediate consequence of Lemma 2. Put differently: Lemma 2 shows that second order axiom systems are not saturated with respect to all assertions of the form $A \in V^2$ ($A \in \mathscr{L}^2$) while under the assumption on α above, there are second order axiom systems which are saturated with respect to all closed formulas whose quantifiers are restricted to C_α: in other words, all such formulas are *decided* (in the sense of second order consequence). Recall that, by Exercise 1(b) of Chapter 3, $\langle C_\alpha, \in_\alpha \rangle$ is the only model of a formula A_α of $\mathscr{L}_E$ itself only if α is finite; so the negative result above corresponds to the fact that $\bar{V}^1$ cannot be defined by a formula whose quantifiers are all restricted to some $\langle C_\alpha, \in_\alpha \rangle$ where α is finite. For reference below observe that $\mathscr{A}$ itself decides all formulas of $\mathscr{L}_E$ whose quantifiers are restricted to (canonical definitions of) $C_{\omega+n}$ for each integer n (and many other α). One such formula is the continuum hypothesis (C.H.) which involves only $C_{\omega+2}$; for C.H. asserts that any subset of $C_{\omega+1}$ is either in 1–1 correspondence with $C_{\omega+1}$ itself or with a subset of C_ω: since 1–1 correspondences between subsets of $C_{\omega+1}$ are elements of $C_{\omega+2}$, C.H. itself is expressed by means of a formula whose quantifiers are restricted to $C_{\omega+2}$ resp. elements of $C_{\omega+2}$.

In short: we *know* somewhat less about $\bar{V}^2$ than about $\bar{V}^1$; but nothing we have said suggests that $\bar{V}^2$ is less well defined than $\bar{V}^1$: in fact, the *same* set theoretic notions are used to define both.

(c) A PRIVILEGED POSITION FOR FINITE FIRST ORDER FORMULAS AND OF FIRST ORDER CONSEQUENCE? (reminiscent of the positivistic doctrine mentioned in the Introduction). Though the purest form of positivism in the theory of foundations is crude formalism, to be considered in Part B, Section 4, a somewhat related, quite common, but even less coherent position may be described as follows:

Roughly, it asserts that Theorem 4 (non saturation) does not establish an *inadequacy* of the axiomatic systems at all: the formulas of $\mathscr{L}_E$ which are not formal consequences of, say, $\mathscr{A}^*$ *should not* be provable! And, hence, the position is bound to reject attempts such as those discussed in Section 3, of discovering new axioms.

The general reason given is this: There is nothing to discover because the notion of set is *defined* by, say, $\mathscr{A}^*$ just as the notion of group is defined by the axioms of group theory. Thus, any structure $\mathfrak{S}$ which satisfies the axioms of set theory chosen is to be admitted as set theoretic; it is then a fact that the axioms are not categorical.

Clearly, if this is to be accepted, first order axiom systems must be tacitly understood since some second order axioms are categorical. So the position is bound to reject the appeal to second order consequence made in Section 3 and at the end of Section 4(b). In particular, it interprets second order decidability, e.g. of C.H.

$$[(\mathscr{A} \to \text{C.H.}) \in V^2] \vee [(\mathscr{A} \to \neg \text{C.H.}) \in V^2] \qquad (\dagger)$$

as follows: it is true that (†) is a theorem of set theory, in fact (†) is a formula of $\mathscr{L}_E$ and consequence of $\mathscr{A}^*$; but every set theoretic structure $\mathfrak{S}$ has its own relation of second order consequence, and (†) merely asserts that, in each $\mathfrak{S}$, *either* the first member of (†) *or* the second member of (†) is verified. The position would compare this to the logical triviality: $\bigwedge x \bigwedge y(x \odot y = y \odot x) \vee \neg \bigwedge x \bigwedge y(x \odot y = y \odot x)$, which holds in each group (with $\odot$ realized by the group operation); one does not conclude that all groups are commutative or all groups are non commutative.

A quite evident defect of the comparison is that the axioms of group theory are not intended to formulate properties of a particular (privileged) structure; and certainly nothing we know about the general concept of group precludes the existence of particular groups such as: integers under addition!

Two less immediate objections to the position go as follows:

1. The very notion of a model or realization of given axioms is defined by means of the basic set theoretic notions. Substituting the word "structure" or "mathematical object" for "set" only transfers the problem of Section 3 to the problem of discovering axioms that are valid for structures. No proposal for doing this has been made.
2. Evidently, if no basic notion of set is accepted, also the notion of second order consequence will be relative because it is defined in terms of the basic set theoretic notions. However, if the property V^2 is to be interpreted relative to *all* set theoretic structures (in the sense above) why not V^1 or D? And Section 2, Lemma 2, shows that D_1, which is an assertion about *first* order consequence, is also not invariant for all set theoretic structures.

Quite generally, the position invites the following objections. First, it is incoherent in accepting abstract structures but not privileged ones, particularly because, for axioms such as $\mathscr{A}^*$, if there is any evidence for supposing that *some* structure satisfies $\mathscr{A}^*$, this is provided, at least at present, by the particular structure $\langle C_{\omega+\omega}, \in_{\omega+\omega}\rangle$). Next, the restriction to first order formulas is evidently simply taken over from combinatorial foundations, cf. Part B, where the assumption of abstract structures is consistently avoided; but the connection is purely superficial as long as one uses the terminology of structures. Of course, $\bar{V}^1 = \bar{D}_0$ (Section 4, Theorem 5): but this is meaningful only if one accepts s.c.t. to which V^1 refers, and without this one has no reduction of V^1 to D_0, because V^1 has no meaning. (The fact that Theorem 5 assumes abstract infinite structures is specially clear from Section 4(b)(i′).) The position tries to get the best from both worlds, and speaks of structures rather than formal rules so as to keep close to mathematical practice (cf. note 2): but it falls between two stools.

The position just described is similar to positivism in two respects: (i) (superficially) in that both positions restrict themselves to first order formulas and the corresponding formal rules; this similarity is superficial because, as already mentioned, the restriction plays quite different roles for the two positions, (ii) more important, neither of these positions provides a positive contribution to foundations at all; but rather, as pointed out in the Introduction, they are merely a consolation for not solving basic foundational questions at all.]

PART B

COMBINATORIAL FOUNDATIONS

The reader will quickly find that the body of mathematical reasoning here considered (and described more precisely in Sections 0 and 2) is quite familiar to him because it is involved in all elementary mathematics. Only the explicit formulation of his knowledge may be new to him. This kind of reasoning, here called: combinatorial, is also called: finitist or syntactic, the difference in terminology reflecting different philosophical views on what is essential about this reasoning.

The present Part B is less thorough than Part A because combinatorial foundations require the use of proof theory, a branch of mathematical logic not treated in this book and therefore not presupposed. However, the reader is supposed to have at least glanced at a formal system such as that of BOURBAKI, Chapter I.

SUMMARY

The basic notions are: *word*, i.e., a finite sequence of symbols of a finite alphabet, *combinatorial function* (whose arguments and values are words), and *combinatorial proof* of identities (between differently defined combinatorial functions such as: $(a \cdot a) - (b \cdot b)$ and $(a + b) \cdot (a - b)$). These notions are supposed to be known here just as the basic set theoretic notions were assumed to be known in Part A (or, for that matter, in the main text). The numbering of sections in Parts A and B brings out the correspondence between set theoretic and combinatorial foundations.

Section 0 analyses the basic notions by means of informal distinctions; Section 0 (a, b) sketches the notions of combinatorial language and combinatorial realization [corresponding to the concepts of language and realization of Chapter 2 for set theoretic foundations], and Section 0 (c) the 'translation' of combinatorial mathematics into set theory.

Section 1 formulates 'adequacy conditions' for a reduction of intuitive mathematical reasoning to combinatorial principles, and relates these conditions to Hilbert's consistency problem (Section 1 (b)). In Section 1 (c) there are examples of substantial parts of mathematics for which Hilbert's problem has a positive solution.

Section 2 (c) describes a formal system $\mathscr{S}_C$ that is related to combinatorial mathematical practice somewhat as Zermelo's axioms in Part A, Section 2 (c) are related to set theoretic practice. Section 2 (d) gives Gödel's incompleteness theorem for $\mathscr{S}_C$, establishing a *combinatorially* valid assertion which is not formally derivable in $\mathscr{S}_C$. [Since there is no reason to suppose that each combinatorially formulated assertion is either combinatorially provable or combinatorially refutable, mere *nonsaturation* of $\mathscr{S}_C$ does not establish inadequacy of $\mathscr{S}_C$ with respect to combinatorial reasoning.]

At the end of Section 2 and in Section 3 the consequences of the incompleteness theorem for Hilbert's problem are analysed.

Section 4 (a, b) reviews the facts established in Part A, Sections 1–4, Part B, Sections 1–3, with respect to the two views of foundations which identify mathematics with (i) the theory of sets and (ii) combinatorial reasoning. In particular, the adequacy conditions of Part A, Section 1 and Part B, Section 1 are related to the possibility of separating mathematical questions from questions about the existence or objectivity of objects other than sets in case (i), and noncombinatorial (abstract) notions in case (ii). An (unavoidable) weakness of each view is that the analysis of the relevant adequacy conditions cannot be formulated in terms of the notions accepted by the view considered [cf. Theorem 5 of Part A]. Section 4 (c) criticises crude formalism, as promised in the Introduction.

Warning. The *proofs* treated here must be distinguished from formal derivations, i.e. from sequences of formulas obtained by mechanical application of formal rules: the distinction is analogous to that between understanding and copying a mathematical proof. In particular, given a (combinatorial) realization of a formal language, a formal derivation *defines* or *describes* a proof. This corresponds in the set-theoretic case to the definition of a set by a formula, namely the set of objects satisfying the formula [its realization in the sense of Chapter 2]. The concept of formula of the predicate calculus is chosen in such a way that the syntactic relations between the parts of a formula correspond to (set-theoretic) relations between their corresponding realizations. In the combinatorial theory, in addition formal rules are chosen in such a way that a combinatorial proof can be associated with every finite sequence of formulas constructed according to these rules; again syntactic relations between parts of such a sequence correspond to natural relations between the corresponding proofs.

Proponents of the formalist doctrine mentioned in the Introduction either refuse to accept the distinction between proof and formal derivation as legitimate (because they do not accept the idea of proof) or alternatively regard it as not precise enough for mathematics. In the Introduction we criticised some assumptions of this doctrine; we shall return briefly to the question in Section 4 after having described the principal consequences of this distinction.

0. Combinatorial reasoning

The objects with which this kind of reasoning is concerned, and whence it takes its name, are finite combinations of concrete objects such as letters of an alphabet, numerals, symbols of a formal language etc.. A combinatorial function of n variables is a mechanical rule *together with* a combinatorial proof of functionality, i.e. a proof establishing that if the rule is applied to any n objects (chosen among the combinations of objects under consideration) it will determine a value after a finite number of steps; to be more precise, the rule is applied to a description (of an object) which, in general, is distinct from the object itself. Finally, for a proof to be combinatorial it must only involve (a finite number of) combinatorial functions and the sequence of the basic objects, i.e. the successive generation of all the finite configurations considered.

The reader will find a detailed analysis of mechanical rules in the theory of recursive functions and a partial analysis of combinatorial proof below. A general idea of these concepts can be obtained by considering a typical example: the combinatorial function of *addition* in *numerical arithmetic.*

(i) *The objects and their description.* The alphabet of numerical arithmetic consists of two symbols: the individual constant 1, and the function symbol S (of one variable). Consequently, the terms (words) are 1, $S1$, $SS1$, ..., also denoted by $S^0 1$, $S^1 1$, $S^2 1$, ..., respectively.

What is typical here, is that it is possible to decide quite mechanically whether or not two terms designate the same object. This decision only involves a finite number of observations of the identity, or non-identity, of the given concrete objects (cf. the act of recognizing a letter of the alphabet). What is not typical is the fact that every object considered here *is* a term, whereas, in the general case, every object has a particular term associated with it, called its canonical description: the structure of this term reflects how the object is (conceived to have been) constructed. It should be noted that the descriptions allowed in combinatorial reasoning are such that the corresponding canonical description can be recovered from any other description by a purely mechanical process: this reduces, *a posteriori*, the importance of canonical descriptions of objects (in contrast to the case of functions: see (a) below).

N.B. It follows from the last remark that as long as only *objects* are considered, the combinatorial theory approximates set-theoretic analysis. The latter, being a *realist* theory rejects, as a matter of *principle,* reference to descriptions of the objects treated (sets with type structure) – a principle which leads to the axiom of extensionality of Part A, Section 2. On the other hand this principle is not satisfied in constructive mathematics in the wide sense of the term (Section 3 below) in which functions and even constructive proofs are admissible as objects.

In (combinatorial) mathematical *practice* the act of recognizing that two expressions are identical is accepted as part of the data without further analysis. Such an analysis is needed here since the importance of combinatorial reasoning for *foundations* depends precisely on the particular (elementary) nature of these acts, which are on a par with the simplest sense perceptions, the objects being conceived as finite spatio-temporal configurations. Thus the only abstract objects which have a place in this theory are proofs, but they are not in turn the subject of combinatorial reasoning. (Proofs, considered as mental acts, are clearly not finite configurations of concrete objects: in particular, it will be seen that they involve the idea of an *infinite* sequence, namely the infinite sequence of all finite combinations.)

The central role of the act of recognizing that two expressions are identical is reflected formally by the restriction to languages whose only relation symbol is $=$.

(ii) *Mechanical rules and their description.* The two place function symbol $+$ is added to the alphabet of (i) (we shall write $t+t'$ instead of $+t, t'$). Starting from the formulas

$$a+1=Sa \quad \text{and} \quad a+Sb=S(a+b) \tag{*}$$

terms are substituted for the letters a and b and the substitution rule for equality is applied, viz: if the equations $t_1=t_2$ and $t'=t''$ have been derived, then in $t'=t''$ one or more occurrences of the form t_1 may be replaced by t_2.

N.B. The formulas (*) define or describe the rule for addition provided one understands the syntactic operation of substitution and, in particular, knows when two expressions are equal. In terms of computers the formulas (*) correspond to the instruction tape and the kind of understanding required corresponds to the mechanism of the computer designed to react to these instructions.

Analysis is full of non-mechanical rules (or, rather, definitions) for mathematical functions (this is one of the essential differences between school and university mathematics). For example, if $r_1, r_2, \ldots,$ is a sequence, ρ, of rationals lying between 0 and 1, then a sequence $A_0, A_1, \ldots,$ of intervals converging to the lower bound of ρ is defined by the following "rule": $A_0=[0, 1]$; A_{n+1} is the left half of A_n if A_n contains an element of ρ, and, if not, then it is the right half. In general we do not know which of these alternatives hold. In the theory of recursive functions it is shown that many of the usual definitions of functions used in analysis are not equivalent to any function defined by a mechanical rule and so certainly not to one defined by a combinatorial rule. (Thus such conclusions do not require any analysis of the concept of combinatorial proof, the definitions referred to being grossly non-constructive: in contrast to the principal problems of Section 3 below.)

(iii) *Combinatorial functions.* In order to show that the mechanical rule (ii) is functional, i.e., can be regarded as a combinatorial function, we have to give a combinatorial proof that for any integers n and m the rule permits one to derive a formula of the form $S^n1+S^m1=S^p1$. The proof proceeds by induction, which, in combinatorial mathematics, comes to this: we visualize the construction of the sequence $S^0 1, S^1 1, S^2 1, \ldots$ and associate with each step in this construction a suitable application of the rules (*). To be combinatorially convincing this sequence of applications must in turn be visualizable. In detail (for given n): If $m=0$, we deduce $S^n1+S^m1=S^{n+1}1$ by replacing a by S^n1 in the first formula of (*); if $m\neq 0$, we replace b by $S^{m-1}1$ in the second formula of (*) which gives $S^n1+S^m1=S(S^n1+S^{m-1}1)$. It remains to be shown that the (particular) rules for equality of (ii) suffice to determine the value; we go back to the sequence $S^0 1, S^1 1$, ...; suppose given a derivation of a formula of the form $S^n1+S^{m-1}1=S^q1$ we extend it to a derivation of $S^n1+S^m1=S^{q+1}1$ by taking $S^n1+S^{m-1}1$ for t_1, S^q for t_2, S^n1+S^m1 for t' and $S(S^n1+S^{m-1}1)$ for t''. To summarize, (the rule defined by) the term $a+b$ is a function on the alphabet of (i) because for any integers n and m, a formula of the type $S^n1+S^m1=S^p1$ is derivable. One shows similarly that, for given n and m, p is unique.

More generally, for any term t of the alphabet consisting of the variables $a, b, \ldots, c$, the constant 1 and the function symbols S and $+$, the mechanical rule which corresponds to t in the sense explained in (ii) defines a function on the words $S^0 1, S^1 1, \ldots$.

N.B. The kind of understanding required for applying a mechanical rule is clearly not sufficient for following the reasoning above; the distinction is reflected by the syntactic distinction between formulas without and with variables.

The explanations given under (i) along with the reader's previous knowledge and intuitive understanding, should suffice to make the combinatorial character of the rule for addition obvious. However it is not so easy to give an explicit formulation of what is *essentially* involved in recognizing this fact: in other words, to formulate in full generality, the possibilities of the combinatorial imagination which are implicitly presupposed in the proof that the addition rule defines a function. (These possibilities determine the combinatorially valid principles of proof. A formulation would provide, inter alia, an enumeration (naturally, not combinatorial) of all combinatorial functions: see Section 3).

(iv) *Proofs of identities and their relation to formal derivations.* Let $\mathscr{R}^+$ be the system of rules obtained by adding the variables $a, b, \ldots, c$ to the alphabet of (ii) and applying the rules of (ii) to all equations of the extended alphabet. Let $t_{(n, m, \ldots, p)}$ be the term obtained by replacing $a, b, \ldots, c$ by $S^n 1, S^m 1, \ldots, S^p 1$ respectively in t, and finally let $\bar{t}$ be the combinatorial function defined by the term t in the sense of (iii).

A combinatorial proof of (the identity) $\bar{t} = \bar{t}'$ shows, by definition, that for any integers $n, m, \ldots, p$, the formula $t_{(n, m, \ldots, p)} = t'_{(n, m, \ldots, p)}$ can be derived by means of the rules of (ii).

(α) It should be noted that a proof of $\bar{t} = \bar{t}'$ can be obtained from a formal derivation (by means of the rules of $\mathscr{R}^+$) of the formula $t = t'$ since $\mathscr{R}^+$ is closed with respect to substitution of terms $S^0 1, S^1 1, \ldots$ for the variables.

(β) On the other hand, although, for example $\overline{1+a} = \overline{Sa}$ is clearly an identity, as can be seen by induction on a, the formula $1+a = Sa$ is not derivable (in $\mathscr{R}^+$) since any derivable formula must be true in the (set-theoretic) model defined as follows: the variables range over the ordinals and the realizations of 1, S and $+$ are the ordinal 1, successor and the usual addition for ordinals. But $1 + \omega \neq \omega + 1$.

(It is quite easy to avoid the use of the abstract concept of ordinal and thus give a combinatorial proof that $1 + a = Sa$ is not derivable: let the variables range over ordered pairs of integers, $\langle p, q \rangle$, where $p \geqslant 0$, $q \geqslant 0$ and $p + q > 0$; put $\bar{1} = \langle 0, 1 \rangle$, $\bar{S}(\langle n, m \rangle) = \langle n, m+1 \rangle$, $\langle n, m \rangle \mp \langle 0, q \rangle = \langle n, m+q \rangle$ and $\langle n, m \rangle \mp \langle p+1, q \rangle = \langle n+p+1, q \rangle$; then $\langle 0, 1 \rangle \mp \langle 1, 0 \rangle \neq \langle 1, 0 \rangle \mp \langle 0, 1 \rangle$.)

N.B. (α) and (β) establish respectively the (combinatorial) validity and incompleteness of the system $\mathscr{R}^+$ with respect to the combinatorial theory of addition. Briefly the development is as follows: starting with mechanical rules for addition (in this case in the form of the formal system of (ii)), we verify that they define a function by means of the argument of (iii); then we construct a formal system containing variables (in this case $\mathscr{R}^+$) and ask whether or not the assertion $\bar{t} = \bar{t}'$ is equivalent to the derivability of the formula $t = t'$ in the system. (Since the very meaning of this question involves the basic combinatorial concepts, a reader who has followed (α) and (β) without difficulty may assume that he has at least a partial understanding of these concepts!)

The reader will note the use of "psychological" terminology which is not in the least surprising since this combinatorial theory is intended to be "idealist".

Finally it should be noted that the combinatorial (though not mechanical) statement

The formula $1+a=Sa$ *is not derivable in* $\mathscr{R}^+$

is similar in character to the identity $\overline{1+a}=\overline{Sa}$ itself; namely, for any sequence of formulas in the language of $\mathscr{R}^+$, it can be ascertained mechanically whether it is constructed in accordance with the rules of $\mathscr{R}^+$ (just as, in connection with the identity $\overline{1+a}=\overline{Sa}$, for any integer n, the values of $1+S^n1$ and of SS^n1 can be mechanically computed) and also whether $1+a=Sa$ is the last formula of the given sequence. The argument of (β) shows that the answer to one or the other of these questions must be negative.

This elementary character of statements of non-derivability is essential to all that follows.

(a) COMBINATORIAL LANGUAGES AND REALIZATIONS. We adopt the languages of the predicate calculus with equality sketched in App. I [see also Chapter 3], modified as follows: no quantifiers are used (and therefore all the variables in the formulas considered are free); each language is supposed to be given by means of combinatorial functions which enumerate, possibly with repetitions, the various kinds of symbols (i.e. we do not allow the sets of symbols to be *arbitrary* disjoint sets). Frequently we shall restrict the languages to ones with a finite number of individual constants and function and relation symbols and an (infinite) sequence of variables enumerated by a specific function.

N.B. These enumerating functions, each of them of course given by a specific definition, constitute part of the definition of the language; consequently two languages with different (descriptions of) enumerating functions will be considered distinct even if the sets of symbols so defined are identical; in particular, we shall distinguish a *finite* enumeration (presented in the form of a finite sequence, i.e., as a combinatorial object) from an *infinite* enumeration of the same set in the absence of a combinatorial proof of their equivalence. These distinctions are needed because, contrary to the case of objects considered in (i) on p. 197, it is not always possible to decide by a purely combinatorial argument whether two functions enumerate the same set, i.e., whether the sets of their values are identical. At this point the combinatorial theory diverges sharply from set theory.

Let $\mathscr{L}$ be a (combinatorial) language. A combinatorial realization $\mathfrak{R}$ of $\mathscr{L}$ consists, by definition of:

(i) a non-empty enumeration U (finite or infinite) of combinatorial objects, called the *universe* of $\mathfrak{R}$, or, alternatively, the *domain* of the variables,

(ii) an element (among those enumerated by U) corresponding to each individual constant,

(iii) an n-place combinatorial function (taking arguments and values among the elements enumerated by U) for each n-place function symbol,

(iv) an n-place characteristic function (taking only two distinct values, $\top$ and $\bot$) for each n-place relation symbol.

N.B. (iv) shows that we could without loss of generality restrict the languages to those having $=$ as their only relation symbol. If $\mathscr{L}$ contains an infinite sequence of function symbols, say of 2 variables, enumerated by the function φ defined over a domain U_0, the definition of realization must be altered as follows: $\mathfrak{R}$ contains a combinatorial function Φ of 3 variables (the first ranging over U_0, the other two over U) such that for every element u_0 of U_0, the function $\Phi u_0 xy$ of the two variables x and y, is by definition, the realization of the symbol φu_0.

(b) COMBINATORIAL REALIZATION OF A FORMULA: COMBINATORIAL VALIDITY. Let $\mathscr{L}$ be a (combinatorial) language, $\mathfrak{R}$ a realization of $\mathscr{L}$ and A a formula of $\mathscr{L}$. A combinatorial proof π will be called a realization of the formula A in $\mathfrak{R}$ if, for two distinct objects, say $\top$ and $\bot$, either

(1) A is [closed i.e.,] a formula without variables, $\bar{A}$ is the truth value of A [i.e., the value of $\bar{A}$ given by the valuation of the propositional calculus in Chapter 1], when we put $\overline{s=t}=\top$ if s and t denote the same element (among those enumerated by U) and otherwise $\overline{s=t}=\bot$; and finally π is a (mechanical) verification that $\bar{A}=\top$ [it should be noted that the valuation rules of Chapter 1 are clearly mechanical]; or

(2) the free variables (i.e. all the variables) in A are among $x_1, \ldots, x_n$ and π is a combinatorial proof of the identity: For any elements $\bar{x}_1, \ldots, \bar{x}_n$ (among those enumerated by U) the calculation of $\bar{A}$ according to (1) gives the value $\top$. (Thus in general, i.e., if U is not a finite enumeration, π is no longer a mechanical calculation.)

It follows immediately that for any $\mathfrak{R}$, one can find a proof (realization) of A if the formula $E \to A$ is valid set-theoretically where E is the conjunction of the axioms of equality for all the terms occurring in A. Conversely, if $E \to A$ is not valid, a realization $\mathfrak{R}$ of the language of A and elements $\bar{x}_1, \ldots, \bar{x}_n$ in the universe of $\mathfrak{R}$ can be found such that $\bar{A}=\bot$. (Clearly we do not assume here that every element enumerated by U has a name in $\mathscr{L}$, i.e., corresponds to a term of $\mathscr{L}$.)

Discussion. Languages with quantifiers are not considered here simply because the familiar logical laws are not valid combinatorially for the obvious extension of the notion of realization to quantified formulas. For example consider a quantifier free formula A whose (free) variables are $x_1, \ldots, x_n$, x and y; and the 'natural' definition:

The pair $(\pi, \bar{f})$ (f a function symbol with $n+1$ arguments, not occurring in A) realizes $\bigwedge x \bigvee y A$ if π is a combinatorial proof of

$$A(x_1, \ldots, x_n, x, f(x_1, \ldots, x_n, x));$$

the pair $(\pi, \bar{g})$ (g a function symbol with n arguments, not occurring in A) realizes $\bigvee x \bigwedge y \neg A$ if π is a combinatorial proof of

$$\neg A(x_1, \ldots, x_n, g(x_1, \ldots, x_n), y);$$

the triple $(\pi, \bar{f}, \bar{g})$ realizes $\bigwedge x \bigvee y A \vee \bigvee x \bigwedge y \neg A$ if π is a combinatorial proof of

$$A(x_1, \ldots, x_n, x, f(x_1, \ldots, x_n, x)) \vee \neg A(x_1, \ldots, x_n, g(x_1, \ldots, x_n), y).$$

Clearly there is no reason to suppose that $\bigwedge x \bigvee y A \vee \bigvee x \bigwedge y \neg A$ (which is valid for all set theoretic realizations) is also valid in the combinatorial sense just defined.

In fact, it is intuitively plausible for certain A that there are no *mechanically* defined functions $\bar{f}$ and $\bar{g}$ such that, for all $\bar{x}_1, \ldots, \bar{x}_n$ and for each $\bar{x}$ and $\bar{y}$ in the universe considered, $A(x_1, \ldots, x_n, x, f(x_1, \ldots, x_n, x)) \vee \neg A(x_1, \ldots, x_n, g(x_1, \ldots, x_n), y)$ be true, let alone combinatorially provable. (This statement will be made precise in the next paragraph.)

(c) SET THEORETIC TRANSLATIONS OF COMBINATORIAL IDENTITIES, NON-COMBINATORIAL PROOFS OF THE TRANSLATIONS. Evidently, in the present section one assumes *both* the set theoretic *and* the combinatorial notions to be known: Combinatorial foundations are independent of this section; but the notions here presented are needed to formulate *adequacy conditions* in the next section.

To any combinatorial language $\mathscr{L}$ and combinatorial realization $\mathfrak{R}$ one associates in an obvious way a language $\mathscr{L}^*$ and a realization $\mathfrak{R}^*$ in the set theoretic sense, cf. Part A, Section 1.

The combinatorial objects of $\mathscr{L}$ and $\mathfrak{R}$ (symbols, alphabet, words in the universe of $\mathfrak{R}$) are regarded as sets; in particular, a word is the set which is the finite sequence of the sets which are the letters of the word considered; $\mathscr{L}$ and $\mathfrak{R}$ being given by (enumerating) combinatorial functions, one associates with each enumeration the set enumerated, and with each combinatorial function its graph. Thus one abstracts from the particular definitions which are used to give us these sets. So,

$\mathscr{L}^*$ is the collection of sets corresponding to the different kinds of symbols of $\mathscr{L}$, $\mathfrak{R}^*$ has as its universe the set of words belonging to the domain of $\mathfrak{R}$, and as realization of a function symbol f or relation symbol R the set corresponding to $\bar{f}_{\mathfrak{R}}$, resp. $\bar{R}_{\mathfrak{R}}$.

The essential role of the particular definitions and enumerations for the combinatorial notions of language and realization can be seen as follows:

(α) there are (set theoretic) languages and realizations $\mathscr{L}'$, $\mathfrak{R}'$ which do not correspond to *any* combinatorial pair ($\mathscr{L}$, $\mathfrak{R}$) according to the correspondence: $(\mathscr{L}, \mathfrak{R}) \Rightarrow (\mathscr{L}^*, \mathfrak{R}^*)$,

(β) there are combinatorial realizations which are set theoretically equivalent (i.e., to which the same set theoretic realization is associated) but not combinatorially (i.e., the isomorphism above can either not be combinatorially defined, or, if defined, not combinatorially proved). The reader should compare this point with the need for a canonical choice of definitions for objects in s.c.t., cf. Part A, Lemma 3.

(α) is an immediate corollary to the following result of the theory of recursive functions: there are sets which are not enumerable by means of mechanically definable functions and *a fortiori*, not by means of combinatorial functions.

(β) follows from a more delicate analysis of combinatorial proofs which shows the existence of two combinatorial functions which have the same graph, but are such that this fact cannot be proved combinatorially.

The *translation* of an identity A for a given combinatorial realization (whose variables are among $x_1, \ldots, x_n$) is, by definition, the assertion: $\wedge x_1 \ldots \wedge x_n A$ is true in the associated set theoretic realization.

It is clear that if $\wedge x_1 \ldots \wedge x_n A$ is not true in the associated set theoretic realization, there is no combinatorial realization i.e., proof, of A.

The general nature of non-combinatorial proofs of (translations of) identities for combinatorial realizations can be formulated as follows: for a given pair $\mathscr{L}$, $\mathfrak{R}$.

First (elementary case): one considers realizations in $\mathfrak{R}^*$ of quantified formulas (to which no combinatorial meaning has been assigned); using the principles which are valid for the *set theoretic* meaning of the extended language, one obtains $\wedge x_1 \ldots \wedge x_n A$. This kind of proof is familiar from the parts of arithmetic or the theory of sequences of rationals which are commonly called "non-constructive"; cf. p. 198.

Second: one embeds $\mathfrak{R}^*$ in a realization which is not associated with any combinatorial realization at all, and appeals in the proof to properties of the extended realization. This is familiar (cf. Part A, Section 3(a)) from analytic number theory where the structure of the natural numbers, a subset of C_ω (cf. Part A), is embedded in the complex plane ($\subset C_{\omega+1}$) or even in the space of functions ($\subset C_{\omega+2}$) on the complex plane. A very simple example of this second process was used on p. 200 where one appealed to the *ordinals* in a non-derivability result about the formal system (i) there described, the non-derivability result being an identity of the kind under discussion.

In this last case, so to speak simply by looking at the proof, one could eliminate the use of these essentially non-combinatorial realizations: instead of the collection of all the ordinals it was obviously sufficient to consider ω^2, and instead of this abstract ordinal, one considered a simple ordering of ordinal ω^2 for which all that was needed of ω^2 could be proved. Similarly, inspection of the existing proofs in analytic number theory shows that, at the cost of some additional explicit detail, one can confine oneself to the rational complex plane, use only approximations to the functions studied, and thus bypass completely the introduction of the non-combinatorial realizations $\langle C_{\omega+1}, \in_{\omega+1}\rangle$ or $\langle C_{\omega+2}, \in_{\omega+2}\rangle$.

It is by no means obvious that the following use of abstract realizations is eliminable. (*Consistency proofs.*) Consider the axioms $\mathscr{A}^*$ of Zermelo's set theory, some formula A and the combinatorial identity: "the formula $A \wedge \neg A$ is not formally derivable from $\mathscr{A}^*$ by means of the formal rules of Part A, Lemma 3". We consider $\langle C_{\omega+\omega}, \in_{\omega+\omega}\rangle$, note that $\mathscr{A}^*$ holds there, that the formal rules preserve truth (in any structure), $A \wedge \neg A$ is not true in $\langle C_{\omega+\omega}, \in_{\omega+\omega}\rangle$, and so it cannot be formally derivable.

Discussion. This argument, though simple, is obviously not empty because it depends on verifying that $\mathscr{A}^*$ satisfies $\langle C_{\omega+\omega}, \in_{\omega+\omega}\rangle$. If one had used the unrestricted comprehension axiom (**) of Part A, Section 1(a), instead of $\mathscr{A}^*$ the conclusion would have been false. (As pointed out in Part A, Section 1(b), this unrestricted comprehension is *evidently* false for $\langle C_{\omega+\omega}, \in_{\omega+\omega}\rangle$.)

The fact that embedding a structure $\mathfrak{S}$ in a richer one often leads to simple proofs about $\mathfrak{S}$ is quite familiar from modern mathematics. Here one uses $\langle C_{\omega+\omega}, \in_{\omega+\omega}\rangle$ to derive a result about $\langle C_\omega, \in_\omega\rangle$, the assertion of formal non-derivability having been translated into an assertion about $\langle C_\omega, \in_\omega\rangle$ by means of the development of arithmetic in $\langle C_\omega, \in_\omega\rangle$ (Part A).

Just because the proof above is so simple, using nothing about the formal rules except that they preserve truth, it is quite implausible that it can be *easily* modified to yield a combinatorial proof of non-derivability, in contrast to the non-derivability result for the formal system on p. 200 or known analytic number theory.

With the informal background provided in the present section, the brief exposition below of the problems of combinatorial foundations should be quite intelligible.

1. How does one analyse intuitive mathematics in terms of the basic combinatorial notions?

Since much of intuitive mathematics presents itself as being about abstract objects (such as $\langle C_\alpha, \in_\alpha\rangle$ for $\alpha \geqslant \omega$) which are not combinatorial at all, the analysis cannot study these objects themselves; a coherent alternative (cf. introduction on "idealist" foundations) is to study reasoning *about* these objects. A precise formulation of such an alternative is *Hilbert's programme*, which states adequacy conditions.

(a) REPRESENTATION (DESCRIPTION) OF MATHEMATICAL REASONING BY MEANS OF FORMAL SYSTEMS. As was pointed out at the beginning of the Introduction, the step from intuitive reasoning to its formulation in a formal language does not proceed by means of mechanical rules because the representation approximates not the external form (the words) of the intuitive reasoning, but its sense or meaning. But granted this step (as being part of the data) the problem remains to establish *combinatorially the basic relations of intuitive reasoning* (such as the consequence relation) i.e., to define combinatorially the corresponding relations for the representation, and to prove, again combinatorially, their properties.

Just what has to be established will be formulated in *adequacy conditions* in (b) and (d) below. Essentially, (b) corresponds to $E^{\mathscr{A}\mathfrak{S}}$ in Part A, Section 1 and (d) to $U^{\mathscr{A}\mathfrak{S}}$. As is to be expected, Theorems 4 and [5, or its particular case] Lemma 3, p. 184 of Part A (or, more precisely, suitable generalizations) will be decisive. The results will be summarized and examined in Section 4(a, b).

Discussion. For the sake of the discussion in Section 4, the reader should compare here the role of (i) [Theorem 5 or] Lemma 3 for combinatorial foundations with (ii) corresponding results in set theoretic foundations. (i) If one *accepts* the basic set theoretic notions in terms of which the notion of consequence can be defined, Theorem 5 provides a *mathematical proof* that a certain combinatorial definition of the consequence relation [for formulas of *first* order] is correct. If one stays *within* the combinatorial framework one only has the "empirical" fact: it so happens that any formula of first order which we recognize as logically valid can also be generated by means of certain formal rules (Lemma 3 of Part A). (Similarly, accepting set theoretic notions one shows by use of the theory of recursive functions, that the relation of *second* order consequence is not definable by means of any mechanical rule. Within the combinatorial framework we could only say that we do not *know* a definition, and for any particular proposal we could exhibit a counterexample, but without, of course, having a *combinatorial* formulation, let alone proof of this general fact.) (ii) A corresponding result for set theoretic foundations, say for the intuitive structure **N** of arithmetic, would be a *proof* that **N** satisfies Peano's axioms $\mathscr{A}_{\mathrm{N}}$. *Within* set theoretic foundations, $\mathscr{A}_{\mathrm{N}}$ is simply accepted; one cannot express the reasoning which shows that **N** satisfies $\mathscr{A}_{\mathrm{N}}$ and one must be content to use suitable informal terminology.

(b) Reduction of intuitive principles to combinatorial principles (Hilbert's consistency problem). A *minimal requirement* can be stated in terms of the translations described in Section 0(d) above:

Consider a combinatorial language $\mathscr{L}$ and a combinatorial realization $\mathfrak{R}$. For any formula A of $\mathscr{L}$ let A_{T} be the canonical translation in $\mathscr{L}_E$ of the (combinatorial) assertion expressing that A holds in $\mathfrak{R}$, i.e., that A is realized in the realization $\mathfrak{R}$ of $\mathscr{L}$.

We wish to know, at least for closed formulas A in $\mathscr{L}$:

(i) If A holds (in $\mathfrak{R}$ combinatorially) can we formally derive A_{T} from $\mathscr{A}^*$ (or even in $\mathscr{A}^*_-$)?

(ii) Given any formal derivation of A_{T}, does A hold in $\mathfrak{R}$?

These questions are so formulated that it makes at least sense to look for purely combinatorial solutions.

Precisely, suppose the formula Dem(s, A_{T}) of $\mathscr{L}$ defines in $\mathfrak{R}$ the relation: the sequence of formulae s in $\mathscr{L}_E$ is a formal derivation of A_{T} from $\mathscr{A}^*$. There is such a formula, e.g. if $\mathfrak{R}=\mathfrak{R}_{\mathrm{C}}$ and $\mathscr{L}=\mathscr{L}_{\mathrm{C}}$, p. 212.

Question (i) is answered by means of a combinatorial function f whose arguments are formulas of $\mathscr{L}$ and values are sequences of formulas of $\mathscr{L}_E$ together with a combinatorial proof of $A \to \text{Dem}(fA,\ A_T)$. Establishing this is nothing else but showing effectively that combinatorial mathematics can be developed in set theory; [this was already used in Lemma 4 of Part A].

Question (ii) simply takes the form, for variable s: do we have a combinatorial proof of: $\text{Dem}(s,\ A_T) \to A$? Note that, for a combinatorial formulation of these questions, one uses essentially the combinatorial character of the relation $\overline{\text{Dem}}$.

A positive solution of question (ii) constitutes a genuine *elimination of the assumptions of set theory*. For, the intuitive basis for the assertion $\text{Dem}(s,\ A_T) \to A$ is simply that of the 'consistency proof' at the end of Section 0(d). One considers the meaning of the formulas appearing in s, i.e. their realizations in s.c.t., concludes the truth of each, hence of A_T, and hence that A holds in $\mathfrak{R}$, at least for closed formulas A. This argument clearly collapses if one does not accept the existential assumptions expressed by $\mathscr{A}^*$. After all, if one does not accept them there is no difference between $\mathscr{A}^*$ and, say, the inconsistent axiom (**) in Part A, Section 2(a), at least before its inconsistency was discovered; and one would be ill advised to conclude that A holds in $\mathfrak{R}$, on being given a formal derivation of A_T from (**)! On the other hand, a combinatorial proof of $\text{Dem}(s,\ A_T) \to A$ (for variable A ranging over all closed formulas of $\mathscr{L}$), does not refer to the meanings of the formulas in s because these meanings (realizations) are not combinatorial at all, but only to their formal (syntactic) properties.

Discussion. The paragraph above shows the necessity of a positive solution of question (ii) if one is to speak of a combinatorial reduction at all: without it, not even the purely combinatorial uses which we make of set theoretic assumptions would be combinatorially justified. But a positive solution is also as much as we can require without further analysis because the formulas A_T are the only formulas in $\mathscr{L}_E$ to which we have associated a meaning in terms of combinatorial notions. (An extension *is* possible provided one extends the notion of combinatorial realization to richer languages in a less naive manner than end of Section 0 (b).)

Even without further analysis (for details see Section 3 below) Theorem 4 of Part A makes a positive solution of question (ii) for the axiomatic system $\mathscr{A}^*$ implausible. However, question (ii) *makes sense* (not only for $\mathscr{A}^*$ but) *for any formal system which represents reasoning about abstract objects* (even for the 'elementary' kind of nonconstructive proof on p. 204

provided only some translation of combinatorial statements into the formal language considered, has been given, analogously to the translation A into A_T above). So Hilbert's programme is not refuted by *general* (positivistic) considerations provided there is *some prima facie* nonconstructive formal system for which question (ii) can be positively solved. This is done in (c) below. This affects the anti-philosophic doctrine mentioned at the end of the introduction, cf. also Section 4(c) below.

Remark on Hilbert's consistency problem. Consistency (of $\mathscr{A}^*$) asserts that, for any formula B of $\mathscr{L}_E$, and variables x, y for sequences of such formulas we have (a combinatorial proof of)

$$\text{Dem}(x, B) \to \neg\, \text{Dem}(y, \neg B) \qquad (\dagger)$$

(where the formula Dem of the combinatorial language $\mathscr{L}$ defines the proof relation for $\mathscr{A}^*$ in $\mathfrak{N}$; cf. Part A, Lemma 3); or, if $\perp$ is the translation of some false combinatorial formula, e.g. of $0=1$, we have

$$\neg\, \text{Dem}(x, \perp), \qquad (\dagger\dagger)$$

where, for the translation of arithmetic in $\mathscr{L}_E$ of Part A, $(0=1)_T$ is $\bigvee y_1 \bigvee y_2[\bigwedge u \neg(u \in y_1) \wedge \bigwedge u(u \in y_2 \leftrightarrow u = y_1) \wedge y_1 = y_2]$.

(($\dagger$), ($\dagger\dagger$) are evidently equivalent by use of the fact that any formula is formally derivable from a false formula.)

Granted (i), *question* (ii) *is combinatorially equivalent to the consistency problem.*

First, consistency is a special case of (ii) by taking $0=1$ for A.

Conversely, by (i), we have $\neg A \to \text{Dem}[f(\neg A), \neg A_T]$; therefore $\neg \text{Dem}[f(\neg A), \neg A_T] \to \neg\neg A$ and so $\neg \text{Dem}[f(\neg A), \neg A_T] \to A$. Joining this to a special case of ($\dagger$) (with A_T for B and $f(\neg A)$ for the variable y) we have $\text{Dem}(x, A_T) \to A$.

The advantage of the consistency statement ($\dagger\dagger$) over question (ii) is merely that one variable in (ii) (over closed formulas A of $\mathscr{L}$) is replaced by a constant $\perp$. But the significance of the consistency problem for combinatorial foundations depends on its consequences, namely the necessary and sufficient conditions mentioned in the discussion, which are obvious for (ii) but not directly for ($\dagger\dagger$).

(c) Positive results on Hilbert's problem. (Naturally, since these results are formulated precisely and established in proof theory, we can only indicate them here.)

Let $\mathscr{L}$ be a (combinatorial) language in the sense of Section 0(b), and

$\mathfrak{R}$ a combinatorial realization of $\mathscr{L}$, and suppose given a combinatorial realization of the formula A of $\mathscr{L}$ whose variables (necessarily free) are among $x_1, \ldots, x_n$; i.e. we have a combinatorial proof of A for the given realization of $\mathscr{L}$.

WEAK RESULT ('weak' for combinatorial foundations because it is formulated by use of *both* set theoretic *and* combinatorial notions):

If all the variables of the formula B of $\mathscr{L}$ are among $y_1, \ldots, y_m$ and if $\bigwedge y_1 \ldots \bigwedge y_m B$ is a consequence of $\bigwedge x_1 \ldots \bigwedge x_n A$ in the set theoretic sense then there is also a combinatorial proof of B for the given realization of $\mathscr{L}$.

To show this we use not merely the existence of *some* formalization of logical consequence, but the following *particular* property of the formal rules indicated in Part A, p. 184 [more precisely, in Lemma 3, based on the Uniformity Theorem of Chapter 2]. If $\bigwedge y_1 \ldots \bigwedge y_m B$ is derived by *these* rules from $\bigwedge x_1 \ldots \bigwedge x_n A$ then B is derived by purely propositional inferences from some conjunction $A_1 \wedge \cdots \wedge A_k$ where A_i is obtained from A by replacing each x by a suitable term. By (b) above such a derivation *defines* a combinatorial proof of $(A_1 \wedge \cdots \wedge A_k) \rightarrow B$ and, together with the given realization of A, also a realization of B.

The particular property of these rules is not satisfied by the usual formalizations, e.g. in Bourbaki, where modus ponens (from X and $X \rightarrow Y$ derive Y) is included among the formal rules, when a derivation of B from $\bigwedge x_1 \ldots \bigwedge x_n A$ may contain formulas with alternating quantifiers; as seen in (b), if the notion of combinatorial realization is extended in the 'obvious' way, some of the formal rules (such as $A \vee \neg A$) are then not combinatorially valid.

COMBINATORIAL VERSION. The general scheme of formulating a combinatorial problem should by now be obvious. The intuitive notion of logical consequence is itself not admitted, but one puts down all formal rules which are evidently valid from one's understanding of this notion. In particular, modus ponens above is certainly included. Let $\mathrm{Dem}_{\mathscr{F}}(s, X)$, with variables X over formulas in $\mathscr{L}$ and s over sequences of such formulas, define the relation (as always, in the realization of $\mathscr{L}$ considered): s is a formal derivation of X in the 'full' system just described. Let $\mathrm{Dem}_{\mathscr{S}}(s, X)$ be the corresponding relation for a *special* system $\mathscr{S}$ of rules (e.g. those of Part A, Lemma 3). We ask: is there a combinatorial function f whose arguments and values are sequences of formulas in $\mathscr{L}$ such that

$$\mathrm{Dem}_{\mathscr{F}}(s, X) \rightarrow \mathrm{Dem}_{\mathscr{S}}(fs, X)$$

is combinatorially provable? (The converse is obvious, because the special rules are included in the 'full' system.)

The weak result (together with completeness of the full system) only allows us to conclude this. There is a mechanical rule which defines a function f for which the *translation* of $\mathrm{Dem}_{\mathscr{F}}(s, X) \to \mathrm{Dem}_{\mathscr{S}}(fs, X)$ is *true*; namely, given s and X, decde if $\overline{\mathrm{Dem}_{\mathscr{F}}(s, X)}$ is true; if not, the implication holds; if it is true, X is valid; enumerate the formal derivations of the system $\mathscr{S}$, until you reach a derivation of X; there must be one because all formal theorems of $\mathscr{F}$ are valid, and all valid theorems are formally derivable in $\mathscr{S}$. But this argument leaves open, first whether there is a *combinatorial* $\bar{f}$ and second, whether, for such an $\bar{f}$, the assertion can be combinatorially proved. Not only is there a conceptual difference between the two results, but the mathematical methods used in proving them are quite different.

Discussion. The result establishes that *elementary non-constructive arguments* (in the sense of p. 204) can be eliminated.

This certainly includes a non-trivial part of current mathematics (which presents itself as non-constructive). [In the case of arithmetic the result applies to the following modification of the system in Chapter 3, Exercise 2(d): we may *add* function symbols and equations (as axioms) for which we have combinatorial realizations, for instance $f(0, y) = 1, f(sx, y) = y \cdot fx$ for exponentiation y^x; but to apply the results above, (i) *we must restrict the induction schema to purely universal formulas A* (in the extended notation) since (ii) for other A, we do not have a suitable notion of combinatorial realization. As to (i), if Ax is $\bigwedge y B(x, y), [A0 \wedge \bigwedge z(Az \to Asz)] \to \bigwedge x Ax$ is a (formal) consequence of $\bigwedge x \bigwedge y[(B(0, y) \wedge \bigwedge z[B(z, y) \to B(sz, y)]) \to B(x, y)]$ and this is a consequence of $\bigwedge x \bigwedge y[(B(0, y) \wedge \wedge (\bigwedge z < x)[B(z, y) \to B(sz, y)]) \to B(x, y)]$. For this we have a combinatorial realization, since, if $B(x, y)$ defines a combinatorial relation, so does $(\bigwedge z < x)\, [B(z, y) \to B(sz, y)]$, for variables ranging over the natural numbers. As to (ii), permitting any wider class of A seems, at least without sophisticated analysis, quite unacceptable because we have not even *defined* a (combinatorial) realization for the induction schema applied to non-universal A. The reader should note that viewed in terms of set theoretic foundations, a restriction of formulas A in the induction schema, as in (ii), is quite artificial (cf. also footnote 3 of Part A); analysed in combinatorial terms the opposite is true.]

(d) REDUCTION OF INTUITIVE PRINCIPLES TO COMBINATORIAL PRINCIPLES (continued). Given an intuitive structure $\mathfrak{S}$ and its language $\mathscr{L}_{\mathfrak{S}}$, a kind of *maximal* requirement on combinatorial foundations is to find a (combinatorially defined) formal system which is *valid* for $\mathfrak{S}$ and *saturated* with respect to $\mathscr{L}_{\mathfrak{S}}$. For, combinatorial foundations concern reasoning *about* $\mathfrak{S}$, and such a formal system would decide all questions about $\mathfrak{S}$ (formulated in $\mathscr{L}_{\mathfrak{S}}$).

[Chapter 4 contains several examples, mainly for *first* order languages, despite the fact that none of the axioms considered is categorical, i.e. none determines the *structure* $\mathfrak{S}$ considered (by Exercise 1, Chapter 3). Note that the non-categoricity result for arithmetic in Exercise 2, Chapter 3, has no interest for combinatorial foundations, while Theorem 4 of Part A shows that the maximal requirement above is certainly not satisfied by the axioms $\mathscr{A}^*$ for set theory.]

The theory of recursive functions allows one to formulate (and then prove) a really conclusive generalization of Theorem 4: no consistent extension of $\mathscr{A}^*_-$ whose set of axioms is definable by means of a mechanical rule is saturated; not even with respect to arithmetic statements, in particular, not even for translations of combinatorial assertions in the sense of Section 0(c).

2. How do we find laws (axioms) for the basic combinatorial notions?

In what follows we use notation from Part A, Section 2(a).

(a) For general orientation on this problem the reader should compare the crude mixture of notions that come under the naive idea of set with the mixture of the kinds of proof that are loosely called constructive: hereditarily finite sets (i) might be compared to mechanical calculations, sets of the hierarchy of types (ii) to combinatorial proofs, and abstract properties (iii) to so-called intuitionistic proofs. We do not go into detail because we cannot expect the reader to be equally familiar with the various notions involved: for instance he will know more about sets in sense (ii) than about combinatorial proofs. On the other hand the literature on intuitionism is much richer than that dealing with abstract properties: see the end of Section 3.

(b) THE LANGUAGE $\mathscr{L}_C$ AND ITS REALIZATION $\mathfrak{R}_C$ ('C' for 'combinatorial' or, alternatively, 'concatenation'). $\mathscr{L}_C$ consists of a single relation symbol ($=$), two individual constants 0 and 1 (or $\top$ and $\bot$), two 1-place function symbols s_0 and s_1, and an infinite sequence of function symbols $f_1, f_2, \ldots$, with two arguments.

The universe of $\mathfrak{R}_C$ consists of finite sequences of two concrete objects: the elements $\bar{0}$ and $\bar{1}$ are the two sequences consisting of a single element: $\bar{s}_0$ and $\bar{s}_1$ are the combinatorial functions which attach $\bar{0}$ and $\bar{1}$ respectively to the end of an element of the universe; the functions $\bar{f}_i (i=1, 2, \ldots)$ are defined by the rules given under (c) below.

N.B. Adequacy of $\mathscr{L}_C$ and $\mathfrak{R}_C$ from the point of view of definability (cf. Part A, Section 1, $X\mathscr{A}\mathfrak{S}$ for the set-theoretic analysis): a systematic exposition will be found in SMULLYAN's monograph, Theory of Formal Systems (Princeton, 1961), in which inter alia, functions of a finite number of variables and words constructed from a finite alphabet are defined in $\mathfrak{R}_C$ by use of the language $\mathscr{L}_C$. (The reader will have to verify the combinatorial character of these definitions for himself since the author does not pay explicit attention to this question.) In particular the language $\mathscr{L}_C$ can itself be defined in $\mathfrak{R}_C$ by means of formulas of $\mathscr{L}_C$ (cf. Theorem 4, Part A) in such a way that a sequence of symbols is the concatenation of those elements (sequences) of the universe of $\mathfrak{R}_C$ to which the symbols correspond.
Example. If we take (the sequence) $\langle\bar{0}\bar{1}\rangle$ for the constant 0, $\langle\bar{0}\bar{1}\bar{1}\rangle$ for 1, and $\langle\bar{0}\bar{1}\bar{1}\bar{1}\rangle$ for $=$, then the formula $0 = 1$ is the sequence $\langle\bar{0}\bar{1}\bar{0}\bar{1}\bar{1}\bar{1}\bar{0}\bar{1}\bar{1}\rangle$ which is defined by the term $s_1s_1s_0s_1s_1s_1s_0s_1 0$.

It can be easily seen that with these definitions of the symbols 0,1 and $=$, we have *unique readability* [cf. Chapter 0], i.e., given the object (element of $\mathfrak{R}_C$) that codes a sequence of these symbols it is always possible to recover the latter from the object. This would not be possible if, for example, we made $\bar{0}$ correspond to 0 and $\bar{1}$ to 1; for then, whatever object a corresponded to the relation symbol $=$, it would necessarily be a sequence of the objects $\bar{0}$ and $\bar{1}$ and would therefore *also* code a sequence consisting of the symbols 0, 1.

(c) A FORMAL SYSTEM $\mathscr{S}_C$, formulated in $\mathscr{L}_C$ and (combinatorially) valid in $\mathfrak{R}_C$. We adopt all the rules valid for all combinatorial realizations (see Section 0(b)). In addition, the following:

(i) axioms for the successor functions: $s_0x=s_0y \to x=y$, $s_1x=s_1y \to x=y$, $\neg s_0x=x$, $\neg s_1x=x$, $\neg s_0x=s_1y$, $\neg s_0x=0$, $\neg s_0x=1$, $\neg s_1x=0$, $\neg s_1x=1$; $\neg 0=1$;

(ii) schema for proof by induction: for any formula Ax of $\mathscr{L}_C$, Ax can be inferred from

$$A0 \wedge A1 \wedge (Ax \to As_0x) \wedge (Ax \to As_1x);$$

(iii) schema for definition by recursion; we let C^n denote the set of symbols $\{0, 1, s_0, s_1, f_r : r<n\}$ $(n=1, 2, \ldots)$, $C=\bigcup_n C^n$; consider an enumeration $(u_0^n, u_1^n, v_0^n, v_1^n)$ of all quadruples of terms (u_0, u_1, v_0, v_1) where

the u are built up on $\{y\}\cup C$, the v on $\{x, y, z\}\cup C$, and, moreover, each u_0^n, u_1^n is built up on $\{y\}\cup C^n$, each v_0^n, v_1^n on $\{x, y, z\}\cup C^n$. (This is evidently possible.)

Writing $v[z]$ for v, we have the axioms:

$$f_n(0, y) = u_0^n, \quad f_n(1, y) = u_1^n,$$
$$f_n(s_0 x, y) = v_0^n[f_n(x, y)], \quad f_n(s_1 x, y) = v_1^n[f_n(x, y)].$$

The *validity* of (i) (in $\mathfrak{R}_C$) is obvious, and the validity of (ii) can be shown by induction (whence the name of this schema). It remains to consider (iii); it can be seen that the model constituted by the universe of $\mathfrak{R}_C$, $\bar{0}$, $\bar{1}$, $\bar{s}_0$, $\bar{s}_1$ can be extended in a unique manner to provide a model satisfying (iii). The mechanical rules involved in the definition of the functions $\bar{f}_n$ ($n = 1, 2, \ldots$) are just those defined in the sense of Section 0(ii) by the axioms (iii) themselves. The fact that these rules define functions (over the universe of $\mathfrak{R}_C$) can be shown by induction: see Section 0 (iii).

N.B. The proof of the validity of $\mathscr{S}_C$ illustrates the relation between combinatorial proofs regarded as mental acts and formal derivations: one has to have understood the method of proof by induction in order to see the validity of the formal rules which are intended to describe these proofs.

It is shown in works on proof theory that the language $\mathscr{L}_C$ and the rules of $\mathscr{S}_C$ are sufficient to formulate most of (informal) combinatorial mathematics so far developed including, for example, the partial solution of Hilbert's consistency problem mentioned in Section 1(c). The position of this system with respect to combinatorial mathematics is therefore comparable to that of Zermelo's axioms (Part A, Section 2) for informal set theoretic mathematics.

(d) DOES $\mathscr{S}_C$ PROVIDE AN AXIOMATISATION OF THE COMBINATORIAL THEORY OF $\mathfrak{R}_C$? $\mathscr{S}_C$ is clearly inadequate for defining all combinatorial functions over the universe of $\mathfrak{R}_C$ if the combinatorial validity of $\mathscr{S}_C$ is granted: (c) above yields an enumeration of the functions $\bar{f}_n$ by means of a combinatorial function and hence, using Cantor's diagonal method, a combinatorial function different from all those defined in $\mathscr{S}_C$. (N.B. This construction involves the *infinite* sequence $\bar{f}_n$; cf. p. 197, line 10.)

Similarly we find a formula of the language $\mathscr{L}_C$ itself which is combinatorially valid but which cannot be derived in $\mathscr{S}_C$: Gödel's method (of Theorem 4 of Part A, but freed from its specifically set-theoretic context) shows that

$$\neg\, \mathrm{Dem}(x, s^*)$$

is not derivable in $\mathscr{S}_C$, where, for a given definition of the language $\mathscr{L}_C$

(see (b) above), $\overline{\mathrm{Dem}(x, y)}$ is the (combinatorial) relation: $\bar{x}$ is a sequence of formulas constructed according to the rules of $\mathscr{S}_C$ and $\bar{y}$ is the last formula of $\bar{x}$, and where s^* is the canonical definition of the formula $0=1$, i.e., of the element of the universe which, on the definition of $\mathscr{L}_C$ considered, is the formula $0=1$.

But, on the other hand, the proof of the validity of $\mathscr{S}_C$ shows that $\neg\mathrm{Dem}(x, s^*)$ is valid in $\mathfrak{R}_C$ (where 'proof' and 'validity' are, of course, taken in the combinatorial sense).

The proof of the validity of $\mathscr{S}_C$ also proves the validity of the following schema of which $\neg\mathrm{Dem}(x, s^*)$ is a special case (with $0=1$ instead of A).

For any formula A of $\mathscr{L}_C$ let s_A be its canonical description (for the given definition of $\mathscr{L}_C$); then

$$\mathrm{Dem}(x, s_A) \to A$$

is valid. This schema, which is formulated in $\mathscr{L}_C$, therefore provides an extension of the system $\mathscr{S}_C$.

There is *another*, stronger, *extension* corresponding to an enumeration of all the functions defined in $\mathscr{S}_C$ or, alternatively, to the operation of associating with every closed term of $\mathscr{L}_C$ its value. That this operation is a combinatorial function follows from the proof that the rules for $\bar{f}_n$ define combinatorial functions.

CONSEQUENCES FOR HILBERT'S PROGRAMME (to be more precise the problem is to carry out Hilbert's programme for *every* formal system suggested by mathematical practice).

The facts just described, show that the principles of reasoning formulated in $\mathscr{S}_C$ are not sufficient to carry out Hilbert's programme for the system $\mathscr{S}_C$, and the analogue applies to, roughly, every formal system which is a valid extension of $\mathscr{S}_C$: this fact is known as Gödel's second incompleteness theorem (for a precise formulation of this theorem, the concept of formal system has to be analysed which requires the Theory of Recursive Functions).

Gödel's Theorem by itself does not at all imply that Hilbert's programme cannot be carried through since it leaves open the following possibility: for every formal system $\mathscr{F}$ suggested by mathematical practice (including set theory) it is possible to find a combinatorial system $\mathscr{S}_{\mathscr{F}}$ and a combinatorial realization $\mathfrak{R}_{\mathscr{F}}$ for which $\mathscr{S}_{\mathscr{F}}$ is valid and such that the consistency statement $\neg\mathrm{Dem}_{\mathscr{F}}(x, s^*)$ is provable in $\mathscr{S}_{\mathscr{F}}$.

Certainly this presupposes that for every $\mathscr{F}$ in question there is a combinatorial proof which cannot be formulated in $\mathscr{F}$ in the sense of Section 0(a)(iv). This latter possibility, though intuitively implausible, cannot be excluded without a deeper analysis of the notion of combinatorial proof; for, just because of the incompleteness theorem, for *all* (consistent) $\mathscr{F}$ there are *correct* proofs which cannot be formulated in $\mathscr{F}$. In other words, the possibility considered cannot be excluded without making use of some more subtle property of combinatorial proofs than, say, their set-theoretic validity.

In the absence of such an analysis we only have the following result: there is no formal system $\mathscr{S}$ such that

(i) there is a formal derivation in $\mathscr{S}$ of every statement formulated in $\mathscr{L}_C$ which is valid in $\mathfrak{R}_C$ (in the combinatorial sense),

(ii) the validity of $\mathscr{S}$ (in $\mathfrak{R}_C$) can be established by combinatorial reasoning.

3. Development of the theory

We shall now consider the hypothesis stated at the end of Section 2. From the discussion above, a *positive* solution to Hilbert's programme would require a case study (cf. Part A, Section 1 concerning $X^{\mathscr{A}\mathfrak{S}}$ and $D^{\mathscr{A}\mathfrak{S}}$) of all the formal systems suggested by mathematical practice (this is the reason why it is of interest for Hilbert's programme to find a single system which covers the whole of mathematical practice).

On the other hand a *negative* solution could be obtained as follows: we first construct a formal system $\mathscr{S}$ satisfying condition (i), but of course not (ii) (end of Section 2); then we try to find a particular system of mathematical practice for which Hilbert's programme cannot be carried through using the methods of $\mathscr{S}$.

In the article on mathematical logic in: Lectures on Modern Mathematics, vol. 3 (ed. Saaty, 1965), a system is described which can be seen to satisfy condition (i) and in which it is not possible to establish the consistency of ordinary [i.e., first order] arithmetic [Chapter 3, Exercise 2]. The idea behind the construction of this system is that combinatorial proofs can be generated by iterations of the type of extension considered on p. 215: the principal problem is clearly that of ensuring that *all* iterations shall be included which are such that every formal derivation has a combinatorial realization. (By Section 2(d)(ii) such a system could not possess a combinatorial model as a whole, i.e., there could be no *combi-*

natorial proof showing that every derivation in such an $\mathscr{S}$ has a combinatorial realization.)

There is a striking parallel to Part A, Section 3: the operation $\mathfrak{P}$ (of forming the set of all subsets of a given set) is the operation which generates the hierarchy of types and the principal problem there is to formulate axioms in the language of set theory which ensure the existence of as many iterations of this operation as possible; in other words to find axioms of infinity which express the existence of high types.

N.B. For a better understanding of the problems presented by Hilbert's programme, the reader should compare it with the problem of squaring the circle: (α) the formulation of a system $\mathscr{S}$ satisfying (i) corresponds to the (mathematical) characterization of the geometrical idea of ruler-and-compass constructions, namely that every point constructed by such means has Pythagorean coordinates (i.e., expressible by means of rational operations and square roots); (β) the proof that $\neg$ Dem (x, s^*) is not derivable in $\mathscr{S}$ corresponds to the proof that $\int_0^1 \sqrt{(1 - x^2)}\, dx$ is not Pythagorean. In modern texts, at any rate those influenced by formalism, there is often no discussion of (α), which requires an axiomatic analysis of geometric concepts, in particular, the introduction of coordinates on the basis of intuitive geometric axioms. The omission is hardly surprising since the very possibility of such an analysis is embarrassing for the formalist doctrine: see the Introduction. (The formulation of $\mathscr{S}$ is more problematic than (α) because the intuitive idea of combinatorial proof is less clear than the intuitive idea of a ruler-and-compass construction.)

The comparison described above suggests the very interesting problem of setting up a theory of proofs which are 'graspable' (intelligible) and not merely valid and, in particular, of intelligible combinatorial proofs. The corresponding geometric problem would be to find a theory of 'feasible' constructions which only involve points 'close' to the starting points and which are stable for 'small' changes in the data (this clearly requires the discovery of the metric appropriate to geometric intuition). Although such a theory of intelligible proofs would not be part of logic in the strict sense of the word, since logic is only concerned with questions of *validity* of one kind and another, it is quite likely that it would make use of the *methods* of combinatorial foundations.

It only remains to say something about the intuitionistic conception of mathematical thought (Section 2(a)): this conception goes beyond combinatorial mathematics since it also admits *abstract objects* such as functions, functions of functions etc. provided that these, in turn, refer only to objects of mathematical thought: in particular, set-theoretic concepts in their realist sense are not included. Thus the intuitionistic conception is idealist; its positive side consists in accepting *abstract constructions* and it is this which distinguishes it from combinatorial mathematics.

N.B. The negative, and better-known, side to intuitionism consists in general polemics directed against set-theoretic concepts; these arguments are no more convincing than those of realists directed against idealists ("What kind of an animal is a proof?") or those of formalists against the others ("Where are those abstract objects?"). All of these critiques are weak because they overlook the fact that there are more things in heaven and on earth than are dreamt of in philosophy (i.e., in the particular philosophical system accepted by the critic). This by no means detracts from the interest of positive results obtained within a limited framework which show, for instance, that the objects accepted suffice for an explanation of the phenomena considered.

Hilbert's programme can obviously be reformulated with intuitionistic concepts replacing those of Section 2. This extension corresponds perhaps to taking the notion (iii) of set in Part A, Section 2(a) instead of Zermelo's. For further details, see the article l.c.

4. Critical summary

(a) COMPARISON BETWEEN SET-THEORETIC AND COMBINATORIAL FOUNDATIONS. Both provide an answer to the question (in old fashioned language): what is mathematics? The former formulates a *particular* "realistic" view, and therefore concentrates on objects, not on the reasoning about them; its answer is that mathematics is the theory of *sets* (for a suitable precise notion of set). The latter formulates a particular "idealist" view, regards abstract mathematical objects as figures of speech, and wants to show that our way of using these figures of speech is coherent. What is particular about this view is that, according to it and contrary to appearances, our mathematical reasoning is 'essentially' combinatorial; 'essentially' in the logical sense (cf. Section 3), namely that the *validity* of our conclusions which can be formulated combinatorially at all, can also be established by combinatorial methods. This view, if correct, not only asserts a *unity* of mathematical reasoning, but one of a very remarkable kind: since school mathematics is typical of combinatorial mathematics, it presents the whole of mathematics as being of the same kind as school mathematics!

Both set theoretic and combinatorial foundations separate mathematical questions from (ontological) questions about the existence, i.e., objectivity, of abstract objects or abstract notions outside the foundational scheme considered. But they draw the dividing line at quite different points. One must therefore not assume from the success of one such separation that also the other separation is correct.

Specifically, consider the separation between set theoretic notions and classical intuitive structures presented, for instance, in our geometric conceptions (continuum) or in our ideas about chance (probability.). *If* the corresponding adequacy conditions of Part A, Section 1(a) are satisfied (for one of these notions $\mathfrak{S}$) *then* we have the required separation (autonomy of set theoretic mathematics). Thus $E^{\mathscr{A}\mathfrak{S}}$ suffices to show that if a purely set theoretic conclusion, i.e., one formulated in $\mathscr{L}_E$, follows by use of intuitive properties $\mathscr{A}_{\mathfrak{S}}$ of $\mathfrak{S}$, then it also follows from set theoretic principles, i.e. those used to establish $E^{\mathscr{A}\mathfrak{S}}$. If in addition $U^{\mathscr{A}\mathfrak{S}}$ is satisfied, this situation is not changed by use of other intuitive properties (formulated in the given language of $\mathfrak{S}$) provided only the intuitive conception is coherent. [As pointed out in the discussion of Part B, Section 1(a), within the set theoretic framework one cannot formulate *why* the adequacy conditions are correct, and therefore the problem of deriving these conditions is properly considered to be foundational (though it is almost always mathematicians who solve it; cf. end of Introduction).]

As pointed out in Part A, Section 1(a), and Section 2(a), the adequacy conditions are satisfied for the *classical* intuitive structures, but in a somewhat weaker sense for ordinals, and, as far as we know, not for the general notion of property, i.e., notion (iii) of Section 2(a).

In contrast, in combinatorial foundations, the separation between combinatorial notions on the one hand and the basic set theoretic notions on the other has been established only in a quite *narrow*, though not at all trivial, part of mathematics (Part B, Section 1(c)). And, modulo the characterization of combinatorial proof mentioned in Part B, Section 3, this separation does not hold beyond ordinary [i.e., first order] arithmetic [Exercise 2, Chapter 3]. For those parts of mathematical reasoning for which the adequacy conditions Part B, Section 1(b) and Part B, Section 1(d) hold, essentially the same conclusions about separation apply as mentioned above for $E^{\mathscr{A}\mathfrak{S}}$ and $U^{\mathscr{A}\mathfrak{S}}$ respectively.

It goes without saying that both set-theoretic and combinatorial foundations are at best auxiliaries for studying the abstract objects themselves which they eliminate!

(b) Doctrinaire foundations, by definition, support their own position largely by criticizing rival foundational schemes. This criticism permits them to ignore those defects (of their own position) whose formulation requires the use of notions not accepted by them, i.e., notions from a rival scheme [for instance, in the case of combinatorial foundations, the defect that the relation of second order consequence is not combinatorially definable; cf. discussion of Part B, Section 1(a)]. – The reader will have noticed in this connection that an interest in combinatorial foundations is often associated with a critique of set theoretic notions, and, incidentally, an interest in set-theoretic foundations with a critique of such notions as that of property in Part A, Section 2(a) or of intuitionistic construction in Part B, Section 3, the reason, obviously, being that we do not have a set-theoretic foundation for these notions.

If a doctrinaire (combinatorial) standpoint is adopted, the importance of Gödel's Theorem 4 of Part A lies precisely in the fact that here the failure of combinatorial foundations can be formulated in combinatorial terms itself. But from a less legalistic point of view a *conceptual framework is defective if it does not allow* (theoretical) *explanations of facts for which an alternative theory has an explanation*, one purpose of theory being the extension of the range of theoretical understanding. [From this point of view, Theorem 5 of Part A, constitutes already a failure of combinatorial foundations, because in terms of set-theoretic notions we have a good reason for the choice of formal rules, while in combinatorial foundations the choice of the formal rules must be taken as part of the data (cf. discussion of Part B, Section 1(a)).]

Another inadequacy of combinatorial foundations (cf. last paragraph of Part B, Section 2) is that within the combinatorial framework one cannot define, i.e., establish the extent of, combinatorial mathematics, but within a wider (constructive) framework one can at least try! (cf. Part B, Section 3).

At the present stage of knowledge we do not have the notions needed to solve, or even to formulate precisely, the analogous question for the whole of mathematics, namely: are there sufficiently abstract, yet precise notions to characterize the extent of the whole of mathematics?

(c) CRUDE FORMALISM, mentioned at the end of the Introduction, is a glorious doctrine, which happily proposes an answer. This doctrine does not even accept the basic combinatorial notions and holds that mathematics consists of assertions of the form: a concretely given configuration has been constructed by means of a given mechanical rule (in terms of Part B, Section 0(b): only *closed* formulas of a combinatorial language are considered). No general statements about such configurations belong to mathematics. Consequently, of course, not even the minimal adequacy condition of Part B, Section 1(b) (Hilbert's consistency problem) can be formulated, since a *variable* x appears in it.

This doctrine is certainly free from failures in the narrow (legalistic) sense of (b) above, by the very simple device that next to nothing can be formulated in the terms it accepts! Obviously, this cult of impotence is based on the conviction that there are no (theoretical) explanations of such basic phenomena of mathematical experience as the validity of (combinatorial) conclusions derived from properties of abstract intuitive concepts[4].

It must have occurred to the reader that, according to this doctrine, what is essential to mathematics are mechanical manipulations, while he learned at school that these are the antithesis of mathematics: "Don't just copy a proof, understand it" (and, moreover, even then he understood the instruction).

So the doctrine certainly does not sound very sensible, besides being inconsistent with mathematical practice. But its most significant fault is this: it has led people to believe in, or at least to assert, the impossibility of explanations where, in fact, there are already explanations to look at, in particular, the positive solutions of Hilbert's problem in Part B, Section 1(c). Evidently, the *general* claim of the doctrine is refuted by any one (non-trivial) theoretical explanation (cf. pp. 208, 209).

The principal problems of the two foundations here considered are these. In set-theoretic foundations we search for new axioms (i.e., properties satisfied by the cumulative type structure); in combinatorial foundations we search for a more detailed analysis of the basic combinatorial notions (and thus a convincing characterisation of the limits of combinatorial reasoning). Based on such research one can then develop new foundational schemes. The limitations of Hilbert's original programme do not exclude other "idealist" foundations satisfying adequacy conditions analogous to those of Part B, Section 1(c); recall Part B, Section 3, where at least one positive proposal beyond Hilbert's original program is mentioned.

Finally it should be noted that (1) realist and (2) idealist foundations in the sence of p. 161 are not *necessarily* in conflict, for even if the objects of (1) are accepted, (2) is also needed to analyze the *kind* of knowledge we have of these objects. But conflicts are likely by p. 174 lines 8 and 9.

[4] Bourbaki flirts with this doctrine and proposes an "empirical" explanation in terms of past experience with formal systems. This is not thought through because it says nothing about the (statistical) principles to be used in evaluating the past experience. Since these principles themselves use at least combinatorial mathematics the examination of such principles leads back to much the same questions as those of Part B. Cf. last sentence of Part A.

Part C

SEMANTIC VERSUS SYNTACTIC (COMBINATORIAL) INTRODUCTION TO MATHEMATICAL LOGIC

N.B. "Semantic" stands, as usual, for: set-theoretic semantic; in syntactic analysis the corresponding basic combinatorial notions have to be understood (those of Part B, Section 2 instead of those of Part A, Section 2).

1. The advantages of a semantic analysis are these:

(a) By Part B, Sections 1 and 4, syntactic or proof theoretic analysis begins where semantic analysis leaves off: The choice of axioms and the relation of logical consequence come from semantic analysis; they constitute the data of the proof theoretic analysis.

(b) By Part A, Section 2 and Part B, Section 3 there are parts of current mathematics which *do* have a semantic foundation in terms of s.c.t., but do *not* have a combinatorial syntactic foundation (and are not known to have a constructive foundation).

[(c) Several of the basic results in first order (classical) predicate logic can be stated and proved combinatorially. But they are more easily proved "semantically", i.e., by using the fact that the rules are valid and complete for the notion of consequence of Chapter 2; cf. Part B, Section 1 (c).

2. The weakness of semantic analysis is that several of the results of 1 (c) hold not only for rules which are semantically sound and complete, but for a wide class satisfying fairly simple combinatorial conditions, for instance the Interpolation Lemma. Therefore the semantic proof hides the full *generality* of the results concerned.]